The best of Britain

D0277558

Devon

SIMON HEPTINSTALL

Contents

The Guide

Photo Essays

Foreword

Michael Caines MBE

People say to me: "Life is slower in Devon." And I say: "What's wrong with that?" It gives you more time to appreciate things around you... like a good local pint in a Dartmoor pub.

I was born and brought up in Devon. In this book you'll read about my restaurant at Gidleigh Park and at the Abode Hotel in Exeter. Obviously I hope this book encourages you to come and visit them. But even if you don't, please try at least to sample some of the great range of local food and drink available all over Devon.

Visiting has changed from the days of simple over-romanticised summer holidays at the seaside. I think that today's visitors want to discover much more depth. And Devon, with all its contrasts and hidden corners, is just perfect for that. Food is a big part of any holiday nowadays. So it must be a good idea to publish an inspiring book that encourages visitors to try some of the great food producers in Devon and the places where you can buy the fabulous local produce.

If Devon was in France or Italy it would be famous as a great food region. Farming and fishing are such an integral part of the culture in the county. In fact, there are more food producers in Devon than anywhere in the west. There are prolific artisans making things like fantastic cheese or wine. Farms are creating such high quality food thanks to Devon's range of wonderful landscapes, including excellent arable land and such lush pastures.

In Devon there's always a food experience to match the location. It may be a Devon ice cream on a sunny beach, a ploughman's with some interesting local cheese or a glass of Sharpham's Devon wine down in the South Hams. And all visitors should try a proper cream tea with clotted cream and homemade scones.

I live with my family in a very small village in mid-Devon. I just feel so lucky to be based there most of the time, working at the thing I love doing. There's outstanding natural beauty everywhere. I think of the contrasts between the granite outcrops of Dartmoor and the softer green rolling countryside, between the high cliffs and long sandy beaches of North Devon and the lush pastures and sandy coves further south. You can easily find yourself in the middle of nowhere but always just a short drive back to civilisation. I'm not surprised people are now choosing to visit Devon instead of going abroad.

Some of my Devon favourites are Dawlish Warren with its nature reserve, views of the Exe Estuary and long beach which can rival anywhere in Europe on a sunny day. Or the unspoilt seaside town of Budleigh Salterton on the dramatic Jurassic Coastline, where I've been going since I was a boy, playing on the pebbles and jumping straight into the deep water. Then there's Plymouth's Barbican, Exeter's shops, Salcombe, Dartmouth, Exmoor... I love it!

One thing I always say to Devon visitors is to try to buy local. Don't turn up at your holiday cottage or campsite with a carload of supermarket groceries. If you eat local and buy local you'll help keep the farmers in business... and that will keep the lovely countryside looking as it does.

Introduction

You might just be strolling under the palm trees along the Torquay seafront with an ice cream or you could be at the end of a bracing walk across a wildly beautiful part of Dartmoor. Suddenly you'll be struck by the feeling that this is more than just another part of the West Country. This is Devon. The realisation that there is something unique about this county strikes different people at different times. It could happen during any one of the classic Devon experiences – a clotted cream tea, a meander along the coast path or a picnic beside a babbling stream on Dartmoor.

Your first 'Devon moment' could come as you're enjoying one of the essential Devon sights – gazing up at the mighty west front of Exeter Cathedral, tottering down through the fishing village of Clovelly to the harbour, or standing on Plymouth Hoe where Drake once decided to finish playing bowls before sailing to defeat the Armada... Or it could happen in a little-known part of Devon, just doing Devonshire sorts of things. Your own heavenly Devon moment could come as you're huddled round the log fire in a cosy thatched village pub or sitting down to dinner of fresh local ingredients in a glamorous boutique hotel, lounging on a perfect sandy beach watching the waves or trying to decipher the broad accent of the assistant at a quirky old farm shop in the middle of nowhere.
This book aims to help you discover those Devon moments as often as possible.

It isn't hard – there is so much in England's third biggest county: for starters there are more than 2,500 square miles, a million people, two coastlines, two National Parks, two World Heritage sites and some of Britain's most popular tourist attractions.

But we're hoping this book makes a fair stab at covering all the best bits in a new and contemporary way. Like all the great regions round the world, you'll mostly find the real Devon not in the famous tourist attractions and well-photographed scenes but in little personal discoveries you make yourself.

So explore the villages, walk around to the next cove, and try something new, even if it's just visiting the pub in the next village. Devon's biggest attraction is that it's full of wonderful surprises.

Unmissable highlights

01 Clovelly

The flower-bedecked fishing village tumbling down a wooded cliff to a harbour is the essential Devon sight, but try to time your visit to miss the crowds, p. 165

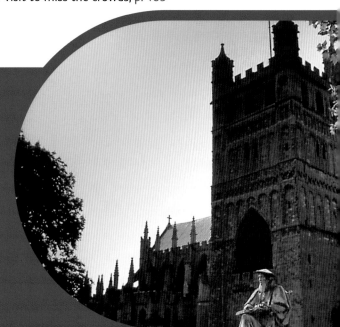

02 Exeter Cathedral

You will have seen a thousand photos of the South West's most famous building in its historic Close, but the ancient reality is so much better, p. 60

05 Climb Haytor

It's worth braving the crowds at Dartmoor's most popular tor for the panoramic views right down to the Riviera coast – and there are plenty more tors where that came from, p.277

06 Lynmouth

Artists and poets have been inspired by England's 'Little Switzerland', and you can be too, especially if you ride the extraordinary Victorian cliff railway, p. 124

Burgh Island

A unique chance to eat, stay or sip cocktails at a surreal art deco fantasy hotel on its own island –
off a beautiful sandy beach and which looks at its best when the tide is in,

08 Dartmouth

One of the best views in England is from the ferry across Dartmouth Harbour. Then wander the old streets of the town for food, history, shopping and sights too, p.222

09 The Torridge Estuary

Appledore has the craft-shops and quayside, Instow the galleries and sands, Bideford the history and bridge... and they've all got the great River Tarka alongside, p. 155

10 Torquay

Still Britain's greatest traditional seaside resort – with beaches, restaurants, grand villas, Victorian gardens, swaying palms and that extra touch of Mediterranean glamour, p. 198

Secret Devon

Local Recommendations

01 The Hunter's Path

Locals love this walk through the woods near Chagford and Fingle Bridge on a well-marked path along the Teign Valley , p. 278

02 The Mason's Arms

The pretty old thatched village pub at Knowstone near Tiverton has a prestigious Michelin star for its superb food, p. 188

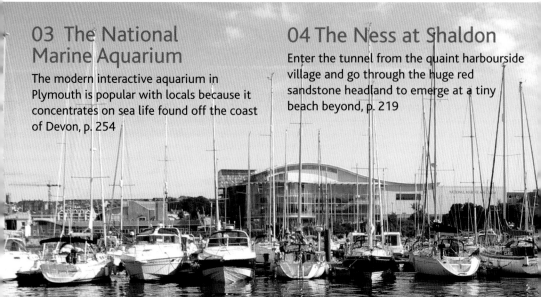

03 The National Marine Aquarium

The modern interactive aquarium in Plymouth is popular with locals because it concentrates on sea life found off the coast of Devon, p. 254

04 The Ness at Shaldon

Enter the tunnel from the quaint harbourside village and go through the huge red sandstone headland to emerge at a tiny beach beyond, p. 219

05 The South West Coast Path

Walking anywhere along either stretch of this great free West Country resource; the local favourites include Beer Head near Seaton, Torquay, Puttsborough in North Devon and Orcombe Point, Exmouth, p. 34

06 Sailing up the Dart

Take a cruise up one of Britain's most picturesque rivers from Dartmouth's historic harbour, p. 224

07 The Warren House Inn

Several locals picked this lonely but cosy pub high on the moor where the open fire never goes out, p. 301

08 Peak Hill near Yelverton

Seth Lakeman's favourite moorland spot is more than 1300ft up, north of Yelverton. It's the best view in Devon, he says, p. 279

09 Go out in the rain

Devon locals choose all sorts of outdoor activities for a rainy day – including water-sports, walking, boating or just strolling on the beach

10 Simon Drew's shop

A favourite among locals – a high quality and friendly art and craft gallery on Foss Street, Dartmouth, p. 225

Factfile

01   Devon is the largest county in the south-west, and the third largest in England.

02   Devon is unique in Britain, having two coastlines. The north coast facing the Bristol Channel is 90 miles long and the south coast facing the English Channel is 110 miles long.

03   The population is just over 1,150,000, and the county town is Exeter (population 117,000) although Plymouth is the biggest city (population 258,000).

04   Dartmoor National Park forms 14% of the county and 3% Exmoor National Park.

05   There are 8,000 miles of road in Devon.

06   The highest point is High Willhays on Dartmoor, at 621m/2039ft.

07   The River Exe is Devon's longest river, flowing from Exmoor more than 50 miles south to Exmouth.

THE FACTS

WHEN TO GO

Whatever time of the year you visit Devon, you can find unspoilt hidden spots and secret routes to avoid the queues. It always pays to ask a local – they rarely get stuck in queues or spend time at the most crowded spots.

It does make sense to minimise the hassles by timing your visit as well as you can. School holidays, and especially bank holidays, are notorious. Even the motorway and trunk roads leading to Devon can turn to gridlock. And despite bad weather, Easter and Christmas can be very busy too. Yet the appeal of a break in Devon is too much to resist for millions of us.

Throughout the year Saturdays are the busiest on the trunk roads, as that's the most popular changeover day for holiday homes, caravans and weekly hotel bookings. It's also one of quietest days on the beaches and at attractions, because everyone is either leaving or arriving.

Mid-week and non-holiday times of the year can be wonderfully quiet, but decide whether that's what you want. Lively resorts can become sleepy without the crowds, and some attractions and facilities close if there is no business.

The big festivals and events attract hordes. Widecombe Fair, for example, involves a special police traffic management plan. At prime times, don't expect to be able to park right next to the beach or the attraction.

Summer

The hottest, driest but busiest season in Devon presents a dilemma. In the school summer holidays accommodation can get booked up, roads can get clogged and car parks full, and the main attractions over-run. But the sea is at its warmest and there is more to do wherever you go. If you don't have children it's easier to avoid the July and August squeeze. If you do have kids, plan your journeys carefully to avoid jams and carry entertainment and supplies in case you do get caught in one.

Autumn

The leaves are changing colour, the days shorten, but there can still be plenty of Devonshire sunshine in September, October and November. There are hundreds of deciduous woods where you can see the turning colours, and wherever you walk in the county you'll find blackberries to pick in the hedges.

Winter

Many Devon attractions and some hotels and restaurants close in the winter – especially in the more touristy areas such as seaside resorts. The cities and more local farming communities are little changed. But away from Exeter and Plymouth, your quiet out-of-season break is likely to involve more activities such as walking, exploring and sitting in the pub.

A little rain won't ruin your holiday. But a lot might. So bear in mind that rainfall on Dartmoor is double what it is on the Riviera coast. Conditions can change quickly on the high ground and you can suddenly be caught in serious weather. But this being Britain, you can enjoy a week of completely dry sunny weather even in the midst of winter. You may not go swimming in the winter, but you may well be eating outside at any time of the year.

Spring

Devon's countryside is bursting with new life in springtime. From the wildflowers in the hedges and fields to the vast banks of colourful flowering shrubs such as rhododendrons, there's a wonderful sense of the change of seasons in the county. With the blossom comes the wave of wildlife: like strains of birdsong that you haven't heard for years or the buzz of insects in long grass.

10... places to avoid in Devon

Even a place as wonderful as Devon has places that it would be better for visitors to avoid.

1 Kingsteignton This small clay-mining village outside Newton Abbot has mutated into a monstrous low-rise sprawl. More than 11,000 people now live in what is officially the UK's biggest village. You won't have your car stolen, you'll just get lost or fall asleep deep in the suburbia of Elm Drive or Darren Close.

2 Union Street, Plymouth By day it's a shabby link between the city centre and Devonport Docks. By night Union Street becomes the wildest, rowdiest, most violent and downright dangerous strip west of Bristol.

3 Beacon Heath, Exeter There's a nice view from these hills to the north of the city but while you're admiring them, you risk having the wheels taken off your car. This large, old council estate has all the social problems you *don't* expect in Devon: poverty, unemployment, young offenders and boarded-up shops.

4 Westward Ho! A great beach and dunes, but the town behind them is the worst seaside resort in the county. The few Victorian homes are submerged beneath bungalows, amusements and cheap modern flats. In fact, the sea is now hidden behind tall blocks of modern holiday apartments.

5 Ellacombe, Torquay Behind the beach, harbour, hotels and shops there is a sadly neglected suburb of cheap, cramped terraces around the town's football stadium. Ellacombe has high unemployment, low educational achievement, and one of the highest rates of teenage pregnancy in the country.

6 Willand One local told us 'the only interesting thing about it is the meat processing factory'. Avoid this characterless Mid Devon village alongside the M5. Go to the Diggerland theme park nearby instead.

7 Bow There's a depressing air about this linear village, as the traffic thunders right through the middle. It had a medieval Royal Charter to hold a market and three-day fair, but it never turned into the town that everyone hoped for. The fair and market have long since died from lack of custom.

8 Wonford, Exeter The big estates around Rifford Road and Burnhouse Lane have a dreadful reputation locally although things have improved in the past decade. It's still not somewhere to spend your holiday.

9 Swilly, Plymouth The city's first council estate was built in the 1920s and by the 1950s it was so deprived that the name 'Swilly' was used across Devon as a derogatory term for any degenerate types. The authorities changed its name to the more estate agent friendly 'North Prospect' but the reputation for petty crime and social deprivation remains.

10 Barnstaple An increasingly smart and enjoyable town centre is failing to mask the fact that the suburbs of Barnstaple are among the most deprived parts of the county. Visitors would be unwise to wander far from the centre. The crime rate here, amazingly for such a rural area, is 1.5 times the national average and double the rest of North Devon.

Across Devon there are hundreds of special spots for walks among the daffodils, primroses and bluebells. Don't hesitate to ask a local for advice – it's usually a matter of Devon pride to be able to point out the best places.

GETTING THERE
By car
If you are travelling from the north or on the M4, simply pick up the **M5** southbound at Bristol and follow it all the way down to the West Country. Without hold-ups, it's about an hour and a half from Bristol to Exeter.

From the south or the M3, choose the **A303**, which meets the M5 at the massive Sowton interchange just east of Exeter. This is the transport hub for the county – with the M5 continuing in all but name as the **A38** south of Dartmoor to Plymouth and the **A30** cutting across the middle of the county above Dartmoor to Launceston in Cornwall.

If you're heading for north Devon, the **A361**, called the **North Devon Link Road**, leaves the M5 before Exeter, at Junction 27, and cuts across Tiverton and South Molton to Barnstaple.

One of the most picturesque portals to Devon is the north coast route – the **A39**. You can pick this up by leaving the M5 at junction 23 or cut across the country from Glastonbury. The A39 is sometimes called the **Atlantic Highway** and can be very busy. There are few safe overtaking spots but from Nether Stowey westwards, you will pass through spectacular scenery with great coastal views, pretty villages and some perfect pubs. This dramatic road across the top of Exmoor from Dunster to Lynton is considered one of the greatest drives in Britain.

Further south it's hard to think that the old **A30** was once the main road from Devon to London. It's now way behind the motorways and A303 in status. While the A303 has been mostly upgraded to dual carriageway, the A30 still winds through Somerset towns such as Yeovil and Chard. The stretch through the Blackdown Hills is worth the wait though and to the east of Honiton the A30 and A303 combine, the older road

asserting its age-old authority by keeping its name from here westwards.

Further south still, the **A35** is a scenic route across southern Dorset, bringing traffic from Poole and Southampton. You'll travel through some nice villages and countryside but don't expect the landscape fireworks of the A39 along the north coast. The A35 stays away from the sea although it gets very busy with seaside traffic in the summer. You'll join the A30 at Honiton or, for a pretty detour that'll add 30 minutes to your journey, switch to the winding **A3052** at Lyme Regis. This will bring you to the M5 at the southern end of that big Sowton interchange at Exeter.

By bus
Again Exeter is the main hub for **National Express** coaches. The city's 1960s Paris Street bus station is scheduled for the bulldozers soon but the replacement will continue to be the centre for Devon bus services.

Usually there are nine services a day from London, taking between four hours and 20 minutes and five hours and 15 minutes. Bristol to Exeter takes around two hours, with four services a day, and Birmingham to Exeter takes about four and a half hours, also four times a day. There are direct services to Plymouth and some of the Exeter buses continue to Torbay. For full details call 08717 818181 or visit www.nationalexpress.com.

Also look for cheap deals. At the time of writing **Megabus** is offering coach seats from London to Exeter for £10 (☎ 0901 331 0031 premium rate line; www.megabus.com).

By train
Devon is well served by trains from all over the country. **First Great Western** trains leave London Paddington regularly, and **South West Trains** start from London Waterloo. **Virgin Trains** runs frequent services from the Midlands and the North, and **Wessex Trains** operate within the South West and Wales region. To book train tickets online, visit www.thetrainline.com or call the individual train companies:

First Great Western: ☎ 08457 000 125;
www.firstgreatwestern.co.uk
South West Trains: ☎ 0845 6000 650;
www.southwesttrains.co.uk
Virgin: ☎ 0845 000 8000;
www.virgintrains.co.uk
Wessex Trains: ☎ 0845 6000880;
www.wessextrains.co.uk

The journey from London Paddington to Exeter is the fastest, only taking around three hours. In fact, some services take just two and a quarter hours. It's another hour to Plymouth.

The trips from Waterloo generally take longer, running via Salisbury and Honiton, but are cheaper. Trains from Birmingham to Plymouth take between three and a half and four and a half hours. To take a bike on any of these trains, first contact the relevant train company. Each company has different rules, prices and availability.

By air

Many UK airports have flights to **Exeter Airport** (☎ 01392 367 433; www.exeter-airport.co.uk), which is about 15 minutes to the east alongside the A30. They include Aberdeen, Belfast, Dublin, Edinburgh, Glasgow, Leeds/Bradford, Manchester, Newcastle, Norwich and the Channel Islands.

There are also flights from international airports – major hubs such as Amsterdam and Paris, and regional airports such as Alicante, Bergerac, Brest Brittany, Faro, Malaga and Salzburg. All flights are operated by budget flyer Flybe (☎ 0871 700 2000 premium rate line; www.flybe.com).

Plymouth City Airport (☎ 01752 204090; www.plymouthairport.com), 20 minutes north of the city at Roborough, is also well served with flights from London Gatwick, Manchester, Leeds/Bradford, Bristol and Jersey. All flights are operated by Air South West (☎ 0870 241 8202; airsouthwest.com).

ENVIRONMENTAL CONCERNS

One of the reasons holidays to Devon are becoming more popular is concern about the environment. More British people are shunning long flights, cutting their impact on climate change and reducing their carbon emissions. By opting to take holidays in the South West they are also helping environmentally conscious businesses in one of the least polluted parts of the country.

Devon officials are working on a concerted campaign to manage their tourism in a sustainable way. As a visitor you may notice the Green Tourism Business Scheme (GTBS) in the county, but it's busy championing environmental best practice in the industry. The South Hams and South Devon areas have already been nationally acclaimed for their progress in managing tourism in a way that benefits both local communities and the environment.

If you see the GTBS symbol anywhere in the county you can be sure that the business is doing its bit, whether that means use of ethical products, promoting alternatives to the car or waste reduction. The symbol is a green oval with the white outline of a leaf on it. To learn more, visit www.discoverdevon.com/site/green-businesses/green-tourism-business-scheme/.

You can also look up the listings of members of the scheme, which will help you plan your holiday accommodation, activities and excursions if you choose to support these greener tourism providers. The South West is the region of Britain with the most GTBS members.

Examples of GTBS businesses include the Royal Castle Hotel at Dartmouth, which encourages guests to arrive by train by offering free taxis from the station, uses refillable bathroom containers and only uses local produce. The self-catering cottages at West Hele Farm at Buckland Brewer in North Devon have geothermal heating, a welcome hamper of local products and a garden producing seasonal fruit and vegetables for the guests. Visit www.green-tourismadvice.co.uk for more examples.

The South West Tourist Board too is keen to work on the sustainability of its tourism. Its special website (visitsouthwest.co.uk/feel-good/love-the-south-west.cfm) encourages visitors to join in the campaign in 10 different ways, admittedly mostly rather obvious, such as: buying local produce, visiting at the less busy times of the year and not dropping litter.

GETTING AROUND

The official discoverdevon.com website promises you that: 'Public transport will get you to all kinds of exciting places in Devon, fascinating spots that can be hard to find by car.'

While well-planned use of public transport could work well for an activity holiday based in one location, the truth is that away from the main commuting routes, public transport is limited, sporadic and not always reliable. For the spontaneous mix of touring, shopping, eating and exploring that most of us enjoy on our holiday, a car is still the most practical means for getting around for most Devon holidays.

Nevertheless, even if you have a car with you, a day out by bus, coach or train can be an adventure in itself. The **Traveline** website (traveline.org.uk) is a useful source of information for travelling around Devon by public transport (or you can call 0871 200 22 33 at 10p per minute). You can also take a look at the detailed Devon County Council website transport pages – (www.devon.gov.uk/index /transport/public_transport). The detailed bus maps are especially useful, although there aren't any timetables.

Buses

The main bus services within Devon are operated by **Stagecoach** (Exeter ☎ 01392 427711 or Torquay ☎ 01803 664500; www.stagecoachbus.com) and **First Group** (☎ 0845 600 1420; www.firstgroup.com /ukbus/southwest/devon). They are particularly useful for getting around within town commuting areas, especially in Exeter, Torbay and Plymouth where summer jams and parking problems are common. Note also that some attractions give a discount for arriving by public transport.

Trains

Railways are a scenic way to travel around Devon, linking its picturesque villages and historic market towns. They'd have been even better if only the government hadn't closed some of the best lines in the 1960s. At least the good ones that remain are being well promoted and services are currently reputed to be pretty reliable. See the panel below for the best scenic trips.

Special one-day tickets are available. These can be a good deal for visitors: **Ranger Tickets** give the freedom of

SCENIC RAILWAYS IN DEVON

The **Tarka Line** runs between Exeter and the North Devon 'capital,' Barnstaple. The 40-mile line follows the valleys of the Taw and Yeo and was named after author Henry Williamson, whose classic tale *Tarka the Otter* was based in this area (see Woolacombe chapter).

On the way the train stops at Crediton, a market town with a great church and some quirky shops, and little villages in the Taw Valley, such as the hamlet of Eggesford, where you can walk from the station into a magnificent Forestry Commission woodland, or Umberleigh, where there is an antique emporium and riverside teashop. Barnstaple is a busy shopping and commercial centre, with the historic pannier market and Butchers' Row shops. Barnstaple is also the start of the Tarka Trail cycle path – so you could combine a rail and bike circuit here.

The **Avocet Line** is named after the elegant bird that spends the winter on the Exe Estuary. The route connects Exeter Central and Exmouth stations, 11 miles along the eastern side of the Exe Estuary. It offers a stop at the historic port, now a suburb, of Topsham. Exmouth itself is a popular seaside resort with a long sandy beach and various watersports. Completing a public transport circle is fairly easy, in the summer at least. Ferries go from Exmouth to Topsham where you can return by train to Exeter or you can cross the estuary to Starcross and take a mainline train for Exeter.

The stretch of the mainline to Plymouth is sometimes called The **Riviera Line**. Brunel's original GWR route is famous across the world. The stretch from Exeter to Newton Abbot sweeps along the sea wall with spectacular views: red cliffs on one side, the sea on the other. The line also passes Powderham Castle's deer park.

The **Tamar Valley Line** runs from Plymouth 15 miles northwards to Gunnislake in Cornwall, through an area of outstanding natural beauty. Passengers get views of the Naval Dockyard and the Tamar Estuary, and cross over the dramatic Calstock Viaduct.

Devon's rail network for a day; **Branch Line Rangers** gives the freedom of one of the local lines – such as the Tarka Line, Tamar Valley Line and Avocet Line. The website www.carfreedaysout.com gives suggestions on days out, maps, walks and ideas on what to do while travelling on some of these lines.

Walking and cycling

From the country's longest footpath (the 600-mile South West Coast Path) to little strolls around a quiet village, Devon is an ideal place for walkers. And it has never been easier, thanks to the county council's website, which now has a wonderful facility for walkers (and cyclists) (see www.devon.gov.uk/index/transport/public_rights_of_way.htm/). The interactive 'path finder' map allows you to zoom into any part of Devon and examine any of the county's **3,200 miles** of public rights of way. You can even find out if there are any stiles, gates or bridges along the paths and how steep or level a route is. There are also lists of walks in each area with map references and details of the walk.

Cyclists should note that Devon is a hilly county and has lots of narrow lanes. There are some really good routes for bikes but for general family pedalling, it's best to plan where you're going. The hills can be very hard work, and the narrow lanes can be dangerous.

A good place to start is www.devon.gov.uk/cycling, where there are maps and details of the county's cycle routes. There are also useful details on how you can combine rail and cycle journeys across Devon. Cycles are carried by all rail companies with a service in Devon, although they all have different policies and availability. Check before you set off.

Each chapter in this book lists cycle hire facilities in that area, and you can get further help on anything to do with cycling from the local tourist information offices – these are listed in each chapter too. Further details about both walking and cycling for pleasure can be found under Activities.

Driving

You would think that driving is much the same wherever you are... but you'd be wrong. Driving in Devon's lanes is a new experience for many visitors. There are hundreds of miles of narrow roads that are only one car wide. The hedges are usually higher than a car so you can't see beyond the narrow green slot. In these conditions you have to be especially careful about pedestrians and cyclists. Sometimes you'll have to stop so they can squeeze past.

If another car meets you head on, one of you has to reverse into a passing place or gateway. The unwritten rule among locals is that the driver nearest to a passing place should reverse. Tempers can fray when outsiders don't follow this rule. Obstinate drivers can sit facing each other, trapped in their cars for as long as 10 minutes, waiting for the other to back down in a bizarre Devonian version of road-rage.

The other Devon hazards are animals. You will sometimes finds animals on the road – either wild or farmed. You could get stuck behind a herd of cows being taken for milking. You'll just have to be patient and follow them at cow walking speed. Don't beep or rev to hurry them. If they get agitated they could hurt themselves or even try to trample your car. And the usual rules about horse-riders apply – don't rev, beep or overtake too closely.

On Dartmoor you'll find sheep wandering freely across the roads. Again be prepared for these additional hazards and be patient. You can be as much at risk as them.

As for route-finding around Devon, you will definitely need a map or a sat-nav. But in spite of a map or sat nav you may end up in a traffic jam the locals would have predicted several days before. So ask people you meet where you are staying for advice, they often know a better way that may not be obvious from a map. There are some sensational driving roads in Devon and the right choices can make your journeys into an entertaining part of the holiday.

Although OS Maps are the most detailed, we recommend Michelin maps and/or the viamichelin.com website for route planning,

10... great Devon drives

1 Dunster to Lynmouth on the A39, the 'Atlantic Highway'

2 Okehampton to Whiddon Down on the old Exeter Road, not the A30. Take the B3260 and then the lanes through Sticklepath and South Zeal

3 Starcross to Torquay along the coast on the A379

4 Sidmouth to Honiton up the Sid Valley on the A375

5 Exeter to Bampton up the Exe Valley on the A396

6 Bampton across Mid Devon to South Molton on the B3227

7 Around the estuaries of Newton Ferrers to Holbeton via the lanes through Noss Mayo, Netton and Battisborough Cross

8 Exeter to Yelverton, right across The Moor on the plunging, winding B3212

9 Tavistock up onto the moor to Dartmeet on the B3357

10 Clyst St Mary to Sidmouth over Woodbury Common on the A3052/B3176

because of one unique facility. Michelin marks in green any roads that are especially scenic. For example, Michelin picks out the B3212 from Exeter to Moretonhampstead on Dartmoor as a 'green' road. Using other maps it might look simpler to take the less interesting A30. You'll find scores of similar examples across the county. We've listed the top 10 beautiful Devon driving roads, as selected by Michelin.

Other transport

We've mentioned ferries and boat trips in each of the relevant chapters. **Horse riding** is available all over the county too. We've mentioned prominent stables, but there are often informal riding arrangements available during peak times, so remember to ask around.

Ballooning is a great holiday treat and plenty of operators are prepared to take you on trips for between £95 and £130 per person. Devon and Somerset Balloons offers flights from Crediton, Bickleigh, Tiverton and Okehampton (☎ 0845 4564201; www.devonandsomersetballoons.co.uk). Aerosaurus offer trips from Rockbeare near Exeter, Ivybridge, Lee Mill near Plymouth and South Brent (☎ 01404 823102; www.ballooning.co.uk). Airtopia balloons fly from Cornwood, Ivybridge, Kingsbridge, Dartmouth, Totnes, Ashburton, Killerton, Exeter and Tiverton (☎ 0845 2262717; www.airtopia.co.uk).

And finally one of the coolest ways to enjoy Devon is in a **VW Camper van**. You'll be a hit at the surfing beaches and the trendiest one in any campsite. O'Connors Campers in Okehampton have started a camper van hire that is ideal for visitors arriving by train or even by 'normal' car. It costs from £75 a day (☎ 01837 659 599; www.oconnorscampers.co.uk).

ACCOMMODATION

There is probably more holiday accommodation in Devon than anywhere in Britain –
yet it can be hard to find somewhere good
to stay in the high season. Whenever you
come, it pays to book as early as you can.
But if you're late and can't find a place, try
the local tourist information centres. Of
course, they won't recommend somewhere
that hasn't paid to join their listings and
won't tell you which on their list is nicest –
they've got their official tourist board ratings
and the centres aren't supposed to express
a personal preference.

Hotels

Hotels are going to be the priciest option
but Devon does have some outstanding
hotels *(see Top 10 hotels)*, some of which
are easily the match of anything in the rest
of the West Country. There are hotels with
two Michelin-starred restaurants, exclusive
luxury facilities or world-class locations.
Obviously you pay for these privileges.

Devon also boasts a vast number of
purely average hotels too and it's worth
checking them out before you pay for something that may not be worth it. Price is not
always the best indicator of quality. And
remember to check the parking arrangements. Parking can be very difficult in some
of Devon's tourist towns. The ABode, Exeter
for example, is one of the best city hotels in
the county but you have to park a long way
away and carry your bags. Exeter's Hotel
Barcelona may not have such a glamorous
location but you can park right outside.

Note that in addition to the prices we've
quoted – the hotel's standard or 'rack-rate' –
there will usually be dinner + B&B deals and
discounts for multiple nights.

Pubs

Often, however, we believe that in much of
Devon, the rooms at pubs and B&Bs are just
as good as the mid-range hotels, but
around half the price. We've included a lot
of pubs and inns in our individual chapters
because we believe they've moved faster to
catch up with social trends than many west
country hotels, restaurants and B&Bs. The
food, atmosphere and accommodation at
the best Devon pubs is often excellent and
they make the best value way to stay in the
county. Apart from the recommendation in
our specific chapters, the best way to find
excellent pubs for eating, drinking or staying
across Devon is the independent *Good Pub
Guide* (£13.49 from goodguides.co.uk).

B&B

Drive along the main road into any of the
Devon seaside resorts and you'll see
dozens of B&B signs. There are thousands
of B&B bedrooms across the county and
obviously they vary greatly. At one end of
the market it's simply the spare bedroom in
someone's house, rented out with a fried
breakfast to earn a few quid on the side.
There are some great bargains at this end,
but some nylon-curtained nightmares too.

At the other end of Devon's B&B world
are some exceptional guesthouses that are
like mini-hotels. Some prices match those at
hotels too. They tend to be cheaper when
they're further from the sea or the main
tourist attractions but prices can vary wildly.
Some of the best deals are on farms, where
the farmer's wife is helping the family business diversify. The houses are usually
historic, the breakfasts memorable. Choose
the right one and you can have a fantastic,
real Devon experience.

Self-catering

Sometimes there are more self-catering
holiday homes than real homes in parts of
Devon. Some villages comprise almost
entirely of holiday cottages and are
deserted out of season. Nevertheless, it
means Devon has some of the most attractive properties to rent in the UK. Some of
the very best are booked years in advance
in the really popular weeks but there is
always something left at the last minute due
to cancellations. Most are rented by the
week but agencies are increasingly offering
short breaks, especially out of season.

We've given examples of some of the
best in the individual chapters but there are
obviously thousands more. You can find
these through internet searches, tourist

The best... Devon hotels and B&Bs

Hotels

1. Bovey Castle, North Bovey – Peter de Savary's luxury country retreat, p.292
2. Burgh Island – an authentic art deco temple on its own private island, p.231
3. Gidleigh Park, Chagford – Michael Caines and Andrew Brownsword together created this opulent gastro hotel, p.292
4. Hotel Barcelona, Exeter – surreal boutique city hotel in former eye hospital, p.68
5. Combe House, near Honiton – this Elizabethan manor was voted 'Country Hotel of the Year 2007', p.97
6. Red Lion, Clovelly – stay on the harbour-side in Devon's prettiest fishing village, p.168
7. Saunton Sands, Saunton – scores highly for its location overlooking the long sandy beach and its superb beach café, p.150
8. Dart Marina Hotel, Dartmouth – modern waterside boutique hotel with its own marina, p.231
9. Orestone Manor, Torquay – beguiling colonial style in rural location overlooking the sea, p.210
10. The Grand Hotel, Torquay – the classic seaside hotel neatly updated for the 21st century, p.210

B&Bs and Inns

1. Galley Restaurant with Rooms, Topsham – stay in a 17th-century cottage next to an acclaimed restaurant, p.68
2. West Colwell Farm, Blackdown Hills – watch the Devon cattle graze from your converted farm dairy, p.97
3. Downderry House, Budleigh Salterton – boutique B&B in a 1920s seaside villa, p.113
4. Westwood, Ilfracombe – luxury contemporary B&B in a Victorian villa overlooking the seaside town, p.140
5. Victoria Lodge, Lynton – sumptuous lashings of Victoriana at this period home, p.128
6. Victoria House, Mortehoe – sleep in a brass bed with a view of the sea, balcony and fresh croissants in the morning, p.150
7. Nonsuch House, Kingswear – great views, award-winning breakfast and Edwardian period charm, p.232
8. Old Chapel Inn, Bigbury – a quirky, cosy and interesting pub/chapel combination, p.232
9. Thomas Luny House, Teignmouth – B&B in the period elegance of the former artist's home, p.211
10. Harton Manor, Hartland – simple but grand village house owned by an artist, p.179

10... Devon campsites

1 Woodovis Park near Tavistock (☎ 01822 832968; www.woodovis.com) – there is an indoor pool and spa, and fresh bread and croissants at this charming small five-star rated camp and caravan site among the trees on the edge of Dartmoor. It won the VisitBritain Rose Award 2007.

2 Beverley Park, Paignton (☎ 01803 843887; www.beverley-holidays.co.uk) – five-star quality seaside site with all the facilities of a holiday camp

3 Hillcrest Farm near Ilfracombe (☎ 01271 863537) – just one six-berth caravan in a pretty garden at the side of a hilltop farmyard

4 Dornafield Touring Park near Newton Abbot (☎ 01803 812732; dornafield.com) – VisitBritain give this leafy site round an old farmhouse the maximum five stars

5 Stoke Barton Farm, Hartland Quay – a wonderfully remote spot overlooking the rugged north-west coast

6 North Morte Farm, Mortehoe – well-equipped site with path down to a little-known sandy beach, p.150

7 Westermill Farm, Exmoor – beautiful remote farm with fields alongside the River Exe, p.128

8 Little Meadow, Ilfracombe – unusually quiet and well-behaved seaside site, see p.140

9 Minnows, Sampford Peverell – pitch alongside the Grand Western Canal with pubs in walking distance, p. 84

10 Exeter Racecourse – a chance to camp in the middle of England's highest racecourse, p. 68

board information, travel/holiday agencies or individual advertisements. Here we've listed the most useful agencies for holiday homes in the county.

Rural Retreats – national upmarket holiday homes with some spectacular properties in Devon; ☎ 01386 701177; www.ruralretreats.co.uk
Helpful Holidays – friendly Chagford-based West Country agency. The Dartmoor selection is particularly good; ☎ 01647 433593; www.helpfulholidays.com
The Landmark Trust – There are a few Devon addresses in this extraordinary national collection of historic properties; ☎ 01628 825925; landmarktrust.co.uk
Coast and Country Cottages – South Hams agency with properties purely in that area; ☎ 01803 839499; www.coastandcountry.co.uk
Classic Cottages – West Country specialist agency with good Devon selection; ☎ 01326 555555; www.classic.co.uk
English Country Cottages – huge national agency with mix of houses across the county ☎ 0870 238 9922; www.english-country-cottages.co.uk

National Trust Cottages – their national range of good quality historic properties includes several excellent locations in Devon; ☎ 0844 8002070; www.national-trustcottages.co.uk

You'll find a longer list of smaller and more locally specialised holiday home agencies on the discoverdevon.com website, under 'The best... places to stay'.

Camping

When the weather's good, camping is popular throughout Devon. But never forget that it's totally weather dependent, and even in Devon good weather is never guaranteed.

The county's campsites vary from the mega parks with waterslides, restaurants and evening entertainment that you'll find in the big seaside resorts to a humble farmer's field with a toilet block.

FOOD AND DRINK

You no longer have to settle for burger and chips in the pubs or gammon steak and pineapple with soggy vegetables in the restaurants. Devon food has finally caught the good food fashion and you'll find some of the finest menus in the west of England. Celebrity chef and Michelin-starred restaurants are now scattered across the county and perhaps more importantly, the general average has improved drastically. A high proportion of pubs now serve decent food, with a small selection dishing up food that would embarrass many expensive London restaurants.

There is still cheap fast food and take-aways everywhere of course, particularly in holiday hot spots such as North Devon's surfing coast or the Torbay Riviera. Even here though, it's possible to find excellent stuff.

Devon has some of the UK's best **pasties**, although it has plenty of the worst type of garage cold-cabinet pasties too. If it has a crimped edge along one side, locals call it 'traditional' and it's enormous and expensive – that is usually a good sign. Don't be afraid to ask the locals – there is a West Country pride in knowing where to find the best pasties. Most towns have a revered pasty baker, and most Devonians will know where their nearest one is.

As for **fish and chips**, there are a few superb ones and we've tried to highlight the best in the relevant chapters. The others certainly have no excuse, with some of the UK's best fresh seafood on the doorstep.

Seafood is the first thing to look for on the menu – the chefs around the south and north coast have their pick of the day's catches. Chefs take mobile calls from boats still at sea offering them something they've just hauled in. You'll see chefs in towns such as Dartmouth and Ilfracombe collecting fish from the quayside or sometimes you'll see fishermen wander into a restaurant in their oilskins carrying a package in newspaper to deliver to the kitchen. Some restaurants and hotels even have their own boat. All this is a good sign. Fresh and local means no hanging around in markets, stores, delivery vans, supermarkets or wasted motorway miles.

Fish can also mean the salmon and trout caught in the rivers, mainly on Dartmoor and Exmoor. The moors also provide plenty of game – pheasant, venison and even wild boar are common on menus around the national parks.

Devonians are just catching onto the fact that their beef is rather special. **Ruby Red Devon** cattle are all over the landscape and graze on some of Britain's lushest and cleanest pastures. So it's no surprise that Devon beef is among the best you can buy. The meat has always been there but now chefs are actually calling it Ruby Red on their menus to point out it's local. We've also highlighted places you can buy it fresh from the farm in each chapter. It can make for a superb Devon holiday barbecue.

Some old specialities such as the **Devon Cobbler** (meat casserole with a scone topping) are rarely seen today but scones are ubiquitous in another guise – the **cream tea**. You'll see these advertised approximately every 100 yards throughout the county. It's a difficult thing to get wrong, so choose places that have lovely locations and pretty views. Ideally the scones will be

10... Devon specialities

1 Clotted cream tea It's best with homemade jam and scones fresh from the Aga

2 Cider Don't believe that it all comes from Somerset – Devon farmers make some of the world's best scrumpy

3 Ruby Red Devon beef Enjoy the tastiest local beef in a traditional Sunday roast sitting by the fire in a country pub

4 Fresh fish It could be sea bass, sole, plaice or mackerel straight from the harbourside... or trout and salmon caught from Devon's fly-fishing rivers

5 Strawberries Pick-your-own or pick up a punnet at the roadside. Eat immediately – preferably with clotted cream

6 Pasties And don't believe they all come from Cornwall either. Devon bakers make them just as well

7 Clotted cream ice cream Is this a local delicacy or just a marketing gimmick? Wait till you've tasted it...

8 Smoked fish and chicken Available all over Devon from the nationally renowned Dartmouth Smokehouse

9 Local beer Microbreweries all over the county are making traditional real ales using Tuckers Malt from Newton Abbot

10 Fresh crab In salad or sandwiches, it always tastes best with a view of the sea

homemade but the only *must* for a proper Devon cream tea is that the cream is clotted. The problem is that it is an entirely unhealthy meal and incredibly filling – so don't have one just before dinner.

Devon also has some of the UK's finest country **pubs**. We've already praised their food and accommodation, now it's time to laud the atmosphere and drink. Open fires, flagstones and beams are the ideal, but ultimately it's the gentle friendliness that counts for most. And that, being a Devon speciality, is everywhere.

Drink-wise there is now a great selection of breweries across the county so many pubs have some local real ale to try. There is usually cider too – often from a Devon farm.

And if the bar staff warn you about a local **scrumpy** don't ignore them or think they're joking. Rough cider has the unique quality of tasting mild and fruity while disguising a tremendous alcohol content.

Finally watch out for the **food festivals** of Devon. They are primarily marketing exercises to promote local restaurants but can be good fun if you happen to be around at the right time. The Exmoor Food Festival in the second week of October (☎ 01458 241401; www.exmoorfoodfestival.co.uk) includes events such as a brewery tour, cookery demonstrations by local chefs and themed evenings around local produce at restaurants on the moor.

Exeter's Food Festival is based in the

Northernhay Gardens amid the ruins of the Norman Rougement Castle. It's always in spring, so check for dates with the tourist office. There are usually celebrity chefs around: Michael Caines and Hugh Fearnley-Whittingstall are likely contenders. There is an on-site Festival Café and Beer Festival of local ales (www.visitsouthwest.co.uk/exeter-foodfestival).

Dartmouth Food Festival in the second week of October is slightly more educational with talks and demonstrations by local producers and cooks, as well as special promotions in the town's restaurants (dartmouthfoodfestival.co.uk). The county council organises a month-long 'Devon Celebration of Food' in October, which has food events all over Devon but is so spread out and varied it's difficult to pin down a theme. Visit devoncelebrationoffood.co.uk for the listings.

FESTIVALS AND ANNUAL EVENTS

There are the traditional fêtes and carnivals in every settlement across the county, and they're nearly always in the summer. We've picked out the best in the relevant chapters. But thanks to the tourist industry there are now hundreds of other 'fairs', 'festivals' and 'weeks' that pop up across Devon throughout the summer season. Some are worthwhile but others are poorly attended marketing exercises. The absolute classics that you can build a holiday around are:

Ottery Barrel Rolling (5 Nov)
Widecombe Fair (second week of Sept)
Dartmouth Regatta (last week of Aug)
Cavaliers' Bonfire at Torrington (whenever they get round to it, probably the Aug bank holiday weekend)
Sidmouth Folk Festival (first week of Aug)

Others to note should you be around the area at this time are given by month below.
January
Second week – the traditional apple-tree 'wassailing' ceremony in the village orchard, Stoke Gabriel, with lantern procession, dancers, singers, Mummers Play and local cider.
February
Second week – Dartmouth Comedy festival at the Flavel Arts Centre.
Second week – Torrington Cavalier March, a torch-lit march, re-enactment and general civil war festivities commemorating the Battle of Torrington.
March
First weekend – Startrek, Ilfracombe, hundreds of people compete in a night-time orienteering exercise.
First two weeks – Exeter Vibraphonic Festival of multicultural urban music.
April
First week – Dartmouth Gig Regatta, not the major summer regatta but teams of locals in rowing race tournament.
Fourth week – Tuckers Maltings Beer Festival, one of the UK's most prestigious, held in a traditional malthouse in Newton Abbot.
Fourth week – Wall of Death Weekend, Dingles Fairground Heritage Centre, near Tavistock, live shows from some of the last surviving riders.
May
First weekend – Blackawton Festival of Worm Charming, 24th year of village fun event.
First Thursday – Torrington May Day processions, funfair and dancing.
First week – North Devon Walking Festival, dozens of guided walks in North Devon and Exmoor over nine days.
Second weekend – Festival of Dartmoor Literature, Tavistock.
Third week – Devon County Show, the area's premier rural show at Exeter's Westpoint Arena.
Third week – Tiverton Spring Festival, some maypoles but mostly an arts festival.
Last week – Exmouth Festival, local live music events.
Last week – Westward Ho! Potwalloping Festival – revival of ancient tradition means crafts, stalls and entertainment at seaside town.
Last week – Appledore Visual Arts festival, arts and crafts extravaganza in waterside village.

The best... restaurants and gastropubs

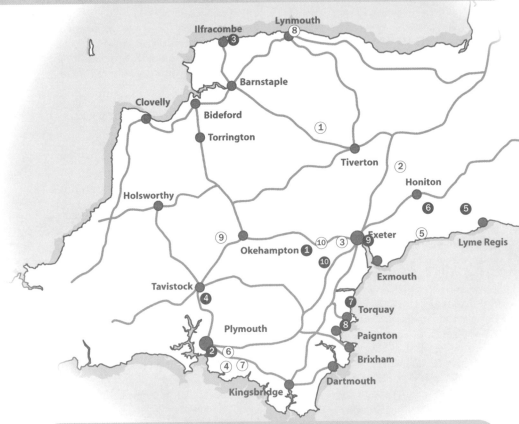

Restaurants

1. Gidleigh Park near Chagford serves two-Michelin star food by celebrity chef Michael Caines, p.297
2. Tanners, Plymouth. The Tanner brothers' 2007 AA Restaurant of the Year is housed in the city's oldest building, p.258
3. No 11 The Quay, Ilfracombe. You must visit Damien Hirst's money-no-object conversion of a harbourside pub into a gourmet restaurant, p.143
4. The Horn of Plenty, near Tavistock. Enjoy traditional Michelin-starred cuisine at this country house hotel, p. 296
5. River Cottage Canteen, Axminster. Hugh Fearnley-Whittingstall's stylishly shabby café-restaurant uses the best local ingredients, p.100
6. Combe House, Near Honiton. You'll find classic fine food in this cosily romantic country house hotel, p.100
7. Orestone Manor, Torquay. You can't help enjoy food served amid colonial splendour in a rural seaside setting, p.214
8. The Elephant, Torquay. Orestone's highly-rated town centre restaurant offshoot overlooking the harbour, p. 214
9. ABode Exeter. Michael Caines stylish restaurant next to the Cathedral, p.72
10. Bovey Castle, near Moretonhampstead. Dress is smart casual at this expensive but fine restaurant, p.296

Gastropubs

1. Mason's Arms, Knowstone. You'll find Michelin-starred pub grub as good as any restaurant here, p.188
2. The Drewe Arms, Broadhembury. It's thatched and white-washed, stands in a picturesque setting and seafood is the speciality, p.100
3. The Nobody Inn, Doddiscombleigh near Exeter. Discover a magical ancient pub atmosphere with acclaimed food and wine, p.73
4. Ship Inn, Noss Mayo. You can't fail with this brilliant estuary-side location, atmospheric décor and fine food, p.259
5. Mason's Arms, Branscombe. Choose between fine restaurant or hearty pub grub in this pretty seaside retreat, p.116
6. The Rose and Crown, Yealmpton. One pub, two restaurants: one modern, one seafood. And both highly rated, p.258
7. Dartmoor Union, Holbeton. Tuck into award-winning food in a lovely old country inn with its own brewery, p.258
8. Rising Sun, Lynmouth. The inn enjoys a superb location on a tiny harbourside, the food's not bad either, p.131
9. Dartmoor Inn, Lydford. Celebrity chef Michael Caines is a regular at this stylish rural pub, p.297
10. Sandy Park Inn, Chagford. Enjoy the food at the good-value part of the Bovey Castle empire, p.297

Last week – The Hunting of the Earl of Rone, Combe Martin – mysterious but entertaining ancient rituals through the town to the beach.

June

All month – North Devon Festival – massive catalogue of events small and big across the North Devon area.

First week – Coast2Coast Endurance Race, 130-mile running, cycling and kayaking challenge over two days.

Second week – Ilfracombe Victorian Week, everyone dresses in period costume for parades, concerts and fireworks.

Second weekend – Lynton and Lynmouth Music Festival, free open-air gigs around the two towns.

Mid-summer – the annual Goldcoast Oceanfest at Croyde Bay includes surfing, live bands and the Red Arrows.

July

Third week – Bread weighing and ale tasting – traditional ceremonies in Ashburton ending in procession and medieval fair.

Fourth week – Hot Pennies Festival, annual fair that ends with crowds trying to catch hot pennies in Honiton.

August

Second week – Dartmoor Folk Festival, a lively annual traditional folk music event near Okehampton.

Second week – Dawlish Carnival, one of the biggest seaside town carnivals that runs for a week culminating in an airshow and a procession.

Second week – Bideford Folk Festival, a week of traditional song, music and dance.

Second week – British Firework Championships, watch the battle of top firework companies from Plymouth Waterfront.

Third week – Orange Rolling, Totnes. Mysterious re-enactment of incident in which Drake bumped into orange delivery boy and fruit rolled down the steep main street.

September

First week – Ilfracombe Folk Festival, weekend of acoustic music around the waterfront.

First week – Bideford Regatta, traditional, serious rowing races.

Third week – Agatha Christie Week, talks, performances and screenings around Torbay.

End of September into October – Appledore Book Festival, nine-day literary event including lessons in the local dialect.

October

Second Wednesday – Tavistock Goose Fair, annual market fair dating back to 12th century. Eat goose, browse hundreds of stalls and enjoy a funfair.

November

Second weekend – Teignmouth Jazz Festival, mainly traditional music events in seaside town

TRAVELLING WITH CHILDREN

With two long coastlines offering scores of sandy beaches and two national parks full of tors to climb and rivers to explore, you'd think there would be enough for the little darlings. But no, they always demand more... So Devon offers you dozens of theme parks and amusement complexes and farm attractions. They're listed in each chapter but we've also listed the very best children's attractions here, just in case parents get to that desperate holiday state of 'something needed to entertain them immediately...'

ACTIVITIES

Interested in activity holidays? You first activity should be to visit the tourist board's website: discoverdevon.com or call 0870 608 5531. Devon County Council produce very useful **free booklets** on walking, cycling and horse riding.

The regional tourist board has some useful information too. Its excellent website for outdoor activities at www.itsadventure-southwest.co.uk lists dozens of activities and where you can do them. Of course being the South West Tourist Board, they're not all in Devon – but many are.

Devon's own subsite, **www.discoverdevon.com/active-devon**, is another good source of activity listings, although the South West website is easier to navigate.

Walking

There are 3,500 miles of footpaths in Devon. With so many to choose from, we think most people will be able to find one that's just right for their needs, wishes and abilities.

The Devon walking booklet mentioned above details the long-distance trails in the county and gives detailed routes and maps for 10 other taster walks around the county. The Devon tourism information service also provides free route-planning booklets for many of the longer trails and sells guides to others. Visit www.discoverdevon.com or call 0870 608 5531.

The network of trails on **Dartmoo**r and **Exmoor** give the best possibilities for hiking. The national parks are criss-crossed with trails and rights of way, with few roads to disturb you.

When walking on the moors treat them as if you were taking a mountain hike. A good map and the right clothes are essential. If you're going for any distance prepare carefully. People do die on Dartmoor – it's higher than many people think and it can take much longer to walk across steep, rocky or boggy ground than you might expect. Rapid changes in weather are common and fog can be a particular hazard. If this warning worries you, there are guided walks available. Contact the **High Moors Visitor Centre** at Princetown (see Dartmoor chapter).

For the rest of Devon, the coast and the estuaries attract most walkers. **The South West Coast Path** is a highlight, the only National Trail in the county. It's comprehensively marked on both north and south coasts, but varies from easy strolling to arduous challenges. It never fails to be beautiful though. The path was created by fishermen, coastguards and smugglers over the centuries and now covers 90 miles along the North Devon coast and 115 miles in the South.

It's difficult to pick highlights but there is no doubting that these are spectacular sections:

Around Combe Martin and Ilfracombe
The rugged rocks around Hartland Point
Plymouth Sound
The South Hams' estuaries
Anywhere on the World Heritage Coast

There are 19 other long-distance trails within Devon. The county's 'walking' booklet details them all. They include:

The popular **Tarka Trail** – a figure of eight route across the central northern part of the county
The **Two Moors Way** – which runs for 100 miles between Ivybridge and Lynmouth, crossing Dartmoor and Exmoor
The **Devonshire Heartland Way** – a 43 mile romp linking Okehampton with the Exe Valley

The www.discoverdevon.com website has another 54 walks that can be downloaded, ranging from 'Plymouth's forts and castles' to 'Devon's Little Switzerland'. And the BBC Devon website (www.bbc.co.uk/devon) lists 25 walks with photos and interesting details along the way.

Climbing

Climbers' hotspots are generally on the coast and Dartmoor. The single best spot is the thin, jagged cliffs at **Sharpnose Point**, in the far north-west. These daunting rocks are considered the match of anything in Britain for single-pitch climbs. The narrow fins extend into the sea and offer 33 different traditional routes – mostly of higher grades.

Other Devon climbing highlights include **Chudleigh Rocks** to the south-east of Dartmoor, the riverside cliff known as the **Dewerstone** to the south-east of Dartmoor; and **Haytor**, which has challenging hidden faces away from the crowds on the south and eastern flanks. For full route information you can't beat the excellent www.rockfax.com/databases

As for courses and guides, here are some of the most useful:

The **Rock Climbing and Caving Centre** at Chudleigh (☎ 01626 852 717; www.rock-centre.co.uk) has with cliffs and caves

The best... things to do with children

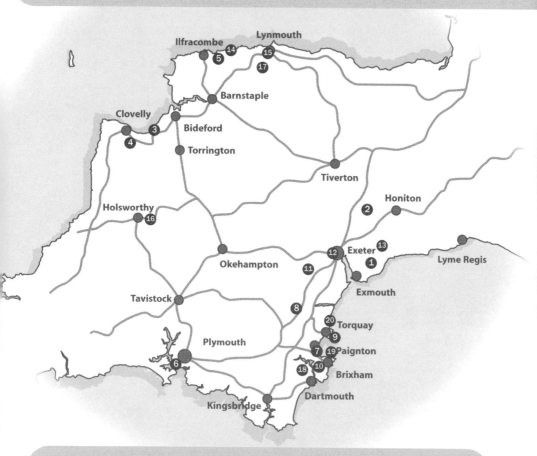

1. Crealy Adventure Park, near East Budleigh – the South West's biggest theme park, with all-weather entertainment for all ages, p.66
2. Diggerland, near Collumpton – lots of mechanical earth-movers and lots of mud, p.82
3. The Big Sheep, near Bideford – light-hearted activity farm themed around sheep. Sounds daft? It is... p.157
4. Milky Way Adventure Park, near Clovelly – all-weather theme park ranging from a rollercoaster to pets corner, p.158
5. Watermouth Castle, near Combe Martin – quirky old-fashioned theme park for younger children, p.138
6. National Marine Aquarium, Plymouth – educational fish zoo with a chance to touch the slimy creatures..., p.254
7. Paignton Zoo, Paignton – the county's biggest and best zoo by miles is a great family day out, p.207
8. River Dart Country Park, Ashburton – riverside adventure parks for children of all ages, p.289
9. Living Coasts, Torquay – get right up close to sea creatures like penguins and seals, p.200
10. Quaywest Waterpark, Paignton – Britain's biggest waterpark with slides and pools for all ages, p.207
11. Miniature Pony Centre, North Bovey – here's a chance to play, ride and watch 150 child-sized animals, p.290
12. Underground Passages, Exeter – don a hard hat to explore the spooky medieval labyrinth under the city, p.66
13. Bicton Gardens, near East Budleigh – indoor and outdoor play areas and a woodland railway keep the children happy here, p.112
14. Wildlife and Dinosaur Park, near Combe Martin – entertaining mix of dinosaur models, scary rides and animals, p.144
15. Glen Lyn Gorge, Lynmouth – entertaining and educational riverside attraction based on the power of water, p.129
16. Dragon Archery Centre, near Holsworthy – serious archery adventure for over eights, p.174
17. Exmoor Zoo, near Bratton Fleming – hundreds of animals to watch and some to hand-feed, p.185
18. Woodland Leisure Park, near Blackawton – theme park with water slides and bumper boats, p.228
19. Goodrington Park, Goodrington – behind-the-beach area full of rides, amusements and attractions, p.208
20. Babbacombe Model Village – a huge and detailed miniature town that will amaze younger children, p.208

within its own site, as well as an indoor climbing wall.

Skern Lodge near Bideford (☎ 01237 475 992; www.skernlodge.co.uk) offers accommodation, courses and many activities, including rock climbing and abseiling. (See Bideford chapter.)

CRS Adventures, Ashburton (☎ 07891 635964; crsadventures.com) also offer caving, climbing and abseiling sessions from £30 per person per day.

Cycling

Devon is hilly and the narrow lanes aren't well suited to a mix of cycles and cars. But there are some excellent routes available with some great traffic-free stretches.

There are more than 150 miles of National Cycle Network (NCN) in Devon. Two NCN routes are fully mapped – the **Coast2Coast** and **West Country Way**. A third, the **South Coast Route**, is still under development, although some sections are open.

The best stretches are on parts of the Coast2Coast route from Ilfracombe to Plymouth and around the Grand Western Canal near Tiverton.

The Coast2Coast has the longest traffic-free sections, mainly on the Tarka Trail on the route of closed down railway lines. It passes through tunnels and crosses viaducts and there are views from the estuaries and beaches of North Devon, across the moor to the busy city of Plymouth. The longest traffic-free section is 32 miles.

Anyone thinking about cycling in Devon should get the free 'cycling' booklet from Devon County Council (via www.discoverdevon.com or call 0870 608 5531). It details the three National Network routes and eight smaller cycle routes across the county. Discoverdevon.com has even more routes you can download and you can buy or order free cycle maps too, including an excellent free cycle map of Exeter.

Further information is available from Mid Devon District Council (☎ 01884 255255; www.middevon.gov.uk) which produces cycle leaflets and information. A five-route pack is available to order online at www.okehampton.co.uk or by calling 01822

813701. And a map of mountain bike routes on Dartmoor (price £7.50) is available from the **National Park Authority** (☎ 01626 832093; www.dartmoor-npa.gov.uk).

For general enquiries about cycling in Devon contact the county council's special cycling department on ☎ 01392 382811.

Horse riding

Such a rural county offers some great scenic opportunities for horse riding, from beginners to the experienced. There are 734 miles of bridleways across the county, so you're never far from an easy route. The *Horse and Hound* magazine has judged Devon as the UK's 'horsiest' county, and indeed there are around 24,300 horses within its borders.

Again, there is an excellent free booklet available from the county tourism department called '*Horse Riding*'. Get a copy via www.discoverdevon.com or call 0870 608 5531. It details nine areas that horse-riders should consider: the two National Parks, four circular trails and three free-riding areas. And the website discoverdevon.com lists more routes with accommodation and places to eat.

Across the county there are all sorts of ways to enjoy riding. Full or half-day treks are available at dozens of stables (listed on www.discoverdevon.com). Some of the best are given in the relevant chapters of this guide.

More specialist centres offer moor or beach riding. There are even courses to learn to drive a horse and carriage at the National Trust's Arlington Court (see Woolacombe chapter).

Surfing

The north coast of Devon has some of Britain's best surfing beaches. Wear a wet suit and they're useable all year round. **Croyde Bay, Saunton** and **Woolacombe** are the epicentres of this cult/sport/craze. These are the spots with the most facilities for surfers too – there are kiosks hiring and selling all the kit you'll need, courses to teach surfing and the all-important après-surf hangouts.

The lesser surf spots are Lynmouth and Westward Ho!, and Bantham, Wembury and Challaborough on the south coast.

The South West tourism website (www.itsadventuresouthwest.co.uk) has all the information you'll need to plan a surfing trip – from surf forecasts (try the impressive www.magicseaweed.com) to surfing schools. **Surf South West Surf School** in Croyde is one of the best with half-day lessons starting at £25. Visit www.surfsouth-west.com or call 01271 890400.

The British Surfing Association's site has plenty of advice and information too. Visit www.britsurf.co.uk or call 01637 876 474.

Watersports

The South West tourist board's outdoor activity site,www.itsadventuresouthwest.co.uk, lists 13 different watersports in its directory of local operators – so there is plenty of choice.

Surfing might be concentrated on the north coast but watersports are more evenly spread between the north and south. For example, you'll find the **Mount Batten Centre** in our Plymouth chapter, Exmouth's watersports operators in our Heritage Coast chapter and the watersports at Tunnels Beach in our Ilfracombe chapter. The sheltered waters of Plymouth Sound and the Exe Estuary are two of the favoured spots for wind-powered watersports.

Exmouth is a centre for **diving** too. Jurassic Coast Diving (☎ 01395 268 090; www.jcdiving.co.uk) offer instruction and trips along the Jurassic Coast ranging from shallow reefs to deep water wrecks. Lundy is another magnet for divers, the Marine Nature Reserve here protects species such as sea urchins, starfish and the red-banded fish, which is only found here. And Plymouth provides several dive operators. Check with the Mount Batten Centre (☎ 01752 406444; www.mount-batten-centre.com) for details.

Exmouth-based Edge Watersports (see Heritage Coast chapter) offer wind-powered **buggying** among other sports.

You'll find more extreme watersports, such as **coasteering, waterfall climbing,**

pier jumping and **rafting** on both coasts. Again consult www.itsadventuresouthwest. co.uk and www.discoverdevon.com/active-devon for specific operators.

Other activities

Such a tourist-friendly area has hundreds of different activities available. We can't list them all but if there is something you fancy doing contact the local tourist board for advice. If it's a bit off the wall try the comprehensive listings on www.itsadventuresouthwest.co.uk/.

Meanwhile, here are some ideas you may not have thought of:

Dartmoor Gliding Society, Tavistock (☎ 01752 848278; www.dartmoorgliding.co.uk) offers a spectacular introductory flight over Dartmoor for £45.

Land Rover Experience, Honiton (☎ 0870 2644471; www.lre9.com) provides 4 x 4 off-road instruction and adventures from £175 per half day.

Skydive UK, Dunkerswell, near Honiton (☎ 01404 890222; www.skydiveukltd.com) gives you a chance to parachute over the beautiful Blackdown Hills from £130 per solo jump, and £225 for tandem.

Devon Mountain Bike Holidays, Dartmoor (☎ 07747 041 596; www.dmbholidays.co.uk) offers guided mountain biking trips across Dartmoor from £40 a day.

ORGANISED HOLIDAYS AND COURSES

The guide section of this book gives the important places where organised holiday centres crop up. There are dozens across the county so it's best to check out the comprehensive listings on the South West and Devon tourist board websites (www.itsadventuresouthwest.co.uk; www.discoverdevon.com). In the meantime, if you can't wait to book something here are the pick of the adventure centres in Devon.

Skern Lodge – near Bideford (☎ 01237 475992; www.skernlodge.com). Families and individuals can do a single session or a residential course on a wide range of activities from climbing to crabbing.
Ashcombe Adventure Centre – near Dawlish (☎ 01626 866 766; www.ashcombeadventure.co.uk). Residential activity breaks, one or half-day activities and team building. Karting, paintball, quad biking, shooting, fishing and archery.
Essential Adventures – Exmouth (☎ 01395 27 11 56; www.essential-adventure.co.uk) runs courses and tailor-made activity holidays covering water and rocks, from kitesurfing to abseiling.
The Mount Batten Centre – Plymouth (☎ 01752 406444; www.mount-batten-centre.com) offers mainly watersports but is increasingly offering land-based adventure activities too in half-day sessions or week-long courses, with accommodation.

FURTHER INFORMATION

By now you should have realised that **www.discoverdevon.com** is a primary source of official information and listings from tourist department at Devon County Council. Parts of it are excellent, parts are awkward to navigate so sometimes we've recommended the South West tourism websites, such as **www.itsadventuresouthwest.co.uk, www.naturesouthwest.co.uk and www.familyholidaysouthwest.co.uk.**

Other great sources of information include maps. You might use sat-nav or GPS to reach Devon but planning routes and touring holidays is impossible without a decent map. The various scale maps produced by the Ordnance Survey (OS) are the most accurate and you can buy maps from the OS website (**leisure.ordnancesurvey.co.uk**) or by calling 0845 456 0420.

Car drivers may find Michelin maps more useful – they are the only ones that show which roads are more scenic than others. You can consult their mapping at **viamichelin.com** and plan routes, but to buy one of their road atlases you'll have to try a general website (such as www.amazon.co.uk).

Local media
Devon's TV stations are based in Plymouth, both BBC and the independent West Country TV, although you are able to pick up Welsh stations in North Devon. The radio stations are more scattered: **BBC Radio Devon** is as staid and authoritative as you'd expect. It broadcasts on AM, FM and digital. The output sometimes varies among the different Devon regions. On AM tune to: 1458kHz (Torbay and South Devon), 801kHz (Barnstaple and North Devon), 855kHz (Plymouth), 990kHz (Exeter and East Devon). On FM you can find it on: 103.4MHz (Plymouth and West Devon), 104.3MHz (Torbay and South Devon), 95.7MHz (Plympton), 95.8MHz (Exeter) and 96.0MHz (Okehampton).

Independent radio stations have more varied output. They can be entertainingly amateurish or really rather good. Tune into:

Lantern FM – covers Barnstaple, Ilfracombe and Bideford, on 96.2 or 97.3 FM.
Palm 105.5 – covers Torbay with its slogan 'All time favourites for South Devon' perhaps indicating how cool its output might be. It's on 105.5 FM.
Plymouth Sound – is a classic 'best of the 80, 90s and today' type indie station covering west Devon. Find it on 96.6 FM (Tavistock) and 97 (Plymouth). Its sister station *Plymouth Gold* is on 1152 AM.

South Hams Radio – covers the southern part of the county. Tune to 100.5 (Totnes), 100.8 (Dartmouth), 101.2 (Kingsbridge) and 101.9 (Ivybridge).
Gemini FM – one of the best and most popular locally, covering Exeter, East Devon and Torbay on 96.4 (Torbay), 97.0 (Exeter) and 103.0FM (Honiton).

The **Western Morning News** is the daily morning newspaper, published in Plymouth and covering the whole south-west. It's a high quality broadsheet-style paper. Its sister evening papers are more tabloid, but still very professional: the **Plymouth Evening Herald**, **Herald Express** in Torbay and Exeter's **Express & Echo**.

Then there are the weeklies, a more varied and quirky bunch, including: the **North Devon Journal** based in Barnstaple; **Mid Devon Star** based in Tiverton; **The Town Crier** in Torrington; **Mid Devon Gazette** based in Tiverton; **The Honiton Advertiser**, and the ancient **Pullman's Weekly News**, which covers East Devon. The liveliest weekly by far is the Plymouth-based tabloid **The Sunday Independent**.

The paper's websites are perhaps the best source of the latest Devon news, information and what's on listings. Visit: **thisisexeter.co.uk**, **thisissouthdevon.co.uk**, **thisisplymouth.co.uk** and **thisisdevon.co.uk**.

THE BACKGROUND

HISTORY

Unlike Cornwall, Devon has always thought of itself as a joined up part of the rest of England. It may be a long way from the centres of power but has always been in touch with the important action. And some major events in British history took place here.

Early history

You could say Devon's earliest history is found in the prehistoric fossils along the Jurassic Coast, which starts on the south-eastern edge of the county. It's one of the greatest spots in Europe to find fossils that pre-date man by millions of years. You can learn about them in guided walks from Lyme Regis (ask at the tourist office at Lyme).

But the history of Devonshire's humans starts at Kent's Cavern in Torquay, which is still a brilliant attraction today. The first sign of human habitation in the county – indeed in Britain – are bones found here that, incredibly, date from 40,000BC. And flint hand axes found here date back a dizzying half a million years.

The next signs of progress are much later – about 2,000BC. Bronze Age tribes left plenty of traces of their time as the dominant culture in Devon – around 1,200 burial mounds, mostly on Dartmoor. Many walks on the moor will pass some signs of Bronze and Iron Age lives – such as stone rows, stone circles and hut circles. The ancient stone clapper bridges, for example the one at Postbridge, are thought to date from this time.

Move forward a couple of thousand years and the Roman invaders marched along the south coast defeating every tribe in their way. In AD48 about 5,000 men of the Second Augustan Legion under Vespasian took over the settlement they called Isca Domnoniorum, now known as Exeter. They built a fort to protect it against the Celtic tribes around them.

And 2000 years later, it's still easy to follow the impressive red sandstone Roman walls of Exeter today. About 70% remain and there are guided walks of the walls available through the Red Coat Guide system (see Exeter chapter).

The Romans' huge stone bath-house is under what is now the Cathedral Close and was excavated in the 1970s. It was found to be an impressive structure with room for hundreds of bathers. It was carefully covered up again and still lies beneath the close.

The Romans also built smaller forts at Lapford near Crediton, Bolham outside Tiverton and Clayhanger near Bampton. They also set up iron-ore workings near Brayford in north-west Devon and a network of roads to connect these outposts.

There was considerable fighting against the Romans in the Taw Valley. In this area were sacred riverside groves of the Celtic Dumnonian people. The Celts called the rivers Taw, Mole and Yeo, the Nemeton, Nemet and Nimet. These ancient names live on in North Devon village names, such as Bishops Nympton and Nymet Tracey. The legionnaires also built forts at Okehampton, North Tawton and Bury Barton (now on the A3072) as the tribesmen fought in vain to protect their sacred sites from Roman desecration.

When the Romans eventually withdrew, it was the Germanic Saxons who took charge, forcing many Celts over the Tamar into Cornwall. The descendants of the Dumnonii tribe who remained integrated with the Saxons and were gradually converted to Christianity by missionaries such as the holy Wynfrith (later St Boniface) from Crediton in the eighth century.

St Boniface was born in Crediton around AD680 and sent to Exeter to be educated by monks. The Cathedral Library's greatest treasure dates from this time. The *Exeter Book* – a collection of illustrated riddles and

THE NAME GAME

It's fun trying to guess how some of the strange Devon village names came into being. It helps to think of the broadest Devonian accent you've ever heard and then imagine that voice saying the name. Even today the local Devon dialect likes to insert extra vowels into words to soften them.

In centuries past Chagford was Chagyford, Dartmoor was Dartymoor and Dartmouth was Dartymouth – hence Chaucer's joke about the corrupt sailor from 'Dirtymouth'. The word Devon itself comes from the Celtic 'Dyfnaint' – the land of deep valleys.

Many old Devon names are like little pictures of what was there hundreds of years ago. The commonest part of Devon surnames is 'cote' or 'cott' – local phonebooks are full of Westcotts, Endicotts, Northcotts and so on. This was once a small humble dwelling of a peasant or swineherd. Another common word is 'beare' or 'beer' – that meant a small wood. So Beer in East Devon is not named after the drink at all...

Saxons called a valley a 'cumbe' or 'coomb' and that lives in place names such as Combe Martin, Ilfracombe and Holcombe. 'Worthy' was a Saxon word for small holding – hence names such as Bradworthy and Holsworthy.

'Ton' and 'don' meant a small community and has become integrated in many town names like Crediton (settlement near the river Credy) and Cheriton (settlement by a church). If the Saxon Devonians put an 'ing' in front of the 'ton' it meant the place was a bit bigger or more important – spots such as Alphington and Kilmington must have been something special back then.

There are about 20 Devon places using 'Buckland' – this just refers to somewhere held by a knight that was recorded in the Domesday Book. So Buckland Abbey was really the abbey mentioned in 'The Book'.

A 'barton' was an enclosed courtyard and has become popular as the name of hundreds of farms all over the county. When in Budleigh or Chudleigh note that a 'leigh' was a clearing, and if visiting Bridestowe and Jacobstow remember that a 'stowe' meant a connection with a saint. The three Sampfords in Devon derive from the word for a sandy ford and the ancient Celtic word for water 'ta' was the root of the Tamar, Taw, Tavy, Teign and probably Torridge rivers. The Dart, however, comes from 'dwr' meaning oak tree and 'clyst' means clear. The River Exe is thought to be a Roman invention.

poems – can still be seen by visitors.

The Danes, who were taking over most of Britain in the ninth and tenth centuries, didn't make many inroads into the far west. The western Saxons, under Alfred the Great and his descendants, kept driving them back. He once marched his army across the country to defeat a Danish army besieging Exeter. Yet marauding Danes did manage to capture and occupy Exeter briefly in AD1003, destroying much of the Cathedral's priceless archive of manuscripts.

The Normans

In AD1066 all that changed. After the Norman Conquest, there were new imposing castles built at Exeter, Totnes and Okehampton, which can still be seen in various states of disrepair today. The French invaders did bring peace and relative prosperity as Devon's cloth trade boomed into the medieval era.

Sheep were grazed across the county's grassy hills, their wool was spun in villages and carted to towns. From there it was exported by increasingly wealthy merchants from towns that grew into important ports, such as Exeter, Topsham, Plymouth, Totnes, Dartmouth and Bideford.

St Boniface's birthplace, Crediton, had been the Cathedral town until 1050. It still boasts a much grander church than you'd expect for a small market town. Lottery-funded excavations in 2007 found traces of the Saxon cathedral underneath it. But back in Saxon times, when Leofric became Bishop he said he didn't want to be stuck in a mere 'village' and transferred the head of the diocese to the booming town of Exeter further south. Thanks to the Normans, work on the city's great Cathedral started soon afterwards.

The Normans were organised enough to start exploiting the west's natural resources. The valuable tin mining towns of Ashburton and Tavistock were made Stannary Towns – which granted financial privileges and their own separate legal system.

At the same time Beer and Brixham were growing as fishing centres. The original medieval layout of their harbour and streets

The best... historical experiences in Devon

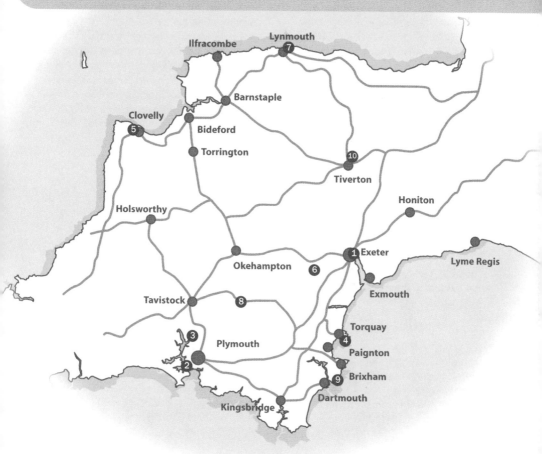

1 Gaze on the medieval splendour of Exeter Cathedral and the ancient buildings of its Close, p.60

2 Sense the seafaring heritage in the cobbled lanes, overhanging Tudor homes and nautical warehouses of Plymouth's Barbican, p.251

3 Experience the relics of a bygone industrial age at Morwellham Quay in the Tamar Valley World Heritage Site, p.268

4 Step into a stone-age family's home – deep underground at Kent's Cavern caves in Torquay, p.207

5 Walk down the tumbling main street of Clovelly – a vision of a Devon fishing village of hundreds of years ago, p.165

6 Explore the extraordinary Castle Drogo – amazingly, Devon's best castle is less than 100 years old, p.281

7 Ride the water-powered Cliff Railway from Lynton to Lynmouth for a memorable glimpse of Victorian ingenuity, p.124

8 Spot the notorious Dartmoor Prison grimly rising from the bleak moorland and enjoy the quirky prison museum in Princetown, p.288

9 Ride aboard the perfectly restored steam train from Paignton to Kingswear, then sail across Dartmouth's historic harbour on a ferry, p.224

10 Enjoy a sedate trip on a horse-drawn narrow boat along the Grand Western Canal at Tiverton, p.79

is much the same today.

From the 13th century, when the first customs duties were enforced, smuggling became a Devon obsession. It was easy to smuggle side by side with fishing. The rugged and complex coastlines were ideal for sneaking past customs inspectors. Smuggling has carried on ever since – today you'll hear of the occasional ambush of drugs shipments off Devon and wonder how much has got through without being ambushed.

This period was also marked by the construction of a weir across the River Exe by jealous aristocrats to stop traders reaching the wool port... and then in retaliation by the building of the Exeter Canal to bypass the weir. It's Britain's oldest canal and is still fully intact today.

A sea change

As trade by sea began to be more important, Devon's seafaring traditions brought it to international prominence. The Elizabethan era was Devon's finest hour. The county bred an extraordinary generation of heroic explorers, adventurers and warriors that included Sir Francis Drake, Sir Walter Raleigh, Sir Humphrey Gilbert and Sir Richard Grenville (see the panels on each of them in the chapters on Plymouth, Heritage Coast, Torbay and Bideford, respectively).

This colourful quartet was to take a leading role in defending and promoting England's interests, although all were also involved in less honourable state-sponsored piracy and slave trading.

Today there are plenty of ways to sample the history of these undoubtedly great men. The highlights include Drake's accurately re-created galleon Golden Hinde in Brixham harbour, his (and Grenville's) home at Buckland Abbey and Gilbert's home at Compton Castle. As good as these though, are the places that retain an air of the great seafaring era – the Barbican at Plymouth, the Close at Exeter, Bideford Quay, and the narrow cobbled streets of Topsham, Dartmouth and Totnes.

This was also the era of fears of foreign invasion. The great sea defences at Plymouth, Dartmouth and Salcombe were started. The great 'invincible' Spanish Armada of 1588 was scuppered by Elizabeth's fleet sailing out of Plymouth Sound, with a commoner, Francis Drake, as second-in-command (see Plymouth chapter).

In the 17th century the Civil War tore the county in half before the last major battle took place at the Royalists' hilltop stronghold of Torrington. The town centre attraction called Torrington 1646 commemorates this decisive battle and the half-timbered Black Horse Inn in the town is

THE PRAYER BOOK REBELLION

Back in the early Tudor times Devon had a rebellious air. Locals had already been involved in two revolts in the years of religious and constitutional upheaval before the Prayer Book Rebellion of 1549. It began in what today is sleepy village of Sampford Courtenay, near Okehampton.

Villagers were roused by the Act of Uniformity which ended the Latin Mass and enforced an English service using the new Book of Common prayer. On Whitsunday, Sampford villagers forced their priest to revert to their old service. When the authorities arrived to try to enforce the changes a man was run through on the steps of the church house with a pitchfork. A plaque marks the spot today.

The rebels marched east, gathering support as they went. For a month they laid siege to the walls of Exeter in vain. Then, just to the west of the city, the rebels met an army of hardened foreign mercenaries under Lord Russell sent to relieve the city. There were three battles, at Fenny Bridges (now near Exeter airport), Clyst St Mary, (near the present M5 junction to Exeter), and, when the Catholic peasants retreated, back at Sampford Courtenay. The protesters were roundly defeated each time, thousands being killed and infamously, 900 prisoners had their throats slit in 10 minutes on Clyst Heath, near Exeter.

In the end the mercenary army stormed Sampford Courtenay despite the amateur attempts of villagers to fortify it... and the rebellion was over. Hundreds of Devonians were executed in the aftermath, including the Vicar of St Thomas' in west Exeter who was hanged from his church tower, which still stands on Cowick Street, although thankfully his body was removed a long time ago.

The best... Blue Flag Devon beaches

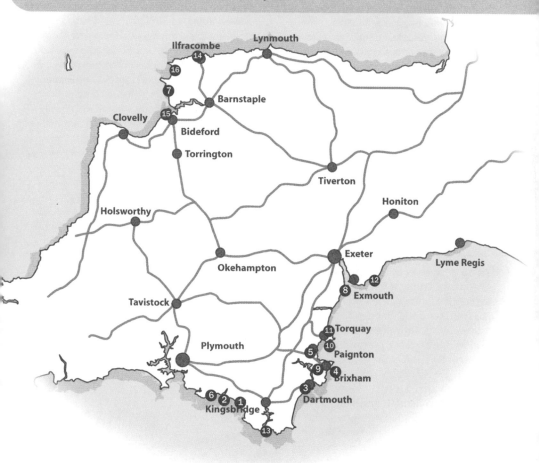

1 Bantham (South Hams)

2 Bigbury on Sea (South Hams)

3 Blackpool Sands (South Hams)

4 Brixham (Torbay)

5 Paignton (Torbay)

6 Challaborough (South Hams)

7 Croyde Bay (North Devon)

8 Dawlish Warren (Teignbridge)

9 Goodrington Beach

10 Meadfoot Beach

11 Oddicombe Beach

12 Sandy Bay

13 Salcombe Sands (South Hams)

14 Tunnels Beach, Ilfracombe (North Devon)

15 Westward Ho! (North Devon)

16 Woolacombe Sands (North Devon)

largely unchanged from its days as head-quarters first to one side, then the other.

The Restoration of the Monarchy soon led to the bloodless Revolution of 1688, when James II was deposed in favour of the Protestant William of Orange. William landed to claim the throne at the harbour in Brixham and a memorial on the harbourside commemorates the day.

The following centuries brought peace and prosperity thanks to the thriving wool trade and mining, which benefited greatly from the new beam-engine to pump water from pits, invented by Dartmouth's Thomas Newcomen. There is still a working New-comen engine on display in the town. Historians consider it a major catalyst for the Industrial Revolution.

The relics of the East Cornwall mining industry are now part of a World Heritage Site that includes the Tamar Valley leading north from Plymouth. Dartmoor and West Devon are dotted with remains of this largely forgotten part of the Industrial Revo-lution. The expertly recreated scenes at Morwellham Quay are the best places to experience this fascinating phase of Devon history.

To the modern day

Through the Victorian era there were the beginnings of a tourist industry. It had started during the Napoleonic War when a hostile continent had prevented the great and good from taking their customary trips to winter in the south of France. Devon made a convenient alternative and genteel resorts grew up along the coast, such as Lynton and Ilfracombe in the north, Sid-mouth and Torquay in the south. Brunel's Great Western Railway arrived in Exeter in 1840 and reached the Tamar by 1859, and North Devon by 1872. Devonshire's tourism soon became accessible for everyone, and not just the idle rich.

Over the years another trend developed – Devon as a retreat for artists. Arthur Conan Doyle, Jane Austen, Thomas Hardy, Charles Dickens, William Turner and Charles Kings-ley all get mentions in the chapters of this guide. And even in the 20th century, Henry Williamson hid in his writing hut at George-ham in North Devon to write *Tarka the Otter* and Agatha Christie tended her garden in the South Hams or sipped cocktails with the fashionable set at Burgh Island Hotel, still the best place in the world to re-create that era.

The Second World War brought the massed bombing of Plymouth and Exeter, as bad as anywhere in Britain. The subsequent hasty rebuilding scarred both cities – only now are their centres recovering some of the character that had been lost.

After the War, Devon's railways were sav-agely trimmed while the M5 finally reached Exeter. Tourism has continued to grow and it dominates much of the Devon coasts.

And in the past few years the county has tried to make its own history by creating its own official 'flag'. You'll see it frequently around the county although it's more popular in the Plymouth and south-west Devon. That's because the BBC Radio Devon poll that settled the design chose exactly the colours of Plymouth Argyle, alienating the supporters of Torquay United (yellow) and Exeter City (red and white). For the record the Devon flag is green with a white cross, outlined in black.

GEOGRAPHY AND GEOLOGY

Devon is Britain's only county with two sep-arate coastlines. These two stretches add up to a total length of around 300 miles and are a perfect opportunity to explore the region's geology through a series of remark-able features, from Slapton Ley to the Valley of the Rocks.

The north coast is characterised by impressive towering cliffs, often with dra-matic folds of rock. The unusual features to look out for include massive dune systems, such as those at Braunton and Northam. Geographic highlights of the North include Lynton's mysterious and beguiling Valley of the Rocks and Hartland's outrageously rugged rocky shores.

The south coast is more gentle and varied, the series of sandy coves is punctu-

10... geographic sites in Devon

1 Slapton Ley
A spectacular ridge of flint and quartz pebbles running for 2 miles, damming an estuary, which has formed the south-west's largest fresh water lake behind, p.47, 239

2 Valley of the Rocks
Geologists gasp over the rock formations, the rest of us scramble over a mysterious collection of pinnacles surrounding a grassy bowl, p.127

3 Dawlish Warren
A strange sandy spit poking across the mouth of the River Exe and backed by striking red sandstone cliffs that are actually fossilised sand dunes, p.220

4 Hartland Peninsular
Those dramatic rocks have put up with that pounding sea for 320 million years – no wonder they're so jagged, p.178

5 Dartmoor's tors
As an alternative to the popular Haytor, discover the crystal-encrusted Blackingstone Rock signed off the B3212 near Moretonhampstead, p.273

6 The Undercliffs
A beautiful stretch of Jurassic Coast from Axmouth to Lyme Regis featuring fossils, landslips, steep valleys and impressive pebble beaches

7 Braunton Burrows
This unique series of dunes at the mouths of the Taw and Torridge rivers is a UNESCO Biosphere Reserve. The dunes stretch for four miles and some are 100ft high, p.148

8 Torrington Common
The inspiring view from this historic hill top show how the River Torridge has cut its valley through the landscape, p.170

9 Lydford Gorge More than a mile long and 100ft high, the lush gorge leads to a spectacular 'White Lady' waterfall, p. 284

10 Kent's Cavern A dramatic cave complex in a type of limestone called 'Devonian' by Victorians after the county where it is found, p. 207

ated by deep estuaries. These are river valleys that have been flooded by a rise in sea levels. To the east lies the Jurassic Coast World Heritage Site with dramatic sea stacks, cliff waterfalls and ancient landslips. At the mouth of the Exe Estuary is the strange sandy spit of Dawlish Warren and further south the extraordinary pebble bar of Slapton Ley, separating the sea from the south-west's largest fresh water lake.

Devon has hundreds of beaches but only 16 were awarded Blue Flags for environmental cleanliness, safety and toilet facilities in 2007. Actually, that was an increase of three on the year before although Preston Beach in Paignton lost its Blue Flag in 2007. The four new beaches on the list are: Sandy Bay, Exmouth; Salcombe South Sands; Bantham Beach in the South Hams; and Goodrington South Sands in Paignton. You'll find a useful index of all the Blue Flag beaches at www.bbc.co.uk/devon/discover_devon/beach_guide. It includes details of each beach, a photo gallery, how to get there and what it's like.

Inland there are wide fertile rolling lowlands that have formed the basis of Devon's successful farmland for centuries. These contrast with the two highland national parks where exposed rocks break from the surface, the result of ancient volcanic activity. Dartmoor is southern England's largest area of exposed granite, which is seen best at the unique tors for example at Haytor or Houndtor. The moors also feature geographic wonders such as bogs, upland oak woods and swathes of heather.

World Heritage sites

Devon is also part of two World Heritage sites. The Jurassic Coast Site runs from Exmouth in East Devon to Studland in Dorset. Geologists explain that it's a special strip of coast because it features a strange tilt in the rock formations. Normally younger rocks are at the top, older rocks underneath. But, in this 95-mile stretch, the rocks have been tilted on their sides so if you started from Exmouth you'd find the rocks getting younger as you walked eastwards. And, whether you're a geologist or not, what a walk it is... There are some stunning seascapes along this stretch – great cliffs above tiny beaches and lone rock stacks standing the sea.

The Cornwall and West Devon Mining Landscape Heritage Site covers the sites of a largely forgotten part of the Industrial Revolution, the west country mining industry in the 18th and 19th centuries. In the Tamar Valley, Tavistock and western Dartmoor, this means a legacy of the search for copper, tin and arsenic. You can still visit the area of Devon Great Consols, which was once the richest copper mine in Europe and the largest producer of arsenic in the world. Morwellham Quay is the best surviving example of how these minerals were mined and transported from quays along the Tamar. Much of the town of Tavistock was elegantly rebuilt by the Duke of Bedford in the mid-19th century on the proceeds of his copper mining investments.

For more information on both heritage sites visit www.jurassiccoast.com or www.cornishmining.org.uk or contact Devon County Council for the free 'Geology' booklet (☎ 0870 6085531; www.discoverdevon.com).

WILDLIFE AND HABITATS

Devon sticks out prominently into the warming Gulf Stream, which laps round its two coastlines, giving it a climate out of all proportion with its latitude. At times it's almost subtropical, with animals and plants to match.

Offshore there is one of the world's richest marine habitats, with a vast variety of creatures from seals to eels. Marine biologists point to the springtime collections of sea campion, kidney vetch and sea lavender as examples of the healthy abundance in the seas off Devon. The National Marine Aquarium in Plymouth is a good place to learn more.

The coastline itself is so varied it also supports a healthy array of wildlife. Seabirds are the most obvious. And it's not just gulls. Gannets, guillemots, puffins, fulmars, kittiwakes and terns jostle for space too. Herring gulls are still worth watching though – you can take a boat trip from Exmouth to see them dropping shellfish onto the rocks from the wing to smash them open. Lundy is the best place to see seabirds; it's famous for the flocks of colourful-beaked puffins that breed there in spring.

There are plenty of places to enjoy wildlife cruises looking for seals swimming or basking on rocks, they may point out jellyfish too. The lucky ones spot dolphins and porpoises. Whales have occasionally been sighted but don't count on seeing one.

Occasionally there will basking sharks and even leatherback turtles too. Boat trips operate from most coastal resorts – the busiest are at Ilfracombe, Torbay, Dartmouth and Plymouth.

Much of the Devon shore is protected by the National Trust. These undeveloped, unspoilt cliffs are often home to rare species such as nightingales, dormice, wild thyme and orchids. And the wild North Devon coast east of Barnstaple and north of Exmoor has dramatic wooded valleys and steep cliffs that harbour winged predators such as ravens and peregrine falcons.

At the opposite end of the county, the Berry Head National Nature Reserve, just south of Brixham, is one of Devon's most spectacular. It's not just a historic stronghold and lookout point, there is a guillemot colony, and skuas and shearwaters can be seen wheeling above the waves. There are rare plants too, and more than 500 species have been recorded here.

Devon's estuaries and reed beds are particularly popular with bird watchers. Rarities found in the Tamar and Exe estuaries include delicate white little egrets, while numbers of the unusual cirl bunting live around the Kingsbridge Estuary.

The Exe in particular is a bird-watchers' magnet. It is home to more than 20,000 wading birds in winter. You may see shelduck, dunlin, curlew, redshank, brent geese, wigeon and large numbers of black-and-white oyster catchers at this time. Many are attracted by the sheltered waters and the flowering marine grass.

One of the best ways to explore these tidal flats is via wildlife boat trips from Exmouth or walking on the north side of Dawlish Warren. Further up the estuary towards Topsham is the favoured winter spot for the elegant curved-billed avocet. Even further north into the reed beds is a small reserve where bearded tits live. And you'll find divers and grebes around the mouth of the river.

Since *Tarka the Otter*, visitors have flocked to the rivers of North Devon expecting to bump into otters everywhere. But despite a recent revival, spotting them in the wild is a rare treat. You're more likely to find kingfishers, herons, dragonflies, salmon and trout, but in the rivers that flow to the south coast.

The National Nature Reserve at Slapton Ley has a fantastic mix of environments – the natural lake and a large freshwater reed area separated from the sea by a long pebble strip. The freshwater habitat is home to rare plants and birds such as the reed warbler. Discover more about the wildlife here at the website of the Ley National Nature Reserve (www.slnnr.org.uk).

Devon's sand dunes are among the country's most extensive. Saunton, Dawlish Warren and Northam have extensive sandy areas but Braunton Burrows is the daddy of all dunes. It's the biggest and most protected range in the country, now with its UNESCO Biosphere designation. More than 400 species of plants have been recorded here ranging from wild thyme to pretty hellebores. The array of unusual wild flowers includes evening-scented sea-stock, marsh orchids and evening primrose.

Inland

Both moors are famous for their wild ponies, a breed that seems hardy enough to survive winter conditions on the high moors. You'll see them all over the moors, in fact drivers have to be careful not to crash into them as they stroll and sometimes lie on the roads.

Among the moors' hillsides of bracken and heath, there are basins of boggy peat that allow heather, cottongrass and bog-mosses to flourish. Rare golden plovers, dunlins and wheatears can be seen here too. Occasionally Britain's fastest bird, the peregrine falcon, nests on the rocky faces. Across both moors, look also for unusually lush lichens and moss on the rocks.

The deciduous woods known as upland oak woods – a mix of oak, holly, rowan, beech, ash and elm – are a rare habitat for butterflies, moths, wood-ants, sparrowhawks, woodpeckers, and the red, roe and fallow deer. Yarner Wood, Wistman's Wood and Trendlebere Down on Dartmoor are the best examples. The bracken hills around Dunsford to the west of Dartmoor have

The best... Devon wildlife sites

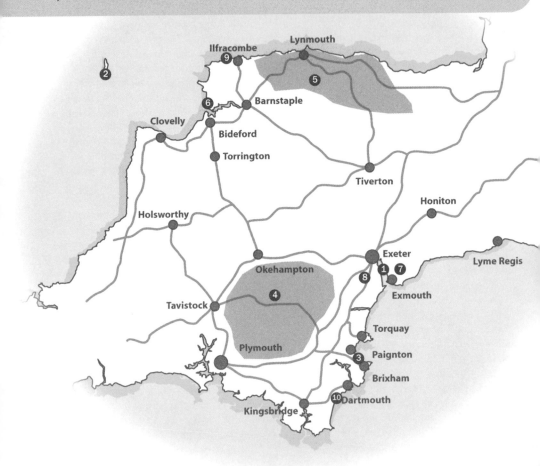

1 The Exe Estuary. See tens of thousands of birds, including gulls dropping shells to break them and flocks of avocets

2 Lundy. Enjoy the puffins, pristine marine environment and thousands of seabirds clustered around the cliffs

3 Berry Head Nature Reserve. It's a short walk from Brixham and you can spot guillemots, skuas and more than 500 types of plants

4 Dartmoor. Various unspoilt and unusual habitats across the moor mean exciting wildlife ranging from rare butterflies to wild ponies

5 Exmoor. See more wild ponies among the heather and gorse, and look out for the wild cranberries too

6 Braunton Burrows. This UNESCO Biosphere Reserve of enormous sand dunes is full of rare wild flowers and plants

7 Woodbury Common. Discover rare butterflies, plants and birds on the trails among these specially protected hills of gorse and heather

8 Haldon Hills. Explore miles of woods and clearings, this is one of the few places where you may see the endangered high brown fritillary butterfly

9 Ilfracombe. Take a wildlife coastal cruise and look out for seals, dolphins, jellyfish and seabirds

10 Slapton Ley. A fabulous National Nature Reserve with a chance of spotting a rarity such as an osprey or a spectacular display by thousands of swallows, swifts and martins

become a special reserve for the Devon Wildlife Trust Reserve, trying to protect a key habitat for the endangered high brown fritillary butterfly.

Exmoor meanwhile is characterised by its upland heath covered with heather, bilberry and gorse. It's closer to the sea than Dartmoor, so slightly less severe in conditions. Among the famous wild ponies and red deer, you may even spot wild cranberry and the heath fritillary butterfly.

Just north of Exmouth, to the east of the Exe Estuary are a series of raised heathlands of heather and gorse, and scattered clumps of Scots pines. This area around Woodbury Common is home for the rarely seen nocturnal bird, the nightjar, and a rare hawk called a hobby. It might, however, be easier to spot butterflies such as the silver-studded blue and the small pearl-bordered fritillary. There is more detailed information on the website of Clinton Estates, the company that manages much of this area (www.clintondevon.co.uk/the_commons).

And a good wildlife walk in the wooded hills to the west of the Exe Estuary may be rewarded with a glimpse of the rare high brown fritillary butterfly or a goshawk. Find out more about this forest park at www.haldonforestpark.co.uk or call 01392 832262.

Devon's rural heartland features those classic small fields rich with wild flowers bordered by thick ancient hedges bursting with life. In the spring, the good old English species such as blackbirds, song thrushes and bullfinches nest in these hedges, which are often grown from hawthorn and honeysuckle.

The county's meadows have what is now considered an unusual density of wildflowers, including orchids. And towards the moorland you may spot the rare marsh fritillary butterflies. Cruising above the fields you'll often spot Devon's commonest hawk, the buzzard.

Devon Wildlife Trust cares for 40 nature reserves around the county, totalling more than 3,300 acres. For more details visit the trust's website (www.devonwildlifetrust.org), including how to find and what to look for at each of their reserves (or call 01392 279244).

CULTURE

Today there are artists and craftspeople in every village in Devon. The county has become a retreat for those seeking rural inspiration while escaping from the worst parts of modern urban life. You'll find art and craft shops selling their work everywhere, and it ranges from embarrassing 'shell wizards' to wonderful fine art.

The greatest concentrations of art and craft are in Appledore, Totnes, Dartmouth, Topsham, Brixham, Bovey Tracey, and the cities of Exeter, Plymouth and Torquay. Generally standards are surprisingly high and prices much lower than equivalent work in London galleries.

The chance to peruse great art in grand civic museums is less common though. As we go to press both Exeter and Plymouth art galleries are shut for refurbishment. Part of Plymouth's – with the west's biggest collection of art – should open in 2008, Exeter's is unlikely to open for several years.

There are plenty of smaller galleries though, including the more avant-garde Spacex in Exeter, the entertaining Broomhill near Ilfracombe and the Dartington 'arts village' in South Devon. Devon's local arts centres have busy programmes too, often serving as the only culture and entertainment for large swathes of the county. The centres at Exeter (Phoenix), Beaford, Torrington, Tavistock and Dartmouth are always worth a visit.

Theatre is available around the fringes of the county. Plymouth has the best theatre, Torbay the most stages. Exeter's Northcott was facing a funding crisis but was rescued from closure at the last moment. Barnstaple and Ilfracombe theatres cater boldly for the northern wastelands. Again it's often the county's arts centres that provide the most exciting and contemporary drama, dance and performance.

Art

Devon hasn't been known through history as the home of great artists, unlike Cornwall for example, but there have been a few highlights through the ages.

The first great cultural figure to emerge

from what was considered a rural backwater was the artist **Sir Joshua Reynolds** (1723–1792). He was born in Plympton, near Plymouth, one of 11 children of the village schoolmaster. He travelled to Italy to study art and returned to paint portraits and historical scenes in a grand heroic style. He was one of the founders of the Royal Academy and is now considered the most important English painter of his era. He is buried in St Paul's Cathedral.

Around 30 years later than Reynolds, the marine artist **Thomas Luny** worked and lived in Teignmouth. Today you can stay in his former home – an elegant period guesthouse (see Torbay chapter). Also in the 19th century, painter **Thomas Danby** (1793–1861) settled in Exmouth to produce his romantic sunsets, landscapes and biblical scenes.

The great British water colourist **William Turner** travelled to Devon to paint at the start of the 19th century. His father had come from South Molton so the artist had family roots in the county. In fact, bizarrely he often told people he came from Barnstaple, even though he was born in London.

During his visits Turner painted a scene of Exeter Quay (see Exeter chapter) and several of Plymouth and the Tamar. His watercolour 'Plymouth from Mount Edgcumbe' was bought by the city's museum for £80,000 with the help of lottery funding in 2006.

More recently, the distinctive long-haired and beared Plymouth painter **Robert Lenkiewicz** (1941–2002) became a well-known figure in the city. He painted the huge mural in the Barbican, which you can still see. In the 1980s he controversially embalmed the dead body of a tramp as part of his studies. He also painted Labour leader Michael Foot (who is from Plymouth) and TV comedian Billy Connolly (live on TV). Some of his works can be seen in the city's art gallery, in the Annexe Gallery on the Barbican, or on his website (www.robertlenkiewicz.co.uk).

Painter **Beryl Cook** has lived in Plymouth for more than 25 years and many of the colourful characters in her work are based on local people, especially the patrons of The Dolphin pub on Plymouth's Barbican. See her work at Plymouth Art Gallery or on her own website (www.berylcook.org).

And one of the world's richest and most famous contemporary artists, **Damien Hirst**, lives with his family in the village of Berrynarbour near Ilfracombe. He personally decorated his restaurant and tapas bar, No 11 The Quay, on Ilfracombe harbourside with a colourful butterfly wallpaper and fish in glass tanks, recalling his famous dead shark in formaldehyde. His official website is www.damienhirst.com.

Literature

Literary talent has long been drawn to the county, from Geoffrey Chaucer to Agatha Christie. While you can still sense the inspiration that they felt, it's more difficult to find actual relics of their time here.

Tourism chiefs are making an attempt to create **Agatha Christie** themed holidays around Torbay – check with the Torbay tourist information centres for more information. Beware that Agatha's garden in the South Hams doesn't have anything to suggest that a writer ever lived there and there is precious little evidence of her presence in the county – just places where she once went. The best of these must be Burgh Island, which captures the atmosphere of her period so well. The Paignton steam railway is another period attraction that lets you, if not follow in the Queen of Crime's footsteps, at least ride on her rails.

Apart from Agatha, **Sir Arthur Conan Doyle** famously stayed here to write *The Hound of the Baskervilles*, Devonian **Samuel Taylor Coleridge** returned to write 'The Ryme of the Ancient Mariner' and 'Kubla Khan' on the Exmoor coast, and **Charles Kingsley** wrote 'Westward Ho!' in 1855, which led to the foundation of a town of the same name near Bideford in North Devon. **Chaucer** visited his roguish friend in Dartmouth (or 'Dirtymouth' as he called it) who later appeared in *The Canterbury Tales*.

Thomas Hardy is mostly associated with neighbouring Dorset but he used Exeter in four of his novels, under the name of Exon-

10... cultural sites in Devon

1 Plymouth Museum and Art Gallery
Devon's biggest and best should be even better when it re-opens later in 2008, p.251

2 Phoenix Arts Centre
The lively and well-run Exeter multi-arts centre includes an obligatory trendy café, p.69

3 Broomhill Sculpture Park near Ilfracombe
Wander through the woodland finding more than 300 sculptures along the way, p.137

4 Spacex, Exeter
You'll find a programme of touring contemporary art in this warehouse gallery, p. 49

5 Dartington
This South Devon village complex includes galleries, cinema, craft centre and an art college, p.230

6 Beaford Arts Centre
A grand old country house hosts an interesting programme of arts cinema, workshops and live shows

7 The Plough Arts Centre
Torrington's friendly town centre café/gallery/cinema/venue serves a wide rural area, p.174

8 Flavel, Dartmouth
Enjoy cinema, music, exhibitions, comedy and drama at this stylish multi-purpose arts centre, p. 29, 230

9 The Wharf, Tavistock
Explore this privately run arts centre with a theatre, concert hall, cinema and art gallery plus a waterside café and bar, p.290

10 Devon Guild of Craftsmen
The largest contemporary craft gallery in the south-west at The Riverside Mill at Bovey Tracey, p.294

bury. His first wife Emma was from Plymouth and he would later recall the proud moment when he first saw his book *Far From the Madding Crowd* advertised at Plymouth Station. So he bought a copy and walked to The Hoe to read the opening pages.

Hardy visited Exeter and Plymouth often. Exeter is featured in *The Trumpet Major, Jude the Obscure, A Pair of Blue Eyes* and *The Woodlanders*. Hardy stayed in Topsham, where his close friend, Tryphena Sparks, is buried (see Exeter chapter). He also made a pilgrimage to Plymouth when Emma died and wrote acclaimed poems about the city.

Charles Dickens' parents lived in a cottage in Alphington, Exeter, and he wrote the opening chapters of *Nicholas Nickelby* there. Dickens described the Exeter area as 'the most beautiful in this most beautiful of English counties'. His favourite pub was said to be The Turk's Head in the city centre. Local Exeter characters were the inspiration behind some of his characters, including the sly Pecksniff, from *Martin Chuzzlewit*, which was based on a resident of Topsham (see Exeter chapter).

Happy memories of a holiday in Devon inspired **Jane Austen** to set her first novel in the county. She wrote *Sense and Sensibility* in 1811 and it was set in the village of Upton Pyne just outside Exeter. Austen also loved nearby Dawlish, which is also mentioned in *Sense and Sensibility* (see Exeter chapter).

The Yorkshire-born poet **Ted Hughes** made the village of North Tawton, just north of Dartmoor, his home in 1961 and following his death in 1998 had his ashes scattered across the moor. He lived with the American poet **Sylvia Plath** in a pretty thatched stone cottage. She later committed suicide, as did his mistress. After these tragedies, Hughes, who was Poet Laureate, kept a low profile locally and spent much of his time walking alone on Dartmoor.

Five years after Hughes' death the BBC tracked down a secret memorial stone in a remote part of northern Dartmoor. It emerged that Hughes had requested his name be carved in a long slab of granite and placed between the sources of the rivers Teign, Dart, Taw and East Okement. Locals think that a slab that heavy must have been airlifted into such a remote place. The spot is on Duchy of Cornwall land, and Prince Charles, a friend of the poet, gave special permission for it.

A film about Ted and Sylvia's life together called *Sylvia* was released in 2003 starring Daniel Craig and Gwyneth Paltrow.

Music

Baroque composer **Matthew Locke** (1621–77), a former a chorister at Exeter Cathedral, later became the favoured composer of Charles II's court and mentor to Henry Purcell. But Devon isn't known as a hot-house of classical music.

It's folk music that is closer to a Devonian's heart. Even today folk is loved across the county. The contemporary duo **Show of Hands**, Phil Beer and Steve Knightly from Topsham, are so popular locally they won the 2006 poll by the county council to find 'The Greatest Ever Devonians'. In the six-month competition, they won a third of the votes cast, beating Sir Francis Drake and Agatha Christie. Despite being successful international music stars now, they often still play small venues in Devon. And one of the hottest new folk acts, Mercury-prize nominee **Seth Lakeman**, still lives on and writes about Dartmoor (see Dartmoor chapter).

The annual Sidmouth Folk Festival is one of Europe's top folk events, and there are smaller folk events scattered around the county including Bideford and Ilfracombe. The best way to catch some local folk though, is not via a big well-lit stage and PA system. It's in the murky surroundings of an informal folk club in an old Devon pub drinking local cider or real ale. Ask locals or the nearest tourist information office – they should be able to recommend the most atmospheric folk night.

Devon has a strong tradition of pop and rock too. The bands **Muse** and **Coldplay** have strong links with the county and international singing star **Joss Stone** is from a small village in East Devon (see Honiton chapter).

As for seeing some music live you'll be taking pot luck. Big bands do include Devon in their tours occasionally – it will generally be a gig in Exeter or Plymouth. There are plenty of smaller venues to catch local bands and up-and-coming tours or tribute bands. The national entertainment site (www.ents24.com) is a fine source of reliable information. The *Western Morning News'* new entertainments website (www.whatsonsouthwest.co.uk) for the south-west has just started as we put this book together – it looks promising at this stage and will be worth a check by the time you get to read this.

The best... book, TV and film locations

1 Tarka country. The rivers around Barnstaple and Bideford have become synonymous with Henry Williamson's classic animal story *Tarka the Otter* (see p.148). You can walk the Tarka Trail, ride the Tarka Line and perhaps, if you're lucky, spot one in the wild

2 Burgh Island. Agatha Christie stayed and wrote at the art deco palace here and her classic *And Then There Were None* was entirely set on the island, which also inspired artists as diverse as Noel Coward and TV's Lovejoy (see p.241)

3 *Fawlty Towers*. Torquay's Gleneagles Hotel was the inspiration for John Cleese's TV comedy – now it's a boutique hotel with a small Basil Fawlty exhibition (see p.210)

4 Westward Ho! Visit a seaside town named after a best-selling Victorian romantic novel by Devonian Charles Kingsley (see p.164)

5 Lyme Regis. Who could forget Meryl Streep standing at the end of the 'Cobb' harbour wall in the film, *The French Lieutenant's Woman* (see p.120)

6 Doone Valley. The map says Badgeworthy Valley, but Exmoor locals say Doone Valley – the setting of R D Blackmore's epic novel *Lorna Doone*

7 Hound of the Baskervilles. Arthur Conan Doyle stayed in Ipplepen to write his most enduring Sherlock Holmes mystery set in the midst of Dartmoor around Fox Tor Mire and Hound Tor (see p.284)

8 Lynmouth. R D Blackmore wrote *Lorna Doone* at the Rising Sun Inn and the romantic poet Shelley stayed at what is now Shelley's Hotel (see p.124). Coleridge and Wordsworth also visited Lynmouth

9 Becky Falls. Poet Rupert Brooke and author Virginia Woolf have stayed at Beckwood Cottage, which is now a rentable holiday home (see p.283)

10 Coulbone Valley. The gorgeous landscape is just over the Somerset border east of Lynton and was the setting for poet Samuel Taylor Coleridge's mystical vision of Xanadu, sometimes described as the greatest ever English poem (see p.132)

LOCAL HEROES

There are more famous names associated with Devon than you'd expect for a lightly populated rural area a long way from the centres of power and glamour. These include some real Devonians who have become famous, such as Joss Stone and Sue Barker, and the rich and famous who have moved to Devon because they like it, such as Damien Hirst and Noel Edmonds.

International singer and model **Joss Stone** comes from Ashill, a small village on the edge of the Blackdown Hills in East Devon, where her family still live (see Honiton chapter). Joss still visits the county regularly and at Christmas 2007 turned on Barnstaple's Christmas lights.

Coldplay star **Chris Martin** comes from the village of Whitstone to the west of Exeter. He met his fellow band members at university but his family still lives in the county. Martin – who is married to actress Gwyneth Paltrow – is a frequent visitor.

Tennis star and TV presenter **Sue Barker** was born in Paignton. In the 1970s Sue was one of the top three women players in the world and was dubbed 'The Paignton Peach'. The convent girl was coached by Arthur Roberts at the indoor court at the Palace Hotel in Torquay. Roberts had also coached Angela Mortimer there and she won at Wimbledon in 1961.

Matthew Bellamy of Muse grew up and met his fellow band members in Teignmouth, although he doesn't remember it fondly. In a recent interview he said: 'The only time the town came to life was during the summer when it turned into a vacation spot. When the summer ended they left and took all the life with them,' he said. 'I felt so trapped there. My friends were either getting into drugs or music, but I gravitated towards the latter and learned how to play. That became my escape. All we used to do was hang around, smoke and listen to music. There wasn't anything else to do.'

Two stars who chose to move to Devon are **Jennifer Saunders** and **Ade Edmondson**. Award-winning comedian, writer and actress Jennifer is famous for her French and Saunders partnership with Dawn French (who went to school in Plymouth) and her own *Absolutely Fabulous* series. Comedian, actor, director and writer Ade Edmondson was one of TV's *Young Ones* and starred in *Bottom* alongside Rik Mayall. More recently he was a star in Holby City. He and Jennifer are married and have three daughters. The family live in a 400-year-old Dartmoor farmhouse with a swimming pool and 45 acres of land. They have cows, sheep, horses, ducks and a boat at Dartmouth.

Jennifer told a recent interviewer: 'Ade and I fell in love with the area on sight. From the start I was so impressed by how accepting the local people were of newcomers. Actually, if I'm honest, when we first moved here I found it a bit frightening thinking of somewhere so large and wild. But the more time I've spent there, the more exhilarating I've found it. Now I love all the little lanes that eventually lead you to this big open space: Dartmoor.'

Jennifer tries to support local farmers. She told a local Devon paper: 'We buy locally where possible, and we also eat our own beef and lamb.'

In 2007 Jennifer and Ade, who have an estimated £11-million fortune, were awarded honorary doctorates of literature from Exeter University.

At Christmas 2007, Jennifer, who is a keen gardener, caused controversy when she rode with the local Mid Devon hunt, although it was a new-style legal hunt. She appeared in many national newspapers on her horse as the hunt gathered in Chagford Square on Boxing Day.

In 2006 Jennifer chose the nearby village of North Tawton to set her TV comedy series *Jam and Jerusalem*. Appearing alongside Jennifer, Dawn French, and Joanna Lumley, were members of the village Women's Institute (WI) branch.

As for the rest of Devon, Jennifer told *Emotion* magazine: 'I love the beaches. Hope Cove and Mothercombe (in the South Hams) are particular favourites. They're so unbelievably beautiful – as are the unspoilt estuaries. Ade had a boat moored at Totnes. We'd potter up and down to Salcombe, another place I love; it's great for kids and really buzzing in the summer.'

Football hero **Steve Perryman** was Spurs FA Cup winning captain and is still the holder of their record number of appearances. After a very successful management career in Japan he moved to Lympstone on the Exe Estuary and a job as Exeter City's Director of Football. The former England international and Footballer of the Year now likes nothing better than a quiet walk in the Devon countryside. See his local recommendations in the Exeter chapter.

Explorer and adventurer **Sir Ranulph Fiennes** lives on a remote farm just over the Somerset border on Exmoor. He's a popular figure locally and can be seen on his daily training runs across the Moor (see South Molton chapter).

TV chef **Hugh Fearnley-Whittingstall** has moved his River Cottage enterprise to Axminster in East Devon – opening a shop and restaurant in the town centre while living and working at a farm in the hills outside. His 2008 TV series about free-range chickens made him a somewhat controversial figure locally (see Honiton chapter).

Millionaire TV presenter **Noel Edmonds** moved down to Devon to escape the media pressures of London, and has become such a part of the local establishment he is a Deputy Lord Lieutenant of Devon. He recently bought a fabulous estate on the northern edge of Dartmoor (see Dartmoor chapter).

Property show TV presenter **Kirsty Allsop** lives in the pretty village of Broadhembury near Honiton. She recently led a local campaign to stop former racing driver Nigel Mansell opening a race track at Dunkerswell nearby. 'As I get to work in and see all parts of the country, I really do appreciate where I live,' she told the *Daily Telegraph*. 'I love its specialness.'

Kirsty and her boyfriend have embraced the local social establishment by joining the Devon and Somerset Staghounds on legal hunts. She told the *Telegraph* she enjoys the less sophisticated lifestyle in Devon. 'If they suddenly opened a shop in Honiton where you can buy swanky shoes and handbags, I'd be horrified,' she says. 'Once I'm past Bristol on the train, any desire to pick up a *Vogue* disappears.'

Alternative comedian **Rik Mayall** lives in a farmhouse near Kingsbridge in the South Hams. He keeps a low profile normally but was lured into public in 2007 to star in a Devon County Council TV advert for the 'Don't let Devon go to Waste' campaign against plastic supermarket bags.

Rik previously starred in *The Young Ones* and *Bottom* with fellow Devonian Ade Edmondson, and *The New Statesman* and has had numerous successful film, stage and TV roles. In 1998 he suffered a serious quad bike crash in a field near his home and was in a coma for several days. He recovered but has kept out of the limelite since the accident. Rik splits his time between his home on London and his Devon farm.

Damien Hirst is mentioned frequently through this book – he and his family live in a village near Ilfracombe. Damien is Britain's wealthiest and most successful contemporary artist but it's his restaurant in Ilfracombe that has raised his profile in North Devon. It's the best-known eatery in the north of the county. Damien is also planning to refurbish some luxury accommodation in the town. He's rarely seen and most locals don't have a tradition of following cutting-edge art, but he is nevertheless popular locally for the positive effect his presence has had on the town.

10... great Devonians through history

1 Sir Francis Drake
Queen Elizabeth's most daring and successful seafarer who sailed round the world, raided Spain incessantly and helped save England from the Armada, p.266

2 Dame Agatha Christie
The world's best-selling crime writer was always a part of South Devon and set many stories there, p.204

3 Charles Babbage
The 19th-century inventive genius from Teignmouth drew up plans for computers and calculating machines way ahead of their time

4 Sir Walter Raleigh
The colourful seaman, explorer, writer and politician from East Devon began our first colonies in America, brought back potatoes and tobacco, but failed to find his fabled 'El Dorado', p.106

5 Thomas Newcomen
Born in Dartmouth in 1663, Newcomen invented the atmospheric pumping engine for mines – one of the most important catalysts for the industrial revolution, p.228

6 Sir Joshua Reynolds
Born in Plympton St Maurice in 1723, one of England's most famous artists went on to found the Royal Academy and to paint for the King, p.50

7 Captain Robert Falcon Scott
Scott of the Antarctic, who died after losing the race to the South Pole, was from Plymouth (his skis are now in Plymouth Museum)

8 Michael Foot
The former leader of the Labour Party is a Plymouthian, former Devonport MP and Director of Plymouth Argyle, p. 50

9 Peter Cook
Comedian and writer Peter Cook was born in near Plainmoor in Torquay and was a life-long supporter of Torquay United

10 Samuel Taylor Coleridge
The poet, journalist and all-round intellectual was born in Ottery St Mary and wrote much of his greatest work on Exmoor, p.94

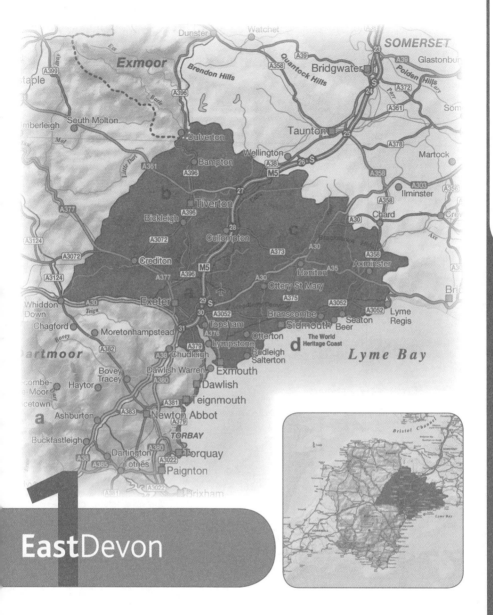

EastDevon

a. Exeter and around

b. Tiverton and the Exe Valley

c. Honiton and the Blackdown Hills

d. Exmouth, Sidmouth and the East Devon coast

Unmissable highlights

01 Stop, gaze and wonder at the magnificent west front of Exeter Cathedral – one of the great sights in England,
p.60

02 Sample the brilliant local ingredients at Hugh Fearnley-Whittingstall's 'Canteen' in Axminster,
p.100

03 Drive a bulldozer through deep mud and dig a big hole with a JCB at Diggerland, near Cullompton,
p.82

04 Stroll along the Regency promenade at Sidmouth, eating an ice-cream made with clotted cream,
p.110

05 Waste a day browsing Exeter's shops, testing pavement cafés and choosing restaurants,
p.70

06 Try a pint of Otter Ale from the barrel in the tiny sitting room of the Luppitt Inn in a farmyard just down the lane from the brewery,
p.101

07 Enjoy a sedate horse-drawn narrow boat trip along the Grand Western Canal at Tiverton,
p.79

08 Walk along part of the fantastic Jurassic Coast – a World Heritage Site that's free to enter,
p.103

09 Order from the award-winning menu at the wonderful old thatched Drewe Arms in the picture-postcard village of Broadhembury,
p.100

10 Hire bikes at Exeter Quayside and work up a thirst riding the towpath to the Turf Hotel for a water's-edge barbecue lunch,
p77

EAST DEVON

This is the first part of Devon most visitors see. As you drive down the M5, A303 or the main rail line, you'll go past the Blackdown Hills at the border with Dorset and Somerset and down into the lush farmland of the Exe Valley. Exeter will appear in the centre of the huge plain between the Haldon Hills and Woodbury Common, and the Exe Estuary will glitter to the south, heading for the sea at Exmouth.

Too many visitors admire these views and continue on their way – heading for the big resorts of the Riviera or the holiday cottages of the South Hams. By skipping East Devon you will miss some of Devon's best countryside, it's most visitor-friendly city and some of the finest seascapes, not just in Devon, but in Europe.

There's no locally accepted definition of what is East Devon. Everyone would agree that the protected World Heritage Coast and rolling countryside between Dorset and the Exe Estuary are included, but we've added Exeter and the Exe Valley right up to the foothills of Exmoor and the Somerset border. And we've drawn an arbitrary line between East Devon and North Devon, from the big north Dartmoor crossroads at Whiddon Down to Dulverton at the southern edge of Exmoor. We've also included the villages to the west of Exeter and north of the A38 before you reach Dartmoor.

EXETER AND AROUND

For a long time the only famous bit of Exeter was its bypass. The holiday bottleneck was nationally notorious in the 1960s and 1970s as a solid summer-long traffic jam. The arrival of the M5 in 1975 helped, but simply sped visitors past Exeter on their way to the coast.

In the past decade, however, the county town has become more of an attractive destination in its own right. The old sleepy backwater has become wealthier with businesses (such as the Met Office) and people moving west. Thanks to more than 15,000 students it has a buzz to the streets and pubs, a lively arts scene and a busy what's-on listing.

And visitors' tastes have changed: people have become more interested in shops and restaurants. Exeter now appeals more as it has the best shopping and eating west of Bristol. And there is a fair bit of history and culture here too.

WHAT TO SEE AND DO

 Fair weather

Exeter has always had one premier league historic sight. **St Peter's Cathedral** is worthy of a detour wherever you're heading. And of course it's still there, dominating much of the city skyline.

The cathedral is one of England's grandest and oldest. The west front in particular is one of the iconic images of Devon, its flying buttresses framed by stout square Norman towers and decorated with 83 carved statues. Stone from the village quarry at Beer in East Devon was carved into the screen above the great west door and was originally painted in bright colours.

It was designed to be so splendid so that the people of the Middle Ages thought of it as the entrance to heaven. Early pilgrims valued the spiritual powers of this building so highly they would carve off chunks of stone, grind it down, mix with water... and drink it.

The building of the two block-like towers started just 50 years after the Norman invasion in 1110. The rest was built 150 years later.

Currently entry is free, but visitors are asked for a donation. and you're encouraged to do so by the information that it costs £2 per minute to run the building. Sadly, as we go to press, the Cathedral bosses are making noises about introducing a compulsory entry charge.

Inside, there is a library of old manuscripts, shop and a café, but they're not what will take your breath away. The cavernous nave soaring to the fan-vaulted

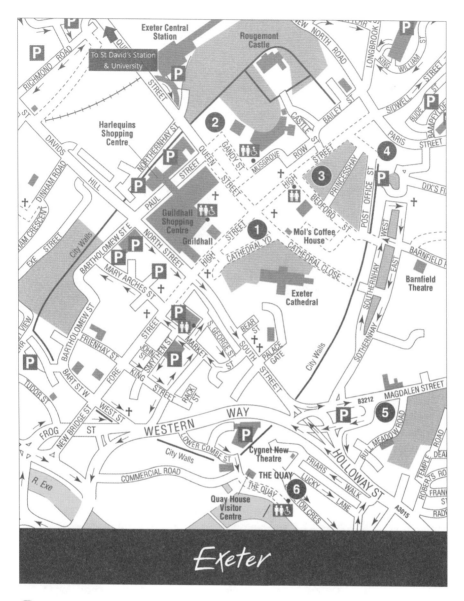

Exeter

1 aBode@Exeter Hotel
2 Phoenix Arts Centre
3 Princesshay Shopping Centre
4 Underground Passages
5 Hotel Barcelona
6 The Quay

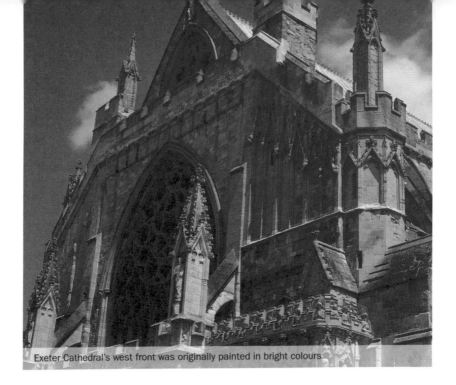

Exeter Cathedral's west front was originally painted in bright colours

roof will do that. The longest gothic vault in the world is superbly atmospheric, especially with a choir and organ echoing around the ancient columns and flagstones.

Details to spot include the 'dog whippers' windows watching down for strays wandering the aisles, recently uncovered medieval wall paintings and the huge organ with more than 4,000 pipes, the longest and deepest of which measures 32ft.

In the east tower spot the giant 1487 clock, in which the sun goes round the earth. Underneath is a small wooden medieval cat flap for the bishop's cat to reach the inner workings, which was installed after mice ate the clock's pulley ropes.

EXETER CATHEDRAL,
☎ 01392 285983; www.exeter-cathedral.org.uk; free (suggested donation £3.50); open daily 9.30am–5pm; free guided tours: Mar to Oct, Mon to Fri, 11.00am, 12.30pm* and 2.30pm; Sat, 11am and 12.30pm* (*only July to Sept).

The Cathedral stands within its **Close** of historic buildings. Most are now shops, cafés and restaurants. In the far corner is Mol's Coffee House, with a distinctive Elizabethan façade. Locals claim it was a favourite haunt of Devon's Elizabethan seadog fraternity, including Drake and Raleigh. Next door, the Royal Clarence Hotel was named after the Duchess of Clarence, William IV's wife, who stayed here. Number Seven, the Close, was the Jacobean town house of the Courtenays, the Earls of Devon from Powderham Castle. On a quiet evening, walking across the ancient cobbles – stones dredged from the bed of the River Exe – it really can feel as if you're walking in the footsteps of the Tudor seadogs and Regency dandies.

Local knowledge

Stuart Nuttall is a prominent local journalist for the *Express & Echo* newspaper, which covers Exeter and the eastern half of Devon. For five years he lived in an isolated cottage between Crediton and Cheriton Fitzpaine. Now he lives in the village of Silverton, 10 miles north of Exeter.

Favourite restaurant: So many great pubs around here offer superb value for money and serve traditional meals using local ingredients. My favourite is the Masons Arms at Knowstone, just off the North Devon Link Road, between Tiverton and Barnstaple.

Favourite pub: For a pleasant pint in pretty surroundings, the Fisherman's Cot at Bickleigh, near Tiverton, alongside the River Exe, takes some beating.

Favourite shop: I use Exe Valley Farm Shop at Thorverton (☎ 01392 861239), between Exeter and Tiverton, on a regular basis. The Darts Farm Shop at Clyst St George, between Exeter and Exmouth, is also well worth a visit. Most Devon farm shops offer a greater variety of locally produced foods than the supermarkets.

Favourite Devon food/drink: Try Haggett's butchers in Newcourt Road, Silverton, for some great pies, pasties and sausages (www.djhaggett.co.uk).

Best view: I love walking and any view from the South West Coast Path in North or South Devon is a favourite. Best of all has to be the view east or west from Beer Head, near Seaton, on the south coast. And the view looking down on Widecombe-in-the-Moor on Dartmoor from the surrounding tors is also breathtaking.

Best-kept Devonshire secret: The many small, traditional villages of Mid Devon.

Favourite thing to do on a rainy day: visit the National Marine Aquarium at Plymouth.

Quirkiest attraction: I like: the National Trust property A La Ronde, at Exmouth; Seaton tramway; Exeter's Underground Passages; the sea tractor that links Bigbury-on-Sea with Burgh Island at high tide; and the Ottery tar barrels event in early November, where locals run through the streets carrying blazing barrels.

Exeter's historic quayside

The quayside

After the Cathedral and its Close there are just lots of nice second-division attractions. Next up is probably the quayside. The walks down there from the cathedral are a mix of interesting old buildings... and horrible busy road junctions and modern developments. But once you're there, the collection of old warehouses turned to bars and clubs, ancient pubs, open-air cafés, the 17th-century customs house and the views along the waterfront make it all worthwhile. Older visitors may recognise it as the setting for TV's Onedin Line series. And for all ages, it's a good place to shop, eat and stroll... and a good starting point for longer walks, bike rides and summer boat trips (www.exeter cruises.com ☎ 07984 368442).

Exeter in art

There is a genteel feel to much of Exeter, and this is reflected in the many arts personalities who have had associations with Exeter. Jane Austen set her first novel here after staying in the pretty village of Upton Pyne on the eastern fringes. She used the area for the setting of Barton Valley in *Sense and Sensibility*. And the marriage of Elinor Dashwood and Edward Ferrars was supposed to have happened at the Upton Pyne village church.

Mrs Fanny Bird, a friend of Anthony Trollope's mother, lived in one of the period houses of Cathedral Close. He often visited Mrs Bird and used her as the model for Miss Jemima Stanbury in *He Knew He Was Right*. Miss Stanbury claims: 'In Exeter, the only place for a lady was the Close'.

One of Britain's greatest landscape painters, JMW Turner, visited in 1827 and painted the quay and Colleton Crescent in typical watery colours. *The Daily*

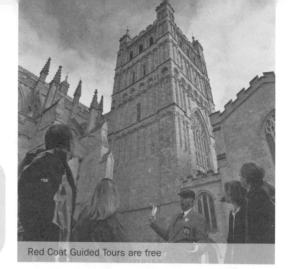

EXETER RED COAT GUIDED TOURS, ☎ 01392 265203; www.exeter.gov.uk/visiting; free 90-minute tours up to five times daily except 25/26 Dec; begin outside Royal Clarence Hotel/Quay Visitor Centre; see website for details.

Red Coat Guided Tours are free

The best route is probably the longest – to the Turf Locks and pub 6 miles south. But there is a bike and canoe hire here and even a separate tourist information centre if you need route guidance.

Walking tours

The tourism-minded Exeter Council has rather embraced the idea of taking tours as many of the city's interesting bits are spread out. So there's a series of self-guided tours you can take following routes supplied by the tourist office – such as the City Wall Trail around the old red sandstone Roman/medieval walls (about 70% remain although you can't walk along the ramparts like in York).

The other tour option is the excellent **Red Coat Guides**. This is a team of highly trained volunteers, usually retired professionals. After six months of training and passing two exams, the Lord Mayor presents them with a prestigious badge and they're off. At the time of writing there are 33 members of this knowledgeable red army and in 2008 the scheme celebrated its 20th

Telegraph recently described the elegant Georgian Colleton Crescent as 'Exeter's answer to Royal Crescent in Bath'. Visitors can still find it in the trees above the quayside.

Thomas Hardy used Exeter in four of his novels and Exonbury and Exeter played a big role in the life of the young Charles Dickens, who thought of the city of Exeter as 'the most beautiful in this most beautiful of English counties'.

Dickens wrote the opening chapters of *Nicholas Nickleby* from his parents' cottage in the village, now a suburb, of Alphington. Many of the Devon characters he met appeared in his work, including the unusual Pecksniff, who was based on a resident of Topsham. The Turks Head pub next to the Guildhall was reputedly Dickens' favourite drinking spot.

Underground Passages beneath Exeter's High Street

birthday. Their walks cover areas such as the remains of Exeter's red sandstone Norman Castle in Northernhay Gardens, the Georgian courthouse nearby, the medieval Guildhall on the High Street and the Tudor 'house that moved' in St Mary's Steps (a half-timbered treasure that was moved on rollers 100 yards out of the path of the new inner bypass in 1963). At some stage you are bound to find or be directed to **Parliament Street**, a ridiculously narrow alley off the High Street that is reputedly the narrowest street in the world.

Wet weather

If the heavens open, then Exeter's **Underground Passages** are a great place to hide away. A unique network of spooky medieval tunnels under the city centre were re-opened by Time Team's Tony Robinson at the end of 2007. Now you can enjoy a smart visitor centre and guided tour's wearing yellow hard hats and look for the memorable sight of a manhole cover... from underneath.

EXETER UNDERGROUND PASSAGES, 2 Paris Street EX1 1GA; ☎ 01392 665887; www.exeter.gov.uk/visiting; adults £5, children £3.50, OAPs/students £4, family £15; June to Aug: Mon to Sat 9.30am–5.30pm, Sun 10.30am–4.30pm; rest of year: 11.30am–5.30pm Mon to Fri, Sat 9.30am–5.30pm, Sun 11.30am–4pm.

What to do with children

We've already mentioned the Underground Passages (suitable for older children) and boat trips from the quayside. But easily the best destination for children is a short drive east out of the city – **Crealy Adventure Park**.

CREALY ADVENTURE PARK, Farringdon EX5 1DR; ☎ 01395 233 200; www.crealy.co.uk, (summer/winter) £9.95/£7.95, OAP £6.50/£5.95, infants under 3ft free, discounts for groups and online booking; summer: open daily 10am—6pm; Nov to Mar: Thur to Sun 10am—5pm.

This giant theme park has huge undercover areas, so it's a perfect all-weather, year-round children's escape. It receives 500,000 visitors a year making it the south-west's biggest family attraction.

There is everything from white-knuckle rides to cutesy animals to feed, and lots in between: a roller coaster, log flume ride, go-karts, bumper boats, soft play and 100 acres of parkland.

From Raleigh to rides

Angela Wright, a mother of five, is not the usual theme park entrepreneur — she was a Devon housewife who launched the south west's biggest theme park as her first business.

Angela actually grew up at Hayes Barton in East Budleigh, the historic house where Sir Walter Raleigh was born. She says this was her inspiration. Some of the rides at Crealy now have Walter Raleigh themes.

When she was a child she had the run of Raleigh's old farm and owned lots of pets. 'I was extremely lucky,' she told *The Times* recently. 'I grew up with an understanding for animals and farming, and a strong sense of the importance of adventurous play.' And every afternoon her parents would show strangers around the house for 20p a time, so Angela was used to sharing her home and adventures with visitors.

Angela told *The Times*: 'Every day at two o'clock it would be: "Oh my goodness, the visitors are coming up the path, quick go and tidy your room." Sometimes I would be too late so I would have to hide things under the bed.' Later she earned pocket money by serving cream teas on the lawn.

Her family later bought their own farm nearby. Angela, who had just had her first child and no experience of running a business, spent six months researching her idea. She then suggested to her parents to turn the farm into a theme park. 'They didn't know if it would work,' she recalled. So she spent another year finding the facts and figures to eventually persuade them.

Crealy finally opened in 1989. It was divided into areas to suit different age groups, including an animal realm where children can hold newborn chicks and feed lambs, and another area with family rides. It was a success from the start.

Angela's family still run the business: her father is chairman, her mother is in charge of buying, her brother is finance director and her husband is in charge of catering. She is the managing director. She says: 'I feel fortunate to be able to deliver some of the most memorable moments in children's lives. When I see a child walking across an aerial walkway or holding a chick, that's quite special.'

The best... **PLACES TO STAY**

BOUTIQUE

Hotel Barcelona
Magdalen Street, EX2 4HY
☎ **01389 281000**
www.aliashotels.com

This exciting contemporary conversion has turned an austere eye hospital into the city's choicest hotel with a popular lively bar, top notch restaurant and handy car park. It's situated on a dreary busy junction, but is probably Devon's most exciting contemporary urban accommodation.

Price: £99 for a single, £119 for a double per night.

ABode Exeter
Cathedral Close, EX1 1HD
☎ **01392 319955**
www.abodehotels.co.uk/exeter

A stylish refurbishment has transformed one of the oldest hotels in Britain, formerly the grand Royal Clarence overlooking the cathedral. It now features Michael Caines' stylish celebrity chef restaurant, modern rooms and a gym, but parking is awkward.

Price: from £125 to £175 for a single; from £125 to £250 for a double; breakfast extra.

HOTEL

Southgate
Southernhay East, EX1 1QF
☎ **01392 412812 www.mercure.com**

The Southgate is a well-equipped but charmless business hotel in a great location, undergoing refurbishment and extension as this guide was going to press.

Price: from £90 to £155; breakfast £13.95.

INN

White Hart Hotel
South Street, EX1 1EE
☎ **01392 279897**
www.roomattheinn.info

Locals love this old half-timbered coaching inn with a popular bar downstairs and oodles of character despite its dated corporate make-over.

Price: from £59.95.

B&B

Galley Restaurant with Rooms
Fore Street, Topsham, EX3 OHU
☎ **01392 876078**
www.galleyrestaurant.co.uk

This 17th-century cottage next to an acclaimed fish restaurant in a historic waterside suburb has only two bedrooms, so book early.

Price: B&B from £95 for a single, £125 for a double.

CAMPSITE

Exeter Racecourse
Kennford, EX6 7XS ☎ 01392 832107

Not many campsites made it into this book, but this one, right in the middle of the racecourse, high above Exeter at the top of Haldon Hill, has superb views and a great feeling of space. Open Mar to Oct.

Price: touring pitches from £8.50 to £19.50.

Entertainment

For all listings check Exeter's daily paper *Express & Echo* in print or online **thisisexeter.co.uk**.

Theatre

Exeter's newly-refurbished **Northcott Theatre** (www.northcott-theatre.co.uk/ ☎ 01392 493493) on the University's leafy campus in the north of the city, has a national reputation and its own full-time company. It started 2008 in a funding crisis, however, and was only saved from closure at the last minute.

More local or smaller-scale productions appear at the **Barnfield Theatre** (barnfieldtheatre.co.uk; ☎ 01392 270891) near Southernhay in the centre and the **New Theatre** in Friar's Gate (☎ 01392 277189).

Cinema

There are various **cinemas** – multiscreen complexes such as the Odeon on Sidwell Street (Odeon.co.uk; ☎ 0871 22 44 007), the Vue in Cheeke Street (myvue.com; ☎ 08712 240240), and the independent Picture Palace in Bartholomew Street (picturehouses.co.uk; ☎ 0871 704 2057).

Live music The Cavern under the shops on Queen Street (cavernclub.co.uk/ ☎ 01392 495370) is for cutting-edge bands while more established names appear at **The Lemon Grove** at Cornwall House on the university campus (www.exeterboxoffice.com; ☎ 01392 263518).

Other possible venues are **Club Rococo** on Mary Arches Street (www.clubrococo.co.uk; ☎ 01392 434411), the **Phoenix Arts Centre** on Gandy Street, (www.exeterphoenix.org.uk; ☎ 01392 667080) and various pubs. Although huge bands such as the Kaiser Chiefs sometimes perform at **Westpoint Arena** at Clyst St Mary to the east of Exeter (www.westpoint-devonshow.co.uk; ☎ 01392 446000), the arena's more likely to host big trade shows and exhibitions.

Clubbers will find the usual variety here – perhaps biased in favour of more indie tastes as one in ten of the population are students. On the quay, **Riva** (www.rivaexeter.co.uk; ☎ 01392 211347) is pretty glitzy and conventional, such as **Arena** at the other end of town in Summerland Street (www.arenaclubbing.co.uk; ☎ 01392 491419) whereas **Club Rococco** (see above) is more studenty. The tiny **Timepiece** in Little Castle Street (☎ 01392 493096) is a long-standing alternative institution, if that's not a contradiction. Joss Stone once hired the whole club for her birthday party.

Shopping

Although Plymouth is the bigger city in Devon, Exeter has the best shopping. The modern precincts lead from the long and busy High Street – the **Guildhall Centre** has more budget, bargain stores such as Primark; the new **Princesshay** development (www.princesshay.com) the more glossy outlets such as Apple, Hobbs and Fat Face. Behind the Guildhall Centre, accessed via a covered pedestrian bridge, is the **Harlequin** precinct, with more upmarket designer stores.

Exeter came bottom of a recent national poll of shopping because of its vast ranks of 'clone' chain stores, and it's true the main shopping areas are devoid of interesting independent shops. But it doesn't take long to find them: there were 350 independent stores at the last count. **Cathedral Close, Gandy Street** and **Fore Street** are all worth exploring and the most bohemian strip is **Sidwell Street**, which has market stalls, charity shops and odd specialists, although this area is the next on the schedule for redevelopment.

The best... FOOD AND DRINK

Exeter has made efforts to become a cosmopolitan eating centre – with its own **food festival** in Northernhay Gardens in April (www.visitsouthwest.co.uk/exeterfoodfestival) and a downloadable eating-out guide on the city council website (www.exeter.gov.uk/index.aspx?articleid=6878).

Eight of the city's restaurants are included in the *Good Food Guide* at the time of writing, and it rates as one of the top 20 cities in the UK to eat out. But it's not just smart trendy restaurants that make it so – the good local produce counts for as much. There is a regular farmers' market and many good suppliers taking advantage of the rich farmland surrounding the city. So Exeter is well placed for fresh meat, seafood, dairy and vegetables, plus specialist treats ranging from traditional cider and pasties to newcomers such as Devon chillies and locally made humous.

 ## Staying in

The **farmers' market** at the top of South Street every Thursday, 9am–2pm, is the easiest way to browse the best of the region's produce. Possible products can include duck and goose eggs, fresh river trout and various cheeses. Try not laugh if some extreme Devon dialect speaker calls eggs 'crackleberries'. Look for traditional local specialities such as Ruby Red Devon beef from the Combe Estate near Honiton.

CELEBRITY CONNECTIONS

Madcap fez-wearing, comic magician **Tommy Cooper**'s mum was from Crediton, and the family moved to Exeter when Tommy was three years old. The Coopers lived in a house behind Haven Banks on the riverside and Tommy went to Mount Radford School in Heavitree. He often helped his parents on their ice-cream van at local fairs at the weekend. At the age of eight, an aunt gave Tommy a magic set and he would spend hours perfecting his tricks. They later formed the basis of his act although he deliberately got them wrong for humorous effect, along with his West Country accent and a sequence of surreal one-liners, such as: 'I slept like a log last night and woke up in the fireplace' and 'I had a ploughman's lunch the other day, he wasn't half mad.' Tommy died after having a heart attack on stage in 1984, but in a 2005 poll of comedians, Tommy was voted the sixth best comic ever.

Another traditional treat is the handmade pasties from **Ivor Dewdney's** shop on Sidwell Street. They cost from £1.24 to £2.32 and the biggest are enormous.

Bon Gout Deli on Magdalene Road (www.bongoutdeli.co.uk; ☎ 01392 435521) has an eclectic range of produce sourced locally and globally. It currently stocks 26 different local cheeses, Dart Valley jams and sauces, farm meats, smoked meats and fish from Dartmouth and clotted cream.

Effings in Queen Street (☎ 01392 211888; www.effings.co.uk) won an award as Devon's best specialist food shop and has a great deli selection of local cheeses and meats.

Out of town, the enormous **Dart's Farm** complex at Clyst St George (www.dartsfarm.co.uk; ☎ 01392 878200) has enough to keep you busy for a whole day and seems to be growing faster than a patch of mushrooms. The food hall is now a supermarket-sized outlet for local producers, and there is a fish shop, butchery, cider maker, and a well-regarded restaurant using the farm shop products, plus interiors shops such as Aga and Fired Earth, an art gallery and plant centre.

EATING OUT

FINE DINING
Michael Caines, ABode Exeter
**Cathedral Close EX1 1HD, ☎ 01392
223638 www.abodeexeter.co.uk;
www.michaelcaines.com**

Celebrity chef Michael Caines has two
Michelin stars at his country house hotel
Gidleigh Park on the edge of Dartmoor but
he doesn't often cook here. Nevertheless
the quality is still high. This understated,
classy restaurant includes a gourmet 'tasting menu' at £58 per head. The rest of us
can enjoy the top notch nosh at £25 for
three courses.

Café Paradiso
**Hotel Barcelona, Magdalene Road EX2
4HY, ☎ 01392 281000
www.aliashotels.com**

Discover a modern menu, exotic décor and
contemporary atmosphere within a former
hospital which is now an acclaimed boutique hotel overlooking its own vegetable
and herb gardens. A three-course meal is
from about £25.

RESTAURANT
Exe-Shed
**Bedford Street, Princesshay EX1 1GJ
☎ 01392 420070
www.shed-restaurants.com**

This contemporary glass building in the new
pedestrian shopping quarter overlooks the
cathedral. Choose from pavement tables,
covered terrace or interior dining rooms. It's
open seven days a week, 10am to midnight.
There is a light modern European menu,
particularly strong on fish and salads.
A three-course set menu is £19.95.

No. 21
**Cathedral Yard, EX1 1HB
☎ 01392 210303
www.21cathedralyard-exeter.co.uk**

An AA rosette restaurant wonderfully sited
next to the cathedral, with an unpretentious
bistro atmosphere. Breakfasts, lunches and
afternoon teas are served before the fine
evening dinners. A three-course dinner is
about £27.

Michael Caines' restaurant is one of Exeter's most stylish

EATING OUT

GASTROPUB

Jack in the Green
Rockbeare EX5 2EE ☎ 01392 8222540
www.jackinthegreen.uk.com

This gastropub is a few miles out of town to the east on the notorious old A30 known to locals as the 'Rockbeare straight', which is now bypassed by a new dual carriageway. The pub features a choice of fine-quality bar snacks or the full restaurant experience with soft leather chairs and dark wood tables. A three-course 'Totally Devon' menu at £25 promotes local suppliers.

Turf Hotel
Exminster EX6 8EE ☎ 01392 833128
www.turfpub.net

It's in sight of the city, but the Turf is so remote you'll need a map to find it. Alternatively, walk/cycle down the towpath from the city. Be warned that it's still almost a mile's walk from the car park. It's hardly a gastronome's menu but the wonderful situation and atmosphere compensate well. And it's worth the journey for the garden barbecues in summer, boat trips to Topsham or Exeter, views across the estuary, simple friendly décor and homely food such as fresh grilled tuna and treacle pudding. There is alot of local produce, with a list of Devon suppliers provided, and the bar has local real ales, cider and even wine. Snacks cost from £4.25, and main courses go up to £12.

The Nobody Inn
Doddiscombleigh EX6 7PS (it can be tricky to find, the easiest route is not the most direct: turn off the A38 at the top of Haldon Hill and follow signs to Doddiscombleigh through the lanes)
☎ **01647 252394 www.nobodyinn.co.uk**

The Nobody Inn is one of the most acclaimed inns in Devon – renowned for its wine and whisky list, selection of local cheeses and creative cooking based on fresh local produce. This ancient village pub was renamed The No Body Inn in the 19th century after an unfortunate episode concerning the remains of a deceased landlord. Low ceilings, blackened beams, inglenook fireplace and antique furniture retain the Old World charm. And there are guest rooms both at the inn and at their manor house Town Barton, a short walk away (single from £25–£40 per night, double from £40–£85). It costs around £19 for three courses.

CAFÉ

Michael Caines, Café Bar
ABode Exeter, Cathedral Yard EX1 1HD
☎ **01392 223626**
www.abodehotels.co.uk

Discover this determinedly stylish café bar in a great location next to the cathedral with tables on the cobbles outside. Meals start from £5.50.

Georgian Tearoom
Broadway House, High Street, Topsham EX3 0ED, ☎ 01392 87346530
www.broadwayhouse.com

Enjoy home-cooked snacks, lunches and award-winning cream teas in a grand relaxing Georgian house or its garden. Main courses cost around £6.

Coolings
Gandy Street EX4 3LS
☎ **01392 43418460**
www.coolingsbar.co.uk

A lively bar in the city centre's most bohemian street, Coolings is a bustling social institution serving everything from cocktails to more than 20 types of salad (from £5.50). Roast lunches are served every day too (£8.25).

Drinking

With local beers, ciders and even wines on the doorstep, Exeter's pubs give visitors plenty of regional interest. As well as the major local breweries mentioned in other regions – such as Cornwall's Sharps and St Austell – Exeter is surrounded by microbreweries.

The Beer Engine at Newton St Cyres (www.thebeerengine.co.uk; ☎ 01392 851282) is a pub that brews its own beer. You'll also find Beer Engine's ales at the **Lamb** in Sandford and the **Black Dog** near Witheridge.

O'Hanlon's beer (www.ohanlons.co.uk; ☎ 01404 822 412) brewed at Great Barton Farm, Whimple, just to the east of Exeter, has recently won several international awards. You can find the O'Hanlon Yellow Hammer at the **Jack in The Green** at Rockbeare (along with Otter ale). Look out too for the ales from **Exe Valley Brewery** at Silverton, **Scatter Rock** of Christow, **Topsham and Exminster Brewery** and **Warrior Brewing Company** of Matford.

Any listing of local pubs will include the **Bridge Inn** at Topsham (☎ 01392 873862), a cranky old place that has been in the landlady's family for five generations. There are lots of local ales, quiet chat and assorted armchairs.

Pub king's locals

The multimillion founder of the fast-growing pub chain JD Wetherspoon lives with his family in the St Leonard's area of Exeter city centre. Tim Martin cuts a distinctive figure – despite his estimated £140 million fortune – with long ginger hair and scruffy clothes. Tim is a graduate of Exeter University, and has been married to his wife Felicity for 30 years and has four children. He founded the pub business in 1979 having originally qualified as a barrister.

Wetherspoon's now owns **The Imperial** in Exeter (The Imperial, New North Road, EX4 4HF; ☎ 01392 434050) and Tim's local, **The George's Meeting House** (South Street, EX1 1ED; ☎ 01392 454250), which was one of the first smoke-free pubs in Britain. He often walks down to the bar from his home.

The Wetherspoon chain takes its named from Tim's primary school teacher, a Mr Wetherspoon, together with 'JD' from the Dukes of Hazzard. It now has more than 500 pubs, renowned for providing good value food and real ale (www.jdwetherspoon.co.uk).

Tim says he models his pubs on a description in a 1946 essay by George Orwell of the imaginary 'Moon Under Water', which offered cheap beer, good conversation, motherly barmaids and solid architecture.

Tim's favourite leisure activities are walking in the Devon countryside or along the coast path plus 'drinking Abbott Ale and eating ham, egg and chips'.

Exeter canal

Medieval Exeter became one of England's wealthiest ports thanks to the early cloth trade. Ships sailed up the Exe to the city's quays to load up with cloth from the surrounding cottage industries.

The Earls of Devon looked enviously from their home at Powderham Castle on the lucrative trading ships passing by. So in the 14th century they unscrupulously built a weir, blocking the river below Exeter... and opened a new quay on the land they owned at Topsham.

It was a disaster for Exeter. Traders couldn't sail up the river now and had to unload at the Earl's quay in Topsham instead. And he charged them heavily for the privilege.

Eventually, in 1563, Exeter traders persuaded Henry VIII – who had just fallen out with the Courtenays – to pass an Act of Parliament so they could build a canal to bypass the weir and restore the direct cargo link with the city.

It was the first canal to be built since the Roman times and is now the country's oldest working canal. Exeter's prosperity was salvaged and at the height of the cloth trade 1,000 bales of cloth a day were exported down the canal from Exeter quay with 500 ocean-going ships a year using the canal.

Express & Echo journalist Stuart Nuttall's favourite city pub is the **Well House Tavern** (www.michaelcaines.com/exetertavern.php; ☎ 01392 223611) on Cathedral Yard, next to the Royal Clarence. It's part of Michael Caines' ABode empire. It serves Otter, O'Hanlons, Exe Valley, Scattor Rock, Branscombe, Skinners, and other local breweries from the cask.

Exeter Tourism Development Manager Victoria Hatfield recommends **The Hourglass** in Melbourne Street (☎ 01392 258722), a semi-circular pub among historic terraces a few steps up from the quay. It has quite a following for its fine food. Victoria also likes the **Double Locks** and **The Turf**, canalside pubs south of the quay.

You can walk or cycle about a mile down the towpath to the Double Locks (www.doublelocks.co.uk; ☎ 01392 256 947). There is good pub grub, local beers and occasional music here. The Turf (www.turfpub.net; ☎ 01392 833128) is even harder to get to (*see Eating out*). But there is a fine collection of local drinks here – including Plymouth Gin, Green Valley's Dragons Tears cider, Topsham Ferryman beer from Topsham and Exminster Brewery and Avocet Ale from Otter Brewery.

FURTHER AFIELD

Topsham

The historic port 4 miles down the river is virtually part of the city now and a sought-after district by wealthy Exonians to live. House prices here are among Devon's highest.

It's a charming place to visit too – with waterfront pubs, good restaurants and antique shops. Many buildings date from the 17th century, including the Dutch-style houses on the Strand, built by wealthy merchants escaping religious persecution in the Netherlands.

Wander through the tiny streets between pastel-painted fishermen's cottages to the quayside – you may spot regular visitor Bob Hoskins – or simply find various boat trips.

Its nautical tradition is based on the location at the meeting of the rivers Exe and Clyst, the start of the Exeter Canal and where the river becomes a wide estuary. Topsham's history involves much shipbuilding, fishing and cargo handling but the estuary here is also a favourite for wildlife enthusiasts. The tidal flats attract a wide range of seabirds and waterfowl such as curlews and avocets. Specialist birdwatching cruises are arranged during the prime season from December to March.

A passenger ferry runs across the estuary to the Exeter Canal (daily in summer, weekends in winter). **The Sea Dream**, a 60-seater launch runs to Turf Lock from Trout's Boatyard near Topsham Quay (daily throughout summer). For information about these services call Exeter TIC on ☎ 01392 265700.

Stuart Line Cruises (☎ 01395 222144; www.stuartlinecruises.co.uk) runs boat trips throughout the summer from Topsham to Exmouth. From there you can take the scenic Avocet train line back to Topsham. You can also do speedboat rides across the estuary or even to Torquay.

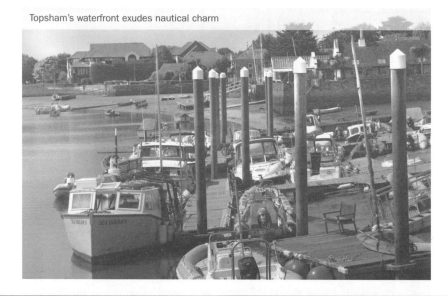
Topsham's waterfront exudes nautical charm

Visitor information

Tourist Information Centres: Exeter *Tourist Information Centre,* Dix's Field EX1 1RQ; ☎ 01392 265700; *Quay House Visitor Centre:* The Quay, ☎ 01392 271611.

Hospitals: The accident and emergency unit is at the *Royal Devon and Exeter* (universally known as the RD&E) on Barrack Road, Wonford EX2 5DW (www.rdehospital.nhs.uk; ☎ 01392 411611).

Websites: www.exeter.gov.uk/visiting; www.essentialdevon.com; thisisexeter.co.uk.

Sport: Exeter City FC plays at St James Park; in walking distance of the city centre (off Old Tiverton Road, EX4 6PS). It's currently in the Blue Square Conference League

(☎ 01392 411243; www.exetercityfc.co.uk); *Exeter Chiefs Rugby Club* (☎ 01392 890890; www.exeterchiefs.co.uk) plays in National League One at the new Sandy Park stadium at Sowton near the motorway interchange.

Bike rental: Saddlepaddle, King's Wharf, The Quay EX2 4AN, www.saddlepaddle.co.uk ☎ 01392 424241. Much of Exeter is hilly, the best place to cycle is by the canal and river – that's where Saddlepaddle is based. It's perfect for rides down to the canalside pubs. You can also hire canoes and kayaks for trips down the canal.

Taxis: Capital taxis, St Davids, ☎ 01392 433433; www.exeter.tc

TIVERTON AND THE EXE VALLEY

In the middle of the rich rolling farmland area above the motorway, Tiverton is the biggest and most interesting town with its historic castle and canal. In this area, you'll find the old market towns of Crediton, Collumpton and Bampton too, which also have good shops, pubs and restaurants. All are worth a visit and across the rest of this patch are scores of classic Devonshire villages of various sizes around the gorgeous Exe valley and its tributaries. It's the iconic Devon landscape – a hilly patchwork of lush green grass, old deciduous trees with dark red soil poking through.

To the south, the villages are full of wealthy Exeter commuters, to the north there is more of an old-money feel, with a traditional hunting-shooting-fishing tweediness as you approach the foothills of Exmoor. Although tourist marketing chiefs are trying to dub this area 'The Devon Heartland', we're sticking to the more accurate Exe Valley description – after all, Tiverton is hardly at the heart of Devon, being only 10 miles from the Somerset border.

WHAT TO SEE AND DO

 ### Fair weather

Nevertheless, we'll agree that the heart of this region is **Tiverton**, a likeable old market town with a castle, canal and colourful history.

Like much of the east of the county, Tiverton grew rich in the Middle Ages thanks to the wool trade. Later the town specialised in lace making. Nowadays, the compact and mostly pedestrianised town centre rising above the river makes for a great stroll. Look out for the Victorian **Town Hall**, **St George's Church** – the only notable Georgian church in Devon and the earlier **St Peter's Church** in pink sandstone.

Tiverton's two great sights are both historic – the canal and castle. The **Grand Western Canal** was built almost 200 years ago for transporting lime from quarries to the kilns to be processed as a building material. It's now the centrepiece of a excellent 11-mile country park, run by the county's council. It meanders between Tiverton and Lowdwells near the Somerset border, following contours because there are no locks. The level

> **GRAND WESTERN CANAL COUNTRY PARK**, The Moorings, Canal Hill, Tiverton EX16 4HX; ☎ 01884 254072; www.devon.gov.uk/grand_western_c anal. Entry: free but permits required for fishing/cycling; book for horse-drawn boat trips (Easter–Oct) and individual boat hire ([tel]01884 253345;

Horse-drawn barge trips from Tiverton

towpath is perfect for walking, cycling, boating, fishing and picnics. Watch out for kingfishers and otters along the way.

The Canal Basin in Tiverton is signposted from the M5 and provides parking, toilets, a visitor centre, tea gardens and a floating shop/café. It is also home to a horse-drawn barge that takes passenger trips along the canal.

TIVERTON CASTLE,
☎ 01884 253200; www.tiverton-castle.com. Entry: adults £5, children 7–16 £2; open Easter to end Oct: only Sun 2.30am–5pm; guided tour: 2.45pm.

The best part of visiting **Tiverton Castle** is entering through the huge 700-year-old red sandstone gatehouse to find a romantic grassed courtyard bordered by the remains of the walls and towers. There is a house and garden too; they're pretty but obviously later additions.

During the English Civil War the castle was besieged by the roundhead General Fairfax and fell to him after a fantastically lucky shot hit the drawbridge chain. Today's visitors can hear ghostly tales and can also try on armour, a plus for older children.

The castle was one of the homes of the Courtenays, the medieval Earls of Devon, who crop up all over the county, but it's is now the private home of Angus and Alison Gordon. They allow visits one afternoon a week but have holiday flats available throughout the year (see *The best... places to stay*).

Two miles north of Tiverton is a classic National Trust country estate: **Knightshayes Court**. It's the striking Victorian mansion and gardens of the wealthy textile barons, the Heathcoat-Amory family. The house is largely the lavish work

Unholy fires

In 1655 Oliver Cromwell issued a charter saying that Tiverton market day would no longer be held on Mondays but Tuesdays. This would avoid 'the profanation of the Sabbath' by traders preparing goods for market. He thought this had clearly provoked God's wrath, and explained the two great fires of 1598 and 1612. The town was destroyed both times. Cromwell's charter is displayed at Tiverton Museum.

Sadly, the Lord Protector's plan didn't work. There was a third fire in June 1731 in which 300 houses were destroyed and more than 2,000 people made homeless. So an Act of Parliament was passed decreeing that in future all Tiverton houses must have roofs built of tiles or slates and not of thatch. And so far, that seems to have done the trick... and the market is still held on Tuesdays as decreed by Cromwell.

Knightshayes was built on the proceeds of the cloth trade

KNIGHTSHAYES COURT, Bolham, EX16 7RQ (signed from the A396); ☎ 01884 254665; www.nationaltrust.org.uk Entry: adults £7.40, children £3.70, family £18.50; garden only: adults £5.90, children £3; open 23 Mar to 3 Nov: Sat to Thur 11am–5pm (4pm from 1 Oct); garden open daily 2 Mar to 3 Nov 11am–5.30pm.

of flamboyant 19th-century architect William Burges, who liked to sit at his desk with a parrot on his shoulder. When you've studied the richly decorated gothic interior and extensive formal gardens, relax in the shop, plant centre and restaurant.

The market town of **Crediton** is much closer to Exeter and it shows. Compared with Tiverton, it's more like a dormitory town for the city down the road. The wide main street lined with period buildings was once grand but feels a little shabby now, although there are some lovely quirky independent stores and a thriving farmers' market (first Saturday of each month).

The one great reason to visit is the extraordinary medieval church. It's as grand as some cathedrals and striking in its red sandstone and creamy Beer stone. Inside, spot the carved stone snakes and birds, the full-sized carving of the knight who fought at the Battle of Crecy and died at the age of 105, and a huge memorial to Victorian hero Sir Redvers Buller, who won a Victoria Cross in the Zulu War (www.creditonparishchurch.org.uk/☎ 01363 773226).

To the east, **Cullompton** is right next to the M5, but not many visitors turn off to investigate. It's a quiet country town on the River Culm, another Exe

Market forces

Cullompton held the south-west's first farmers' market 10 years ago and since then the number of stalls has grown to 28 and buffalo ice cream, trees, cider, honey and fudge have been added to the wide range of local produce on sale. The town's markets have a unique atmosphere helped by music provided by local school bands. Hot food is available and the local scouts group sells teas and coffees.

All the stall holders at the market travel less than 40 miles to get there and sell produce they grew, reared or created themselves. Cullompton Farmers' Market is the only one in the UK to be set up by local volunteers rather than by a local authority.

Crediton 'village'

Crediton is the birthplace of the early missionary St Boniface, and originally the town was the site of the Devon Cathedral. St Boniface began life as Winfrith in Crideton in 680. He became a Benedictine monk in Exeter and became one the greatest early Christian missionaries. He was given the name St Boniface by the Pope. Legend says that he once cut down a tree associated with the pagan god Thor. A fir tree grew from the roots and this became a symbol of the new Christian religion and eventually our familiar Christmas Tree.

Years later, in 1046, Leofric was appointed bishop of both Devon and Cornwall in Crediton. He quickly decided that the cathedral should be moved to the larger, more culturally active community of Exeter. The reason he gave to Edward the Confessor was that Exeter was more easily defended from marauding Danes, but Leofric confided to the Pope that his main motive for the shift was that he didn't want to be stuck in a 'mere village'.

tributary. There is a lively **farmers' market** (Station Road car park on the second Saturday of each month (January being the only exception) 9.30am–12.30pm) and a red sandstone church, but the main attraction is the marvellous **Diggerland** Theme Park (see *What to do with children*).

The small town of **Bampton** to the north is the most attractive in the area. It's close to the south-east corner of Exmoor and stands on the River Batherm, another tributary of the River Exe. During the Civil War, Royalists from Tiverton Castle burnt down the whole town, so there are few surviving buildings from earlier than the 17th century. But there still seem to be dozens of old stone cottages with a leat running down the main street and almost 100 listed buildings. You'll spot flower baskets, window boxes and flower beds everywhere – the town has won the Britain in Bloom competition six times and takes its floral

Tracy Frankpitt, who runs Peverstone Cheese on her dairy farm near Cullompton, had the idea for the market. 'We wanted to sell our award-winning cheese at the farmers' market in Bath but they said we were too far away', she says. 'Cullompton was looking for something that would bring more people into the town and I suggested we started our own farmers' market.'

The organisers of Cullompton farmers' market have been helping others start up across the county. Tracy – whose long-standing family dairy farm is based in the luxuriant river meadows of the Exe Valley – says: 'We are working together to make sure that all farmers' markets across Devon are a success both for the farmers and local people.'

Killerton House stands among fabulous gardens

displays very seriously. At the time of writing it had just won the 2007 South West in Bloom trophy.

Midway between Exeter and Tiverton on the A396 is the pretty hamlet of **Bickleigh**, with a picture postcard bridge over the Exe, thatched cob cottages and a picturesque red stone castle surrounded by thick woods. Over the years the hamlet has become a centre for tourists and visiting locals so there is now a good mix of attractions here.

In the castle gardens, there is a sixth-century thatched chapel, one of Devon's oldest buildings, but you'll have to get married to see it – the chapel is a very popular private wedding venue (☎ 01884 855363; www.bickleigh-castle.com).

But anyone can visit **Bickleigh Mill** – a collection of shopping, crafts and children's activities. There is a railway theme park, a maize maze and a vineyard too (see *What to do with children*... And *how to avoid them* and *Shopping*).

Killerton House and Garden can be spotted on a hill to the west of the M5, just north of Exeter. It's another grand National Trust estate, featuring an 18th-century house containing a costume collection of more than 9,000 pieces.

> **KILLERTON**, Broadclyst, EX5 3LE; ☎ 01392 881345; www.nationaltrust.org.uk
> Entry: adults £7.40, children £3.70, family (2+2) £18.50; garden only: £5.60/£2.80 (reduced rate Nov to Feb); open most of the year, see website or call for details.

The hillside garden has attractive walks among the flowering rhododendrons and magnolias, and there is a plant centre, restaurant and shop.

 ## Wet weather

Tiverton Museum is better than the average municipal collection. It's actually an archive of Mid Devon life through the ages with an eccentric array of artefacts in 15 galleries, including the last steam train to arrive in Tiverton, 400-year-old cider-making equipment and a horse-drawn fire engine.

> **TIVERTON MUSEUM**, Beck's Square, EX16 6PJ (just off the Great Western Way opposite the bus station); ☎ 01884 256295; www.tivertonmuseum.org.uk. Entry: adults £4, concessions £3, children 5–16 £1; open Feb to Christmas: bank holidays, Mon to Fri 10.30am–4.30pm, Sat 10am–1pm.

 ## What to do with children

Diggerland is designed for children to indulge their muddiest Bob the Builder fantasies. This small theme park is like a dirty Disneyland giving you a chance to dig a hole in a muddy field with a JCB, take scary rides in a digger's shovel, drive

> **DIGGERLAND**, Verbeer Manor, Cullompton EX15 2PE; ☎ 08700 344437; www.diggerland.com. Entry: £12.50, over 65s £6.25, under 3s free; open weekends and school holidays 10am–5pm (see website for details).

your own dumper truck, ride pedal-powered diggers, and enjoy gentle trips on a 'digger train'.

There is lots of mud, big tyres, frantic lever twiddling, and children screaming with terror/epiphany. The action spreads from the shed-like café, shop, soft-play and amusements across big fields, artificial ponds, off-road tracks and extremely muddy digging areas reminiscent of the First World War. Remember to take wellingtons.

DEVON BADGER WATCH, East Stoodleigh Barton, Stoodleigh, Tiverton EX16 9PT; ☎ 01398 351506; www.devonbadgerwatch.co.uk. Entry: adult £10, children 7–16 £6; Apr to Oct opens 7.30pm, Mon to Sat.

THE AMAZING MAIZE MAZE, Bickleigh Hill, Bickleigh; ☎ 01363 772567. Entry: £4, under 5s free; open 10am–5.30pm when maize has grown, until when maize is harvested.

DEVON RAILWAY CENTRE, The Station, Bickleigh EX16 8RG; ☎ 01884 855671; www.devonrailwaycentre.co.uk. Entry: adults £5.60, OAPs £4.80, children 3–16 £4.60, family (2 adults + 3 children) £17.30; entry includes unlimited train rides; open May–Sept: daily 10.30am–5pm.

Devon Badger Watch offers a rare opportunity to observe these secretive nocturnal animals. From the edge of their natural set, visitors watch their antics in the comfort of the purpose-built hide. Children must be able to sit still and quietly for an hour and a half.

In a field next to Bickleigh Mill, the 10-acre **Amazing Maize Maze** is open in July and August. Farmer Nick Lees and his family have created themed mazes celebrating annual events such as the Queen's Golden Jubilee, the 200th anniversary of the Battle of Trafalgar and the bicentenary of the birth of Victorian engineer Isambard Kingdom Brunel.

Another option for entertaining bored children is the **Devon Railway Centre**. Enjoy rides on a narrow-gauge and a miniature-gauge railway, or play with a huge train set, explore a model village (with trains), play area or railway-themed crazy golf... it's all a clever re-use of a station on the South Devon line that was closed in 1963. A local family bought the site and lovingly restored everything. The station building itself is now the café.

 ## Entertainment

There are occasional pub gigs and events in village halls but most entertainments require a trip to Exeter or Taunton. **Remedies** is a small night club in Gold Street, Tiverton (☎ 01884 253347), but at the time of writing the only cinema in the whole area has closed and one Cullompton local described the town's live music scene with typical Devon wit as 'driving up the road with dance music playing loud'.

The best... PLACES TO STAY

HOTEL

Bark House 🏃 🏠 🍴

Oakford Bridge, Near Bampton EX16 9H
☎ **01398351236**
www.barkhouse.co.uk

This 200-year-old tanning store is now a charming wisteria-covered guesthouse in the Exe Valley with open fires and simple furnishings.

Price: B&B from £49 to £62 per person per night.

Barton Cross Hotel and Restaurant 🏃 🍳 🍴 ♿

Stoke Canon, Exeter EX5 4EJ
☎ **01392 841245**

Five miles north of Exeter, you'll find this 17th-century country house hotel with old fashioned, homely décor and rooms and highly rated food.

Price: from £69 to £75 for a single, from £98 to £110 for a double.

FARMSTAY

Hornhill 🏃 🏠 ♿

Exeter Hill, Tiverton EX16 4PL
☎ **01884 253352**
www.hornhill-farmhouse.co.uk

Sleep in a Victorian four-poster and eat homemade bread, although probably not at the same time, in a five-diamond rated farmhouse B&B with panoramic country views and walks among the 75 acres.

Price: from £30 to £32 for a single; £60 for a double (no credit cards).

CAMPSITE

Minnows 🏃 ♿

Holbrook Lane, Sampford Peverell EX16 7EN. ☎ **01884 821770**

Alongside the Grand Western Canal, this small site has a children's playground. There are two pubs about 15 minutes' walk along the towpath; fishing and boating permits are available on site. Open 10 Mar to 3 Nov.

Price: tent pitches from £9.95 to £13.00 per day.

SELF-CATERING

Tiverton Castle 🏃

Park Hill EX16 6RP ☎ **01884 253 200**
www.tivertoncastle.com

There are four luxurious period holiday apartments in the main castle building, approached through a turret door. Guests are entitled to free tours, use of the garden and fishing on the Exe.

Price: from £270 to £600 per week for a flat sleeping two. Short breaks are available.

Otter's Holt 🏃 🏠 📺

3 miles north of Tiverton
c/o Classic Cottages ☎ **01326 555555**
www.classic.co.uk

A two-bedroomed former cider barn now has under-floor heating and wifi. The river is 100 yards across a field, farm animals abound but the nearest pub is 3 miles away.

Price: from £336 to £756 per week.

Fisherman's blues

Where should you go to stay when you're weary, feeling small? How about a room in a picturesque thatched inn next to a river in a pretty Devon village? It certainly did the job for **Paul Simon** 30 years ago. He had temporarily split from singer Art Garfunkel and came to England, playing in small, provincial folk clubs. While he was playing in the Exeter area, Paul is believed to have stayed at the Fisherman's Cot in Bickleigh.

The half-timbered pub looks the archetypal Devon thatched long house but it was only built in 1933 as a fishing lodge for Bickleigh Castle in the woods behind. It stands by a 16th-century stone bridge over the Exe. When Simon was staying the river was in flood. Some locals scoff at the Paul Simon story, but they do say there had been a drowning nearby at that time. Whatever, the Exe can turn very nasty at Bickleigh, families have been evacuated from cottages many times and the Cot itself has been waterlogged.

Yet it was while gazing at the turbulent waters under the bridge outside the window of Room Six that Simon was said to find the inspiration he'd been looking for. A few years later the world heard the result.

Bridge Over Troubled Water topped the UK and US charts simultaneously, won six Grammy awards and the eponymous LP stayed in the UK charts for 41 weeks. The record's hugeness may have faded over the past 30 years, but the pub that inspired it is still there. The Fisherman's Cot is so pretty and has such a spectacular location that it has become a tourist pub – indeed it's almost a tourist attraction. The restaurant serves everything from burgers to sea bass and Room Six is still there with its inspirational view. The rooms are comfortable, modern and neat but without great character. Like in Simon's day, it's the view that's memorable.

On most sunny days the banks slope down to a tranquil sparkling river. Customers eat cream teas on picnic tables as the river flows by, untroubled. But the flood danger continues with regularity.

The best... FOOD AND DRINK

From the foothills of Exmoor in the north to the edge of Dartmoor and the outskirts of Exeter in the south, this slice of Mid Devon is a rural food factory. Dairy and livestock farming is the keystone of the Mid Devon economy so expect the local produce in shops and restaurants to mirror that. But it's a quiet area too, culinary tradition is conventional rather than experimental, hearty rather than fashionable; you won't find many examples of contemporary cuisine.

Taking the cream

At some stage you will give in to temptation and sample a Devon cream tea. It's difficult not to – with so many signs on farms, shops, pubs and lay-bys.

The secret of this afternoon speciality is the clotted cream. This is made by leaving the cream on the most gentle of heat. As the fat rises, it is creamed off to create the very opposite of skimmed milk – a tasty cream so thick it has a slight yellow crust on top.

A proper cream tea consists of clotted cream instead of butter and homemade scones with either raspberry or strawberry jam. And note that slightly runny strawberry jam is a good sign. Strawberries are low in natural pectin and don't gel really well when making jam.

Staying in

There are plenty of opportunities to sample the fine fresh produce from the area. We've already mentioned the fantastic **farmers' market** in Cullompton (Station Road car park on the second Saturday in each month, January being the only exception, 9.30am–12.30pm). And we've mentioned the stalls in Tiverton's refurbished **Pannier Market** (☎ 01884 243351; www.tiverton-market.co.uk). There is a farmers' market here on the third Wednesday of every month, 9am–2pm, and the general market all day on Tuesday, Friday and Saturday has plenty of local food too.

Regulars include Alister Strachan, who sells fresh vegetables grown in the walled garden at Knighthayes Court, Chris Hamilton, who sells stiltons and cheddars from West Town Farm, and Anne Petch from Heale Farm, who makes and sells sausages, bacon and ham from old breeds of pig.

Yeoford, just west of Crediton, has just started a local produce **market** too – 10am–12pm on the first Saturday of each month in the car park of the Mare and Foal pub, or inside if it's raining.

There are farm shops and delicatessens across the area selling their selection of what's being produced locally. Here are some of the most interesting:

- **The Country Cupboard** in Bampton Street, Tiverton (☎ 01884 257220) stocks local cheese, wine, butter and cream.
- **Mrs Gill's Country Cakes** in Leat Street, Tiverton (☎ 01884 242744) sells homemade cakes.
- **Treloars**, 38 High Street, Crediton (☎ 01363 772332) stocks homemade pies and around 15 local cheeses, including Quickes Cheddar from a farm on the A377 at Newton St Cyres.

EATING OUT

FINE DINING

Barton Cross Hotel and Restaurant
Stoke Canon, Exeter EX5 4EJ
☎ **01392 841245**

This thatched country house hotel has a cottagey feel in its candlelit restaurant with a huge fireplace. The AA rosette menus include fresh local produce including plenty of Brixham fish. A three-course dinner costs about £25.

Bark House
Oakford Bridge, Near Bampton EX16 9H
☎ **01398351236**
www.barkhouse.co.uk

Bark is a wisteria-covered guesthouse in the Exe Valley and has a restaurant with open fires and simple furnishings. The chef uses produce from local shops and farmers' markets when possible and the cooking style is a mix of traditional oven dishes and meals cooked to order with either fresh vegetables or salads, followed by homemade desserts. Three courses cost £29.95.

RESTAURANT

The Fisherman's Cot
Bickleigh, EX16 8RW
☎ **01884 855237**

The Cot is a picturesque thatched riverside pub/hotel where Paul Simon once stayed (see panel). B&B costs from £69.95 per room. The food is secondary to the mouth-watering view of the river and bridge, especially from the tables outside. The carvery is popular with locals (adults £8.45, children £4.95), while the main menu can feature Exe mussels and River Dart trout, with three courses at about £21.

Woods Bar and Dining Room
Banks Square, Dulverton, Somerset TA22 9BU ☎ **01398 324007**

It's worth crossing the border to find this little bar in the centre of Dulverton that does top-quality modern British food. It has won an AA rosette and has more than 450 wines – all available by the glass (from £3.50 to £100 a glass!). Main courses cost from £10 to £18.50.

GASTROPUB

Mount Pleasant
Nomansland EX16 8NN (on the B3137 from Tiverton to South Molton)
☎ **01884 860271**

The only *Good Pub Guide* recommended spot in this whole area is a welcoming old whitewashed roadside inn, with open fires and old wooden furniture. Sadly the pub is for sale as we go to press, so we can't predict the quality of food in the future. At present the food is homemade and homely, ranging from steak and kidney pies to lamb with redcurrant and orange sauce. Three courses cost about £20.

Exeter Inn
Tiverton Road, Bampton EX16 9DY
☎ **01398 331345**
www.exeter-inn.com

It's hardly gastro, but this popular riverside food pub serves everything from tapas to fish and chips and Sunday roasts in front of log fires or on tables outside. Local Exmoor venison and trout feature regularly on the menu. There is also B&B upstairs. Meals cost £3–£10.

• **Haigh's Bakehouse** (☎ 01363 774234) in Crediton High Street is run by fifth-generation baker Mel Curran, who makes bread, cakes, pastries, pies and croissants to sell in the shop and at farmers' markets.

DJ Haggett's family owned butcher's shop in Newcourt Road, Silverton (☎ 01392 860226; www.djhaggett.co.uk) is renowned for its prize-winning sausages made from local meat and available in 40 different flavours. **Exe Valley Fishery** right up at Exebridge rears trout that you can catch yourself or buy from their on-site smokery – along with smoked duck, salmon, chicken and pheasant (☎ 01398 323328; www.exevalleyfishery.co.uk). **Exe Valley Farm Shop** at Thorverton, just off the A396 (EX5 5LZ; ☎ 01392 861239), is highly recommended by locals.

🍸 Drinking

You'd think that this sleepy rural area would be exclusively a real ale and cider province but there is a surprise on the sunny hills of the upper Exe Valley. **Yearlstone Vineyard** near Bickleigh (☎ 01884 855700; www.yearlstone.co.uk) is open to visitors 11am–4pm, Fri–Sun, and has a café and shop. Among the still and sparkly white wines, the 2006 Vintage Brut is recommended by Oz Clarke. There are also scores of fine real ale pubs. Here are a few of the best:

• **The Exeter Inn**, Bampton (Exmoor Ale and good food)
• **The Trout** at Bickleigh (Exmoor Ale and hearty grub)
• **The Three Tuns**, Silverton (Exe Valley beer and period furniture)
• **The King's Arms** at Tedburn St Mary (Otter beer and farm cider)
• **New Inn** at Coleford (monthly pig roasts and resident parrot)
• **The Globe Inn** at Sampford Peverell (Otter ale and good food)
• **Crediton Inn** in Crediton (Sharps and St Austell beer from Cornwall)

FURTHER AFIELD

The Exe factor

The **River Exe** is Devon's main river – it rises near Simonsbath on Exmoor and runs for more than 50 miles to Exmouth. It stretches almost all the way from the Bristol Channel in the north to the English Channel in the south passing through many towns and villages including Tiverton, Topsham and Exebridge and, of course, the county town of Exeter. The landscape changes from windswept moorland at its source, through deep wooded valley to rich farmland, and finally to a broad sandy estuary.

In AD50 the Romans had founded their stronghold at the river's lowest crossing point. And historically, this first bridging point was always at Exeter where

Visitor information

Tourist information centres:
Devonshire Heartland Tourist Association, www.devonshire
heartland.co.uk; *Crediton Tourist
Information Centre,* Old Town Hall,
High Street, Crediton EX17 3LF, ☎
01363 772006, crediton.co.uk; *Tiverton Tourist Information Centre,*
Phoenix Lane, Tiverton EX16 6LU, ☎
01884 255827, www.discovertiverton.co.uk.

Hospitals: for accidents and emergencies go to *Tiverton and District
Hospital,* Kennedy Way, Tiverton
EX16 6NT, ☎ 01884 235400; *Crediton Hospital,* Western Road, Crediton
EX17 3NH, ☎ 01363 775588; 24-hour
accident and emergency facilities are
available at *Royal Devon and Exeter
Hospital* (Wonford), Barrack Road,
Exeter EX2 5DW, ☎ 01392 411 611.
Websites: bampton.org.uk;
www.cullompton.org
Supermarkets: Tesco Superstore,
Blundells Way EX16 4DB, ☎ 08456

779672; *Morrisons,* Kennedy Way,
EX16 6RZ, ☎ 01884 255301;
Somerfield, Phoenix Lane, EX16 6
☎ 01884 258962; *Spar* Newton
Square, Bampton EX16 9NE,
☎ 01398 331200; *Somerfield,* Mill
Street, Crediton EX17 1EY,
☎ 01363 773475; *Tesco,* High Street,
Crediton EX17 3JP, ☎ 0845 0269151;
Somerfield, Exeter Road, Cullompton
EX15 1EY, ☎ 01884 32958.

Bike rental: Abbotshood Cycle Hire,
Greenway, Halberton, Tiverton EX16
7AE, ☎ 01884 820728, www.abbotshoodcyclehire.co.uk. Bicycles are
delivered to/collected from holiday
cottages or the Tiverton Parkway Station free of charge.

Taxis: Devon Link Taxis, Tiverton
☎ 01884 243104; Arrow Cars, Crediton ☎ 01363 777 714; *Jolly Jaunts,*
Uffculme, Cullompton
☎ 01884 840979.

the river narrows considerably. Further south the 10-mile estuary between
Exeter and the sea widens to at least a mile.

The Exe has been the scene of major flooding in the past, sometimes in a
devastating way, destroying churches and homes in Exeter and causing chaos
in Tiverton. Flooding is still a problem along some stretches but Exeter's flood
defence scheme has prevented serious flooding in the city.

The river has traditionally been popular with anglers. In 1924 a monster
salmon weighing 64lb was caught by Topsham fisherman Richard Voysey. It
became known as the '**Exe Salmon**'. It was 5ft long and took three men to lift
for the photo. Sadly, today's fishermen are unlikely to be so lucky.

HONITON AND THE BLACKDOWN HILLS

The countryside of East Devon, between the M5 and the coastal strip, is rich green traditional farming land, well watered by the rivers Otter, Yarty and Culm. To the east are the inspiring Blackdown Hills, designated as an Area of Outstanding Natural Beauty with their dramatic steep-sided valleys and windy crests. To the west is flatter productive farmland punctuated by the heights of Woodbury Common.

The old market towns of Honiton, Ottery St Mary and Axminster are the main centres in this quiet quarter of Devon. Inland, East Devon's countryside is less developed, the pace is slower and most visitors merely pass through on their way to the sea or further west. But that means you're missing some of the county's finest countryside, delightful villages and fascinating towns and attractions. When Daniel Defoe, author of *Robinson Crusoe* visited in the 18th century, he considered this 'the most beautiful landscape in the world'.

WHAT TO SEE AND DO

 ### Fair weather

The east of Devon may not have the famous resorts of the coast, but it has perfect walking, exploring and picnicking countryside. The best part is one of the least well known: the 360sq km of the **Blackdown Hills** Area of Outstanding Natural Beauty between Chard and Honiton. It's a flat, high plateau deeply gorged by rivers and around two-thirds of the area is in Devon.

The hills offer a sequence of great views and the valleys are dotted with ancient villages surrounded by patterns of enclosed fields, isolated farms and a maze of winding high-hedged lanes, largely unchanged for 200 years. The hills are so valuable to naturalists that there are 16 sites of special scientific interest. Rare species include barn owls, nightjars, orchids, butterflies, dormice, lizards, kingfishers, otters and bats.

One of the best spots for views is **Culmstock Beacon**, a mile to the west of the pretty village of Culmstock. It's one of the chain of Elizabethan beacons built to warn of invasion by the Spanish at the time of the Armada. Fires on the coast would be lit and then one by one a network set ablaze. This was the signal for all able-bodied men to arm themselves and assemble at their local church. Culmstock's is the only beacon hut in the country to have survived.

CELEBRITY CONNECTIONS

International singing star **Joss Stone** comes from the tiny Devon village of Ashill on the northern edge of the Blackdown Hills. She grew up in this very rural spot, the third of Peter and Wendy Stoker's four children. Her parents still live in Ashill. There are reports that Joss has bought a house at Culmstock to use when she's back in the UK.

Joss's father sells dried fruit and her mother used to rent out holiday cottages but is now her manager. Joss was in the county before Christmas in 2007 to turn on Barnstaple's Christmas lights and seems to return every April for her birthday. In 2007 she celebrated her 20th at the Ilminster Stage pub in Culmstock and even helped out behind the bar when things got busy.

Joss went to Uffculme Comprehensive School 5 miles from Ashill. She socialised in Exeter, hanging out at the Real McCoy Arcade café and vintage clothes shop off Fore Street (www.therealmccoy.co.uk). Blaming dyslexia, Joss left school aged 16 with just three GCSEs. But she made her first public singing appearance at the school, singing Jackie Wilson's 'Reet Petit' at a fifties-themed variety show in the school hall. Her early performances included a gig at Exeter University and a collaboration with a near neighbour, Portisheads Beth Gibbons, who lives near Exeter.

Since then she has had international success, including winning two Brit awards, one Grammy, appearing at Live 8 and in the film *Eragon*. Joss entered *The Sunday Times* Rich List in 2007 with an estimated personal fortune of £10 million... at the age of 20.

Apart from her voice and looks, Joss is known for singing barefooted and being a vegetarian. She has been chosen to represent Gap and is the new Cadbury's Flake girl. When she first appeared in the USA, MTV described her as the '16-year-old girl from the little English town of Devon'.

When asked by *The Guardian* about how such an innocent teenager coped with the American music industry, Joss said: 'Honestly, I haven't really seen any dodginess. I've seen more dodgy stuff in Devon. People think it's all flowers and sheep – well, it ain't. It's a funny old world, isn't it? They're all like: "And you come from lovely Devon, and you're an English rose, and so perfect." And I'm like: "Oh, you don't know..."'.

A slit window allowed observers to watch for a light at Upottery Beacon to the south.

In the village of **Hemyock** there are the ruins of a medieval castle include a dungeon, gatehouse and moat that's only open on bank holiday afternoons or at other times by arrangement (☎ 01823 680745; www.hemyockcastle .co.uk). There are also attractive self-catering holiday cottages within the walls (£236 –£460 per week).

In the woods north-west of Honiton is the massive **Hembury Hill Fort**. This was first built in the Neolithic period and was re-fortified during the Iron Age. It's Devon's biggest hill fort, and was dubbed 'The Fort of the Dead' by the invading Romans, probably because the residents had fled before they arrived. Just the massive earth ramparts are left now, but it's an evocative spot to visit and the views are awe-inspiring.

For more information about the Blackdown Hills, visit the excellent independent website (www.blackdown-hills.net).

For riding fans hacks and instruction for all ages are available at East Devon stables such as:

- **Heazle Riding Centre**
  at Hemyock in the Blackdown Hills (☎ 01823 680280)
- **Devenish Pitt Stables**
  near Farway (☎ 01404 871355; www.zen63696.zen.co.uk)
- **Hitts Barton**
  near Whimple (☎ 01404 822 335; www.hittsbarton.co.uk).

Then there are the towns of East Devon – each with good reasons to visit. **Axminster** may be a sleepy market town but its name is world famous, thanks to its carpets.

Axminster carpets were first produced in 1755 by Thomas Whitty, whose factory made high quality, custom-made carpets for stately homes. These original hand-tufted carpets took so long to finish that the church rang its bells every time one was completed. Their quality was due to 'the pliant fingers of little children' according to 18th-century locals. A factory in Woodmead Road still makes Axminster carpets and there is an outlet shop too (see *Shopping*).

The best recent news for Axminster was that after moving his **River Cottage HQ** to a nearby village, TV chef Hugh Fearnley-Whittingstall opened a farm shop and restaurant in the town. See *Shopping* and *Eating out* for details.

Apart from that, Axminster is a pleasant, unspoilt market town with attractive streets radiating out from the town square. It's worth looking out for the minster church of St Nicholas and a weekly Thursday market dating back to 1210. The small local history **museum** in the old Victorian police station in Church Street is open between June and September.

Local knowledge

Former world-class footballer **Steve Perryman** now lives in the picturesque village of Lympstone on the Exe Estuary. He is Director of Football for Exeter City. As a player Steve holds the record for most appearances and most medals for Spurs, winning two league cups, two UEFA cups and two FA cups alongside being voted Football Writers' Player of the Year in 1982 and playing for England. He later became Assistant Manager to Ossie Ardiles, was awarded the MBE, and managed Brentford and Watford.

Best view: There are two. The first is from the top of Hunters Path, around Fingle Glen in the Teign Valley. The second is from the cliffs above Exmouth Beach up along coast towards Torquay and up the Exe Estuary.

Favourite shop: Darts Farm, Topsham. And my favourite Devon food is any fish from the Fish Shed (it sells fish and chips and has a fresh fish stall) at Darts Farm. And I love the wine from the Kenton Vineyards to the west of Exeter.

Best things about living here: Peace and quiet, nature on your doorstep, the feeling of safety and the beauty everywhere. And 'The smell of the sea' – that's quoting our daughter Ella!

Best kept Devonshire secrets: Shears Café in the middle of Lympstone village, Eastcote Guesthouse in Clyst St Mary, and Home Farm Hotel and Restaurant near Honiton.

Favourite thing to do on a rainy day: Walk along Exmouth beach, especially in the winter.

Favourite hotel: My favourite beach hotel is the Saunton Sands Hotel in North Devon, and my favourite city hotel is aBode Exeter.

Favourite beach: Exmouth is the best beach for families, especially those with small kids. Saunton and Croyde are great for those who like watersports.

Best place for children: The River Dart Country Park, near Asburton, is great in the summer for kids – with canoeing, high ropes, a big adventure playground, lake with pirate boat and tyres on ropes where you can get very wet. You can even camp there.

Shute Barton Gatehouse is available for holiday lets

SHUTE BARTON MANOR,
near Axminster EX13 7PT;
☎ 01297 34692; www.national-trust.org.uk. Entry: adults £2.70, children £1.30; open 4 Apr to 31 Oct: Wed/Sat 2–5pm.

Shute Barton Manor nearby is an ancient National Trust house dating back to 1380. It has been occupied by the Carew Pole family for 500 years. The manor claims to have the largest fireplaces in England (and possibly the world). It stands 22ft wide and 7ft tall.

Just off the A35, east of Axminster, you'll find **Burrow Farm Gardens** – an interesting woodland site with unusual plants, pergola walk, spectacular borders and views. The café is a calm spot for a cream tea.

BURROW FARM GARDENS,
Dalwood, Axminster EX13 7ET;
☎ 01404 831285; www.burrowfarmgardens.co.uk. Entry: £3.50; open 1 Apr to 30 Sept: daily 10am–7pm.

The central town of East Devon is **Honiton** at the western edge of the Blackdown Hills and alongside the A30 trunk road. Honiton grew wealthy on the medieval cloth trade, and then specialised in lace making. Its long High Street is lined by attractive 18th-century buildings and is worth a wander for its antique, book, pottery and lace shops.

While Honiton is a main road stop-off for travellers, **Ottery St Mary** requires more of a journey; it's not really on the way to anywhere. So it's much quieter but no less interesting. The town's narrow streets wind between some fine Georgian buildings and the twin-towered church of St Mary is surprisingly impressive. That's because a medieval bishop of Exeter decided to model it on Exeter's Cathedral.

During the 18th century, Rev. John Coleridge became the vicar and fathered 13 children, the youngest of whom was the famous poet and philosopher Samuel Taylor Coleridge. 'STC', as his friends called him, spent some of his most creative time in North Devon and Exmoor, where he wrote 'Kubla Khan' and the 'Rime of the Ancient Mariner'.

Ottery, as it is known to locals, is famous across Devon for its riotous **barrel-burning ritual** on the night of 5 November (see www.tarbarrels.co.uk). Perhaps dating back to an ancient pagan ritual of burning evil spirits, each town centre pub sponsors a barrel.

Ottery's barrel burning Is notorious across Devon

These are soaked in tar for weeks, set alight and carried on the shoulders of brave/foolhardy local volunteers who run through the thronging streets. Often generations of the same family have assumed this dangerous task. Injuries are common, there is a huge bonfire and fun fair on the picturesque river banks and crowds come from all over Devon.

Wet weather

Coldharbour Mill is not what you'd expect from a Devon tourist attraction. It's a 200-year-old textile mill in a sleepy village with a history you'd be more likely to find in West Yorkshire. Nevertheless, it's an interesting way of seeing how wool was produced with steam-powered machinery. In the 19th century, many children worked 14 hours a day here for a few pence a week. The chil-

COLDHARBOUR MILL, Uffculme, Cullompton EX15 3EE; ☎ 01884 840960; www.coldharbourmill.org.uk. Entry: £4; open Apr to Oct: daily 10.30am–5pm; Nov to Mar: Mon to Fri, times vary (call for details).

dren have long gone, but the mill still produces worsted on its period machines powered by the south-west's largest water wheel. And Coldharbour houses the largest stitched embroidery in the world – The **New World Tapestry** is 264ft long, with 39 million stitches. It took an army of local volunteers 20 years to create. There is a licensed café and shop too.

What to do with children...

ESCOT PARK, near Ottery EX11 1LU; ☎ 01404 822188; www.escot-devon.co.uk Entry: adults £5.95, concessions /children 3–15 £4.95, family (2+2) £18.50, dogs on leads 50p (access to pet and aquatic centre free); open daily from 10am–5pm.

This isn't difficult when you're sandwiched between two of Devon's greatest family attractions: **Crealy Adventure Park** – see Exeter chapter and **Diggerland** – see Tiverton chapter. But if you need more there is always **Escot Park**, 200 acres of restored Capability Brown gardens with good family fun factor, including a beech maze, falconry displays, play areas, off-road tours, wild boars and red squirrels, blacksmith, award-winning aquatic centre with seahorses and piranhas, pet centre with rabbits and birds, and a decent café.

And how to avoid children

A day spent on a craft course or at an open workshop could be the perfect holiday escape from noisy children. Local professional craftspeople run all sorts of classes at **The Old Kennels** – from woodcuts to millinery in this quiet rural spot.

THE OLD KENNELS, Stentwood, Dunkeswell EX14 4RW; ☎ 01823 681138; www.theoldkennels.co.uk. Courses from about £35 a day.

95

Carpets fit for a king

Axminster's original carpet factory was founded in 1755 and its products quickly became the undisputed choice for wealthy English country homes and town houses. Axminsters were found in Chatsworth House and Brighton Pavilion as well as being bought by King George III and Queen Charlotte – who also visited the factory here.

After the factory was destroyed by a fire, the Axminster company folded and the name and tradition became just a historical footnote. About 70 years ago a businessman relaunched carpet manufacturing in the town. Now carpets from Axminster can be again found in royal residences, in top hotels around the world, in train carriages and even on British Airways aircraft.

To celebrate 250 years of carpet weaving in Axminster, a huge commemorative rug was produced in 2005. The carpet was paraded by the town's weavers to the Minster Church where it was blessed by the Bishop of Exeter, and then presented to the Earl of Devon. Its final resting place was Clarence House, home of the Prince of Wales.

The same sense of peaceful retreat comes in a very different way at **Hollies Trout Farm** (☎ 01404 841428; www.holliestroutfarm.co.uk). The Downer family provide course and fly fishing on their lake with everything laid on – 24-hour hot drinks and snacks, an all-weather cabin, easy parking, tackle store and hire. There is even a self-catering log cabin or B&B in their farmhouse. You can buy smoked trout and homemade fish pate here, and the family also runs a stall at Crediton and Wellington farmers' markets.

Shopping

Axminster is famous for one thing – carpets. And you can still buy them here, thanks to the new **Axminster Factory Outlet** shop on the A358 Seaton road. There are some bargains too – factory seconds, remnants, end of lines, discontinued rugs and underlay at factory prices (www.axminsterfactoryoutlet.co.uk; 9am–5.30pm Mon to Fri, 10–5 Sat).

Honiton is also famous for making things that carry its name. For centuries Honiton has been renowned for Honiton lace and Honiton pottery. The town still has plenty of shops dedicated to both. And Honiton has also become the main centre in the West Country for antiques and antiquarian books. It's a magnet for antique dealers and bargain hunters from all over the world, who come to browse in 30 different shops, one of the auction houses or the twice-weekly street markets (Tues and Sat).

The best... **PLACES TO STAY**

BOUTIQUE

Combe House

Gittisham near Honiton EX14 3AD
☎ **01404 540400.www.thishotel.com**

The 2007 'Country Hotel of the Year' isn't cheap but is a perfect example of a sumptuous country house hotel. The Elizabethan manor is set in farmland and gardens where Arabian horses and pheasants roam, near a pretty village with a babbling brook and village green. Push open the ancient oak door to find an award-winning restaurant, crackling log fires, squashy sofas, old oil paintings and dark wood panelling.

Price: B&B from £165 to £320 for a single; from £180 to £335 for a double; dogs £7pn, children (12 and under, in an extra bed) £27 B&B.

Woodbury Park

Hotel, Golf and Country Club, Woodbury Common, EX5 1JJ. ☎ **01395 233 382 www.woodburypark.co.uk**

Racing driver Nigel Mansell and his wife Roseanne built this 500 acre luxury resort near their home on Woodbury Common. Late in 2007 they sold the Park to their next-door neighbour and moved to the Channel Isles. Property developer Robin Hawkins, who lives in Merehaven Manor next to the Park, has taken over and promises to improve the standard. Mansell has vowed to continue to be a figurehead for the resort but don't expect to bump into him in the car park too often. Robin has bought a modern resort with exceptional facilities – two restaurants, two golf courses, outdoor tennis courts, a top-quality football pitch, squash court, a gym, spa and indoor pool and a hotel with classically styled rooms and individual lodges.

Price: from £105 for a double.

HOTEL

Home Farm Hotel

Wilmington, Nr Honiton EX14 9JR
☎ **01404 831278**
www.thatchedhotel.co.uk

A cosy and classic old, thatched Devon long-house converted to a hotel and restaurant with fine food, leather Chesterfields, wifi, open fire but some slightly dated features. It's a favourite of football legend Steve Perryman and his family.

Price: B&B from £60 to £77 for a single; from £90 to £125 for a double.

B&B

Glebe House

Southleigh, Colyton EX24 6SD
☎ **01404 871276**
www.guestsatglebe.com

Glebe House is set in grounds of 15 acres, including a heated pool and tennis court. There are only three well-equipped en suite bedrooms with fridges for fresh milk, hair dryers and free wireless broadband. Eat breakfast under the vines in a conservatory with views over the valley.

Price: B&B £40 for a single; from £60 for a double; from £80 for a family room.

West Colwell Farm

Offwell EX14 9SL. ☎ **01404 831130 westcolwell.co.uk**

In the beautiful Blackdown foothills, this farm's dairy has been tastefully converted to three highly rated, award-winning B&B rooms. No dogs or children allowed, just some Devon Ruby Red cattle grazing around the farm. Breakfast is served in the garden or by a wood-burning stove inside.

Price: B&B from £50 for a single; from £70 to £75 for a double.

SELF-CATERING

Cadhay House

Near Ottery St Mary, EX11 1QT
☎ **01404 813511**
www.cadhay.org.uk

Cadhay is a beautiful Elizabethan mansion with magnificent gardens converted to luxurious self-catering accommodation for large parties of up to 22 people. The stables and coach house have recently been converted into a holiday cottage that sleeps six.

Main house prices: from £2952 to £6063 for a week.

Honiton lace

Lace making was the main industry of Honiton for hundreds of years. In all the villages around the town, women would sit outside their dark cottages using the sunlight to see while weaving the highly complicated, delicate pieces of lace.

Lace making was extremely labour intensive, with even the smallest piece requiring skill and precision. In 1841, lace makers from the Honiton area were commissioned to supply lace for Queen Victoria's wedding dress. The Queen was so impressed by the quality, she commissioned a christening robe for her eldest son, later King Edward VII. This delicately woven lace gown is still used by the Royal Family.

The lace makers were mostly single workers making lace from their cottages and their products were brought to Honiton as a centre for dispatch. Eventually, machine-made lace forced Honiton's lace-making industry into decline.

The Queens Adelaide, Victoria, Alexandra and Mary all tried to support production of local lace through patronage but the industry never returned to its previous high point.

The Allhallows Museum in Honiton features interesting displays of Honiton lace making.

The best... FOOD AND DRINK

The Blackdown Hills and East Devon have been virtually self-sufficient over the past few centuries as the landscape provides perfect growing conditions for a wide variety of crops and animals. The farmers still employ traditional methods that help keep their food produce tasting so special. For visitors this means that fresh local produce can be found in a variety of farm and specialist shops or markets. Many village shops also stock local produce.

The area also has scores of country pubs and small family-run hotels and guesthouses that serve homemade food using the best of the regions produce. Many B&B providers pride themselves on producing breakfasts using eggs, bacon and sausages from neighbouring farms.

Staying in

There is one star ingredient in the East Devon area that is worth hunting down – TV celebrity chef Hugh Fearnley-Whittingstall. His River Cottage HQ is the 60-acre Park Farm near Musbury in the Axe Valley (☎ 01297 631 862; www.rivercottage.net).

Hugh's most recent project is the conversion of an old inn in Trinity Square, Axminster, to an organic produce shop and 'canteen' that opened in late 2007. Hugh crusades for the use of the best local produce so it's no surprise that his shop is full of the best produce from East Devon and west Dorset.

As an example, Hugh has recently helped develop Stinger Beer, a nettle-flavoured ale, with local brewers Hall and Woodhouse (www.hallwood house.co.uk/beers/badgerales/stinger.asp). You can buy the beer in the shop.

Hugh says: 'We have set up this store as a real alternative to the supermarket. We stock a wide selection of everyday food items such as milk, cheese, eggs, meat and poultry. Virtually all of our produce is sourced locally.' The shop is open seven days a week.

And it's not the only high-quality farm shop in the area. **Royal Oak Farm** (Cotleigh, near Honiton EX14 9LF; ☎ 01404 831 223; www.royaloak farm.co.uk) is the ultimate example of farm diversification with B&B, pick-your-own, cream teas and a farm shop. The shop provides beef, pork, lamb, venison and chicken from the farm or local Stockland Hill neighbours – all naturally reared and free-range. You'll also find homemade pies and pasties, cakes and preserves, and fresh vegetables, flowers and plants. B&B is available in a well-sited caravan with its own garden from £80 to £300 per week.

Wallace's Hill Farm Shop (Hemyock EX15 3UZ; ☎ 01823 680307; www.wel-cometowallaces.co.uk) near Hemyock is so comprehensive it has won the title of the best farm shop in the country. The shop and restaurant specialise in homemade food thanks to their own kitchens, bakery, butchery, curing unit and smokery. Specialities include their award-winning pork pies, soups and free-range pork sausages. The farm supplies many local shops and farmers' markets too. Wallace's traditional working farm has bison, Highland cattle, red deer and sheep. There are pigs, miniature ponies and pygmy goats to entertain children, and there is also a small museum featuring historic farming tools.

Drinking

In keeping with East Devon's traditional rural lifestyle, there are plenty of micro-breweries and cider makers in the patch. Real ale fans should look out for **O'Hanlons** from Whimple, **Blackdown** from Honiton and **Branscombe Vale** from Branscombe. Perhaps the most distinctive and popular local brewery is **Otter** at Luppitt. This was started in 1990 by David and Mary Ann McCaig, on a 16th-century farm in the Blackdown Hills. David had brewed with Whitbreads for 17 years and Mary Ann's family have been brewers for generations. The original plan was for a small microbrewery, using its own spring water, yeast and locally malted barley to supply a few real ale houses with a cask-conditioned beer. But demand led to growth and now the brewery consists of a state-of-the-art 80-barrel brewing plant designed by David.

🍴 EATING OUT

FINE DINING
Combe House
Gittisham near Honiton EX14 3AD
☎ **01404 540400. www.thishotel.com**

Being voted the best restaurant in the south-west in 2006 launched this country house hotel into the premier league of eateries. The same year it was voted the county's best restaurant by readers of *Devon Life* – the ultimate judgement from the locals. Outsiders began to notice the menu that specialises in local meat and fish, and includes vegetables and herbs from the hotel garden and well-kept wine from ancient underground cellars. You eat in wonderful surroundings, either inside or outside, but it isn't cheap: a three-course dinner is £39.50, and a two-course lunch is £20.

Woodbury Park
Hotel, Golf and Country Club EX5 1JJ
☎ **01395 233 382**
www.woodburypark.co.uk

This luxury resort designed and built by Nigel Mansell has an AA rosette restaurant in an atrium with a high glass roof, marble floor and comfortable chairs. You can eat more casually in the hotel's Conservatory restaurant but in the Atrium the high-quality food is modern with a simple presentation and formal service. Sunday lunch costs £8.95, and a three-course dinner is around £29.

RESTAURANT
Wallace's
Wallace's Hill Farm, Hemyock EX15 3UZ
☎ **01823 680307**
www.welcometowallaces.co.uk

Wallace's a working farm, with a restaurant that serves produce from the farm and its neighbours. The Wallace family's idea has proved very popular with locals so it's best to book. Every meal in the restaurant is freshly made on site, including the bread, cakes and puddings. And it's fully licensed. Breakfasts are popular, thanks to the home-cured bacon and free-range pork sausages; the highlight of afternoon tea is freshly made scones. Wallace's is open seven days a week, 9am–5pm (Sun 10am–5pm).

GASTROPUB
The Culm Valley
Culmstock EX15 3JJ. ☎ 01884 840354

This is a quirky whitewashed riverside pub with menus on blackboards, local paintings for sale, board games, newspapers, local cider and beers, including Branscombe Vale, Blackawton, Cotleigh and O'Hanlons. The extremely popular food – with lots of fresh local ingredients – ranges from tapas and sandwiches to Ruby Red beef in red wine and Ladram Bay crab. Snacks start from £5, and main courses start from £8.

Tuckers Arms
Dalwood EX13 7EG. ☎ 01404 881342
www.tuckersarms.co.uk

Another typical East Devon thatched long-house pub with good homely food in the beamed, flagstoned bar. There is Otter ale and Wadworths 6X, farm cider and a big open fire. The kitchen specialises in fresh fish and game, and locally caught crab, lobster and lemon sole. Meals cost £8.95–£17.95.

Drewe Arms
Broadhembury EX14 3NF
☎ **01404 841267**

The *Good Pub Guide* selected Drewe Arms as their 2007 Devon dining pub and it's not the first time the lovely old thatched Drewe Arms has won awards. There are a few local drinkers among the old settlers and good real ale from the cask but it's now mainly a top-quality restaurant in a idyllic village setting. The speciality is fish, ranging from smoked haddock chowder to lobster. A three-course dinner costs about £30.

CAFÉ
River Cottage Canteen
Trinity Square, Axminster
☎ **01297 631 862. www.rivercottage.net**

Hugh Fearnley-Whittingstall's 'canteen' is open for breakfast every day except Sunday, for lunch every day, and dinner from Thursday to Saturday. All the ingredients are local and seasonal, and the décor is trendy and basic. Snacks start from £3.50, and a three-course dinner is around £25.

Hugh's chicken run

Otter beer has developed into a highly popular brand and is currently supplying more than 450 free trade outlets and all the major national pub groups. This amounts to over 180 brewer's barrels or 52,000 pints per week.

The best place to try Otter ale is at the amazing one-room **Luppitt Inn** in a farmyard just down the road from the brewery (Luppitt Inn, Luppitt EX14 4RT; ☎ 01404 891613). Otter is supplied to this old farmhouse in the barrel and the landlady is an eccentric, cantankerous 85-year-old who hands out puzzles to test new customers.

Cider drinkers aren't neglected in this area either. East Devon has **Bollhayes Cider** from Clayhidon, **Green Valley** in Clyst St George and **Tay's Farmhouse** from Hawkchurch.

Perhaps the best place to get a taste is at **Lyme Bay Winery** at Shute, near Axminster (EX13 7PW; ☎ 01297 551355; lymebaywinery.co.uk). They offer tastings, and sales of course, throughout the year. If you dare, try their own Jack Ratt Vintage at 7.4% – it's named after notorious Lyme Bay smuggler Jack Rattenbury.

In addition to all the pubs we've mentioned above here are a plenty more good ones in East Devon. Here are some of the highest rated: **Merry Harriers** at Clayhidon, **Five Bells** at Clyst Hydon, **Kings Arms** at Stockland, **Golden Lion** at Tipton St John and the **Diggers' Rest** at Woodbury Salterton.

FURTHER AFIELD

Further to the west, and much smaller than the Blackdown Hills, is the raised heathland of **Woodbury Common**. This untamed area between Woodbury and Newton Poppleford is an attractive upland of bracken, gorse and heather with breathtaking panoramic views stretching right round Lyme Bay and up the Exe Estuary.

In a clump of trees at the centre of the common, there is a half-mile-wide pre-historic hill fort. An easy network of paths leads through the trees and heathland, which forms another Site of Special Scientific Interest. Rare species here include 24 different species of dragonflies and damselflies.

Nigel Mansell's Woodbury Park resort is the luxury place to stay and eat here, although village pubs in Woodbury and Woodbury Salterton provide good value alternatives.

 Visitor information

Tourist information centres:
Lace Walk Car Park, Honiton EX14 8LT, ☎ 01404 4371;,
www.honiton.com; *The Old Courthouse*, Church Street, Axminster EX13 5AQ, ☎ 01297 34386; *Broad Street*, Ottery St Mary EX11 1DJ, ☎ 01404 813964, www.ottery-tourism.org.uk
Hospitals: Honiton Hospital, Marlpits Road EX14 2DD, ☎ 01404 540540;
Axminster Hospital Chard Street, Axminster, Devon EX13 5DU, ☎ 01297 630400; *Ottery St Mary Hospital*, Keegan Close EX11 1DN, ☎ 01404 816000; 24-hour A&E facilities available at *Royal Devon and Exeter Hospital* (Wonford), Barrack Road, Exeter EX2 5DW, ☎ 01392 411 611.
Websites: www.blackdown-hills.net.
Supermarkets: Tesco superstores: Battishore Way, Honiton, EX14 2XD, ☎ 0845 677 9459; Shand Park, West Street, Axminster, EX13 5NG, ☎ 0845 677 9019.
Bike Rental: Cycle, 1 King Street, Honiton, ☎ 01404 47211.
Taxis: Horseshoe Taxis, Honiton, ☎ 01404 850800; *A 1st Call Taxis*, Axminster, ☎ 01297 35007.

EXMOUTH, SIDMOUTH AND THE EAST DEVON COAST

The spectacular stretch of East Devon shore from Exmouth to Seaton is Devon's 'Heritage Coast'. Ever since UNESCO declared the strip from Swanage to Exmouth a World Heritage Site, tourist officials have worked overtime to promote this East Devon coast as a natural wonder of the world. They claim it ranks alongside the Great Barrier Reef and the Grand Canyon and so they have grandly renamed it the UK's 'Jurassic Coast'.

The website (www.jurassiccoast.com) will give you all the details about the Triassic period and so on, but sadly geology and fossils make poor promotional points for tourists.

Perhaps it would be better to put it into simple language: this length of East Devon coast does have world-class spectacular scenery, but don't go there expecting dinosaurs and fossils at every step.

Instead, the 40-mile coastal strip includes dramatic golden sandy beaches, red sandstone cliffs and sea stacks, white chalk cliffs, unusual pebble beaches, river mouths and estuaries and a series of lovely characterful seaside resorts and villages. It's one of the best stretches of the Devon coast and still one of the least crowded.

Sleepy Sidmouth sits amid World Heritage Site scenery

WHAT TO SEE AND DO

 ## Fair weather

Given that **Exmouth** is a classic family seaside resort with a genuinely nice sandy beach that's 2 miles long, it's surprising it's not more popular. This is certainly one of the best beaches on the whole of the South Devon coastline, framed between the busy harbour at the mouth of the Exe and the National Trust's grass-topped red sandstone headland.

The beach itself is the number one attraction – 2.5 miles of soft sand with dunes, rock pools and beach huts. Exmouth's **Esplanade** entertains families with swing boats, crazy golf, miniature railway rides and a lifeboat station. At the eastern end, a zigzag path leads up the cliff to the **High Land of Orcombe** for fine views of Torbay and the mouth of the Exe, plus a wonderful clifftop walk eastwards to find smaller sandy coves.

Behind the beach, Exmouth town is a mix of sprawling bungalow suburbs, some lingering Victoriana and a few old Georgian terraces. The best of these is the elegant **Beacon**, where both Nelson and Byron's widows came to live and grieve while admiring a sea view. Lady Nelson is buried in nearby Littleham Church.

Two eccentric spinsters created A La Ronde

Local knowledge

Watersports mad, that's **Steph Bridge**. In 2007 the young Devonian, who was already British Champion, became Women's World Kiteracing Champion. And Steph is determined to defend her title in 2008 too. If you're in Exmouth look out for her practising off-shore – it can be quite spectacular. Steph also runs kitesurfing holidays with her husband Eric, and owns and runs Edge Watersports in Exmouth.

She was born in Exmouth and bought up in a boatbuilding family. 'Sailing and making sails was what I did all my youth,' she says. 'I love windsurfing, big boat sailing and more recently kitesurfing. I have tried to move away from Exmouth but there is something about this place that always drives me back.'

Favourite restaurant: The Seafood Restaurant, Tower Street, Exmouth

Favourite pub: The Turf Locks, Exminster, Exeter

Favourite Devon food/drink: Sea bass caught locally and Devonshire cider

Favourite Devon activity: Kitesurfing of course...

Best view: Standing at Orcombe Point at the eastern end of Exmouth beach and looking back towards Start Point across Lyme Bay

Quirkiest attraction: Exe Wake, Exmouth (wakeboarding and boat hire centre on the Exe Estuary)

Best thing about living here: The temperature is warm, there's plenty of sun and it's the best place for watersports with wind and surf so close to wherever you live

Favourite thing to do on a rainy day: I love to be out on the water – kitesurfing, paddle-boarding, sailing, wakeboarding, whatever. It can be even better in the rain!

Anything else you'd like to recommend to Devon visitors? Talk to the local people, they are a wealth of knowledge and information about what to do and where to go. And enjoy the fantastic watersports that are on offer...

105

Sir Walter Raleigh

One of the greatest Elizabethan seadogs, Raleigh was born at Hayes Barton in 1552. This wonderful old farm still stands just outside the village of East Budleigh but isn't open to the public.

Sir Walter's always been a controversial character – even his name is said to be spelt wrongly and should be pronounced 'rawley', but don't worry, few locals follow that advice.

In 2006, a bronze statue of Raleigh was unveiled opposite the church in East Budleigh after 12 years of controversy. Protesters objected to the fact that the 6ft £30,000 statue had been part-funded by British American Tobacco. Local MP Hugo Swire who campaigned for the statue said: 'If anyone is seriously suggesting a statue to Walter Raleigh, an extraordinary renaissance man, glorifies smoking, frankly they should get a life.'

Sir Walter's real life was even more colourful. As a young man he fought with French protestants in their Wars of Religion before sailing to America with his half-brother Sir Humphrey Gilbert. Raleigh twice tried to establish settlements in North Carolina and Virginia, but he's more famous in the UK for bringing tobacco and potatoes back from the New World. After going to Ireland to help suppress an uprising during which he supervised the slaughter of 700 surrendered mercenaries, the Devonian became a favourite of Elizabeth I. He was knighted and appointed Captain of the Queen's guard.

Portraits show a dashing looking courtier with a pointed beard and flared moustache. He was an acclaimed poet and writer, and many myths are attached to him – such as the story of his servant pouring water over his head when he found him smoking for the first time. In the Armada year of 1588 he was employed as Vice Admiral of Devon, looking after coastal defences.

When the Queen discovered he had secretly married one of her ladies in waiting, she locked them both in the Tower. When Her Majesty calmed down and released them, Raleigh tried to win back her favour. He set sail for the South American jungle to find the mythical golden land of El Dorado. Later he somehow got involved in an English attack on mainland Spain and was wounded.

Elizabeth's successor James I wasn't as susceptible as her to Raleigh's charms. Raleigh was rather harshly accused of plotting against the king and imprisoned for 12 years in the Tower. In 1616 he was released to lead another expedition to find El Dorado. He failed again and infuriated James by attacking the Spanish against his instructions. On his return James promptly had him executed to appease the Spanish. On the scaffold Raleigh famously asked to touch the executioner's axe and made one of his best-remembered jokes: 'This is a sharp medicine, but it is a physician for all diseases and miseries'.

Exmouth's most memorable sight is just north of the town – the bizarre National Trust house, **A La Ronde**. It's a whimsical 16-sided, 45-foot high tower house built in 1795 by two eccentric spinsters. It has 20 rooms around an octagonal hall decorated with shells, seaweed, feathers and souvenirs from their grand tour of Europe.

A LA RONDE, Summer Lane, Exmouth EX8 5BD; ☎ 1395 265514; www.national-trust.org.uk. Entry: adults £5.20, children £2.60; open 17 Mar to 4 Nov: Sat to Wed 11am—5pm.

Boat trips and birdwatching

Walter Raleigh often set sail from Exmouth's harbour – nowadays you can take **boat trips** up the estuary or along the coast. Ferries cross to Starcross and Dawlish Warren in the summer. In the winter, birdwatching cruises sail up the estuary. It's a prime spot for seabirds. Around 25,000 birds and 40 different migrant species congregate here. Part of the nature reserve upstream from Exmouth is a mussel bed where you can see gulls that have learnt to drop shellfish from 10m to crack the shells, then quickly swoop to eat the insides. In the summer the same company, Avocet Cruises (☎ 01803 898 280; www.avocetcruises.co.uk), offers cruises along the Jurassic Coast to Studland in Dorset.

In addition, Stuart Line Cruises runs various trips from Exmouth harbour throughout the year. The itinerary includes a relaxing river cruise, guided wildlife cruise and day trips to Torquay and Brixham. They even run speedboat taxis to Torquay's Princess Theatre (summer ☎ 01395 222144; winter ☎ 01395 279693; www.stuartlinecruises.co.uk).

EDGE WATERSPORTS, Royal Avenue, Exmouth EX8 1EN; ☎ 01395 222551; www.edgewatersports.com. Prices: taster half-day of kitesurfing for £75, two four-hour windsurfing lessons at £125 and three-day kitesurfing course £285.

Watersports

Thanks to the estuary, river and beach, Exmouth has more **watersports** opportunities than any other East Devon resort. Edge Watersports is one of the best operators, offering kitesurfing, windsurfing, powerkiting, powerboating, sailing, water skiing, wakeboarding, landboarding and buggying. Owner Steph Bridge was British Ladies Kitesurfing Champion 2006. An alternative is Waterfront Sports (☎ 01395 276599; www.waterfront-sports.co.uk).

Raleigh Country

The coast between Exmouth and Sidmouth is optimistically dubbed **Raleigh Country** by some tourist organisations. But sadly the seadog's birthplace and boyhood home, Hayes Barton near East Budleigh, is no longer open to the public. So there isn't much to see about Raleigh. There is the Raleigh family

Budleigh Salterton's beach

pew at the Church of All Saints at East Budleigh and you can see the spot in Budleigh Salterton where the famous painting 'The Boyhood of Raleigh' was sited. (It's the sandstone wall between the road and the seafront.) There is a statue of Raleigh in East Budleigh and you can see Exmouth Harbour, where he sailed from. But perhaps most importantly, in the timeless rolling hills and lush farmland you can get a feel of what the countryside was like when Raleigh lived here.

Budleigh Salterton
Heading west from Exmouth it's a short drive or a memorable cliff walk to **Budleigh Salterton**, the only town within the East Devon Area of Outstanding Natural Beauty.

The best-selling smuggler

Beer was once known as the smuggling capital of East Devon. Jack Rattenbury, Devon's most notorious smuggler was born there in 1778. Jack's wild career was documented in his doubtlessly exaggerated best-selling biography *Memoirs of a Smuggler* in 1837, which was written by a Unitarian Minister from Seaton.

Jack started as a fisherman, then progressed through a succession of close scrapes and daring escapes, which landed him in a French prison, had him hiding up chimneys to avoid press gangs, single-handedly kidnapping a boatload of French smugglers and once fighting off nine soldiers with a scythe.

Jack and his gang often used Beer Caves to hide booty. They are also believed

This sleepy retreat couldn't be more different from Exmouth. For starters, there is no sand. Instead the beach is a steep crescent of 440 million-year-old oval quartzite pebbles, which are much older than the crumbly red cliffs. The beach was leased to the council by Lord Clinton for a shilling a year for 999 years with the proviso that there shall be no trading on the beach nor any 'untoward developments'. With just a couple of cafés (one of which serves Ovaltine), a few wooden beach huts and some fishing boats drawn up on the beach, Lord Clinton's wishes have been fully met. Budleigh is a uniquely unspoilt seaside spot where at least half the population are retired.

At the eastern end of the promenade lies the Otter estuary, an Area of Special Scientific Interest. Here on the salt marshes that give the town its name, you can spot kingfishers, egrets and herons.

FAIRLYNCH MUSEUM,
Fore Street, Budleigh Salterton EX9 6NP. Entry: adults £2.50, concessions £2, children and students free; open Easter to Oct: daily 2–4.30pm.

The only thing that's remotely like a visitor attraction in this strange undisturbed time-capsule is the **Fairlynch Museum** on the main street. This pretty thatched museum houses a costume collection of over 3,000 items plus displays of local history and geology.

BUDLEIGH SALTERTON RIDING SCHOOL, Dalditch Lane EX9 7AS; ☎ 01395 442035; www.devonriding.co.uk
Price: adult group hack £28 for two hours/children £27, one-hour lesson from £20/£19.

Just out of town, on the edge of the perfect hacking tracks of Woodbury Common, there is one of the largest, best-equipped riding stables in the area. **Budleigh Salterton Riding School** has two large all-weather ménages with jumping facilities. All standards and ages are welcome. There are also two holiday cottages sleeping up to six and eight and a shared heated swimming pool (£250–£935 per week).

Just up the Otter Valley is a converted watermill complex that has become a centre for arts and crafts with a gallery, farm shop, bakery and restaurant.

to have also stored contraband at Bovey House, an Elizabethan house in the village connected to the caves by a tunnel.

Smugglers also dug pits in the fields between Beer and Branscombe to hide goods. Things could turn ugly and in 1755 a customs officer was pushed off the cliffs and killed. The lookout, which stands behind Branscombe beach, once housed a dozen excisemen as the government tried to clampdown on this notorious smuggling hotspot. In the end even Jack Rattenbury gave up smuggling, died in his bed, and is buried in Seaton churchyard.

Otterton Mill (☎ 01395 568521; www.ottertonmill.com) has four resident artists who can be seen at work and it's a regular music venue (see *Entertainment* and *Eating out*).

Sidmouth and Branscombe

Heading east, the red cliffs rise to mountainous peaks before you drop down into the next resort – the grand old Regency town of **Sidmouth**. Spot the elegant wrought iron balconies and white painted facades on the traditional seafront – just like Budleigh, this is a delightfully sedate seaside apparently stuck in time warp.

Sidmouth has 500 listed buildings, from thatched cob cottages to imposing Victorian mansions dating from its period as a posh 19th-century resort. Many of the fine public gardens and hotels look like something owned by the National Trust. Some of the hotels have excellent traditional restaurants (see *Eating out*) and the town has some delightful old-fashioned shops too. There are two beaches, the main town beach, a steep pebble ridge, and Jacob's Ladder to the west, with a wide stretch of red sand at low tide.

Further east, as the red sandstone cliffs suddenly change to chalk, is the tiny village of **Branscombe**. This spreadeagled collection of cottages spreads along a gorgeous valley surrounded by lush green National Trust land. There are two acclaimed pubs, an ancient church, and a National Trust teashop, mill and forge. The pebble beach is about a mile further down the valley from the village. There is a car park, café and shop.

The village hit the headlines in 2006 when a large cargo ship, *MSC Napoli*, went aground. Locals were accused of scavenging washed-up cargo, including new BMW motorbikes. Later the ship was dramatically split in two by salvage experts using explosives. As this book went to press, sections of the ship remain just offshore and there is still pollution on the beach after heavy weather. The last parts of the *Napoli* are expected to be towed away during 2008.

Beer and Seaton

Whether or not the *Napoli* is there, the cliff scenery and walks in both directions are some of Devon's finest. The walk to the next village – **Beer** – passes **Hooken Cliff**, where 10 acres of cliff suddenly shifted towards the sea one night in 1790. The rocks now stand as spectacular pinnacles with paths through the vegetation between them.

Whether you walk or drive to Beer, you'll find one of the south coast's best fishing villages – with a notorious smuggling tradition. The houses stand in a steep valley leading to the sea. A small stream runs down the main street to the sea. The pebble beach is sheltered by steep chalky limestone cliffs and overlooked by a Victorian park that's a perfect suntrap. There is still a bit of fishing here so expect to pick your way through boats, nets, winches, floats and ropes. You may be able to buy fresh fish fresh off the boats here too. But don't get too excited about the name of this village – 'bere' is the old English word for woodland.

The lively small seaside town of **Seaton** has a mile-long pebble beach, and things that don't often occur along this stretch of coast: fast-food and amusement arcades. At the eastern end of the beach is the attractive mouth of the river Axe curving through the pebble banks. Quieter **Axmouth** on the far bank has picturesque cottages, a tiny harbour and a nice pub, The Harbour Inn.

> **SEATON TRAMWAY**, Harbour Road, Seaton EX12 2NQ; ☎ 01297 20375; www.tram.co.uk Entry: Seaton/Colyon return for adults £7.95, seniors/students £7.15, children 4–14 £5.55; open daily in summer, for other times check timetable.

Seaton's most popular attraction is a rather incongruous 25-minute **electric tram** ride following the former branch line along the Axe Valley to Colyton. The trams were introduced 50 years ago by an enthusiast from London who owned a company that made electric milk floats. It had previously been operating in Eastbourne. Now you can catch the tram next to Seaton Tourist Office or at Colyton's restored railway station. From Colyton Station there is often a wagon ride available, drawn by shire horses.

Wet weather

If it's raining on Exmouth's two-mile seafront, the **model railway** is guaranteed to be busy. There is not much else under cover. Even if you don't like the sound of it, you may be surprised. The amazing model railway has taken 14 years to build and is the world's largest 00 gauge train sets, with nearly 1.5 miles of track winding round its shed.

> **EXMOUTH MODEL RAILWAY**, Queens Drive EX8 2AY; ☎ 01395 278383; exmouthmodel-railway.co.uk. Entry: adults £2.25, children 3–16 years £1.25, OAPs £1.75; open Easter to Nov.

And when it's raining in Beer what could be better than to shelter in quarter of a mile of **underground quarries**. These vast caves have been dug out by people over 2000 years. The chalky limestone here has been prized by stonemasons since the Romans because it is soft, easy to carve and creamy white in colour. Beer stone was used for 24 cathedrals including Exeter and St Paul's, parts of Westminster Abbey, the Tower of London, Hampton Court and Windsor Castle. And the huge vaulted caves have a colourful history as a smugglers' hiding place.

> **BEER QUARRY CAVES**, Beer EX312 3JG; ☎ 01297 680282; www.beerquarrycaves.fsnet.co.uk Entry: adults £5.50, children 5–16/OAPs £3.95, family (2+2) £16.50; open Easter to Sept: daily 10am–5pm; Oct 11am–4pm.

What to do with children...

THE WORLD OF COUNTRY LIFE, Sandy Bay EX8 5BU; ☎ 01395 274533; www.worldof-countrylife.co.uk. Entry: adults £9, OAPs 7.50, children 2–17 £7.50.

The World of Country Life is a sort of mini-theme park, where the theme is simply being in the country. So you'll get a chance to feed baby animals, explore deer and llama paddocks, see the owl centre, plus enjoy some more standard stuff such as an adventure playground, indoor soft play, a full-sized pirate ship and museum of old vehicles.

BICTON GARDENS, East Budleigh EX9 7BJ; ☎ 01395 568465; www.bictongardens.co.uk Entry: adults £6.95, children over 3 £5.95; open summer: daily 10am–6pm; winter: daily 10am–5pm.

The Donkey Sanctuary (Sidmouth EX10 0NU; ☎ 01395 578222; www.thedonkeysanctuary.org.uk) is always a hit with younger children. You'll find lots of rescued donkeys in paddocks here – the donkeys clearly love the attention and most kids love giving it. There is a visitor centre, café and maze but note that you're not allowed to feed the animals. Bags of carrots are removed at the entrance. It's free to get in but the really donkey-daft can pay to work as a volunteer for a day (for £150).

In the rolling countryside 3 miles north of Budleigh Salterton, **Bicton Gardens** could be just another boring garden for the kids, but thankfully they go to great lengths to entertain them. So, as well as 63 acres of gardens and an exquisite 1820 glass palm house, the gardens have a woodland railway, indoor and outdoor adventure play areas, mini-golf, nature trail, all-weather football and a countryside museum. For parents there is a plant and gift shop and a restaurant in the orangery.

BICTON COLLEGE GARDENS, East Budleigh EX9 7BY; ☎ 01395 562400; www.bicton.ac.uk; Entry: adults £2.00; open Nov to Mar: weekdays 10am–4pm; Apr to Oct: daily 10am–4pm; closed Christmas week.

 ## And how to avoid children

Confusingly, right next to Bicton Gardens (see above) is **Bicton College Gardens**, a very specialist garden that makes absolutely no concession to children. It's the superb garden and Grade I listed estate of a horticultural college, mostly planted in 1832. The arboretum includes Britain's largest monkey puzzle tree which was planted here in 1843 and a 37m poplar that's also Britain's tallest. The garden has many rare plants and the shop sells many unusual specimens.

The best... **PLACES TO STAY**

HOTEL

Royal Beacon Hotel

The Beacon, Exmouth EX8 2AF
☎ **01395 264886**
www.royalbeaconhotel.net

This grand whitewashed period hotel on Exmouth's finest Regency terrace features two restaurants and gardens overlooking the sea.

Single room from £60 per night, double £90–£120.

The Salty Monk

Church Street, Sidford EX10 9QP
☎ **01395 514722**
www.saltymonk.co.uk

Just a mile from Sidmouth, this 16th-century house is now a restaurant with rooms. The modern rooms are smart and well equipped, some with spa baths and water beds.

Price: B&B from £50 to £90 per person. The three-course dinner costs £32.50.

B & B

Downderry House

Exmouth Road, Budleigh Salterton EX9 6AQ. ☎ **01395 442 663**
www.downderryhouse.co.uk

This 1920s seaside house is more like a boutique B&B with luxury décor and furnishings and an acre of gardens.

Price: B&B £65 for a single; from £75 to £95 for a double.

Masons Arms

Branscombe EX12 3DJ
☎ **01295 680300**
www.masonsarms.co.uk

Once a simple old village inn, the Masons has grown to 21 rooms spread out over two buildings and eight garden cottages. It's virtually a hotel, with a rosette-winning restaurant, and all about a mile down a lane from the sea.

Price: B&B from £80 to £165 for a double.

SELF-CATERING

The Thatched Cottage Company

☎ **01395 567676**
www.thethatchedcottagecompany.com

A holiday cottage company based in Colaton Raleigh offers high-quality thatched cottages at various spots along the East Devon coast, such as East Budleigh, Budleigh Salterton, Otterton and Woodbury.

Guinea Royal Cottage

Pound Street, Exmouth, EX8 1AT
www.palm-house.co.uk

This two-bedroomed pink cottage built in 1850, stands between the town centre and seafront. Inside all is stylish and simple, with wooden floors and pale colours.

Price: from £375 to £600 per week.

Entertainment

With live performances by top folk acts such as John Renbourn, Gordon Giltrap and Martin Carthy, plus Devon locals such as the Strawbs and Show of Hands, **Otterton Mill** (☎ 01395 568521; www.ottertonmill.com) has become a major roots music venue. Gigs are usually on a Thursday and often sell out, so book in advance.

- **Sidmouth Manor Pavilion** has a busy programme but mainly amateur dramatics (☎ 01395 514413; www.sidmouth.ws/sidmouth_theatre.htm).
- **Exmouth Pavilion** hosts a lot of live music, much of it by tribute bands (☎ 01395 222477; www.ledleisure.co.uk/index/Exmouth_Pavilion/index.asp).
- **Strand Inn** in the Parade, Exmouth, has weekly live bands (☎ 01395 263649).

There is a cinema in Exmouth at the Savoy in Strand Gardens (☎ 01395 268220/www.scottcinemas.co.uk) and in Sidmouth at the Radway in Radway Place (☎ 01395 513085; www.scottcinemas.co.uk). Lyme Regis just over the Dorset border also has a cinema and a theatre.

Festivals

The highlight of many locals' year is **Sidmouth Folk Festival** in the first week of August, which has an international reputation. The names are usually big but the atmosphere in the town is even better. The promenade becomes an impromptu stage for Morris dancers, musicians, fire-eaters and buskers. Pubs host informal jam sessions and the whole town turns into a musical street party on the last night of the festival (www.sidmouthfolkweek.co.uk).

In comparison, **Budleigh Salterton Festival** in the last week of July is a sedate selection of operatic, classical and world music in churches or on The Green at the top of Fore Street (www.budleigh-festival.org.uk). **Exmouth Festival** in the last week of May (www.dtnetnt.net/exmouthfestival.org.uk) is mostly a mix of local acts, street parades and community events. The town's illuminated carnival in mid October is usually a spectacular night.

The best... FOOD AND DRINK

The coastal strip is obviously less committed to farming than the rural hills further north but there are still fields leading to the water's edge in some parts of the coast. The National Trust stewardship of land at Branscombe means, for example, there is open countryside behind the beach here.

In Branscombe you'll spot the local breed of Ruby Red Devon cattle reared entirely on grass grown in flower-rich pastures managed for nature conservation. All over Devon you'll see cows raised in this traditional way, living out-doors in the fields and woods all year round. Local farmers claim that this kind of animal husbandry produces better tasting meat. And you can be the judge because there are plenty of opportunities to buy and eat Ruby Red beef in East Devon.

The other regional specialities to look for come from the sea. Line-caught fish are landed right along the coast as are pot lobsters and crabs. Often fish-ermen call restaurants while still at sea to try to sell what they've caught, but if you see a fisherman unloading his catch it's considered normal to ask to buy something there and then. If you're trying to be eco-sensitive look for line-caught fish rather than netted.

▶ Staying in

If you're shopping for self-catering meals, picnics or barbecues, you'll find **farmers' markets** at Seaton Town Hall on the second Friday in the month and in the Strand Gardens, Exmouth, on the second Wednesday of the month (both 9am–1pm). And there are good delis and farm shops in each of the resort towns. At the **Food Shop** in the High Street, Budleigh Salterton (☎ 01395 443182; www.devonheaven.co.uk) you could pick up clotted cream, salmon pate and local chocolate, whereas at **Exmouth Fisheries** on the Pierhead at Exmouth (☎ 01395 272 903) you can buy local wet fish and shellfish, plus eggs from a nearby farm. **Chris Downs** in Chapel Street, Exmouth makes and sells award-winning traditional meat pies.

Broom and Son at Logshayne Farm near Colyton (☎ 01297 552101) spe-cialises in fresh free-range, hand-plucked turkeys while the excellently named **Crackling and Feathers** next to the post office in Sidford (☎ 01395 512874; www.cracklingandfeathers.co.uk) sells local pork, poultry and game, plus their chicken and venison sausages, Otter Vale preserves and Sidmouth honey.

To buy Ruby Red Devon beef from the gate at **Gay's Farm** at Branscombe you have to call first so they can prepare your order (☎ 01297 680352). You also have to ring to buy at **Smallicombe Farm** at Northleigh near Colyton (☎ 01404 831310; www.smallicombe.com) – it's worth it for their award-win-ning Dorset Down lamb, Devon Ruby Red beef, rare breed pork, award-win-ning sausages, gammon and smoked bacon. They also provide B&B and self-catering accommodation and even run weekend courses that teach about pigs.

Otterton Mill is the place for bread, biscuits and cakes made from their own stoneground organic flour from the mill. They also supply Luscombe ciders and soft drinks, O'Hanlon's beers, Lyme Bay wines and ciders, Devon Hills water, local free range eggs (☎ 01395 568521; www.ottertonmill.com).

EATING OUT

FINE DINING

The Salty Monk
Church Street, Sidford EX10 9QP
☎ **01395 514722**
www.saltymonk.co.uk

This is a two- AA rosette restaurant in a 16th-century house just outside Sidmouth. Seafood is delivered daily from Brixham and lots of fresh local produce features on a modern British menu. A three-course dinner costs £32.50.

The Hotel Riviera
The Esplanade, Sidmouth EX10 8AY
☎ **01395 515201**
www.hotelriviera.co.uk

This old-fashioned hotel on the seafront offers totally traditional food and service but with excellent quality cuisine which has won spoonfuls of awards. Lunch is £25, and a six-course dinner costs £36.

Moores' Restaurant and Rooms
High Street, Newton Poppleford EX10 0EB
☎ **01395 568100**
www.mooresrestaurant.co.uk

It looks like a teashop from the outside but Jonathan and Kate Moore's restaurant is good enough to win two rosettes from the AA. Dishes are well presented modern British. Is it local? Well, Jonathan catches much of the fish himself... . Lunch costs £10, and dinner £19.50.

RESTAURANT

Otterton Mill
Otterton, Budleigh Salterton EX9 7HG
☎ **01395 568521**
www.ottertonmill.com

We've mentioned Otterton Mill a lot in this chapter so far, and it's a great place for eating out too. The licensed restaurant only uses seasonal vegetables and tries to use organic produce if available. Eighty per cent of ingredients are from Devon, most from within 10 miles. The eggs are free-range, the fish is wild and the meat comes from local, naturally fed and reared stock. It's open seven days a week but only until 5pm

except on music nights (usually Thursdays) when it's open for dinner too. Main courses cost £6–£14.

Steamers
New Cut, Fore Street, Beer EX12 3JH
☎ **01297 22922**
www.steamersrestaurant.co.uk

A former bakery in a seaside village has been converted into an interesting modern restaurant/bar. Food is modern too, with lots of local seafood, including line-caught sea bass and River Teign mussels. It's open for morning coffee, lunch and dinner. Main courses cost £10.00–£16.00.

The Victoria Hotel
The Esplanade, Sidmouth EX10 8RY
☎ **01395 512651**
www.brend-hotels.co.uk/TheVictoria

This is another grand seafront hotel with period décor, high ceilings and top-quality traditional cuisine using plenty of local seafood and Devon meats. A three-course dinner costs £32.

GASTROPUB

Mason's Arms
Branscombe EX12 3DJ
☎ **01295 680300**
www.masonsarms.co.uk

There is both an AA rosette restaurant with fine modern cuisine and a hearty bar menu in this historic village pub. Sometimes lobster and crab come straight from the beach a mile away. A three-course dinner costs £27.50.

The Barrel o' Beer
Fore Street, Beer EX12 3EQ
☎ **01297 20099**
www.barrelobeer.co.uk

A freehouse that serves both real ale in its bar (Exe Valley's Devon Glory) and fine food in its restaurant. The chef has worked with some of the best so be prepared for the contemporary quality. All fish is from local day boats and all meat is free-range or organic from local farms. A three-course dinner costs around £20.

Drinking

You'll find that the more cosmopolitan tastes of the seaside strip mean there are less real ale pubs compared with a few miles further north (see Honiton chapter). Nevertheless there are some high spots, notably **Branscombe Vale Brewery** that makes beer at Great Seaside Farm in the village using local spring water in two picturesque barns leased from the National Trust. The brewery owns one pub, the **Old Inn**, Kilmington, near Axminster and the beer is always available at **The Fountain Head** in Branscombe and **The Bridge Inn**, Topsham, two lovely real old Devon pubs, and appears as a guest in many others. The brewery does sometimes allow tours in the winter – call 01297 680511 for details.

Four Elms Fruit Farm at Harpford near Sidmouth produces an apple juice recently judged the best in the country. All fruit is grown on their own farm and is hand picked. The juice and plenty of fruit is available from the farm shop (2pm–5pm Mon to Sat; ☎ 01395 568286). You can pick your own soft fruit from June to August and apples from September to February.

Enjoy shellfish from the beach at the Mason's Arms

The Visitors' Book

Things to do in Lyme Regis

'Lyme Regis really is the most picturesque English seaside town we've ever visited. We were spoilt for choice: there's a dinosaur museum, town museum, crazy golf and fossil hunting; boating and fishing; and a theatre and cinema as well as a whole variety of cafés, takeaways, restaurants and pubs.

'We found the main high street has lots individual shops to poke around but I preferred to explore the smaller streets and alleyways to discover unexpected gems like a most fantastic dress shop.

'Our favourite thing to do whenever we visit is to walk out onto the Cobb. If I'm feeling brave, I'll walk along the top looking out to sea and then back at the pale candy colours of the cottages and hotels that line the promenade.

'To either side of the town the cliffs rise up golden and spectacular whenever the sun is shining. I love to walk around the harbour, stop and watch the boats going in and out or visit the Lifeboat Station.

'Or I like to stroll the length of the front — you will be surprised how far it is and explore the rock pools or search for fossils on the beaches. If you are feeling really energetic then take the opportunity to walk along the South West Coast Path towards Seaton. You won't be disappointed — the views over Lyme Bay are breathtaking.'

Annette Roffey, Somerset

Visitor information

Tourist information centres:
Exmouth Tourist Information Centre,
Alexandra Terrace, EX8 1NZ,
☎ 01395 222299, www.exmouth-
guide.co.uk; *Budleigh Salterton*
Tourist Information Centre, Fore
Street EX9 6NG, ☎ 01395 445275,
www.visitbudleigh.com;
Seaton Tourist Information Centre,
Harbour Road Car Park, Seaton
EX12 2QQ, ☎ 01297 21660,
www.seatontic.com; *Sidmouth*
Tourist Information Centre, Ham
Lane, Sidmouth EX10 8XR, ☎ 01395
516441, www.visitsidmouth.co.uk.
Hospitals: Exmouth Hospital, Clare-
mont Grove, Exmouth EX8 2JN,
☎ 01395 279684; *Seaton and Dis-*
trict Community Hospital, Valley
View Road, Seaton, EX12 2UU,
☎ 01297 23901; *Budleigh Salterton*
Hospital, East Budleigh Road,
Budleigh Salterton EX9 6HF, ☎

01395 442020; 24-hour A&E facilities
available at *Royal Devon and Exeter*
Hospital, Wonford, Barrack Road,
Exeter EX2 5DW, ☎ 01392 411 611.
Supermarkets: Somerfield, Magno-
lia Walk, Exmouth EX8 1HB
☎ 01395 278956; *Tesco*, Salterton
Road EX8 2NP, ☎ 0845 6779265;
Spar, Fore Street, Budleigh Salterton
EX9 6NG, ☎ 01395 442003;
Waitrose, Stowford Rise, Sidmouth
EX10 9GA, ☎ 01395 519416; *Tesco*,
High Street, Sidmouth EX10 8EJ,
☎ 01395 578039; *Somerfield*, High
Street, Sidmouth EX10 8EQ,
☎ 01395 515143.
Bike rental: Knobblies Bike Hire, 107
Exeter Road, Exmouth, ☎ 01395
270182.
Taxi: Clapps Taxis, Seaton,
☎ 01297 20038; *Sid Valley Cars*,
Sidmouth, ☎ 01395 577633; Phone
a cab, Exmouth, ☎ 07792 628512.

FURTHER AFIELD

Lympstone

North of Exmouth, the east side of the estuary runs for 10 miles up to the M5
bridge just south of Exeter. The historic village of Topsham is virtually a suburb
of Exeter now (see Exeter chapter). But there are some attractive spots on this
east shore (for the west shore see Torbay chapter).

The village of **Lympstone** is famous for the Royal Marine training camp on its
outskirts but the village itself is really a collection of pretty cottages around a
sleepy harbour.

The lively **Redwing Inn** (☎ 01395 222156) next to the railway station has jazz on Tuesdays, local bands on Fridays, homely food and farm cider every day. Opposite is **Shear's Café** (☎ 01392 223663), a favourite of football legend Steve Perryman and his wife Kim, who live in the village.

Lympstone **Furry Dance** on the first Saturday in August involves a dance right though the village starting near the river at about 7pm and ending with a firework display.

Just along the main road, in Exton the next village, is a popular gastropub recommended by locals and the *Michelin Guide*. **The Puffing Billy** (☎ 01392 877888; thepuffingbilly.com) has a stylish interior and serves fine modern British food with main courses from £7.95 to £17.95.

Heading north there is a luxury B&B just outside Clyst St Mary. **Eastcote Guest House** (☎ 01392 873006; www.eastcoteguesthouse.co.uk) is an average-looking bungalow from outside, but inside it's like a magazine feature on interior décor. B&B (double room) costs £60.

Lyme Regis

The county sign is just on the hill as you drive down into Lyme Regis, so technically it's out of Devon... but we wouldn't want you to miss it.

'Lyme' as locals call it is a period seaside resort with sandy beaches, an interesting harbour and old winding streets with quirky shops and caf[eacute]s. Its literary connections include being the hometown of novelist **John Fowles** (author of *The Magus* and *The French Lieutenant's Woman*). *The French Lieutenant's Woman* was filmed around the town including the memorable scene with Meryl Streep standing on the end of the harbour wall (known as the 'Cobb') that formed the poster for the film.

Jane Austen spent a whole summer in Lyme too and it features in her novel *Persuasion*. The dramatic demise of Louisa in *Persuasion* caused a flow of fans to Lyme. The Poet Laureate Alfred Lord Tennyson went straight to the Cobb on his arrival in the town demanding to know the spot where she fell into the sea.

The pretty and interesting old town has a theatre, cinema, museum, arts centre (☎ 01297 443579; www.townmill.org.uk), aquarium, fossil shop and regular guided fossil walks along the beach. The town has a good sandy family beach with attractive, recently laid-out gardens behind.

The Tourist Information Centre is at Guildhall Cottage, Church Street DT7 3BS (☎ 01297 442138; www.lymeregistourism.co.uk).

2

NorthDevon

a. Lynton and Lynmouth

b. Ilfracombe and Combe Martin

c. Woolacombe, Croyde, Barnstaple and around

d. Bideford and the Torridge Estuary

e. Clovelly

f. Torrington and north-west Devon

g. South Molton, Mid Devon and Exmoor

Unmissable highlights

01 Walk down the tumbling main street of Clovelly – the prettiest and most iconic West Country fishing village, p.165

02 Take the amazing cliff railway from Lynmouth to Lynton for one of the most awe-inspiring views of cliffs, rivers, moors and seascape in Britain, p.124

03 Escape to Lundy Island: sail on the MS Oldenberg from Bideford's historic quay to explore the old smugglers' island, p.160

04 Eat seafood on the quayside at Appledore gazing across the Torridge to Instow... or walk the Promenade and sands at Instow looking across to Appledore, p.156

05 See the Atlantic smashing against jagged rocks at Hartland Quay – or any far north-western spot such as Welcome Mouth, Peppercombe or Bucks Mill (especially during a storm) , p.178

06 Enjoy a leisurely pub lunch at The Mason's Arms, Knowstone – a thatched village boozer serving Michelin-starred food, p.188

07 Ride the waves – or just let them knock you over – at one of the three great surf beaches: Woolacombe, Croyde and Saunton, p.145

08 Walk along the grassy cliff path to North Devon's best 'secret' sandy cove – Rockham Beach near Mortehoe, p.146

09 Explore the hilltop town of Torrington – from the ancient town centre to the amazing views south from The Commons, p.170

10 Eat at Damien Hirst's No 11 restaurant on Ilfracombe Harbour – great food, great views, just don't think about the bill... , p.143

NORTH DEVON

In the major population centres in the south of Devon, locals call anything above Exeter 'north'. We've tried to be a bit more scientific about it but our north Devon area is still by far the biggest area of the county.

Our 'north Devon' includes the small strip of inspiring Exmoor that falls in the county, the vast area of classic rolling Devonshire farmland between Dartmoor and the north coast, and the wonderful north Devon beaches, ports and fishing villages. This is a huge area, bordered by the north coast, the western border as far as Launceston, the A30 to Whiddon Down, and a line from there, heading north-east to Dulverton.

North Devon is quieter, more rural and less developed than the southern half of the county. The only big town is Barnstaple but there are plenty of smaller market towns and hundreds of villages. Most visitors head for the wonderfully rugged coast – the surf beaches, the resorts of Ilfracombe and Westward Ho!, and the fascinating sights of Lynmouth and Clovelly. There are two major estuaries in the north – the Taw and the Torridge, with the pretty waterfronts of Bideford, Appledore and Instow.

Inland you'll find mile after mile of rolling Devon scenery dotted with charming quiet villages, great local pubs and some memorably quirky attractions. With less outside influence, it's hard to escape the conclusion that North Devon is more 'real' than the more popular south coast.

LYNTON AND LYNMOUTH

The most northerly pair of towns in Devon are really one place – Lynmouth's ancient cottages huddle down in the gorge around the mouth of the river Lyn, while Lynton's Victorian villas peer over the high cliffs above.

Exmoor meets the sea here with an abrupt drop from rugged moorland to rocky seaside. The awesome views of steep wooded gorges, mossy waterfalls and England's highest cliffs inspired the first celebrity visitors 200 years ago: romantic poets Shelley, Coleridge, Hazlitt, Southey and Wordsworth all made the arduous journey to what was an almost inaccessible spot. These hippies of their day wrote passionately about some of the finest landscapes to be found, not just in Devon, but in the whole of the UK.

By the Victorian era word had spread and tourism to Lynton and Lynmouth really took off. In their top hats and long dresses they arrived by boat, carriage and train... and left a wonderful legacy of Victoriana among the trees, terraces and ravines. The legions of 19th-century admirers called this area of mountainous cliffs 'Little Switzerland'.

Gainsborough called the towns 'the most delightful area for a landscape painter this country can boast'. And that genteel Victorian atmosphere is still one of the great attractions. Forget karaoke or amusement arcades, there's not even a supermarket or nightclub here. It's an area that's great for walking or just sitting and gazing at those panoramas.

WHAT TO SEE AND DO

 Fair weather

The single best thing to experience in Lynton and Lynmouth is the extraordinary **Cliff Railway**. This was built by Victorian entrepreneur George Newnes (see panel), to link his new holiday mansion to the port 500ft below. Previously, pack-horses used to struggled up the precipitous cliff path. More than 120 years later, Newnes' railway still works perfectly.

It's a memorable testament to Victorian engineering and ingenuity. Two carriages are pulled by steel cables almost vertically up the wooded cliff, like lifts. The best thrill comes from standing

CLIFF RAILWAY, ☎ 01598 753908; cliffrailwaylynton.co.uk. Entry: adults £1.85, children £1.00; returns and day tickets available; open: mid Feb to mid Nov: daily from 10am to dusk.

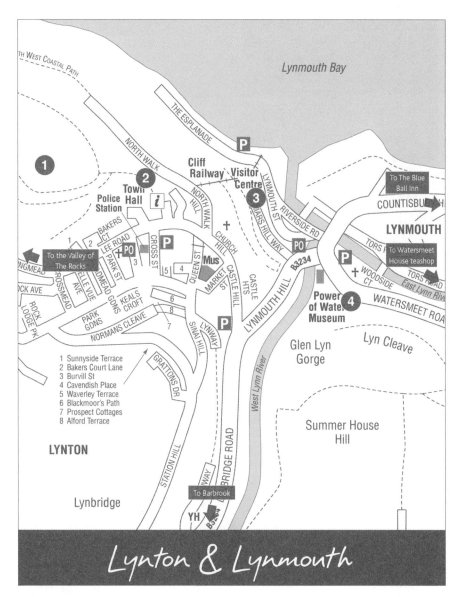

Lynmouth Bay

THE ESPLANADE

NORTH WALK

TH WEST COASTAL PATH

1

2

Town
Hall

Police
Station

Cliff
Railway

Visitor
Centre

3

North WALK HILL

CHURCH HILL

BAKERS CT

LEE ROAD

1

2

PO

3

ELLE VUE

LDMEAD GDNS

PARK ST

CROSS ST

QUEEN ST

Mus

MARKET ST

5

4

CASTLE HILL

CROSSMEAD

NGMEAD

CK AVE

ROCK LODGE PK

PARK GDNS

KEALS CROFT

NORMANS CLEAVE

6

8

7

MARS HILL WAY

LYNMOUTH ST

RIVERSIDE RD

PO

B3234

COUNTISBURY H

LYNMOUTH

TORS P

To The Blue
Ball Inn

To Watersmeet
House teashop

WOODSIDE CT

TORS ROAD

East Lynn Rive

WATERSMEET ROA

Power
of Water
Museum

4

CASTLE HTS

LYNMOUTH HILL

Lyn Cleave

To the Valley of
The Rocks

1 Sunnyside Terrace
2 Bakers Court Lane
3 Burvill St
4 Cavendish Place
5 Waverley Terrace
6 Blackmoor's Path
7 Prospect Cottages
8 Alford Terrace

LYNTON

Lynbridge

GRATTONS DR

STATION HILL

SINAI HILL

LYNWAY

WAY

BRIDGE ROAD

West Lynn River

Glen Lyn
Gorge

Summer House
Hill

To Barbrook

YH

B5234

Lynton & Lynmouth

1 Hollerday Hill

2 Town Hall/Cinema

3 Rising Sun

4 Shelley's Hotel

George Newnes built the cliff railway to reach his house

on the open platform at the front. Incredibly, the whole system is powered by a simple stream of water – there isn't a single emission to worry about. For the squeamish or exercise-mad, the alternative is a steep **zigzag** walk up through the trees.

After you've recovered from the excitement of the cliff railway, take a stroll at the top – Lynton – or the bottom – Lynmouth. The shops, restaurants and teashops up in Lynton are generally smarter than Lynmouth's more touristy and cheeky offerings.

Spot the grand **town hall** on Lynton's Lee Road – it's so pompous it's like something from Trumpton. The hall is a working civic building but take a free peep inside, the wooden ceilings are especially spectacular.

Lynmouth has a small **harbour** at the mouth of the trickling Lyn River. The quay is a remnant of an 18th-century herring industry that has long been lost. The ornate tower at the end of the harbour wall was a 19th-century folly – it's an imitation of towers on the Rhine.

The **East Lyn and West Lyn** rivers may look innocuous on a summer's afternoon but the rains of Exmoor can quickly turn them into raging torrents. All around town you'll see mementoes of the great flood in 1952 when the river swelled and a terrifying flash flood washed away 98 houses and killed 34 residents.

Don't bring buckets and spades expecting a day at the seaside. Lynmouth's dark rocky beach has a few patches of shingle and occasionally some gritty

The man behind Victorian Lynton

Any Lynton local will tell you the story of **George Newnes**, the Victorian MP who made a fortune as publisher of the *Strand Magazine* printing Arthur Conan Doyles' Sherlock Holmes stories. Newnes took such a liking to 'Little Switzerland' that he financed Lynton's grand town hall, the convent further up Lee Road and the intriguing cliff railway.

He also built himself a grand mansion at Hollerday Hill in Lynton. It burnt down 100 years ago and sadly there is nothing left except some odd stones and an old tennis court. Locals often walk on the wooded hill behind the Town Hall to enjoy the same spectacular views that made Newnes choose this spot. Take the path up the right hand side of Lynton Town Hall in Lee Road.

Head west on the coast path for dramatic scenery

sand is exposed. The best rock pools are on **Blacklands Beach** towards the east under the looming cliffs of **Countisbury**. There is a sort of half-hearted civic park on the east side of the river mouth that sometimes has events such as shambolic historic re-enactments or local musicians playing but most of the time it's simply a softer, flatter place to have a picnic than the rocks beyond.

It's better to bring walking shoes and head out of town on some of Devon's best trails. The Coast Path west leads to the **Valley of the Rocks**, a mile away. (The incurably lazy can drive along Lee Road instead to get there.) This is a sheltered grassy bowl surrounded by strange steep rocky outcrops. Barmy wild goats and adventurous humans roam across grey boulders and bracken, more sedate visitors wander the maze of paths or sit and gaze across the sea to Wales. You can almost see the starry-eyed romantic poets reaching for their adjectives...

 ## Wet weather

LYN AND EXMOOR MUSEUM,
www.devonmuseums.net/lynton
Entry: adults £1, children 20p; open
Easter to end Oct: Mon to Fri 10am–
4.30pm/Sun 2–4pm.

The **Lyn and Exmoor Museum** in a pretty cottage in Market Street, the oldest house in Lynmouth that has an interesting collection of curios, including pictures of the 1952 flood disaster and the amazing tale of the 'Overland Launch'. This happened one wild night in 1899. The storm was so strong the Lynmouth lifeboat couldn't launch from the harbour to save a struggling ship. So 100 villagers and 20 horses dragged the 10 tonne lifeboat to Porlock's sheltered harbour 13 miles east, including climbing over Countisbury Hill. They did it, launched, then rowed for an hour to find the stricken ship and saved everyone on board. You can also see displays about the heroic story at the Glen Lyn Gorge.

The best... **PLACES TO STAY**

HOTEL

Shelley's Hotel

Watersmeet Road, Lynmouth (overlooking crossroads at foot of cliff), EX35 6EP
☎ **01598 753219**
www.shelleyshotel.freeuk.com

It's now a friendly hotel neatly decorated in pastel shades with period furniture, but 200 years ago the rebellious Romantic poet honeymooned in this picturesque spot at the heart of the town 'commanding a fine view of the sea with mountains at the side and behind us'. Shelley, however, left without paying his bill... nowadays, you'll even have to pay to use the car park across the road.

Price: from £90 to £130 for a double

B & B

Victoria Lodge

Lee Road, Lynton EX35 6BS
☎ **01598 753 203**
www.victorialodge.co.uk

This sumptuous five-diamond rated temple to Victoriana in the town centre has lavish fabric-draped bedrooms, a huge breakfast menu, and serves packed lunches but no evening meals.

Price: from £70 to £140 for a double.

CAMPSITE

Westermill Farm

Near Exford, Exmoor ☎ **01643 831238**
www.westermill.com

The farm is at the end of a long track in a remote but beautiful steep-sided Exmoor valley. Choose from three fields bordered by the River Exe. Children can play safely in the river and there is a great farm shop too.

Price: adults £4–£4.50, children £2–£2.50.

SELF-CATERING

Glen Lynn Gorge

Lynmouth (at the crossroads, next to Shelleys Hotel), EX35 6ER
☎ **01598 753207**
www.theglenlyngorge.co.uk

Quirky self-catering cottages and apartments with log fires, kitchen ranges and four-posters. Single nights available off-peak.

Price: from £99 for a single night, or £395 for a week, up to £795 for a week.

Barbrook Cottage

Helpful Holidays, ☎ **01647 433593**
www.helpfulholidays.com

Devon-based Helpful Holidays have several holiday cottages in the area. The pick is in nearby Barbrook – a riverside stone house that sleeps 11, with exposed beams and a cooking range.

Price: from £298 to £1248 per week.

What to do with children

Glen Lyn Gorge is a locally owned attraction based in the steep valley of the gushing West Lynn River. The entrance is right at the crossroads in the centre of Lynmouth. There is plenty for all ages here – from firing water cannons to making your own rainbows and using water to make electricity (the whole town is powered by hydroelectricity). Adults will enjoy the walks in the lush forest and local history exhibitions.

> **GLEN LYN GORGE**,
> ☎ 01598 753207; www.theglen-lyngorge.co.uk. Entry: adults £4, children/senior citizens £3; open Easter to Oct.

There are plenty of great walks of varied difficulty around the steep landscape here. One of the best is to the National Trust's teashop at **Watersmeet House** ☎ 01598 753348; tea shop open mid Mar to Oct) along the east bank of the babbling East Lyn River gorge through deciduous woods, giant ferns and grey boulders. Built in 1832, it's one of the UK's oldest tea gardens.

Entertainment

The flower-bedecked **cinema** (☎ 01598 753243; www.lyntoncinema .co.uk) based in a former Methodist chapel next to Lynton's Town Hall in Lee Road shows recent films in Dolby stereo surround sound and seats 68 in air-conditioned comfort. It makes Lynton the UK's smallest town with a full-time cinema.

The best... FOOD AND DRINK

The food revolution hasn't quite reached Lynmouth and Lynton yet – expect mostly conservative fare at most restaurants. But that old-fashionedness is balanced by excellent quality produce from local farms. This is one area where the farms are closer to you than the supermarket. Exmoor is just down the road so look out for regional specialities including whortleberry jam, smoked trout and locally made Cheddar cheese.

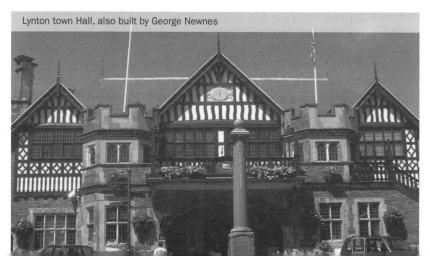
Lynton town Hall, also built by George Newnes

The Visitors' Book

A regular visitor to Lynton & Lynmouth

'My love affair with Lynton and Lynmouth began over 25 years ago. I recall driving down the impossibly steep gradient of Countisbury Hill gasping at the sweeping views across to Wales and then seeing the first glimpse of the town in all its glory.'

'The twin towns are only separated by a 500ft cliff but are as different as chalk and cheese. At the bottom is Lynmouth, the seaside resort: with cafés, gift shops, ice cream parlours and narrow streets where motorists and coaches jostle for parking spaces. Here's the lower end of the Cliff Railway which has whisked visitors up to Lynton since 1890 without a single accident.'

'"Upstairs" is Lynton. I find this area more relaxed and peaceful; it has an air of a bygone time about it. Elegant Victorian houses that are now hotels have gardens adorned with palms, yuccas and ferns; there are glass-ceiling tea-rooms as opposed to cafés; galleries rather than gift shops. Lynton has an ornate Town Hall and steep backstreet full of bookshops, antique shops and well-tended private homes.'

'The High Street leads down into the eerie Valley of the Rocks which, unlike most other valleys, runs parallel to the coastline. There are rugged peaks with massive, well-weathered boulders balanced at ridiculous angles, while wild goats trot along tamely. The views here are wonderful. Foaming waves crash onto the rocks that have slipped from the cliffs over thousands of years — it's a truly wild and spectacular sight.'

Graham Brown, Wiltshire

EATING OUT

FINE DINING
Rising Sun
Harbourside, Lynmouth, EX35 6EG
☎ **01598 753223**
www.risingsunlynmouth.co.uk

They say R D Blackmore wrote some of *Lorna Doone* in this ancient thatched inn overlooking the harbour entrance. It looks pretty from the outside and you'll eat the classiest food in town. A three-course dinner costs around £30.

RESTAURANT
Greenhouse Restaurant
6 Lee Road, Lynton, EX35 6HW
☎ **01598 753358**

This appears to be yet another large Victorian teashop but its quirky international menu includes an excellent range of meals from pizzas to a three-course dinner, and at good prices too. The Sunday roasts with their huge selection of fresh vegetables are particularly good. The owner is Indian and his curries are highly commended locally. Snacks cost from a few pounds, and main courses up to £15.

GASTROPUB
The Crown Inn
Market Street, Lynton, EX35 6AG
☎ **01598 752253**
www.thecrown-lynton.co.uk

Everything from hearty pies to fresh lobster salad, washed down with real ales, attracts locals to this stylishly modernised traditional coaching inn. The menu ranges from snacks to main courses costing from £4.95 to £14.95.

 Staying in

The best place to buy any local produce is at the **farmers' market** on the first Saturday of each month in Lynton Town Hall, Lee Road, from 10am. Most local shops sell some regional goodies. Try the **Post Office** in the nearby village of Barbrook (1 mile south on B32234), which has spring water from Nutcombe Spring in Combe Martin, chutneys from South Devon, honey from South Molton and clotted cream from Torrington. There are Chinese, Indian and fish and chip takeaways in Lynton.

Further afield, **Hindon Organic Hill Farm shop** between Porlock and Minehead in Somerset sells a wide range of local meat including the farm's own lamb and handy barbecue packs, plus bread, eggs, jam, fruit and vegetables (☎ 01643 705244; www.hindonfarm.co.uk).

 Drinking

The **Rising Sun** serves Exmoor Ales from Wiveliscombe in Somerset and **The Crown** serves St Austell beer from Cornwall. Both these inns (see *Eating out*) have lively public bars.

Visitor information

Tourist information centres:
Lynton-Lynmouth Tourist Information Centre, Town Hall, Lee Road, Lynton EX35 6BT, ☎ 0845 6603232 (UK local rate), ☎ 01598 752225 (national rate); www.lynton-lyn-mouth-tourism.co.uk.

Websites: www.visit-exmoor.co.uk
Supermarkets: Lynton has a *Costcutter* and *Londis*
Taxis: Lynton Private Hire, Lynton, ☎ 01598 753853; Carol's ☎ 01598 653501, *Luke's Taxi* ☎ 01598 753301

The newly renamed and neatly refurbished **Blue Ball Inn** (previously The Sandpiper) at the top of Countisbury Hill and the **Hunters Inn** off the A39 to the west are popular for food and drink both at lunch time and evening. The Blue Ball serves local Proper Job beer and its own Blue Ball Ale (made by St Austell brewery), while Hunters has Exmoor Ales from Wiveliscombe just over the border in Somerset.

FURTHER AFIELD

Follow the coast path a mile further west and you'll walk past **Lee Abbey**, a wonderfully located Christian retreat, before reaching the unspoilt 'secret' sandy beach at **Lee Bay**. You can drive here, but there is a toll road (costing £1) through the Abbey's land and parking for only a handful of cars. A short drive over the next headland is **Woody Bay**, another small unspoilt sandy stretch (at low tide) surrounded by steep wooded hills. It's owned by the National Trust so there are few buildings and wonderful views.

To the east the coast is wild, rugged and beautiful but difficult to access between Lynmouth and Porlock Weir, well into Somerset. The **A39** is a marvellous road, with fabulous views as it weaves across this northern part of Exmoor. You'll need a map to explore either side of the main road but it's worth it. To the north, the seaward side, the lanes lead to **Culbone**. This is the valley that inspired poet **Samuel Taylor Coleridge** to write his mystical masterpiece 'Kubla Khan'. He woke from an opium-induced sleep in a farmhouse overlooking the valley and immediately scribbled out what he had dreamt – a strange haunting vision of a land called Xanadu and its arcane pleasure dome. The farmhouse has long gone but the valley is still there. It may not inspire you to fabulous poetry but the walk down into the woods is marvellous and there, down a muddy track, you'll find Culbone Church, the smallest in England.

ILFRACOMBE AND COMBE MARTIN

The biggest resort in North Devon is a strange but beguiling mix of wild rocky coast, peeling Victorian grandeur, kiss-me-quick seaside tartiness and contemporary chic.

The town radiates out over steep hills surrounding the well-protected harbour. These slopes rise almost 900ft above the sea within a short distance –meaning there are brilliant views around every corner.

There was an ancient fishing village huddled around Fore Street leading up from the perfect natural harbour but most of Ilfracombe's buildings date from its heydays in the 19th century. Tens of thousands of miners and factory workers took steamers from south Wales or trains from Barnstaple to stay in the elegant crescents of tall guesthouses and grand hotels. There was even a fashionable sea spa here for a while.

Eventually the spas fell out of favour and the foreign package holiday boom of the 1960s and 1970s left resorts such as Ilfracombe catering to a market that wasn't there any more. Soon all that Victoriana started looking pretty tired. There was a time when Ilfracombe had serious social problems and very downmarket appeal. For a while the resort's decline looked terminal but some serious action by the authorities and private investment has addressed some of the problems, although many locals still feel resentment. With its isolated position away from the centre of power in Exeter, even Ilfracombe politicians say they haven't always got their fair share of attention.

For the visitor, however, that sense of isolation can be rather attractive and in the past few years Ilfracombe has started re-inventing itself in a more contemporary way. Outsiders have been moving in, attracted by some of the cheapest property in Devon. There is a feel of something new happening all over the town.

The wonderful traditional seaside **public gardens** have been spruced up and empty hotels are being converted into scores of luxury self-catering flats. Signs of a new modern resort are emerging – the extraordinary theatre complex, the excellent Tunnels Beaches and much better quality B&Bs and restaurants.

And as the icing on the cake, super-rich artist Damien Hirst bought a farm in the picturesque village of **Berrynarbour** nearby and started investing heavily in Ilfracombe. He now owns a glamorous quayside restaurant and tapas bar, plus Victorian property that at the time of writing is said to be on the way to becoming luxury accommodation. Local tourist chiefs are starting to talk of 'Ilfracool' and making comparisons with Rick Stein's Padstow. But expect that and you'll be disappointed – Ilfracombe is still quirkier and has a much wider range of good and bad than the trendy Cornish fishing village.

WHAT TO SEE AND DO

As you round the final bends coming into Ilfracombe, the first thing to spot is the distinctive **Lantern Hill** at the harbour's entrance, topped by the 600-year-old **St Nicholas' Chapel** (open Easter to October, entry free). This quaint landmark has always doubled as a warning beacon for sailors, making it the UK's oldest working lighthouse.

Lantern Hill overlooks the harbour

The Harbour is great for a wander: peer into the lifeboat house – it always looks ready for action and gawp at the prices on the menu of **No 11**, Damien Hirst's swanky restaurant. The stylish tapas bar downstairs isn't too pricey though and his arty décor makes it all worthwhile.

It's easy to spend half a day browsing the quayside gift shops, cheap cafés and busy bars, and the quaint aquarium housed in a former lifeboat house. Crowds often form to watch fishing boats unloading their catch on the south quay, while on the north quay the local boatmen tout noisily for punters for their wildlife cruises or fishing trips.

Fair weather

Several little sandy beaches are dotted around the town's complex of inlets and headlands but the best is **Tunnels Beaches** on Granville Road. There is a big seawater pool that's safe for children and a gritty, greyish sandy beach with rock pools, gardens and shop. The stylish modern café now has a very handy children's play centre. The

TUNNELS BEACHES,
☎ 01271 879882; www.tunnels-beaches.co.uk. Entry: adults £1.90, children £1.50, concessions, family tickets; open Apr to Oct: daily; winter: Fri to Mon.

whole area has been tastefully renovated – take time to look at the entertaining displays dotted around explaining the beach's history. There is also a centre here for kayak hire and adventurous coasteering expeditions along the shore. (For more on the beach's owners, see the panel.)

The harbour is the centre of **boat trips** of all sorts, including the official ferry to Lundy Island. (For details, see the Bideford chapter, where the Lundy office is based.)

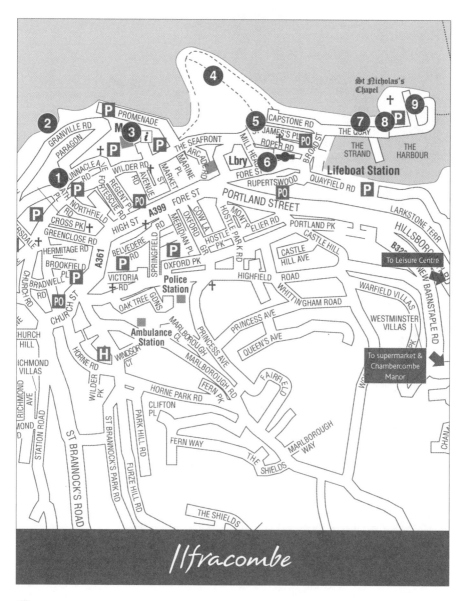

Ilfracombe

1. Entrance to Tunnels Beach and Cafe Blue
2. Tunnels Beach
3. Landmark Theatre
4. Capstone Hill
5. Expresso Bar
6. La Gendarmerie and the Terrace Tapas Bar
7. Damien Hirst's Number 11 Resturant
8. The Aquarium
9. Lantern Hill

Art is scattered through the woods at Broomhill

BROOMHILL ART HOTEL,
10 miles south of Ilfracombe on the B3230; ☎ 01271 850262
www.broomhillart.co.uk.
Entry: adults £4.50, under 16s £1.50, concessions and family tickets available; open Sept to June: Wed to Sun 11am–4pm; July/Aug: daily.

The historic **pleasure steamers**, the *Waverley* and *Balmoral*, often call into the harbour. Get the latest dates and times from the tourist office or from www.waverleyexcursions.co.uk. It's a chance for a cruise, with food and drink, amid the polished brass and varnished wood of a classic ship. The *Waverley* is the last sea-going paddle steamer in the world.

THE ILFRACOMBE PRINCESS, ☎ 01271 322858;
www.ilfracombeprincess.co.uk
Prices: adults £10, children £5;
Easter to Oct: 90 min cruises daily from 10.30am.

Other possibilities include sea fishing expeditions, wildlife cruises and sightseeing trips. One of the best organised is the distinctive locally owned yellow vessel, ***The Ilfracombe Princess***. The owners have a small ticket kiosk opposite the entrance to the aquarium. The boat is specially designed to navigate close to the rocks to look at birds and sealife. You'll be unlucky if you don't see seals, and maybe

We bought a beach

Jamie Mclintock and wife Zoe, in a lifestyle change worth a TV series, gave up office jobs and sold their small house in the Midlands in 2001 to return to their childhood home of Ilfracombe... and bought a beach.

Amazingly an unwanted 1.5 mile stretch of coast, known as **Tunnels Beaches**, with five tunnels, two private beaches, three Victorian tidal pools, and a clifftop plot with planning permission for a new house had been languishing on an estate agent's books for nine years.

The couple, both 24, who previously worked in design and marketing jobs, were able to snap up the whole lot for the price of an ordinary family house.

At first they lived with relatives while they worked on renovating the town's most unique attraction. 'We didn't just want to take over a beach – we wanted to create something high quality,' says Jamie. 'People would say things like 'What do you know about running a beach?' recalls Zoe. 'Well, what does anyone know about running a beach?'

They've succeeded – and not just in building a dream house for their own young porpoises or dolphins but whatever happens, you'll see some spectacular coastal scenery.

You may not see seals but you will spot some extraordinary things down in the woods at

Broomhill Art Hotel. This eccentric Victorian house in a secluded wooded valley has an amazing 10-acre garden, dotted with more than 300 sculptures by 30 different artists. Wander round the woods and find a giant red stiletto shoe, a snow-white figure on horseback and tall glass mushrooms. Inside there is a full-sized gallery. The restaurant is also good, and although it's a quiet, scenic place to stay, the hotel bedrooms are now a little dated.

Wet weather

AQUARIUM ☎ 01271 864 533; www.ilfracombeaquarium.co.uk; adults £3, children £2.25, concessions, family tickets; open Feb to Nov: daily 10am and Christmas holidays.

The quaint harbourside **Aquarium**, in the old lifeboat house, was opened by a former London zookeeper. It's very family friendly and focuses on what lives in the sea around Ilfracombe.

A mile out of town, off the Combe Martin road, discover a real Scooby Doo experience at **Chambercombe Manor**. It's shrouded in ghost stories and has starred in TV shows about the paranormal. Hear legends of skeletons in secret chambers and ghouls emerging from sealed rooms on the

family on the clifftop above. Their beach received its first Blue Flag award within a year and has won one every year since, their café is one of the best in town and the young couple have turned the Tunnels into an intriguing attraction with dozens of signs explaining the weirdest parts of its history.

The Tunnels were cut through cliffs in 1823 to allow access to previously inaccessible coves. Ilfracombe Sea Bathing Company built a driftwood-powered pump to send seawater back into a smart spa bathhouse. Ilfracombe became one of the most popular spots in the country for 'taking the waters' – literally drinking a cup of seawater for its supposed health benefits.

The displays include passages from Victorian newspapers including the advice to beach-going ladies that 'corsets should be left at home' while gentlemen were warned that 'great care must be taken not to splash the ladies'. One poster concerned the bugler who was stationed on the rocky outcrop between the gentlemen and ladies' bathing areas. His job was to blow an alarm to the ladies if any of the gentlemen strayed too close.

Ilfracombe's aquarium in a former lifeboat station

memorable guided tours. Overnight paranormal investigations are available too... if you're brave enough.

You wouldn't normally classify a town's swimming pool as a visitor attraction but Ilfracombe's **Leisure Centre** is so well situated in the greenery on the east side of the harbour, overlooking the sea, it makes a great escape for families if the weather's poor. You'll find a 33m pool, sauna, sun room and handy car park.

CHAMBERCOMBE MANOR, Chambercombe Lane, Ilfracombe EX34 9RJ; ☎ 01271 862624; www.chambercombemanor.org.uk Entry: adults £6, children £2.50; open Easter to Oct: Sun to Fri.

LEISURE CENTRE, Hillsborough Road EX34 9QG; ☎ 01271 864480. Entry: adults £2, children £1.65, OAPs £1.70; open daily all year.

 ## What to do with children...

WATERMOUTH CASTLE, ☎ 01271 867474; www.watermouthcastle.com. Entry: over 14s £10.50, 3–13s £9, includes all attractions and rides.

KEYPITTS FARM, Oxpen Lane, Ilfracombe; ☎ 01271 862247; www.keypitts.com Price: quad bikes from £10 for 15 min, riding from £15 for 30 min, paintball from £10 an hour, 4 x 4 drives £32 for 30 min.

Watermouth Castle, 3 miles from Ilfracombe on the Combe Martin road, is a quirky old-fashioned theme park best suited for younger children. There is nothing hair-raising, just gentle rides including a water-squirting shooting gallery and an aeroplane roundabout.

Keypitts Farm has been in the Chugg family for 600 years but they've never had anything like this before... there are now quad bike tracks, horse trekking, off-road driving and paintball at a rugged adventure centre. It's best to book in advance.

Local knowledge

Lawrence Raybone is owner of Ilfracombe Aquarium and lives in the town with his wife Martha. 'It's sad really', says Lawrence, 'I love my work so much I think of it as an extension to a hobby'. When Lawrence was second-in-charge at London Zoo sealife department he one day hoped to have his own aquarium. 'And I realised that I was destined to live by the coast,' he says. 'I did some research into North Devon and Ilfracombe seemed most logical location, the old lifeboat station became available through liaising with the district council and I was open to the public in June 2001...'

Favourite restaurant: In Ilfracombe either Damien Hirst's 11 The Quay, or La Gendarmerie. For a real treat we go to Andrews-on-the-Wier, Porlock, over the border in Somerset.

Favourite pub: The Reform Inn, Pilton, has its own microbrewery on site, live music and pub games. Barum and Exmoor are my favourite local beers.
Favourite local shops: The Farm Shop, Blakewell Fisheries, Muddiford; Cool, Calm and Collected gifts, Barnstaple.
Best view: Across Braunton Burrows from the coast road to Croyde, the B3231.
Quirkiest attraction: Watermouth Castle near Combe Martin, it's eccentric but great fun for all ages.
Best thing about living here: The natural environment and the lack of traffic.
Anything else you'd like to recommend to Devon visitors? Walking anywhere on the South-West Coast Path and visiting one of the Devon pannier markets – like Barnstaple, Bideford or South Molton.

The best... PLACES TO STAY

HOTEL

Poplars

Woodlands, Combe Martin, EX34 0AR
☎ **01271 882241**
www.poplarshotel.co.uk

This hotel is right next to the beach at the small resort of Combe Martin but on a busy road. It's a strange small hotel where the proprietor is liable to pick up an electric guitar and start serenading guests. There is a bar, restaurant, pool and games room but some of the décor is depressingly old-fashioned.

Price: B&B from £25 to £28 per person.

B & B

Westwood

Torrs Park, Ilfracombe, EX34 8AZ
☎ **01271 867443**
www.west-wood.co.uk

Here is luxurious contemporary B&B in a grand Victorian villa on the heights of The Torrs. It's as near as Ilfracombe gets to a boutique hotel.

Price: B&B from £80 for a double.

Norbury House

Torrs Park, Ilfracombe, EX34 8AZ
☎ **01271 863888**
www.norburyhouse.co.uk

Another imposing Victorian house and garden offering an artful mix of modern and period style.

Price: B&B from £65 for a double.

CAMPSITE

Little Meadow Camping and Caravan Site

Watermouth, Ilfracombe EX34 9SJ
☎ **01271 866862**
www.littlemeadow.co.uk

Once rated the 36th-best campsite in the world by the *Independent* newspaper, this pretty and strictly peaceful site allows you to camp in the stunning countryside close to the shore between Ilfracombe and Combe Martin. Static caravans are available to rent too.

Price: from £10 for one car and tent per night.

SELF-CATERING

The Admiral's House

Quayfield Road, Ilfracombe, EX34 9EN
☎ **01271 864666**
www.theadmiralshouse.co.uk

Five self-catering flats in a prominent historic house overlooking harbour have great views, over-the-top furnishings, quirky period details and rambling communal garden.

Price: from £241 for a week.

Lower Cowley Farmhouse

**Parracombe near Combe Martin
c/o Helpful Holidays**
☎ **01647 433593**
www.helpfulholidays.com

This classy 18th-century farmhouse can be rented in a secluded valley just west of Parracombe. It sleeps 14 (seven bedrooms), has a big indoor heated pool, 10 acres, three ponds and a grand piano.

Price: from £1,272 to £3,117 for a week.

Why the Kaiser hated England

One little-known snippet of history is a very popular tale among locals... and demonstrates the classic isolated, but determined, Ilfracombe spirit.

In the summer of 1878 Prince William of Prussia was enjoying a holiday in Ilfracombe. He was later to become the 'Kaiser Bill' who fought Britain and the Allies to a standstill in the First World War. Back then he was a spoilt 19-year-old staying in the Ilfracombe Hotel, which stands where the Landmark Theatre is now.

The Prince was caught throwing stones at beach huts by Alf Price, the 16-year-old son of the beach attendant. Alf tried to tell the stranger to stop but the Prince snapped 'Don't you know who I am?'. Alf replied: 'I don't care a dash who you are.' With that the German lashed out at Alf's jaw, knocking him to the sand. Alf leapt up and the two became locked in rather undignified teenage mêlée. Locals watched, presumably silently cheering the local lad on, but no-one intervened until the horrified Prince's retinue arrived a few minutes later. The future Kaiser, sporting a bleeding nose, was separated from the plucky Ilfracombe lad. The Prince's tutor promptly paid Alf 30 shillings to keep quiet about the incident.

He did keep quiet... until the war broke out 36 years later. Then Alf's story was printed in a small leaflet and handed out to British troops at the front as a morale booster called 'Why the Kaiser hates England'. You can see more about this story in **Ilfracombe Museum** (entry: adults £2, children free; open daily 10am–5pm, Apr to Oct, 10am–1pm Nov to Mar) in the seafront Runnymeade Gardens, including a photo of Alf happily still working on the beach in 1916.

 ## And how to avoid children

Plod up any part of the hilly coastline for rewarding views. **Capstone Hill** to the west of the harbour is a good start, with great views from the top. If you survive that try the hill to the east – **Hillsborough Hill**. It's four times higher.

Best of all, tackle the coast path west across **The Torrs**, a strange series of bumpy hills protected by the National Trust. It's 2 miles to the little beach and village of **Lee Bay**. Bracing sea views along the way make it worthwhile, and there are two good pubs in Lee to help you recover (The Grumpus and The Lee Bay Hotel).

 ## Entertainment

The distinctive modern architecture of the **Landmark Theatre's** twin cones was called 'Madonna's bra' by locals when it opened in 1988. The concrete has grown a bit grubby now but there is much more acceptance of the striking design. The bar opening out onto the sea behind is a good place to eat and drink whether you're seeing a show or not. The complex also has the town's tourist office.

There is a varied year-round programme in the excellent auditorium with everything from Bill Bailey to classical concerts (☎ 01271 32 42 42; www.north devontheatres.org.uk).

The Marlboro Club in the High Street hosts a surprisingly interesting line-up of rock bands. Damon Albarn played recently and there are several gigs a week here. Check the club's myspace page (www.myspace.com/themarlboro-club) or call 01271 863001.

Festivals

And in such an isolated community the locals learn to create plenty of their own entertainment – Ilfracombe's main **Carnival** in August is one of Devon's biggest, but watch out too for the **May Day** walking celebration, June's **Victorian Festival**, the **Birdman Festival** in August (entrants try to fly from the harbour wall) and **Folk Festival** in September. For more details, visit the tourist office.

The best... FOOD AND DRINK

Ilfracombe is an old-fashioned seaside resort. You can still find rock and candy floss in the shops around the harbour. So expect plenty of fish and chips, cheap fast food and a variety of international takeaways. But there are now some excellent restaurants among the average ones, so take your time to make sure you find a good one.

The countryside around Ilfracombe is very rural with hardly a village bigger than a hamlet for 10 miles in all directions. This means there is plenty of good fresh produce available in the town's shops. Plus, of course, there is fresh seafood from the small fishing fleet based in the harbour.

▶ Staying in

Locals in-the-know drive to **Besshill Farm Shop** (☎ 01271 850311) on a 270- acre farm at the nearby village of Arlington, just south of the A39. The award-winning farm sells its own Limousin beef and Bluefaced Leicester lamb, locally grown vegetables and fruit, and pork from a neighbouring farm.

A local **farmers' market** is held on the third Saturday of the month at the Village Hall, High Street, Combe Martin between 9.30am and 12pm.

🍴 EATING OUT

FINE DINING

No 11
The Quay, Ilfracombe
☎ **01271 868090**
www.11thequay.com

Damien Hirst's fabulously converted harbourside pub has a gourmet restaurant upstairs with stunning sea views. It's one of North Devon's best and certainly its most famous restaurant. There is usually plenty of local fish on the menu. Downstairs is Ilfracombe's trendiest bar decorated by Damien and serving coffee, drinks, tapas from £2.20, as well as main courses costing around £10. Upstairs, a three-course dinner costs around £40.

La Gendarmerie
Fore Street, Ilfracombe
☎ **01271 865984**

A stylishly converted former police station on the town's oldest street next to the lively tapas bar. La Gendarmerie is more cool and contemporary, with an open kitchen and quality food using local produce where possible. It's only open Wednesday to Sunday throughout the season but the honey-roasted scallops are worth waiting for. Three courses cost around £25.

RESTAURANT

The Terrace Tapas Bar
62 Fore Street, Ilfracombe, EX34 9ED
☎ **01271 863482**

Family-run bar with good-value Spanish food, beer and wine on hill above the harbour. The atmosphere is lively and the bar is popular with locals. You can eat out under umbrellas on terrace or in spacious rambling interior that was once the town bakery. The set four-course meal costs £14.95.

CAFÉ

Expresso Bar & Grill
1 St James Place, Ilfracombe, EX34 9BH
☎ **01271 855485**

You can choose between fresh seafood, snacks and coffee in this lively new continental-style café at the foot of Capstone Hill. It's one of the favourites of Jamie and Zoe Mclintock, owners of the Tunnels Beaches and Café Blue.

Café Blue
Tunnels Beaches, Granville Road, Ilfracombe, EX34 8AN
☎ **01271 879882**
www.tunnelsbeaches.co.uk

At the entrance to the Tunnels Beaches, Café Blue's informal style and children's play facilities make it Ilfracombe's coolest café for families.

🍷 Drinking

Ilfracombe has a huge number of pubs and some can get rowdy, so choose carefully. The **Royal Britannia** on the harbour has a sense of history and nice terrace at the back over the water. It's claimed Lord Nelson once stayed here. Further along the harbour the **Pier Hotel** sometimes has live music. Around the corner at the bottom of Fore Street is the ancient **Prince of Wales** with low ceilings, a wishing-well outside the gents and wifi. And of course the bar at Damien Hirst's **No 11** is the coolest place to drink.

Visitor information

Tourist information centres:
*Ilfracombe Tourist Information
Centre* is housed inside the Landmark Theatre on the seafront, ☎
01271 863001, www.ilfracombe-
tourism.co.uk.
Hospitals: Ilfracombe Hospital, ☎
01271 863448; 24-hour A&E facilities

are available at *North Devon District
Hospital*, Raleigh Park, Barnstaple
EX31 4JB, ☎ 01271 322577.
Bike rental: Ilfracombe Cycle Hire,
5 St James Place, ☎ 01271 863108.
Taxis: 1st A.B.C Taxis, ☎ 01271
867777; Ace Taxis,
☎ 01271 866688.

Out of town, the **Grampus Inn** in Lee Bay is a cosy village local incorporating the village shop. There is usually a great array of local real ales including Black-awton from Saltash and Barum from Barnstaple.

FURTHER AFIELD

Five miles east is **Combe Martin** – essentially just one long street running down a 'combe' or valley towards the sea for 2 miles. It's reputedly the country's longest high street. At one end, the sheltered sandy cove is one of the best beaches in North Devon and the cliffs to the east (Great and Little Hangman) are among the country's highest. For more information contact the town's tourist information centre in Cross Street (☎ 01271 881319; www.visitcombe-martin.co.uk).

One village pub, **The Pack o' Cards**, was built by a gambling-mad landowner to celebrate a win at cards in 1690. It has 52 windows, 13 rooms and four floors to match a pack of playing cards. The rooms may be standard pub qual-ity but it makes a quirky place to eat, drink or stay (☎ 01271 882300; www.packocards.co.uk; B&B from £27 per person for one night). **The Fo'c'sle Inn** may not have such a unique history but it serves excellent pub grub on a terrace overlooking the beach (☎ 01271 883354).

A stroll among the postcard cottages and garden of the nearby village of **Berrynarbour** can end in the cosy comfort of the village pub, Ye Olde Globe Inn, or a traditional teashop.

Heading south out of Combe Martin you'll pass the **Wildlife and Dinosaur Park** (☎ 01271 882486; dinosaur-park.com; entry: adults £12, children £7; open daily mid Mar to early Nov 10am,). It's an entertainingly eccentric theme park with animated full-size dinosaurs, white-knuckle rides, and a selection of animals that appeal to youngsters, such as monkeys, penguins and wolves, but beware the crowds on a gloomy day during the high season.

The best of... DEVON'S COASTLINE

DEVON IS THE ONLY COUNTY WITH TWO SEPARATE COASTS –
MEANING THERE ARE TWO COMPLETELY DIFFERENT SEASCAPES TO
EXPLORE. THE NORTH IS WILDER – WITH HUGE CLIFFS, LONG
SANDY BEACHES AND UNTAMED DUNES. THE SOUTH HAS GENTLE
GREEN ESTUARIES, SHELTERED COVES AND THE DRAMATIC AND
ANCIENT ROCKS OF THE WORLD HERITAGE COAST.

Top: Jurassic coast; Middle: Brixham Heritage fleet; Bottom: Sidmouth's coast

Top: Bucks Mills at low tide; Bottom: Woolacombe coast

Plymouth Hoe lighthouse

Top: The Hoe, Plymouth; Middle: Clovelly at Christmas; Bottom: Buddleigh beach

WOOLACOMBE, CROYDE, BARNSTAPLE AND AROUND

With miles of flat golden sands where Atlantic breakers continuously roar towards the shore... is it any wonder the trio of beaches between Ilfracombe and Barnstaple are so popular with surfers?

Of course there is more to this area than big waves – starting with the UK's biggest dunes, a pretty village with a literary history and North Devon's biggest town. But whether you're surf mad or just fancy a day at the seaside, those Blue Flag beaches are the main attraction.

Note that the beaches at Woolacombe, Croyde and Saunton are very flat. You walk a long way to get to a swimming depth by which time the waves have usually knocked adults from their feet – so it's not always easy for small children. The good news is that the sand flats are venues for all sorts of activities from nudism to sand-yachting. Kids will love flying kites here – it's usually plenty windy enough.

Among all the dreadlocks and VW camper vans, it's easy to get caught in the surfing frenzy around these resorts. There are plenty of shops selling and hiring the gear you'll need, and many courses and instructors offering to teach the finer skills.

If the beaches are best for spotting surfers in their natural habitat, the grass and gorse headlands between them are where you'll spot even wilder life – such as cormorants, gannets and grey seals. Between and behind the beaches this area is criss-crossed with great trails for walking.

It's a chunk of countryside that seems to inspire outdoor activity, with non-stop opportunities to hire bikes, ride horses, learn a new adventure sport... or simply picnic on National Trust clifftops gazing at the view of Lundy Island.

WHAT TO SEE AND DO

 Fair weather

Beaches and surfing

Woolacombe's famous three-mile beach is framed between two National Trust headlands whose cliffs slope down to child-friendly rockpools. At low tide the sea is a long way away – and so is the other end of the beach.

There's always room on the beach at Woolacombe

The south part of the beach has a different name, **Putsborough**. This end is best to escape the crowds – as there is not much more than a car park and a couple of bungalows; the busier north end, close to Woolacombe village, is best for facilities and entertainment. Speedboats and jet skis are banned, but there are excellent facilities for surfing, windsurfing, sailing and sea canoeing.

Woolacombe village itself doesn't feel like a real place, just a collection of hotels, shops and cafés around a car park and crazy golf course. It's buzzing with visitors in the summer, deserted and windswept in winter. The beach, however, never loses its charm.

South of Woolacombe, beyond Putsborough and over Baggy Point headland there is another surfers' favourite: **Croyde**. It's a smaller sandy beach, also backed by huge dunes, but it's almost exclusively the domain of surfers. The waves are fast and 'hollow' here because of the shape of the bay. It's quite demanding, especially at low tide. Saunton and Woolacombe's gentler waves are better suited to beginners.

If you're just sampling surfing for the first time, surf lessons can be good fun and useful. Family-run Barefoot Surf School (☎ 01271 891231; wwwbarefoot-surf.com) holds lessons on Putsborough Sands. Nick Thorne Surf Coaching (☎ 01271 871337; www.nickthorn.com) is right on Woolacombe Beach. And Surf South West Surf School operates at Croyde and Saunton (☎ 01271 890400; www.surfsouthwest.com). Expect to pay around £25 for a half-day's coaching in a group.

The ancient village of **Mortehoe** that almost joins Woolacombe to the north is a more appealing community, with stone cottages, a friendly pub with real locals, an interesting medieval church and a decent local shop that sells good homemade pasties. From Mortehoe there are paths across National Trust land to the lovely hidden sandy cove at **Rockham**.

Croyde village retains some cuteness despite the summer hordes; its thatched whitewashed cottages and rambling gardens stand alongside a trickling brook although towards the sea there is a serious outbreak of surf shops.

The best walk from Croyde is the coast path to see the views from **Baggy Point**, the best cycle is through the lanes to **Georgeham**. This is the prettiest

The Visitors' Book

Summer weekend in Croyde

'Whenever I visit Croyde I know I am nearly there when I start to see people walking along the road with surfboards under their arms. When we went there last, it was a summer weekend. My friend and I camped on a site near the centre of town.'

'A good day in Croyde starts with cooked breakfast on the campsite. Then it was onto some beginners' surf lessons. It's possible to surf at Croyde but we went up the coast to Putsborough as it's apparently... better for beginners. It's a lovely beach — quieter than... Croyde.

'We booked surf lessons through the Barefoot Surf School with Nigel. I definitely recommend them. All the equipment is included in the price for a two-hour lesson. After the lesson, shattered and out of our wetsuits, we tucked into a well-deserved snack lunch in the beach café. Parking at Putsborough lasts all day so we took a walk along the beach.'

'Woolacombe is a good couple of miles but there is plenty of flat sand and it's an enjoyable walk. The town is slightly more touristy than Croyde but just as devoted to surfing and with more shopping opportunities.'

'It's a great atmosphere in Croyde where everyone seems to know each other, even though there are many tourists. When we finally we hit the sack, we were still able to hear the waves down on Croyde beach.'

Isabelle Utley, 25, from Hertfordshire, stayed in Croyde

village for miles, well worth an aimless wander among the pastel painted cottages and the thatched **Rock Inn** (see The best... food and drink).

The third of the surfers' trio is **Saunton Sands** – another three-mile stretch with big waves and a long walk to get there. There is not really a village here, just a few houses, the region's top hotel and a slick beach café.

The beach is backed by **Braunton Burrows**, the country's biggest dune system. It's a Site of Special Scientific Interest and was declared Britain's first UNESCO Biosphere Reserve, ranking alongside Vesuvius in Italy and the Danube Delta in Eastern Europe. The impressive stretches of sand are so much like the long Normandy beaches that the US army practised D-Day landings here.

The four miles of Braunton Burrows includes two highly rated golf courses and a restricted military training area, the red flags warn of any firing. There are wooden paths through the dunes – look for some of more than 500 species of wild flowers and 33 different butterflies, many of them extremely rare.

The south end of the beach can sometimes attract nude bathers while fishermen and birdwatchers (usually with their clothes on) head for **Crow Point** right at the mouth of the estuary. It's an atmospheric spot with a chance to spot seals, curlews and flocks of migrating birds.

Tarka the Otter

Georgeham's claim to fame is that controversial author **Henry Williamson** lived here while writing *Tarka the Otter* more than 80 years ago. It's one of the most enduring wildlife stories ever written, a worldwide best-seller.

The story was set in North Devon, between the Taw and Torridge estuaries. Henry made up the name but now Tarka has become more famous than his creator. You'll see the Tarka Line (railway), Tarka Trail (walking and cycling path) and Tarka Country (around the Taw and Torridge estuaries). Visitors might go home with a Tarka T-shirt, but few get to know anything about the man who created the loveable fictional otter.

Henry had visited Georgeham as a schoolboy on holiday before the First World War. After serving with distinction in the trenches he argued with his strict father, rode to Georgeham from London on his motorbike and rented a cottage for one-and-sixpence (12.5p) a week.

A small blue plaque outside Crowborough Cottage commemorates Henry's residence. You can see the window of the upstairs writing room where he wrote *Tarka*. Henry had once kept an orphaned otter cub as a pet and claimed he rewrote the book 17 times to get it right. And this cottage is where Henry's great pal Lawrence of Arabia came to visit.

Inland from the Burrows is **Braunton**, which only gets noticed by thousands of holidaymakers because of the traffic jams at the gridlocked crossroads in the centre. But it has plenty to justify a stop and not just the convenience stores, takeaways, delis, cafés and bars along the busy main roads. The surf shops, bike hire and watersports tuition can be very useful but turn into the back streets and it's immediately quieter, with grand Georgian houses and pastel-painted cottages. There is a gallery, museum and award-winning chip shop but also have a quick peep to the west of town, before the Burrows, where you'll find **Braunton Great Field**, a 340-acre area farmed according to medieval strip methods.

Wet weather

Put on a wet-suit and ignore it, say the surfers. The rest of us head for Barnstaple's shops and facilities or further to Ilfracombe or Torrington.

There isn't much to do undercover at the surf beaches other than hide in a bar.

The **Elliott Art Gallery** in Hillsview, Braunton has the largest art collection in the area but won't

ELLIOTT ART GALLERY,
☎ 01271 812100; www.elliottart-gallery.co.uk; open April to Oct: Mon to Sat 11am–5pm; 11am–4pm Thur/Sat rest of year except closed in Jan/Feb.

A biography written by his daughter-in-law Anne Williamson in 1997 revealed how Henry secretly planned to take his friend Lawrence to see Hitler and prevent the outbreak of the Second World War. The plan faltered when Lawrence was killed when he was racing back on his motorbike after sending a telegram to Henry about the barmy peace mission. The book also revealed that Henry was a lifelong womaniser who lived with his wife, mistress and their children all in the same house. But it seems likely his pre-war pro-Hitler comments were the naive musings of a country eccentric. At the time suspicious villagers thought he was signalling to Nazi bombers and had him arrested.

Williamson is buried in Georgeham churchyard 1977. Sadly his evocative writing hut in a field nearby isn't open to the public so the best place to get a flavour of Williamson is the Rock Inn, his favourite pub – referred to as 'The Upper House' in many of his 50 books. Several faded black-and-white photographs of Henry drinking there still hang on the walls.

Ask elderly locals if they remember the eccentric wildlife lover. 'He was a right naughty so-and-so,' one old lady told us. 'He'd sit in the pub and when it all went quiet he'd make cuckoo noises.'

The best... **PLACES TO STAY**

HOTEL

Saunton Sands Hotel

Saunton EX33 1LQ
☎ **01271 890212**
www.sauntonsands.com

The white art-deco hotel stands prominently above one end of the beach. The location, indoor pool and crèche make it a great place for families even if the level of luxury doesn't always match the prices.

Price: B&B from £87 to £200 per person per night.

Watersmeet Hotel

Woolacombe EX34 7EB
☎ **01271 870333**
www.watersmeethotel.co.uk

Yet another great seashore location and some fine Edwardian period details such as stained glass and open fires, but the floral drapes, patterned carpets and pendant lights make it feel somewhat dated. The restaurant is very traditional – a jacket and tie is required, but it's highly-rated all the same.

Price: Rooms are sold on the basis of dinner, B&B and cost from £75 per person per night.

FARMSTAY

Combas Farm

Putsborough, near Croyde EX33 1PH
☎ **01271 890398**
www.combasfarm.co.uk

Farmer's wife Gwen Adams has been taking paying guests for 52 years at her wisteria-clad 17th-century farmhouse. The sheep farm is a 20-minute walk from Putsborough Sands. Breakfast includes homemade yogurt and jams, and water from the farm's own spring.

Price: B&B from £29 per person.

B&B

Victoria House

Chapel Hill, Mortehoe EX34 7DZ
☎ **01271 871302**
www.victoriahousebandb.co.uk

Actually it's Edwardian but it's still one of the most attractive places to stay along this coast. Features like an antique brass bed, freestanding bath, sea-view balcony, plush sofa and fresh-baked croissants make it special.

Price: B&B from £85 for a double room.

Sandunes

Beach Road, Woolacombe EX34 7BT
☎ **01271 870661**
www.sandwool.fsnet.co.uk

This small guesthouse close to the beach doesn't look much from the outside but has great sea views. Inside it's cheap and neatly decorated and two rooms have balconies. And the owners fill your breakfast plate with local produce.

Price: B&B from £22 per person per night.

CAMPSITE

North Morte Farm

Morthoe EX34 7EG
☎ **01271 870381**
www.northmortefarm.co.uk

Judged one of the *Guardian's* top 50 camp-sites in Britain, these terraced fields lead from the edge of Mortehoe down towards little-known but lovely Rockham beach. It's like the site's private beach. The site is quiet but well-equipped and perfect for families with a playground and shop.

Price: from £6 per adult per night.

keep you dry for long. There is plenty of local work for sale but much of it is of the soft focus pictures of cats variety. There are sometimes striking pieces in there though.

Entertainment

Barnstaple has a lovely old theatre for music, drama and events. The **Queens Theatre** is in the pedestrianised Boutport Street (☎ 01271 324242; www.northdevontheatres.org.uk). Barnstaple's multi-screen **cinema** is the only one in the area (☎ 0871 230 3200; www.scottcinemas.co.uk).

Apart from that it's pubs, with plenty of live music especially in the summer. Try the **Red Barn** on the seafront at Woolacombe or the **Agricultural Inn**, East Street, Braunton (called the Aggi by everyone).

The best... FOOD AND DRINK

There is less of the fresh local seafood influence on this stretch of coast. The surfing invasion means lots of fast food and quality is not always high, so shop around. Don't expect gastropubs either, hearty pub grub is more likely. Local shops and restaurants do, however, get the pick of plenty of great local farm produce, especially dairy and fruit. And of course, there will always be chances to sample the famous Devon clotted cream tea.

▶ Staying in

It would be a mistake to drive past **Squires** award-winning fish and chip shop on Exeter Road, Braunton, heading for an anonymous takeaway in Barnstaple. Celebrity chef Rick Stein recommends this two-storey restaurant and takeaway. The secret of their success is evidently that chips are made from local Maris Piper spuds and cooked in groundnut oil.

For self-caterers **West Hill Farm Shop** (☎ 01271 815477; www.westhill farm.org) near Braunton is a good source of organic dairy produce, including pots of their award-winning fresh organic chocolate sauce (Green & Black's choc plus cream from their organic herd). And there is some succulently fresh fruit at **Ashford Inn Fruit Farm** (☎ 01271 344457) on the Braunton Road into Barnstaple. You'll also find local cream, cheese, yoghurt and honey.

Blakewell Fisheries at Muddiford, just north of Barnstaple, is a favourite for catch-your-own trout which will then be prepared for you. The farm shop sells fresh or smoked trout too, plus meat, vegetables and diary produce from within a 15 mile radius (☎ 01271 344533; www.blakewell.co.uk).

 **EATING OUT**

FINE DINING

The Courtyard Restaurant
South Street, Woolacombe EX34 7BB
☎ **01271 871187**
www.courtyardrestaurant.co.uk

It's worth tracking down this locally run restaurant tucked away in streets behind the beach. On sunny days the roof can be opened to the sky and it's one of the few Woolacombe eateries rated by locals. It costs £35 for a three-course dinner.

Zena's
Market Square, Barnstaple EX31 1BX
☎ **01271 378844**

In a courtyard next to the pannier market this smart trio grouped around a courtyard shows how far the previously dour centre of Barnstaple has moved in the past decade. The mother-and-son partnership own a coffee shop serving tables in the courtyard, a French-style patisserie and a continental bistro with waiters in crisp black and white and regular live music.

RESTAURANT

Sands Café Bar
Saunton Beach EX33 1LQ
☎ **01271 891288**
www.brend-hotels.co.uk/TheSaunton-Sands/SandsCafeBar.cfm

The best beach café along this coast is above a row of surf hire shops right next to the beach. It's owned by the Saunton Sands Hotel but feels like the hotel's trendier little sister, with stylish metal furniture inside the wooden interior or on decking outside. There is classy bistro food day and night with great views – it's one of the best spots in Devon to enjoy a great sunset. Menu ranges from snacks to three-course meals at around £20.

The Quay Café
Fremington, near Barnstaple EX31 2NH
☎ **01271 378 783**
www.fremingtonquaycafe.co.uk

This restaurant/café right on the Taw estuary and the Tarka Trail is in a converted railway station. It's difficult to find but very popular with locals. Binoculars are supplied to admire the view and the food is exciting and contemporary. Lunches, dinners and cream teas are served. Local beer, cider and wines are available too. Main courses cost around £12.50.

🍷 Drinking

The old thatched **Rock Inn** at Georgham is an atmospheric place to drink and eat, (☎ 01271 890 322; www.croyde-bay.co.uk/Business/rockinn.htm) The pub grub includes the '16 inches of pure pleasure Rock-Inn-Roll' – an enormous filled baguette. There are usually eight different real ales on tap too.

It couldn't be a more different setting in **The Red Barn**, on The Esplanade at Woolacombe (☎ 01271 870264). This is a large scarlet-painted wooden seaside bar that's convenient for the beach, so it can get very crowded. It's owned by a local keen surfer and many staff are surf life-savers. Watch out for regular live music from local acts such as the Elderly Brothers or the Food Fighters,

The sloping cliffs on Woolacombe coast

plus a music festival for the first weekend in December.

The Reform Inn at Pilton on the west side of Barnstaple is popular with locals. It has its own microbrewery producing Barum ale, regular live music and plenty of pub games.

FURTHER AFIELD

Barnstaple is the biggest town in North Devon so can be very handy for shopping, supermarkets, cinema, nightlife and practicalities such as a hospital, railway station and sports centre, but there isn't a lot of seaside charm in its straggling suburbs.

The town centre has been revitalised in the past few years though. The busy **High Street** has been pedestrianised; there are good-quality pavement cafés and new shopping malls. Highlights include the huge wooden Victorian covered **pannier market** selling different types of goods each day (Tuesday is food) and **Butcher's Row** alongside, an ancient row of traders' stalls which is another great way to pick the best of local food produce.

Barnstaple has two great ideas for rainy days too: **North Devon Leisure Centre** (Seven Brethren Bank, ☎ 01271 373361, open daily up to 15 hours a day), has a swimming pool, indoor bowls, squash, solariums, steam room, gym, café and soft play for toddlers.

ARLINGTON COURT,
Arlington, nr Barnstaple, Devon EX31 4LP; ☎ 01271 850296; www.nationaltrust.org.uk; Varied opening times and prices for house, gardens, carriages and bat-cam.

And **Arlington Court**, a short drive north, is a classic National Trust property with impressive gardens, quirky mansion and a major collection of horse-drawn carriages, including the tiny one specially built for midget celebrity Major Tom when he visited the area. It's the former home of

Visitor information

Tourist information centres:
**Woolacombe Tourist Information
Centre**, The Esplanade, Woola-
combe,☎ 01271 870553; **Braunton
Tourist Information Centre**, The
Bakehouse Centre, Caen Street,
Braunton, ☎ 01271 816400; **Barn-
staple Tourist Information Centre**,
The Square, Barnstaple, ☎ 01271
375000.
Hospitals: 24-hour A&E facilities
available at *North Devon District
Hospital*, Raleigh Park, Barnstaple
EX31 4JB, ☎ 01271 322577.
Websites: www.woolacombe-
tourism.co.uk;

www.brauntontic.co.uk;
www.staynorthdevon.co.uk.
Bike rental: Bike Trail Cycle Hire,
Stone Barn, Fremington Quay, Barnstaple, ☎ 01271 372586; *Tarka Trail
Cycle Hire*, Barnstaple Junction Station, Junction Yard, Barnstaple, ☎
01271 324202; *Otter Cycle Hire*, The
Old Pottery, Station Road, Braunton
☎ 01271 813339.
Taxis: Trevor's Taxi, Braunton,
☎ 01271 815353; A&S Taxis, Braunton, ☎ 01271 813334; *T&T's Taxi
and minibus service*, Braunton,
☎ 01271 816882.

the Chichester family, yet another adventuring and seafaring lot. The last owner's nephew was one of Devon's most famous 20th century heroes, **Sir Francis Chichester**. Sir Francis was born at Shirwell near Barnstaple and was knighted after sailing solo round the world in his yacht *Gypsy Moth* in 1967.

Don't miss the exquisite collection of model ships made by French Napoleonic Prisoners of War, and down in the cellar there is also an intriguing 'bat cam' to spy on Devon's largest colony of lesser horseshoe bats.

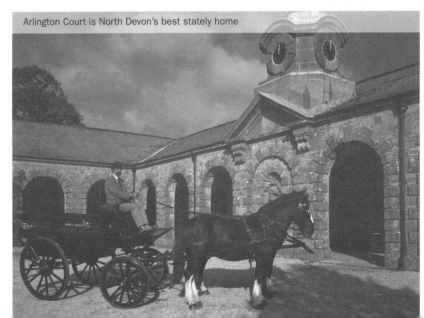
Arlington Court is North Devon's best stately home

BIDEFORD AND THE TORRIDGE ESTUARY

This historic river port has an ancient nautical air, with narrow streets leading up to the town centre, a long medieval bridge and even longer quayside. It's at the centre of excursions around the attractive Torridge Estuary, which can include the pretty villages of Appledore and Instow, the beach at Westward Ho! and the breathtaking island of Lundy.

WHAT TO SEE AND DO

Strolling along the neatly restored tree-lined **Quay** today it's hard to imagine Bideford was once the third busiest port in the country (in 1699 only London and Topsham, near Exeter, surpassed the number of vessels sailing).

The Conqueror's son, William Rufus, had given this hillside town to the Grenville family. They remained lords of the manor until 1744. In Tudor times, the adventurer Sir Richard Grenville, cousin of Francis Drake and Walter Raleigh, colonised Carolina, meaning Bideford enjoyed lucrative transatlantic trade. Some say Sir Walter Raleigh landed his first tobacco cargo here.

Bideford means 'by the ford' but there is no ford today, instead the stately **Long Bridge** across the Torridge is one of the distinctive sights of the town. It was built in 1460, copying exactly a previous oak bridge constructed by an early Grenville. This is why the stone bridge has 24 arches varying between 12ft and 25ft wide – they mimic the varied lengths of original oak lintels supplied by various parishes according to their wealth.

A new high-level **Torridge Bridge** has carried the A39 Atlantic Highway traffic since 1987, bypassing Bideford. There are great views of the estuary driving or walking over this and Bideford has become a nicer, quieter place without the A39's traffic.

Fair weather

The 17th-century quay and waterfront **Victoria Park** are the best places to start any stroll. There is usually something to see: cargo ships carrying clay, fishing and pleasure boats, the town rowing club practising to and fro or the MS Oldenberg leaving for Lundy.

At the time of writing, *Kathleen and May*, a magnificent three-masted schooner is permanently moored and visitors can look around below decks. But the world's only remaining three-masted schooner is for sale following financial problems. Locals are currently petitioning to stop the historic ship

The genteel period charm of the banks of the Torridge

being taken from the quay. After this book is published you'll see whether or not they've been successful.

Further north, old and new nautical worlds meet at the pretty village of **Appledore** on the west shore at the mouth of the Torridge. It was made a free port by Elizabeth I in gratitude for its contribution of ships and men to fight the Spanish Armada and later had a grand smuggling tradition. Writers Henry Williamson, Jerome K Jerome, Charles Kingsley and Rudyard Kipling all found inspiration here.

Unlike most of Devon's traditional seafaring spots, it's not all history at Appledore. Away from its narrow cobbled lanes of brightly-painted cottages, restaurants and craft shops, you can see the largest covered dock in Europe. Here local craftsmen uphold the village's reputation for boat building, even though it's not galleons they're working on today but new container ships.

Facing Appledore on the east side of the Torridge is **Instow**. Instead of Appledore's tiny cottages and quayside, Instow has grand period villas and a smart yacht club. There are dunes and tidal sands here too – the west facing promenades have a sunnier seaside feel compared to Appledore's more craftsmanlike heritage. Yet Instow's unlikely tourist attraction is a Grade II listed 1873 **Signal Box**. Visitors can climb inside and operate the signals themselves.

SIGNAL BOX, Instow;
☎ 01237 423585;
www.instow.net/7a.htmEntry: free; open Sun and bank holidays.

In the hills behind Instow is **Tapeley Park**, the impressive semi-tropical and formal gardens of a beautiful stately home. House tours have to be arranged in advance but a children's play and pets area, tearoom and woodland walks are open to all. It's the home of farmer, environmental campaigner and novelist Hector Christie whose family own much of the land at Saunton, including Braunton Burrows. Hector is a keen local footballer and

TAPELEY PARK, EX39 4NT;
☎ 01271 860897; www.tapeley-park.co.uk. Entry: adults £4, children £2.50; open Apr to Oct: Sun to Fri.

Sir Richard Grenville

The least known of the trio of Devonian Elizabethan seafaring cousins, **Richard Grenville** was born in Buckland Abbey near Yelverton. But records show that he was just as full of daring as Raleigh and Drake. In 1562, for example, he got in an argument in the Strand in which he ran another man through with his sword and left him to die.

And here's a contemporary description of his behaviour while dining with Spanish captains: 'He would carouse three or four glasses of wine, and in a bravery take the glasses between his teeth and crash them in pieces and swallow them down, so that often the blood ran out of his mouth without any harm at all unto him.'

Grenville asked Queen Elizabeth if he could lead an expedition around the world but she gave the job to Francis Drake instead. To add to the insult, Drake returned fabulously wealthy, was knighted and bought Buckland Abbey from Grenville.

After being made Vice-Admiral of the English fleet, Grenville's demise came in typically swashbuckling fashion in 1591. Off the Azores, his lone ship, the *Revenge*, formerly Drake's ship, refused to retreat when confronted by a Spanish fleet of 53 vessels. Grenville held them off single-handed for 15 hours, heavily damaging 15 Spanish galleons, until he was 'wounded in the brain'. He tried to blow the ship up rather than surrender but was over-ruled by what was left of his crew and died soon after.

won notoriety for barricading Tapeley against Ministry of Agriculture officials to protect his pedigree herd of Aberdeen Angus cattle during the 2001 Foot and Mouth crisis.

On the opposite side of the estuary from Tapeley, in the midst of Northam Burrows north of Bideford, is the oldest golf course in the country. The **Royal North Devon Golf Course** also has the oldest ladies' club in the world. It is regarded by locals as the 'St Andrews of England'. The Royal North Devon is ranked number 61 in *Golf Monthly*'s Top 120 Courses, and visitors are welcome.

ROYAL NORTH DEVON GOLF COURSE, EX39 1HD; ☎ 01237 477598; www.royal-northdevongolfclub.co.uk Price: a one-off 30 min lesson with one of the club professionals costs from £17.50.

Wet weather

You'll see plenty of posters and leaflets advertising **The Big Sheep**. It's an imaginative and extensive undercover family attraction with a sense of humour that includes sheep races with little soft

THE BIG SHEEP, just off A39, two miles west of Bideford; ☎ 01237 472366; www.the-bigsheep.co.uk. Entry: prices vary with season, adults from £5, children under 3ft free; open Easter to Oct: daily 10am–6pm.

toy jockeys on their backs, sheepdogs trying to round up ducks and the Ewe-topia soft-play zone. You'll also get chances to bottle-feed lambs, cuddle kittens and puppies and learn the secrets of horse whispering.

What to do with children...

When they've had enough of The Big Sheep, Lundy and Westward Ho beaches, try **Atlantic Village** – a glossy factory shopping complex rather incongruously sited in the windswept heights to the west. For families there is an additional attraction: there are excellent facilities for children to run wild at the **Atlantic Adventure Zone**. It includes a full-size galleon to clamber around, maze (claimed to be Devon's biggest hedge maze), crazy golf, trampolines, soft play, train, bouncy slide and pirate shows in high season.

ATLANTIC VILLAGE, off A39, 3 miles west of Bideford; ☎ 01237 422544; www.atlanticvillage.co.uk
Entry: £7.50; open until 6pm except 4.30pm Sun, 8pm Thur.

MILKY WAY ADVENTURE PARK, just off the A39 west of Bideford; ☎ 01237 431255; www.themilkyway.co.uk
Entry: £6–£9; online discounts available; open Apr to Oct: daily 10.30am–6pm; winter: open weekends and school holidays 11am–5pm.

Further west **Milky Way Adventure Park** is the ultimate farm diversification – a 205-acre farm turned into an all-weather theme park. It has saved many a rainy family holiday. There isn't really a theme – just plenty of park. The activities easily last a day, including Devon's biggest rollercoaster, dodgems, huge adventure play area for children and adults, under-5s play area, falconry displays, ferret racing, owl show, pets corner, farm museum, railway, maze, archery centre, putting course, golf nets and laser target shooting.

Appledore language

Outsiders to Devon, or 'grockels' as the locals will call you behind your back, may struggle to understand the local accents anywhere in the county. But in Appledore they may have the most trouble of all...

Over the centuries the tight-knit community of fishermen and boat-builders evolved a vocabulary of its own. Even people from Bideford just 3 miles away can be baffled by Appledore-speak. In 2007 the village started holding lessons in their language, mainly to preserve it in the face of an invasion of outsiders' holiday homes. Here are few Appledorian words to give you a taster:

ory tory – a posh person, *zamzoid* – rotten, *fraped up* – makeshift, *orts* – left

And how to avoid children

BURTON ART GALLERY,
EX39 2QQ; ☎ 01237 471455;
www.burtonartgallery.co.uk
Entry: free; open Easter to Oct: Mon
to Sat 10am–5pm, Sun 2–5pm; winter: closes at 4pm.

Burton Art Gallery and Museum in Victoria Park is a surprisingly good little museum and gallery founded by local grocer and philanthropist Thomas Burton in memory of his daughter. Mary Burton was a talented artist who died young – some of her drawings are on display, including one of her father. There is a changing programme of art and craft exhibitions, coffee shop, displays about the history of Bideford bridge, Sir Richard Grenville, the townswomen who were the last 'witches' to be executed in England and fabulously decorated cider jugs – a 17th-century local speciality.

 ## Entertainment

There is often live local music in pubs around Bideford including the **Blacksmiths Arms** in Torrington Street, **Joiners Arms** in the Market Place and **The Tavern in the Port** at the west end of Bideford Bridge. The town's clubs draw crowds from a wide area but don't expect big city sophistication. **Caesar's Palace** in King Street (☎ 01237 478022) is thought by locals to be the town's 'main nightclub'. But at the time of writing, the **Palladium Club** (☎ 01237 478860; www.palladiumclub.co.uk) in the town centre is running live music nights up to four times a week and some of these you will of heard of, bands such as John Otway and Nine Below Zero.

The week-long **Bideford Folk Festival** in August includes many free sessions. And across Devon, Bideford is renowned for **New Year's Eve on the Quay**, when thousands traditionally celebrate in fancy dress.

overs, *missledraught* – small things, *eel taps* – chips, *cat's mother* – an ory tory with a high opinion of themselves, *miniter* – very clean, *hannah macdonald* – dressed up (after the name of an old lifeboat), *westby stranner* – someone from the west side of the village

Walter Fowler, one of the few who can still speak pure Appledorian, was born in the village in 1943 and has lived there all his life. He recently told the *North Devon Journal*: 'There are only a few of us left that still speak the language and it would be wonderful to see it resurrected.'

The Lundy experience

The **Lundy** Shore Office is on Bideford's Quay and the **MS Oldenberg** ferries passengers to the island from here and from Ilfracombe between March and October. It's a handsome polished brass-and-wood type of ship with a shop, café and bar on board. On a calm day the trip is a great two-hour cruise and you'll enjoy views of the North Devon coast. On a rougher day it's... a more challenging experience. (☎ 01271 863636; www.lundyisland.co.uk; www.landmarktrust.org.uk; day return £30 adults, £15 children; sailings dependent on weather).

Lundy is 12 miles off-shore and you'll find a population of just 26 humans, hundreds of sheep and thousands of seabirds. It's just 3 miles long, half a mile wide, but seems bigger when you trek around it.

You'll find plenty here to keep you going for a day or longer, including wandering the formidable cliffs, exploring the rugged grassland on top, poking around the castle

The tiny island of Lundy is well worth a visit

and lighthouses, looking for puffins (spring), sharks (mid-summer) and seals (best in autumn), or just escaping from the rest of the world for a while. Visitors get up to all sorts of activities, like diving, rock climbing, fishing, walking or painting. You'll have a chance to learn about the island's colourful history, which ranges from being a pirates' lair to a religious retreat. And the granite for the London Embankment was once quarried here.

The granite was also used to build the island's pub, the **Marisco Tavern**. This is the heart of any visit, with its own beer and wholesome food. The **Lundy Shop** is interesting too and here you can buy cuts of Lundy lamb. This meat from animals grazed exclusively on wild pastures of untreated grasses is said to produce a unique flavour. You can usually sample some on the menu at the Marisco too.

In the winter, an extravagant six-minute **helicopter trip** costs £87 for an adult return, and £46 for a child, but you have to stay over on the island. You can get to Lundy on private charter boats from various spots along the north coast. They're usually quicker and cheaper than the Oldenberg but you have to pay a landing fee of £5 when you get there (see Clovelly chapter).

It's possible to stay on the island. You can either camp or rent one of the historic buildings from the Landmark Trust, see *The best... places to stay* below.

The best... PLACES TO STAY

HOTEL

Commodore Hotel 🍴

Marine Parade, Instow EX39 4JN
☎ **01271 860347**
www.commodore-instow.co.uk

Pay a little extra for one of the new luxury 'Marine bedrooms' – the estuary views make them seem more luxurious than they really are. The sunsets above Appledore on the shore opposite will help you forget the anonymous décor and rather high prices.

Price: B&B from £66 per person per night.

Yeolden House Hotel 🐾 🍴

Durrant Lane, Northam EX39 2RL
☎ **01237 474400**
www.yeoldonhousehotel.co.uk

Red carpets, stained glass, four-poster, rich floral wallpaper and polished wood make this Victorian home more like a mini country house hotel in gardens overlooking the Torridge above the river, and there is an impressive restaurant.

Price: B&B from £72.50 for a single; from £110 for a double.

B & B

The Mount 🐾 ♿

Northdown Road, Bideford EX39 3LP
☎ **01237 473748**
www.themount1.cjb.net

This eight-bedroomed Georgian cottage has an immaculate period ground floor and modern bedrooms upstairs.

Price: B&B from £30 per person per night.

SELF-CATERING

Huish Moor 🐾 🍴

Huish Lane, near Instow EX39 4LR
☎ **01271 860450**
www.silverstreamukfishing.com

This farmhouse offers the choice of B&B or self-catering in a converted barn. Décor is a bit uninspiring but the views are great from the hills behind Instow – you'll see Lundy on a clear day. Food includes homemade cream teas, local sausages and bacon, Dartmouth smoked kippers, fruit, eggs and jam from the farm, and fish caught by the owner. He also offers fly fishing tuition and trips.

Price: B&B £32–£50 per person, self-catering £300–£700 per week, sleeps seven; short breaks available.

SELF-CATERING, B&B AND CAMPING

Lundy Island 🏊 ⚓ 🍴 🚗

☎ **01628 825925**
www.landmarktrust.org.uk

There are 23 quirkily historic buildings on Lundy offering self-catering accommodation, ranging from a 13th-century castle to a lookout hut without electricity. Prices range from £147 for a week in the one-bedded Old Light Cottage in January, to £2,569 for an August week in Millcombe, a Georgian mansion that sleeps 12. Short breaks are available out of the high season from around £30 a night and B&B is occasionally offered at the last minute if there are unbooked properties. You get breakfast in the pub. Contact the Lundy Shore office in Bideford (see panel).

Camping is also available on the island from £7 per night, but be warned it can get pretty wet and windy out there.

The best... FOOD AND DRINK

There is lots of fly-fishing in rivers around here so look for fresh trout and salmon. And as with the rest of the Devon coast there will always be seafood on offer. Bideford is surrounded by rural farming land with a strong theme of traditional farming practice, which means some excellent quality local meat, veg and dairy products are available. The town itself has a less gastronomic tradition with a plethora of Chinese (and other) takeaways.

▶ Staying in

- **Barton Farm Shop** at South Stroxworthy, west of Bideford, is tricky to find but is an honest source of home-reared beef, lamb, and locally sourced chicken, pork and vegetables (☎ 01237 431690; www.bartonfarmshop.co.uk).
- **Marshford Organic Foods** at Northam only sells local organic produce – vegetables, salad and herbs from their own gardens and eggs, dairy and meat from other local farms (☎ 01237 477160; www.marshford.co.uk).
- **Burgess Farm Butchers** in Butcher's Row at the pannier market in Bideford, (www.burgessfamilybutchers.co.uk or ☎ 01237 473957) sells pork and bacon from its own herd of free-range pigs plus other high-quality meat.
- Another well-thought-of local meat supplier is **Honeys** family butchers in Mill Street who also rear their own livestock (☎ 01237 463334).

At **Blackwell's Pastys** in Meddon Street, Bideford (☎ 01237 4721103) you can pick up some fresh local holiday snacks. Andrew Blackwell's handmade savouries use only local produce and have a huge following in the area. They're so popular they're 'exported' to Cornwall. A standard traditional pasty is £1.60 with 20% discount if you're hungry enough to buy more than 12.

🍷 Drinking

Like the **Royal George**, **The Beaver** in Irsha Street, Appledore, does good seafood. This quirky-looking place also has St Austell beer and local farm cider. The quiet and unspoilt **Heavitree Arms** in Mill Street, Bideford has colourful floor tiles bearing a striking resemblance to the cargo of an Italian ship that ran aground in the Torridge many years ago. The **Kings Arms** on the Quay has low ceilings with beams and real ales. Across the estuary the **Wayfarer** on Instow's waterfront serves beer from the cask and has its own boat available for fishing trips.

🍴 EATING OUT

FINE DINING
Yeolden House Hotel
Durrant Lane, Northam EX39 2RL
☎ **01237 474400**
www.yeoldonhousehotel.co.uk

A mini country house hotel overlooking the Torridge, with an AA rosette restaurant run by the chef/owner who boasts a collection of over 2,000 cookbooks. It costs £27.50 for three courses.

9 The Quay
Appledore EX39 1QS
☎ **01237 473355**
www.9thequay.co.uk

Downstairs is an art gallery and coffee shop, but upstairs in this pink-painted waterfront building is where serious diners head. Ask for a window table for the estuary views. Local specialities include Clovelly crab Thermidor and Taw mussels. Three courses cost £30.

RESTAURANT
The Boathouse
Marine Parade, Instow EX39 4JJ
☎ **01271 861292**
www.instow.net/boathouse/

This waterfront seafood restaurant and bar has great views across Torridge and a varied menu from chicken and chips to fresh local lobster. Three courses cost about £20.

Bensons on the Quay
20 The Quay
Appledore EX39 1QS
☎ **01237 424093**
www.bensonsonthequay.com

Bensons specialises in fish landed on the quay outside – the menu could include sea bass, brill, turbot, plaice, John Dory, lobster, crab or oysters. And there are great views across the estuary. Three courses cost about £25.

GASTROPUB
Westleigh Inn
Westleigh EX39 4NL
☎ **01271 860867**
www.westleigh-devon.gov.uk/sites/westleigh_inn.htm

This is an ancient whitewashed pub in a picturesque village above Instow that serves great value home-cooked pub grub like sausage and mash and ham, egg and chips as well as crab and salmon tartlets and lamb on leek mash. It's very popular with locals, so it's best to book. Three courses cost around £20.

Royal George
Irsha Street, Appledore EX39 1RY
☎ **01237 474335**

This old quayside pub's restaurant is built into the seawall. It's small and very popular, so again, it's best to book. There is a good mix of pub grub and fresh seafood. It's recommended by Bideford-based Liberal Democrat politician Baroness Sue Miller. Three courses cost about £20.

Visitor information

Tourist information centres:
Bideford Tourist Information Centre,
Victoria Park, ☎ 01237 477676,
bidefordtic@torridge.gov.uk.
Hospitals: There is a minor injury
unit at *Bideford Hospital,* Abbot-
sham Road, ☎ 01237 420200; 24
hour A & E facilities are available at
North Devon District Hospital,
Raleigh Park, Barnstaple EX31 4JB,
☎ 01271 322577.
Supermarkets: the biggest is
Morrisons just round the corner
heading north from Bideford Quay.
Bike rental: Bideford Bicycle Hire,
☎ 01237 424123.
Taxis: Quay Cars, Bideford,
☎ 01237 472027.

FURTHER AFIELD

Westward Ho! is the only place in Britain named after a novel and whose name
includes an exclamation mark. Westward Ho! has a long sandy beach with a
pebble strip behind, then an expanse of dunes and marshes. Although the
waves can be big, the sands are flat and wide and it's often called Devon's
safest beach.

The 2 mile stretch is popular with surfers, watersporters and adventure sport
seekers of all kinds. There are plenty of hire shops and instructors on hand.

The town itself is a disappointing mix of cheap amusement arcades and peb-
ble-dash bungalows, Victorian villas with UPVC windows and a smattering of
swish new luxury apartments. There is not much to detain visitors, but the area
behind the beach is **Northam Burrows**, a Site of Special Scientific Interest
because of the distinctive two-mile pebble ridge between the beach and the
burrows, and because of rare plants found here. The Burrows are common
land still grazed by the 'Potwallopers' of the ancient manor of
Northam. Between May and September there is a £3 toll charge for cars but
it's worth it for the walks when you get there. And at the heart of the Burrows
is a small visitor centre and shop.

Clovelly is an archetypal Devon village

CLOVELLY

It's such an important, iconic and simply wonderful place, we've decided to give little Clovelly its own section. The flower-decked whitewashed cottages tumbling down a narrow chasm to the sea must be Devon's most reproduced image, out-scoring even Haytor and Exeter Cathedral. It's so photogenic it has become one of the most famous village images in Europe.

And if the whole village seems like it's stuck in the feudal era, in some ways it is. Clovelly is all owned by 'Lord of the Manor' John Rous. John was educated at Gordonstoun Public School, like Prince Charles, and qualified as an accountant. He is a Deputy Lord Lieutenant of Devon (along with Noel Edmonds) and his family have owned the village since 1738. He and his Indian wife and their daughters live in Clovelly Court, the grand stone house behind the church. Its **Walled Victorian Garden** is open to visitors. See how the maritime microclimate allows peaches, melons and apricots to grow and flowers to bloom year round.

In some ways Clovelly is totally unspoilt – there are no modern buildings, amusements or racy bars. The Rous family are not as strict as the National Trust would be, however, so there are a few TV aerials and overhead cables. But in many ways, Clovelly *is* completely spoilt. It's a museum village maintained purely for and by tourists.

In summer there is an enormous flood of visitors trooping up and down the steep cobbled path, peering in windows, eating ice-creams and buying postcards. No-one who lives here can have a 'normal' life.

Yet out of season or when the crowds have left for the evening, Clovelly can be magical. Sea mist often hangs in the thick woods either side of the village, gulls wheel around looking for crumbs dropped during the day, the cobbles and slates shine wet in the damp air and, beyond the harbour, a bad sea

Clovelly through the ages

Clovelly was there for centuries before anyone thought it was cute or pretty. The sturdy 14th-century breakwater of gigantic boulders created the only safe harbour in the notorious shipwreck corridor between Appledore and Boscastle in Cornwall.

Not only was the village impossibly remote and usually accessed by sea, it was impossibly steep too. Horse and carriages couldn't get up the challenging street made from pebbles, just as cars couldn't now. Pack donkeys used to haul everything up, right until the 1990s. Before tourism, the community survived from fishing, smuggling, piracy and wrecking (luring ships onto the rocks, then plundering the cargo).

Then the Victorians arrived. It was all the fault of writer Charles Kingsley. He was bought up in Clovelly because his father was rector. He returned as an adult and wrote much of *Westward Ho!* here – a massive seafaring novel that became a best-seller. Kingsley's other big success, *The Water Babies*, was inspired by Clovelly too.

It's not unusual for artists to be awestruck by Clovelly. Novelist Charles Dickens, painters Whistler and Turner, and former poet laureate Ted Hughes came to Clovelly and left raving about the place. Turner painted the wonderful 'Clovelly Bay', now in the Irish National Gallery.

Kingsley's books encouraged ordinary Victorians to visit. It wasn't easy, so most came on steamships from resorts like Ilfracombe. What they saw is little different emphasises how remote and precarious life once was here.

Whatever your thoughts about Clovelly, it's probably Devon's most vital sight. If you can see through the car park charges and camera-toting crowds, there is a glimpse here of a real Devon seaside village from long ago before tourism, before second homes and before the car. It's a unique eye-opener and can help you understand much of the spirit of the rest of Devon too.

PARKING COSTS, £4.95 per adult, £3.25 per child, or £14.50 for a family (2 adults/2 children). Covers entry to the Visitor Centre (☎ 01237 431781, open daily 9am–6pm summer, 10am–3.30pm winter, whether you like it or not.

WHAT TO SEE AND DO

Turn off the A39, 11 miles west of Bideford at Clovelly Cross. There is no parking or even stopping all the way into Clovelly, where you are shepherded into the official car park at the top of the cliff. It's handy but very pricey, considering you are just stopping outside a village for a walk.

The cavernous **Visitor Centre** contains gift shops and cafés but has the great benefit of keeping the worst of the commercialised nonsense out of the village itself. Once you've got over the shock of the entry fee some of the exhibits are interesting, especially the 20-minute film about Clovelly's history.

You can avoid this charge by walking along the coast path for about four miles from either direction... or simply arrive out-of-hours. There is a car park attendant until 7pm in the high season, collecting money even when the Visitor Centre is shut. But the parking is open 24 hours, so you can visit at all other times for free.

The other visitors who get away without paying are those staying overnight at the New Inn, Red Lion or one of the B&Bs, and visitors taking fishing trips, who can use a fisherman's car park hidden in the woods.

Fair weather

Visiting Clovelly is simply a matter of a walk through a village with around 80 cottages. But it is made special by the plunging, twisting stone **High Street** that drops 400ft in half a mile. You totter between, round and under impossibly cute 16th-century cottages and their colourful gardens with trailing fuchsias, geraniums and nasturtiums. It's so steep you can see down the chimneys of cottages below. Don't be too shy to explore the narrow side passageways too; you'll peep behind village homes and see carefully tended vegetable patches teetering on the cliffside.

Clovelly is Devon's most inspiring sight

The best... PLACES TO STAY

HOTEL

Red Lion Hotel 🔋 🟦
Clovelly, EX39 5TF
☎ **01237 431237**
www2.clovelly.co.uk/red_lion

The ancient inn perched on the quay is pitched slightly upmarket of the New Inn. The extra few pounds buys waves splashing your windows in a storm. There is an ambitious French chef and bedrooms have an interior designer's feel, with lots of cream paint and quality fabrics.

Price: B&B from £58.50 per person per night.

INN

New Inn Hotel 🔋 🟦
Clovelly, EX39 5TQ
☎ **01237 431303**
www.newinn-clovelly.co.uk

Halfway up the High Street, this looks like the definitive Olde Worlde pub but has been renovated inside in a refreshing William Morris style. Some rooms have balconies, all have great views. And you have the unique memory of your luggage brought to the hotel on a sledge.

Price: B&B from £51.50 per person per night.

Note: there are also two tiny B&Bs in the village: Donkey Shoe Cottage (☎ 01237 431601; donkeyshoecottage.co.uk, from £23 per person per night) and 55 The Quay, from £55 per person (☎ 01237 431436).

You can't help admiring the villagers through the centuries who have coped with this life on an angle. With typical Devonshire understatement they call the High Street 'Up-along' or 'Down-along'... depending on the direction they're heading. They used to use donkeys but now pull their own wooden sledges to carry everything home, from supermarket shopping to rubbish bags.

On the way down you'll see the former load-lugging donkeys' sanctuary; a restored 1930s fisherman's cottage; a pottery workshop and silk shop; two chapels, one pub, the Charles Kingsley Museum, and a tea shop and a pasty shop.

Don't turn around before you reach the bottom. There is a harbour, pebble beach, lifeboat station, a few fishing boats and lobster pots down there – and it's the only place to see the waterfall pouring down the cliff. Village legend says that Merlin was born in the cave behind the falls. And those bollards on the quay – they are upturned cannons, taken from a Spanish Armada ship, or so says another village legend.

Wet weather

Watch out for those slippery cobbles! Wear sensible shoes and be pleased that rain is keeping the crowds away. When you get to the bottom, dry out in the bar of the Red Lion. If you really can't face the walk, there is a **Land Rover taxi** from Easter to October that chugs you down the service road to the west of the village (£2.50). Hotel guests can use it with their luggage too.

What to do with children...

They'll like the donkeys and the beach but the steep village trek may be a struggle, especially for prams and pushchairs. Best buy an ice cream/sweets/toy at the start and that may keep them happy while you're gawping at the views.

And how to avoid children

If you need a day away, there is a choice of intrepid **boat trips** from the harbour. Part-time potter Clive Pearson's boat 'Jessica Hettie' for example, runs trips to Lundy twice as fast and cheaper than the 'official' MS Oldenberg (it only takes an hour for £30 return) or a chance to dive and swim with seals off Hartland Point (£42.50). Clive is proud that his boat was once featured on Bill Oddie's TV wildlife programme (☎ 01237 431405/07774 190359; www.clovelly-charters.ukf.net).

The best... FOOD AND DRINK

This is essentially one big tourist attraction so you're lucky it's not just a few fast food outlets. In fact there is only a pasty shop that qualifies as fast food. Instead why not try a traditional cream tea at the **Cottage Tea Rooms** or **Temple Bar Cottage**. For a main meal or drink, your choice is either the traditional English fare at the **New Inn** (three-course dinner costs £20) or the more adventurous continental style of the **Red Lion** (three courses cost £25).

Visitor information

Tourist information centres:
Clovelly Visitor Centre,
☎ 01237 431781.
Websites: www.clovelly.co.uk.
Hospitals: The nearest hospital providing 24 hr A & E facilities is in Barnstaple.

Supermarkets: There are no supermarkets in Clovelly, but there is a general Store/Post Office on 23 High Street.

TORRINGTON AND NORTH-WEST DEVON

The rolling hills of this vast north-west corner of Devon form one of the least spoilt, least crowded parts of the county. Apart from Dartmoor, it's among the quietest parts of the south of England. In an area bigger than Greater London, there are only three small towns (Torrington, Holsworthy and Hatherleigh) – the rest of the space is made up of a network of ancient lanes linking scores of scattered villages and hundreds of remote farms. More than any exciting resorts, modern attractions or Michelin stars, it's this simple unchanged way of working and living close to the land that forms much of the attraction of Devon's north-west.

The far corner around Hartland is especially wild, windswept and rugged, with an edge-of-the-world feel. Further south the landscape becomes more gentle but never lush, as it heads towards Dartmoor, looming on the horizon.

WHAT TO SEE AND DO

 Fair weather

No local uses the prefix 'great' but **Torrington** deserves it. This is one of the undiscovered gems of Devon. You'll find a small, quiet, historic town perched high on an inland cliff with memorable views down to the **River Torridge** below. The streets of the **old town centre**, loop round a Victorian **covered market**, porticoed **town hall**, lively **arts centre** and ancient pubs. Through side streets and alleys you emerge at the top of the hillside to gasp at the great view south.

In fact, to the south and west you can step straight from the town centre into **The Commons** – 365 acres of wild heath given to the townspeople 900 years ago. It's still an unkempt area of woods, wild pasture and pathways leading down to the river.

Torrington's rebuilt **St Michael's Church** is worth a peep. See if you can tell the original medieval bits from the post-explosion reconstruction. Note that the list of vicars on the wall includes Thomas Wolsey, later a powerful cardinal in Henry VIII's reign.

Further south, the town of **Hatherleigh** is prettier, but smaller. Its rows of cob and thatched houses climb the hill above the Torridge. There are pubs, craft galleries and teashops to browse and good walks to explore. There has been a livestock market here on Tuesdays since 1693.

Holsworthy is a bigger town but more earthy working community. The busy

Torrington and the Civil War

Torrington's hilltop location was strategically vital during the English Civil War. This Royalist stronghold was known as 'Cavalier Town' as the population sided with the King, while all the countryside around was Parliamentarian. It took until the last big bloody battle of the war for it to fall to the Roundheads in 1646. King Charles was captured shortly afterwards and the war was over.

The gruesome battle for Torrington involved 17,000 men fighting through the streets: Royalists under Lord Hopton, the New Model Army under General Thomas Fairfax and Oliver Cromwell.

Around 200 Royalist soldiers were rounded up and imprisoned in the parish church. The Roundheads didn't known it had been the Cavaliers' arsenal and there were still 80 barrels of gunpowder hidden inside. No-one knows how or why it was set off but the whole lot went up, all 200 Royalists were killed and the church destroyed. The cobbled mound in the new St Michael's churchyard is the burial place of what was left of the Royalists.

Market Square is at the heart of everything, surrounded by colour-washed houses, shops and pubs.

Then there are the villages, too many to list here, but you'll find interesting pubs, quirky shops, old churches and lovely walks at most of them. **Dolton**, for example, has a church with a 1,000-year-old stone front and the walking trails of **Halsdon nature reserve** along the banks of the Torridge nearby. If you're very lucky, you may spot otters (☎ 01392 279244; www.devonwildlife trust.org).

Shebbear has a quaint village square with **The Devil's Stone** (see *The best... places to stay*) pub at one end, the church at the other. That's where you'll find the '**Devil's Stone**' in the churchyard. This ancient and hefty pagan relic was 'placed there by the devil' according to village legend. He challenged villagers to move it or their village would be destroyed. So every fifth of November, there is a peal of bells from the church, then ringers come outside to tackle the stone with sticks and crowbars. Once it's turned over they return inside to ring another round of bells.

The village of **Sheepwash** west of Hatherleigh still looks perfectly Olde Worlde today with white-washed thatched cottages round a green with cherry trees. The **Half Moon** pub has a log fire hung with horse brasses and homely restaurant (see *The best... places to stay*). And the church at the tiny hamlet of **Monkeigh** has an intriguing monument to the Lord Chief Justice of England in the 15th century who was shot when he was taking a night-time walk in his estate by his own gamekeepers who thought he was a poacher.

The rural charm of Rosemoor Gardens

ROSEMOOR GARDENS, Great Torrington EX38 8PH; south of Torrington on A3124 Exeter Road; ☎ 01805 624067; www.rhs.org.uk/whatson/gardens/rosemoor. Entry: adults £6, children 6–16 £2; open Apr to Sept: daily 10am–6pm; Oct to Mar: daily 10am–5pm.

Formerly the grounds of a wealthy family's fishing lodge, **Rosemoor Gardens** have grown under the Royal Horticultural Society's guidance into one of the great West Country gardens. Its wonderful setting in the Torridge valley features year-round colour in its formal, lakeside and semi-tropical gardens, including a rose garden with 2,000 roses and a surprisingly picturesque 'bog garden'. Rosemoor also includes a shop, plant centre and restaurant.

The well-known **Tarka Trail** walking and cycling track runs for 30 miles from Braunton to Meeth using the railway lines that were closed in the 1960s (☎ 01237 423655; www.devon.gov.uk /tarkatrail). The popular route passes through the countryside where Tarka, Henry Williamson's fictional otter, was supposed to live. Torrington is a good place to pick up the trail. It's six miles north to Bideford along the river, 11 miles south to the village of Meeth through unspoilt countryside.

Bikes can be hired next to the trail at **Torridge Cycle Hire**, in the Old Station Yard a mile to the east of town (☎ 01805 622633). The Victorian station is now **The Puffing Billy** (☎ 01805 623050) with food and drink served all day in the former waiting room.

The Tarka website above includes 21 downloadable audio clips for mp3 players relating to specific spots with information boards along the trail recorded by local conservation workers.

The Tarka Trail

TAMAR LAKES, EX23 9SB;
☎ 01288 321712;
www.swlakestrust.org.uk
Price: parking £2 all day.

Further west, right on Devon/Cornwall border, are the two **Tamar lakes**, with well organised sports and leisure facilities. The Upper Lake has a watersports centre with sailing, windsurfing and kayaking tuition and hire. The teashop (☎ 01288 321607) overlooks the lake, a visitor centre explains the flora and fauna. There is a children's play area and a campsite here too (£5 per adult per night). A path round the lake provides an hour's picturesque walk and coarse anglers can buy permits to fish here. Lower Tamar lake is smaller and managed as a nature reserve. There are walking trails, bird hides and picnic tables. Both lakes have car parks and linking footpaths.

 # Wet weather

DARTINGTON CRYSTAL,
Torrington EX38 7AN; ☎ 01805 626262; www.dartington.co.uk.
Entry: adults £5, OAPs £2, children free; open all year: Mon to Fri 9.30am–5pm, Sat 10am–5pm, Sun 10am–4pm.

There are a couple of options in this part of Devon if the rains come. **Dartington Crystal** on the north side of Torrington is a modern glassworks where you'll be able to watch craftsmen blowing contemporary glassware and of course, buy as much of it as you want afterwards.

Another slightly more eccentric option is **Barometer World**, a north-west Devon oddity. Retired bank manager Edwin Banfield set up an eccentric collection of weather predicting devices more than 30 years ago. It's now the largest barometer collection in the world and includes barmy examples such as the Tempest Prognosticator from 1851 that used live leeches to tell if a storm was coming.

BAROMETER WORLD,
Quicksilver Barn, Merton, EX20 3DS;
☎ 01805 603443; www.barometer-world.co.uk;
Entry: adults £2.50, children £1;
open Tues to Fri 9am–5pm, also first and third Sat of the month.

 # What to do with children

GNOME RESERVE, West Putford, near Bradworthy EX22 7XE;
☎ 01409 241435; www.gnomereserve.co.uk Entry: adults £2.75, children 3–16 £2.25; open Mar to Oct: daily 10am–6pm.

It will be hard resisting the pull of **Milky Way Theme Park** (see Bideford chapter) but if you're determined to stay in this area try the bizarre **Gnome Reserve** at West Putford.

It's best to suspend disbelief, put on your free gnome hat and set off into the woods to enjoy one of Devon's strangest attractions. Artist Ann Fawssett Atkin has made more than 1,000 gnomes and pixies, who can be seen fishing, posing and loafing on toadstools around the gardens, which

Shoot monsters at Dragon Archery

include a wildflower area with 250 labelled specimens. It's so surreal that the Reserve was proposed by the *Daily Telegraph* as a candidate for The Turner Prize.

And if that's not weird enough, how about the **Dragon Archery Centre**, near Holsworthy? This is a serious archery experience that's only suitable for over 8s. You spend half a day learning archery, then shooting monstrous velociraptors, orcs and finally – even more horrific – French knights.

Perhaps the least eccentric place to take the children is **Torrington 1646**... but you may still find yourself dressing in civil war armour and talking to a man boiling up herbal remedies in a cauldron. You'll find this quirky attraction at Torrington's Castle Hill car park. There are some odd displays and chaotic re-enactments, but the best bits are when guides in period costume tell you about their lives. They'll help you try on costumes and show you the weapons, herbs, food, clothes, medicine, cooking and town gossip of the time.

DRAGON ARCHERY, Westcott Cottage, Holsworthy EX22 7YQ; 4 miles east of Holsworthy; [tel]0800 0372466; www.dragonarcherycentre.co.uk . Entry: adults £29, children £14; open all year.

TORRINGTON 1646, Castle Hill, Torrington EX38 8AA; ☎ 01805 626146; www.torrington-1646.co.uk Entry: adults £6.95, children 5–16 £4.95; open Mar to Sept: Mon to Fri 10am–5pm, Sat 10am–3pm; Oct/Nov/Feb: Tues to Fri 10am–4.30pm.

Entertainment

Torrington's **Plough Arts Centre** in Fore Street has impressive listings of films, events and live music. There is a nice café inside too (☎ 01805 62424; www.plough-arts.org). A charity group called Torrington Cavaliers periodically build huge full-size wooden replicas on the Commons. The complete Houses of Parliament and *HMS Victory* have been highlights of the past decade. Then they set fire to them in front of huge crowds, fireworks and a carnival-like atmosphere. If you hear of a **'burning'** from locals go along... it's a spectacular night out.

The best... **PLACES TO STAY**

HOTEL

Court Barn Hotel

Clawton, Holsworthy EX22 6PS
☎ **01409 271 219**
www.hotels-devon.com

This charming but old-fashioned country house hotel sits in five-acre gardens and is furnished with antiques. The atmosphere is helped by log fires and candlelit dining in the AA rosette restaurant. Painting courses are available and walkers can order pack-lunches.

Price: B&B from £50 per room per night.

Blagdon Manor

Near Ashwater, EX21 5DF
☎ **01409 211224**
www.blagdon.com

Blagdon is a tastefully decorated dog-friendly country house hotel and restaurant. It's a Grade II listed house with lots of cushions and cream paint, ancient oak beams and flagstones but modern conservatory, set in 20 acres, 4 miles south of Holsworthy.

Price: B&B from £125 per double room per night.

INN

The Devil's Stone Inn

Shebbear EX21 5RU
☎ **01409 281210**
www.devilsstoneinn.com

Lovely old flagstone-and-beams pub with eight en suite letting rooms, simply furnished with wooden floors and white bed linen. It's said to be connected to the church by a secret tunnel and is one of the 12 most haunted pubs in Britain. The pub owns prime fly-fishing rights on nearby Rivers Torridge and Oakment. These are available exclusively to guests.

Price: B&B £35 per person per night.

Half Moon Inn

Sheepwash EX21 5NE
☎ **01409 231376**
www.halfmoonsheepwash.co.uk

Similar fishing arrangements are available just down the lanes at the Half Moon at Sheepwash, another whitewashed pub in a very rural village. All the food is homemade in the pub kitchen, apart from pasties from the local baker. Dinner is announced by a gong at 8pm.

Price: B&B from £45 per person per night.

FARM STAY

Buttermore Farm

Milton Damerel EX22 7PB
☎ **01409 261314**
www.buttermorefarm.co.uk

Why not stay in a converted duck house? It's on a pretty 17th-century farm with award-winning cattle and home-cooked food, sourced locally or fresh from the farm.

Price: B&B £40 for a single; £60 for a double); children under 12 half price, under 2s free. Evening meal costs £15.

SELF-CATERING

Combe Cottage

Peppercombe
c/o The National Trust
☎ **0870 4584422**
www.nationaltrustcottages.co.uk

The National Trust rents three pretty former Victorian coastguard cottages that are hidden in a wooded valley (or 'combe') quarter of a mile from the rocky beach. Combe Cottage is the biggest, sleeping four in one double and two singles.

Price: from £167 for three nights in January to £815 for a week in August.

The local independent website (www.great-torringtoncrier.co.uk) is a good place to check on what's happening.

For Torrington's **May Fair**, on the first Thursday of May, schools close and children dance round a maypole outside the town hall and a May Queen is crowned. There is a procession and a banner hung across the High Street saying: 'Us be plazed to see 'ee '.

It's a bit more racy at **Hatherleigh Carnival** on the second Saturday in November – the highlight is when flaming tar barrels are pulled through streets. With at least 300 floats, the procession is one of Devon's biggest parades. Traditionally 52 flaming torches accompany floats, one for each week of the year, while a frame carrying 12 flaming torches (one for each month) leads the way.

In early July Holsworthy holds the three-day **St Peter's Fair**, which includes live music, processions and the presentation of a 'Pretty Maid' to the towns-people. There is a major one-day **agricultural show** at the end of July.

The best... FOOD AND DRINK

The food of north-west Devon reflects its rural setting. There is very little con-temporary cuisine but masses of traditional fresh local produce. The quality of the meat, dairy and vegetables are particularly high. For self-caterers buying food for picnics, barbecues and cooking, the quality is temptingly high, even if the choice is limited. Holsworthy and Torrington have a range of takeaways, elsewhere eating out usually centres round the village pub.

Shopping in Torrington is a delight

EATING OUT

FINE DINING

Percy's
Virginstow EX21 5EA
☎ **01409 211236**
www.percys.co.uk

Enjoy acclaimed gourmet food in this stylish restaurant-with-rooms. Dine amid oak floors, a zinc bar and crisp table linen. Specialities include chef Tina Bricknell-Webb's home-reared organic lamb and pork, home-grown vegetables, game and wild mushrooms from the grounds, and locally sourced meat and fish. Three courses cost £40. Also luxurious accommodation is available in a converted granary (from £125 per person per night).

Blagdon Manor
Near Ashwater EX21 5DF
☎ **01409 211224**
www.blagdon.com

In this country house hotel restaurant, dishes feature ample local produce and modern presentation. Children under 12 are not permitted. Open to non-residents Tuesday to Saturday for dinner (three courses £35) and Wednesday to Sunday for lunch (two courses £17).

GASTROPUB

Black Horse Inn
High Street, Torrington EX38 8HN
☎ **01805 622121**

Explore this ancient black-and-white coaching inn at the heart of Torrington that was a Civil War headquarters for first one side, then the other. There is still a 17th-century atmosphere with black-oak panelled rooms inside, real ales and hearty pub food.

Hoops Inn
Horns Cross, EX39 5DL
☎ **01237 451222**
www.hoopsinn.co.uk

A bar snack or a three-course dinner in the AA rosette restaurant? Eat outside in the garden or inside the thatched pub? Whatever, this inn has a good reputation with locals – and the French-trained chef is the landlord's daughter. A three-course dinner is £30, and bar snacks cost from £9.

(There is also rather pricey B&B accommodation from £65 for a single and £95 for a double.)

 ## Staying in

Holsworthy holds one of the UK's biggest livestock and pannier markets every Wednesday in the Market Square. There is a huge range of fresh local farm produce with around 50 stalls. Torrington's pannier market on Thursdays and Saturdays has a smaller range of fresh produce.

There is a good organic farm shop at **Blackberry Farm**, Milton Damerel, near Holsworthy (☎ 01409 261440; www.Lizzyslarder.co.uk; open daily except Mon), which stocks a wide range of local food and crafts, including free-range eggs (chicken and duck), Angus beef, grass-fed lamb, duck meat, home-cured bacon, fresh fish, local cheeses, fruit and veg, and homemade pickles.

Visitor information

Tourist information centres:
Torrington Tourist Office, Castle Hill
car park, ☎ 01805 626140,
info@great-torrington.com; Holsworthy Tourist Information, *Manor car
park,* ☎ 01409 254185,
vic@visitholsworthy.co.uk.
Bike rental: *Ride On Bike Hire*
(between Hatherleigh and Holsworthy), ☎ 01409 231100, www.rideon-
southwest.co.uk; Will have bikes
waiting at your accommodation;
prices per day: adults £16, child's
bike £12, trailer £8.
Taxis: *R&D Travel,* Torrington,
☎ 01805 622707; *Holsworthy Taxis,*
☎ 01409 259420

 ## Drinking

You'll find lots of real ale available in the dozens of village pubs across this region. Some good ones we haven't mentioned already include the **Bell Inn** at Monkleigh, which has decent food and accommodation and beers from Clear-water Brewery in Torrington, Burrington Brewery, and Countrylife Brewery near Bideford.

The Tally Ho on Market Street, Hatherleigh, does food and accommodation too and the bar stocks Clearwater's Cavalier and St Austell beers. The 13th-century thatched **Bell Inn** at Parkham also contains the village shop. It's another good place for real ales and cider from Winkleigh.

Torrington's **Torridge Inn** and **Holsworthy's King's Arms** both serve the increasingly popular Sharps beer from Rock in Cornwall.

The **Hoops Inn** on the A39 near Clovelly serves Hoops ales specially brewed by Burrington, plus local guests like Countrylife's 'Golden Pig' and Jollyboat Brewery's 'Grenville's Renown' from Bideford.

Choose local bottled water if you get the chance. **Tarka Springs** is bottled at its source on a farm at Langtree, near Torrington.

FURTHER AFIELD

The **Hartland Peninsular** is Devon's most remote corner. This wild square of north-west Devon has a dramatic coast but no bathing beaches. It's best for bracing walks rather than sunbathing or sandcastles. There are miles of daunting cliffs and scary pointed rocks, but **Bucks Mill, Peppercombe** and **Welcome Mouth** are the best places to reach the shore at interesting but rocky beaches.

Hartland is the only village bigger than a hamlet. The fortress-like grey stone parish church, **St Nectan's**, is worth a quick look – its 600-year-old carved wooden screen is nationally renowned among church historians. Older Devonians call it 'the Cathedral of North Devon' – its 128ft tower serves as a landmark for ships struggling round the dangerous headland.

> **HARTLAND ABBEY,**
> ☎ 01237 441264; www.hartland-abbey.com. Entry: house and gardens, adults £8, children £2.50; cheaper for gardens only; open Apr to Sept.

Visiting **Hartland Abbey** to the west of the village is a eccentric stately home experience, with a drawing room modelled on the House of Lords, corridor inspired by the Alhambra in Granada and peacock-filled parkland.

To the south of the village are the pretty gardens of **Docton Mill** in a sheltered valley beside an ancient watermill. There is a teashop with homemade scones and local clotted cream – and you can buy from a huge range of plants.

> **DOCTON MILL,** EX39 6EA;
> ☎ 01237 441369; www.docton-mill.co.uk. Entry: adults £4, OAPs £3.75, children free; open Mar to Oct 10am–6pm.

Follow the lanes to the west to reach the end of the road at **Hartland Quay**. This feels like the very end of Devon, with the Atlantic bashing against a gnarled jaw of rocks below. An old stone quay was destroyed by the constant waves 100 years ago and no-one has dared try again since. Discover great walks here – north to the lighthouse at **Hartland Point** and south to the cliff waterfall at **Spekes Mill Mouth**.

Right on the rocky headland, **Hartland Quay Hotel** is a wonderfully sited hotel/pub with atmospheric bar, shipwreck museum and gift shop selling great local ice cream from a farm near Holsworthy (☎ 01237 441 218; www.hartlandquayhotel.com).

In the heart of Hartland village is a charming place to stay. **Harton Manor** is a whitewashed grand house with a cool, minimalist air. The stylish bedrooms have nice art everywhere and that's not surprising, the owner also runs woodcut printing courses here. You can take a day course at short notice (☎ 01237 441670; www.twohartonmanor.co.uk; B&B from £25 per person per night).

The newly opened **Downe Health Spa** in Hartland is a sign that the 21st century is finally reaching this remote corner (☎ 01237 441881; www.devonspa.com). There are five listed Victorian farm buildings converted into luxury self-catering accommodation, with treatment rooms, sauna, spa, gym, steam room and restaurant in the farmhouse. Prices start at around £225 per person for a couple sharing a four-night 'pamper break'. It might be the only place in the world where you can get all those health treatments and then enjoy a clotted cream tea in the garden.

SOUTH MOLTON, MID DEVON AND EXMOOR

Despite its rolling lush farmland, steep wooded valleys and remote picturesque villages, this area of Devon is one of the least visited parts of the county. Outsiders probably won't have heard of any of the places here and the quiet little town of South Molton is the only place that could be described as slightly urban. So don't expect nightlife and shopping excitement – this is a wide slice of unspoilt countryside around the valleys of the Taw and its tributaries, between Dartmoor and Exmoor.

There are few things you'd call major attractions too – this isn't a spot for ticking off well-visited sights. Its appeal is more varied than that: visitors enjoy relaxing country breaks, activities such as walking, fishing or riding, and pottering around dozens of pretty villages. We've tried to pick the best of them for you, but it's worth exploring; most of Mid Devon's settlements offer something memorable, whether it's a historic church, friendly pub or teashop, or just a pretty village green surrounded by thatched whitewashed cottages.

WHAT TO SEE AND DO

Fair weather

You'll hear locals talk of going to **South Molton** as if it's some sort of throbbing metropolis. And on the map it's certainly the biggest place in a wide area between Tiverton and Barnstaple, between Okehampton and Minehead. Villagers and farmers for many miles around rely on South Molton's services and facilities. But don't expect too much: South Molton, with a population of just 4,000, is much smaller and quieter than any of those big places. But it's nevertheless a likeable little historic market town.

South Molton was built on the wealth of the wool trade, but the axing of the Barnstaple to Taunton railway in the 1960s and then the upgrading of the North Devon Link Road (A361) mean it was bypassed by travellers heading for the coast. So it's been left a bit high and dry, like something from a different age. This makes it a nice quiet place to wander, looking at shops and pubs and at pretty colour-washed terraced houses and grand buildings around the central market square.

South Molton's pannier market

Start in **The Square**: the 1743 **Town Hall** houses the town's quirky but free **museum** on the ground floor. Star exhibits include a huge 18th-century cider press and one of the oldest fire engines in the country, dating 1736.

Next door is the **pannier market** built in 1860 with an impressive assembly room above. There are still markets here twice a week (Thursdays and Saturdays). The **Medical Hall** with its ornate balcony supported on classical columns stands on an island in the square and has housed a chemist's shop for over 100 years.

To the south and west of South Molton the **Tarka Line** railway and **A377** Exeter–Barnstaple road follow the attractive Taw Valley. It's a beautiful drive or

SOUTH MOLTON, MID DEVON AND EXMOOR

The charming market town of South Molton lies at the heart of rolling hills

ride. (For more information about the Tarka Line contact any rail information service, eg National Rail Enquiries: ☎ 08457 484950; www.traveline.org.uk).

The countryside around these routes is highly thought of by naturists. The grasslands are renowned by scientists for having one of the world's highest concentrations of different species. The rivers have England's biggest population of wild otters. If you're very, very lucky or are Bill Oddie, you may be able to spot rarities such as dormice, barn owls, curlews, kingfishers and unusual butterflies.

Around **Eggesford** there are good walking trails through high firs and birches on the steep valley sides. Look out for wild deer. The village itself has a station, pretty Norman church and **garden centre** (☎ 01769 580250; www.eggesfordgardens.com) on the hill above the river with a popular restaurant, craft shop and unofficial tourist information point. If you've only time for one walk, locals recommend the path from the garden centre past the church and then curving up the hill for great views of the valley.

Picturesque villages

Chulmleigh is one of the prettiest villages in Mid Devon. It's an ancient hilltop settlement of cob (walls of Devon clay mixed with straw) thatched cottages that prospered from the Middle Ages' wool trade, then declined into sleepy rural contentment... like much of Mid Devon. There is an interesting church, St Mary Magdalene, decent pubs and cafés, and a lively annual fair in the first week of the summer holiday that dates back to 1253. On the outskirts are a

182

Local knowledge

Frank Adey and his family run the Gables Tea Rooms and the village websites in Umberleigh and Croyde (www.umberleigh-northdevon.co.uk and www.croydedevon.co.uk).

It may seem unbelievable to outsiders but the Adeys moved from the village of Croyde 'because we wanted a slower pace of life'. The old tea rooms in the village of Umberleigh right alongside the River Taw and Tarka Line seemed ideal. 'We invested lots and now have a beautiful conservatory with the 150-year-old grapevine and an art gallery, as well as our B&B house and tea rooms. It's reported that Henry Williamson visited the old tea rooms many times.'

Favourite restaurant: Weirmarsh Farm Restaurant, Umberleigh

Favourite pub: The George, High Bickington near Umberleigh, and The Bell at Chittlehampton

Favourite shop: Murchs' Antiques Emporium in Umberleigh

Favourite Devon food/drink: Pint of Exmoor ale (the best local brew) and Christine's Clotted Cream Scones at Gables Tea Rooms

Favourite Devon activity: Walking and surfing, photography

Best view: Firstly the coast, that's looking down across Putsborough Sands, and secondly hills, that's anywhere up on Exmoor.

Quirkiest attraction: Cobbaton Combat Collection in Chittlehampton

Best thing about living here: The wilds and the old villages

Best kept Devonshire secret: The Umberleigh area in the Taw Valley, including Chittlehampton village, Chittlehamholt and High Bickington

Favourite thing to do on a rainy day: Walking and then sitting by an open fire or painting

183

golf course with great views (☎ 01769 580519; www.chulmleighgolf.co.uk), friendly riding stables (Bold Try Equestrian Centre ☎ 01769 580366) and plenty of walks.

King's Nympton and **Burrington** are two more pretty villages with nice churches and pubs. King's Nympton's Saxon church has unusual wooden carvings of 'the green man' – a pagan fertility symbol. Burrington's cottages stand around a village square and a 500-year-old oak tree.

Chittlehampton's ancient church attracted medieval pilgrims who trekked to its shrine to St Hieritha, a 6th-century martyr cut to pieces by heathen locals with scythes. Chittlehampton also has an award-winning pub (see *Drinking*). In the lanes of the Exmoor foothills, in the hamlet of **Molland,** you'll find the charming old London Inn next to a 15th-century church with high-sided 'horse-box' pews. And the pretty old church of St James at **Swimbridge** is considered by experts to be one of Devon's best, with a lead-covered spire, ancient carvings and stone pulpit.

 ## Wet weather

Local farm contractor Preston Isaacs began collecting motorised military memorabilia 40 years ago and his private army base has just grown and grown. The **Cobbaton Combat Collection** is an engrossing informal museum packed inside

COBBATON COMBAT COLLECTION,
north of the B3227;
☎ 01769 540740;
www.cobbatoncombat.co.uk.
Entry: adults £5.75, OAP £5.25, children £4.25; open July/Aug: daily 10am–5pm; Apr to Oct: closed Sat; winter: by appointment only.

Cobbaton Combat Collection

The origin of Jack Russells

Swimbridge was home of the eccentric Reverend John 'Jack' Russell for more than 50 years from 1832. The parson was mad on hunting, bred the first Jack Russell terriers and set up The Kennel Club. Rev Jack still rode with hounds into his late seventies and was renowned for delivering brief sermons while his groom waited outside the church with his horse saddled and ready to go.

You'll find his grave in the churchyard... and the sense that his spirit lives on among locals. The village pub is even called the Jack Russell Inn. The pub is known locally for its huge sandwiches but it's worth looking up as you go in – its sign is a reproduction of a painting of Trump, the Parson's beloved terrier who was crossed with a Devon hunting dog to create the first Jack Russell puppies. The painting was commissioned by the then Prince of Wales (later King Edward VII) and the original still hangs at Sandringham.

his sheds. They're sometimes dragged out for a moment of glory in TV and films like *Dr Who* and *The Land Girls*. You'll find the whole range of war relics here: from tanks, guns, helmets, artillery, grenades and bombs to ration books, gas masks, Home Guard uniforms and blackout lamps – with background music from Vera Lynn.

Quince Honey Farm, just outside South Molton, started with just three hives in a cottage garden – it's now the biggest honey farm in the UK with 1,500 hives. You can see how bees make honey through glass fronted hives and of course there is a shop selling many varieties of the sticky sweet stuff.

> **QUINCE HONEY FARM,**
> ☎ 01769 572401; www.quince-honey.co.uk. Entry: adults £4, OAPs £3.50, children 5–16 £3; open daily Easter to Oct.

What to do with children

There are more than 200 different species of animals at **Exmoor Zoo**, a surprisingly good little menagerie in the foothills, including cheetahs, wolves, penguins, monkeys, wallabies and mongooses. They seem to be happy, and many have bred successfully. In the summer look out for falconry displays, snake handling and a chance to hand-feed small animals.

> **EXMOOR ZOO,** South Stowford, Bratton Fleming, EX31 4SG; ☎ 01598 763352; www.exmoor-zoo.co.uk. Entry: (summer/winter) adults from £6.95/7.95, children over 3 £4.50/5.50, family tickets; open daily 10am, closes 4pm–6pm depending on season.

The best... **PLACES TO STAY**

HOTEL

Northcote Manor

Burrington, Umberleigh, North Devon EX37 9LZ
☎ **01769 560501**
www.northcotemanor.co.uk/

This highly-rated wisteria-clad country house hotel stands in a 20-acre estate above Taw Valley. The food is good – thanks to a two-rosette restaurant. Occasional special events include murder mysteries, aromatherapy, watercolours and casino evenings. Although it's pricey, the baby listening and baby food hearing service and sofa beds make it good for couples with very young children.

Price: B&B from £155 for a double.

INN

The Bell

The Square, Chittlehampton, EX37 9QL
☎ **01769 540368**
www.thebellatchittlehampton.co.uk

The en suite bedrooms rooms are quite basic but the fabulous views of the church and rolling farmland make up for it. There is a kitchen and lounge too for those opting for self-catering. The pub itself is good too, with local food and real ales.

Price: B&B £30 for a single; £25 per person for a double or twin.

FARMSTAY

Higher Biddacott Farm

Near Chittlehampton EX37 9PY
☎ **01769 540222**
www.heavy-horses.net

This old stone farmhouse offers B&B in three double bedrooms upstairs. The farm is owned by a couple of shire horse enthusiasts. Downstairs you'll find log fires, evening meals with homegrown produce, cream teas, picnic hampers and horse-drawn wagon rides. The farm is worked sustainably with heavy horses, using traditional methods.

Price: B&B from £25.00 per person; evening meal £12.50.

B & B

The Old Bakehouse

South Molton St., Chulmleigh, EX18 7BW
☎ **01769 580074**
www.colinandholly.co.uk

This medieval whitewashed cob and thatch bakery is reputed to be Chulmleigh's oldest building – it's now a guesthouse with a well-regarded restaurant. 'Well-behaved' children over 5 are permitted to stay.

Prices: B&B from £45 for single; from £65 for a double; children 5–11 sharing parents' room £10; three course dinner costs £25.

SELF-CATERING

Rose Cottage

Wembworthy Down Farm, Chulmleigh, EX18 7QP
☎ **01769 580593**
www.devon-farm-cottage.co.uk

A pretty stone cottage with clean, modern décor attached to a working farm with walks among pigs, sheep, chickens and horses. It sleeps a maximum of five in two bedrooms.

Prices: from £206 to £615 per week.

Eggesford Barton Holiday Cottages

Eggesford, EX18 7QU
☎ **01769 581250**
www.eggesford-barton.co.uk

These three holiday cottages arranged around a courtyard attractively converted from farm buildings on what used to be the Earl of Portsmouth's estate. They are well equipped and sleep six, eight and ten respectively or they can be joined for large parties. There are exposed beams, bare stone walls, wooden floors and each has a garden area. The smallest costs from £603 a week to £1326; the largest from £931 to £2088.

Entertainment

The **George Hotel** in East Street, South Molton has live bands and comedians once or twice a week (usually Wednesdays and Saturdays). And a few annual events are worth watching out. **South Molton Olde English Fayre**, around midsummer's day includes stalls, crowning of the Queen, a floral dance and a family evening in the Assembly Rooms. The town's carnival at the end of August is another colourful day.

 Shopping

South Molton has some interesting little independent shops to browse, such as **Snapdragon Antiques** in South Street (☎ 01769 572374; www.snapdragondevon.co.uk). And **Murch's Antique Emporium** in Umberleigh is recommended by locals for finding small oddities (☎ 01769 560522). **Roger Cockram Ceramics** in Chittlehampton (☎ 01769 540420; www.rogercockram-ceramics.co.uk) is a gallery of this villager's high quality bowls and plates. The exquisite flower paintings are his wife's work.

The best... FOOD AND DRINK

Some of Devon's finest farming land is in this area, so you'll find plenty of the best farm produce to buy and eat. There isn't a gourmet tradition but there is a custom for doing things the right way. However your homemade clotted cream tea or Ruby Red beef steak is served, expect the ingredients to be perfect. Incidentally, don't believe the 'Ruby Country' tourism marketing in the Holsworthy area, this is really where the distinctive red North Devon cattle originates.

You're most likely to find the best food in the few top hotels and pubs. For locals, pubs are increasingly the places to eat out. And happily, there are plenty of good country pubs around Mid Devon, with home-cooked food, local real ale and real atmosphere too. Some of the pub chefs are sensational, surpassing any of the restaurants in the region.

Staying in

This is a great area for visitors to buy barbecue meat. The organic meat from **Higher Hacknell Farm** at Burrington has been widely praised. 'Melt-in-your-mouth texture and real flavour,' according to the *Mail on Sunday*. The farm shop is open Mondays to Fridays 8am–4pm, on weekends you'll need to call

EATING OUT

FINE DINING

Northcote Manor
Burrington, Umberleigh, North Devon
EX37 9LZ
☎ **01769 560501**
www.northcotemanor.co.uk

This two-rosette restaurant in an elegant country house hotel serves local specialities such as Lundy mackerel with vine tomato butter sauce, Exmoor venison Wellington and slow-cooked North Devon beef. A three-course dinner costs £38.

The Crown Hotel
Exford, Somerset TA24 7PP
☎ **01643 831554**
www.crownhotelexmoor.co.uk

The Crown is a lovely old inn in the heart of Exmoor long favoured by hunting, shooting and fishing locals. The two-rosette candlelit restaurant serves fine traditional English food with Somerset pork and cider, Exmoor venison and local seafood featuring regularly. Main courses cost from £10.95 to £21.50.

RESTAURANT

The Old Bakehouse
South Molton St., Chulmleigh, EX18 7BW
☎ **01769 580074**
www.colinandholly.co.uk

You'll find a well-regarded restaurant in this medieval village guesthouse. It's renowned for ingredients like Ruby Red beef, Mid Devon lamb, locally smoked chicken and fresh seafood. The restaurant is open Tuesdays to Saturdays. A three-course dinner costs £25.

Weirmarsh Farm
Umberleigh, EX37 9BE
☎ **01769 560338**
www.weirmarsh-big-barn-devon.co.uk

This converted barn is only open on Thursdays to Saturdays but locals rave about the food here. A five-course set menu costs just £25.50 with plenty of local meat, fish and vegetables. They also offer B&B and a luxury four-bedroomed self-catering barn (£600 to £1000 per week).

GASTROPUB

The Grove Inn, Kings Nympton EX37 9ST, ☎ **01769 580406**
www.thegroveinn.co.uk

This thatched and whitewashed inn has won an award as North Devon's best pub for two years' running. There are specials and snacks on a blackboard and villagers love Tuesday 'Fish & Chip Night' with haddock in homemade local real ale batter. They use lots of Devon suppliers from potato chips from Kingsbridge to beef from Lakehead Farm just down the road.

The Mason's Arms
Knowstone EX36 4RY
☎ **01398 341231**
www.masonsarmsdevon.co.uk

This thatched village inn is one of Devon's top-rated food pubs, with a Michelin star and three AA rosettes. The restaurant serves the finest contemporary cuisine. Owner/chef Mark Dodson worked for 18 years with Michel Roux at the famous Waterside Inn at Bray. You'll need to book though. Main courses cost from £12.50 to £17.50 and three courses cost about £33.

Tarr Farm Inn
Hawkridge TA22 9PY, ☎ **01643 851507**
www.tarrfarm.co.uk

Tarr Farm is a characterful beamed pub in wonderful riverside woods on the edge of Exmoor. The fine contemporary restaurant makes the best of local ingredients such as Ruby Red beef, Exmoor lamb and game, local honey, West Country fish and seasonal vegetables. Main courses cost £12.95 to £17.50.

CAFÉ

Gables Tea Rooms
Umberleigh, ☎ **01769 560461**
www.gablestearooms.co.uk

This family business serves mum's fresh homemade cakes and scones, local clotted cream and a range of meals just on the River Taw by Umberleigh Station and bridge. Eat in the lounge hung with local art or out in the riverside garden.

The couple who bought a pub

The Dodsons were fed up of living under the Heathrow flight path. Chef Mark and wife Sarah looked for a new start in the country and found what they were looking for in 2005: a pretty thatched village pub in the foothills of Exmoor.

'Its potential struck us as soon as we walked through the door,' Sarah told *Devon Today* magazine recently. 'It felt absolutely right – we could see ourselves at home here.'

The speed of their success was unprecedented. Within a year The Masons Arms had been awarded a Michelin star for their food – one of only a handful of British pubs ever to get the great culinary accolade. They have kept the star since. The latest Michelin guide calls the pub 'delightful' and their chief UK inspector is among the fans of Mark's 'superb, flavourful modern dishes'.

'We just wanted our own place to be successful and for it to happen so quickly is amazing,' said Sarah who runs the pub restaurant after a career working on P&O cruise ships. The couple and their three daughters now live above the pub.

It's a long way from when Mark started work in the galley of a cross-channel ferry after school. After 14 years of marriage Sarah has finally found out what Mark was up to for all those years working at Michel Roux's three-star Waterside Inn, the Savoy in London and the Clivedon Hotel. 'It's been a real eye-opener to see what Mark's been doing all this time. I love working with him especially after so many years of not being together much. He's a brilliant chef – even when he makes a bacon sandwich.'

first (Higher Hacknell Farm, Burrington EX37 9LX; ☎ 01769 560909; www.higherhacknell.co.uk).

Clannaborough Barton Farm (☎ 01363 84217), on the A3072 between Copplestone and Bow, has won awards for its Ruby Red cattle and the May family's farm shop is a great place to try different beef cuts or their homemade burgers and sausages. It's open every day except Tuesdays and Sundays.

And if you've wondered where Northcote Manor restaurant gets its superb beef and lamb from, here's the secret: **Bonners Farm** also in Burrington (☎ 01769 520601; www.bonny-beef.co.uk). You can buy yours there too. Their animals are reared in a well-cared for environment, butchered locally and very well hung – hence the quality taste. For more general produce, **Moorland Larder** in South Molton specialises in making traditional handmade pies, pasties and sausages using locally reared venison and wild boar (Moorland Larder, East Street, South Molton EX36 3DB; ☎ 01769 573554).

On Handsford Farm near Chulmleigh, **Gratton and Oldridge** make and sell a range of homemade jams, marmalades, chutneys and pickles (☎ 01363 83279; www.grattonandoldridge.co.uk).

Plenty of honey, honey ice cream, marmalades, mustards and chutneys are made and sold at **Quince Honey Farm Shop**, North Road, South Molton EX36 3AZ (☎ 01769 572401; www.quincehoney.co.uk). Just down the road **Chanters Bakeries** make and sell its own distinctive bread and cakes (Chanters, Barnstaple Street, South Molton EX36 3BQ; ☎ 01769 572651).

South Molton is the best place for general food shopping – apart from the cattle market on Thursdays and **farmers' market** on every fourth Saturday, there is the **pannier market** on The Square. Every Thursday and Saturday you'll find local meat, fish, cheese and vegetables here from 8am to 1pm.

And if you don't feel like cooking you can still visit South Molton's **Honeycomb Restaurant** (☎ 01769 572594) on The Square for an extensive takeaway menu including vegetarian meals, **Pagoda Wok** (☎ 01769 572503) in New Road for Chinese takeaways and **Baker George** in George Arcade off The Square, for sandwiches, baguettes, cakes and pasties (☎ 01769 573133).

And finally **Heal Farm Shop** near Kings Nympton hit the national headlines at Christmas 2007. Farmer's wife Anne Petch created a record-breaking medieval-style monster roast containing 48 birds of 12 different species that weighed four stone and served 125 people. It took eight hours to cook in an industrial oven. She told the *Mail on Sunday*: 'The True Love Roast has a different bird for each of the 12 days of Christmas.' It included layers of quail, duck and pheasant stuffed inside a giant turkey. You can order one of these for a mere £665, or some of the more reasonably priced local produce at the shop, which is indicated by brown signs from the B3226, 5 miles south of South Molton (☎ 01769 574341;www.healfarm.co.uk).

Drinking

It may not be renowned as a gourmet area for foodies but locals are justifiably proud of the quality of the pubs around the South Molton/Mid Devon area. In this area you can expect most pubs to offer a good choice of local real ales and ciders, good pub food with plenty of local produce and often a couple of simple B&B rooms upstairs.

There is local cider right on the doorstep and for beer drinkers, there is a microbrewery in the heart of the patch: **Burrington Brewery**, which makes Newt real ales, such as 'Black Newt', a richer porter style brew and a lighter bitter called 'Azza Newt'.

Cider lovers will find local cider in most pubs. **Hancock's** is the most local of all, based at Clapworthy Mill EX36 4HU, three miles west of South Molton (☎ 01769 572678; www.hancockscider.co.uk). Visitors to the shop can see a film of how it's made – the Hancocks should know, they've been making it here for five generations.

And there is a surprising treat for wine-lovers hidden deep in the valley of the River Yeo in Mid Devon. **Down St Mary Vineyard** (☎ 01363 82300; www.eng-lish-vineyard.co.uk) stands on a steep, sunny, south-facing slope. Grape varieties chosen to match the climate and soil have flourished here since 1986 and make for fresh, fruity white wines and a sparkling wine. There is a shop for tasting and buying, and a public footpath runs along the top of the vineyard with glorious views across the valley. The shop opens Easter Saturday to 31 October and throughout December (Tues to Sat 10.30am–5pm, Sun 12.30–4.30pm).

Devon Hills, a bottled spring water brand that sells in supermarkets and stores nationwide, comes from a spring on a farm near Chulmleigh. Its source is near its bottling plant at West Brushford Farm. The spring was mentioned in the Domesday Book and has been supplying drinking water for over 1,000 years. The area is among the least polluted in the country and the water comes from deep underground, filtering through rocks for years before being bottled.

As for specific pubs, we've already mentioned the **Grove Inn**, Kings Nympton (☎ 01769 580406; www.thegroveinn.co.uk) which has won an award as North Devon's best pub for two years running. The Grove is a great example of what you can find in some of these Mid Devon villages. It stocks a wide range of local drinks, including Exmoor Ale and Cotleigh ales brewed in Wiveliscombe by the Exmoor and Cotleigh Breweries, respectively, Jolly Boat Ales from Bideford, Oakford Vinyard beers from Tiverton, Otter beer from Honiton, Tarka Ales from Fremington near Bideford, Plymouth Gin from Blackfriars Distillery in Plymouth and Sam's Real Dry Cider from Winkleigh Cider Co.

Other pubs worth a detour are **The Bell** at Chittlehampton (☎ 01769 540368; www.thebellatchittlehampton.co.uk) which was CAMRA (Campaign for Real Ale) North Devon pub of the year for 2007; the **Barnstaple Inn** in Burrington, which stocks Azza ale but calls it 'Burrington Best Bitter'; **The George Hotel**, Broad Street, South Molton (☎ 01769 572514; www.georgehotelsouth-molton.co.uk) feels like the centre of the universe on Thursday lunchtime, market day. Try the Freeboater or Mainbrace beers from Jollyboat, and there is Winkleigh Cider too. **The London Inn** in the hamlet of Molland (☎ 01769 550269) is a lovely old fashioned hunting pub with rugs on flagstones and stuffed animals everywhere. It does B&B too. The thatched **Kings Arms** at Winkleigh (☎ 01837 83384; www.hatherleigh.net/kingsarms) is recommended by the *Good Pub Guide* and the *Good Food Guide* and has bedrooms upstairs. Brayford's **Poltimore Arms** (☎ 01598 710381) on the road up to Exmoor from the village is so remote it generates its own electricity; it serves Exmoor Ale from the cask. At Morchard Bishop just off the A377, the 16th-century **London Inn** has homemade food and a lively local atmosphere; and the **Black Venus** at Challacombe (☎ 01598 763251; www.blackvenusinn.co.uk), is known for traditional roast on Sundays and the children's play area in the garden. The thatched **Old George Inn** at High Bickington near Umberleigh has log fires, a sofa and highly rated Sunday roast lunches.

FURTHER AFIELD

Exmoor

Only a thin ribbon of Exmoor falls into the county of Devon – the rest is in Somerset. But we don't imagine that county boundaries will stop you exploring further into Britain's smallest National Park (see Day trips chapter).

Compared with Dartmoor, Exmoor is less forbidding, less bleak. There is more farmland, more roads and villages. And it's closer to the sea. It's a rolling highland of heather, grass and bracken sliced by deep valleys. The views are inspiring, particularly towards the north when you can see the sea and often the Welsh coast.

Exmoor is less busy and easier to explore than Dartmoor too. Simply take a drive across the heather-covered hills or walk on any of the comprehensive network of paths. The upland area is also famous for riding; there are plenty of stables offering trekking.

The highlights of Somerset's Exmoor include the pretty village teashops, pubs and shops of **Dunster**, with its National Trust castle watching over it from a wooded hill, the smart and busy little town of **Dulverton** around its market

The author's wife explores an Exmoor wood near Porlock

CELEBRITY CONNECTIONS

Take a walk on Exmoor and you may bump into an elderly chap out for a run. Look a bit closer – because it could be one of the world's greatest living explorers. **Sir Ranulph Twisleton-Wykeham-Fiennes**, 3rd Baronet, OBE (born 7 March 1944), usually known simply as Ranulph (Ran) Fiennes, lives at Greenlands Farm just north of Exford and for 25 years has run on footpaths on the moor preparing for his expeditions.

When Fiennes married his childhood sweetheart Ginny they bought the farm and raised a herd of 200 pedigree Aberdeen Angus cattle and a flock of 100 black Welsh Mountain sheep. At 1,400ft, their farm had no electricity when they arrived and is one of the highest working farms in the South West. Over the years they acquired more grazing land, including some over the border in Devon.

Ranulph has become very attached to the farm and says that he would never sell it. He has become a respected hill farmer in the Exmoor area and the former SAS officer likes to tell how he was once auditioned for the role of James Bond, but was rejected by film producer Cubby Broccoli because his hands were too big and he had 'a face like a farmer's'.

When he returned from having run seven marathons in seven days while recovering from a heart attack he received a hero's champagne welcome in Exford with banners strung across the local garage saying 'Welcome home'.

After Ginny died, Ranulph remarried, and he still lives on the moor with his wife Louise and daughter Elizabeth.

The first man to visit both the north and south poles by land told an interviewer recently: 'My favourite view is of the remoter parts of Exmoor. They're a bit on the bleak side but the colouring and light you get there I've never seen anywhere else. Up on top you can go for 16 miles and not see anything man-made and yet you're in the south of England.

square in the southern foothills, and the picture-postcard National Trust village of **Selworthy**, with its ochre-washed matching thatched cottages.

The longest footpath of them all starts here at West Somerset's biggest seaside resort, **Minehead**. The **South West Coast Path** is one of the great resources of the region – a wonderful free outing wherever you meet the coast anywhere between Minehead and Poole, 630 miles away. For more information visit www.exmoor-nationalpark .gov.uk or www.visit-exmoor.co.uk.

Visitor information

Tourist information centres:
South Molton Tourist Information Centre, 1 East Street, EX36 3BU, ☎ 01769 574122.
Hospitals: 24-hour A&E facilities available at *North Devon District Hospital*, Raleigh Park, Barnstaple EX31 4JB, ☎ 01271 322577.

Websites:
www.visitsouthmolton.co.uk; see the community websites for village information, three of the best are: www.eggesford.net; www.chulm-leigh.org; www.btinternet.com/~tyl-coat/burringt.htm
Supermarkets: Somerfield, New Road, South Molton.
Taxis: South Molton Taxi Service ☎ 01769 573636.

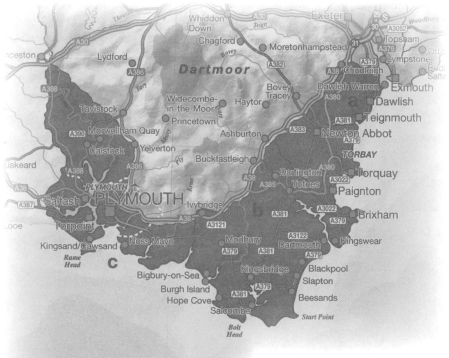

SouthDevon

a. Torbay from Brixham to Dawlish Warren

b. Dartmouth and the South Hams

c. Plymouth and the Tamar Valley

Unmissable highlights

01 Stand on Plymouth Hoe and simply soak up that monumental view,
p.249

02 Stroll under the fairy lights and past the illuminated gardens of Torquay waterfront after dark,
p.200

03 Take the restored steam train from Paignton to Kingswear, then sail across to Dartmouth on the ferry,
p.229

04 Make a brilliant sandcastle – Torbay's sand is said to be Britain's best for building,
p.201

05 Explore the cobbled lanes, overhanging Tudor homes and converted warehouses of Plymouth's historic Barbican area,
p.251

06 Sip a cocktail under the stained glass dome of the Palm Court Bar at the extraordinary art deco Burgh Island Hotel,
p.231

07 Say 'hello' to cheeky-looking penguins and puffins at the Living Coasts attraction right on Torquay's harbourside,
p.200

08 If you're going to lounge on the beach why not pick Britain's best: Blackpool Sands?
p.239

09 Pick your own fresh seafood from the seawater tanks at Beesands and have it cooked for you on the beach,
p.234

10 Play with the fish at the innovative National Marine Aquarium at Plymouth,
p.254

SOUTH DEVON

It's an old travel-writing cliché to say there is something for everyone, but there can't be many visitors who leave South Devon unable to find their own perfect spot somewhere along this coastal stretch.

This is one of England's most popular tourist areas and it's easy to see why. Yes, it gets crowded and yes, some of it's over-developed, but here we've tried to steer you towards spots that are less well known.

We've defined South Devon as the part of the county west of Exeter and underneath Dartmoor, stretching from the Tamar to the Exe. It's a horseshoe shape of some very different types of seaside — from the full-on tourist resorts of Torbay to the exclusive estuaries of the South Hams, from the extraordinary panorama of Plymouth Sound to the exotic art deco hotel at Burgh Island.

TORBAY FROM BRIXHAM TO DAWLISH WARREN

Driving along the A380 heading for Devon's biggest seaside resort, you'll pass a giant civic flowerbed on the verge spelling out the words: 'Welcome to The English Riviera'. You may be stuck in one of the summer traffic jams at the time; it may even be raining. You'll certainly wonder why Torbay has such a high opinion of itself. But once you reach the sea at Torquay you'll realise it's not just marketing gobbledegook. This stretch of coast really is a 'riviera' – and most Devonians would pick it as the most glamorous part of their county.

The Victorians originally coined the term 'Riviera', thinking of Torbay as an alternative to the south of France. It doesn't mean it's always going to be sunny or posh but there really is a certain atmosphere about this part of South Devon.

Torquay has a genuinely exciting holiday aura created by palm trees and grand white hotels, fairy lights along the promenades and Mediterranean-style gardens, sandy beaches and wooded coves. This period glamour at the heart of Torquay spreads out across **Paignton**'s more homely and traditional seaside appeal and the slightly manufactured quaintness of **Brixham**'s fishing village.

Devon's hot spot

Torbay forms a horseshoe lined by the towns of Torquay, Paignton and Brixham. The semi-circular bay faces south-east, sheltered from prevailing winds by the heights of Dartmoor behind. It makes Torbay a perfect suntrap.

Tourism chiefs boast that the English Riviera has more hours of sunshine than any other place in the UK. Whether that's true (and other tourist boards make the same claim) the Torbay microclimate is noticeably milder when you arrive from the north or east. Winters are short, snow is rare, spring comes earlier and November is often mild enough for sitting outside cafés and bars.

This climate allows many sub-tropical plants to flourish, in particular the **Torbay Palm** that lines the streets and brings an exotic touch to parks and gardens. The Palm was introduced to Torquay around 1820 from New Zealand by early plant collectors. The scientific name is *Cordyline australis* but it's also known in New Zealand as the rather less exciting sounding Majestic Cabbage Tree.

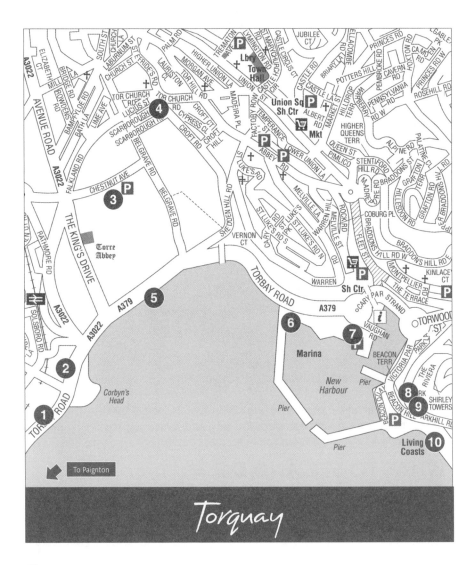

Torquay

1. Corbyn Head Hotel & Orchid Resturant
2. Grand Hotel
3. Riviera Leisure Centre
4. Mulberry House
5. Torre Abbey Beach
6. Princess Theatre
7. Pavilion
8. The Elephant
9. Number 7
10. Beacon Cove

Walk among penguins at Living Coasts

The trio have almost merged into one city but retain their identities.

This is Devon's biggest resort area but no matter how busy and developed it gets, there is always a feeling of something special about being on the 'Riviera'.

WHAT TO SEE AND DO

 Fair weather

The English Riviera

Torbay is Devon's biggest holiday attraction, with more than 500 hotels, 20 beaches and scores of things to see and do. The town of **Torquay** is the centrepiece of the resort – famed for its location among the seven green hills, from where whitewashed Victorian villas and Italian-style terraces gaze out to sea. Palm-lined promenades lead to the town's pavement cafés, boutique shops and restaurants. The wide, long esplanade with parks, beaches and harbour is perfect for strolls particularly in the evening when fairy lights drape across the seafront and the semi-tropical gardens are colourfully illuminated.

So it was a brave decision to build a new £7m wildlife attraction right on the seafront, but **Living Coasts** pulled it off with style. This offshoot of

LIVING COASTS, Beacon Quay, Torquay TQ1 2BG; ☎ 01803 202470; www.living-coasts.org.uk; adults £6.75, children 3–15 £4.70; open daily from 10am; winter: closes 4.30pm; summer: 5.30pm.

Paignton Zoo is a well-designed way to see shore dwellers such as penguins, seals, puffins, ducks and waders. Visitors use tunnels for underwater viewing and wander under a big meshed aviary roof as birds fly around. Feeding times are the highlight, and there is a good café with sea views.

Within the 22 miles of Torbay's coast there are 20 **beaches**. They vary considerably – Maidencombe and Watcombe are hidden among the wooded cliffs to the north, Oddicombe Beach is reached by a cliff railway, Torquay's Torre Abbey and Paignton Beach are at the centre of their towns, but Preston Sands, Broadsands and Goodrington are also fine sandy beaches without much of a town behind them. And there are five less-visited sand and shingles coves around Brixham too. The water is usually clean safe and calm... and the even the sand is highly rated. Visit www.whats ontorbay.co.uk/beach for a detailed beach-by-beach guide.

In 2007 the BBC TV coast series conducted a test of Britain's seaside sands for their sandcastle suitability... and Torquay's won easily.

In the summer, the bay hosts around 50 regional, national and international watersports events. Two marinas at Torquay and Brixham and the harbours of Torquay, Paignton and Brixham together offer a wide-range of watersport amenities including stores selling chandlery, specialist clothing and equipment. The facilities for sailing, sail-boarding, scuba diving, powerboats, kayaking, waterskiing, jet skiing, kite surfing and sea fishing are so numerous that we won't list them all – it would fill the rest of the book! For full details of how to do each activity contact the tourist information centres.

These harbours all offer **boat trips** around Torbay, between the resorts, as far as Exmouth and Totnes, and wildlife, evening and after-dark cruises. There are plenty of **fishing** trips too – popular species found around the bay include bass, mackerel, mullet, dogfish, pollock and conger. Visit www.torbay fishing.com for more information, including a list of secret fishing hot spots and a guide to identify your catch. Specialist wreck and shark fishing is available too. More details are available the free leaflet 'Angling on the English Riviera' available from tourist information centres. And for detailed information on each of the harbour facilities, boat trips, tides, berthing and anchorages visit www.tor-bay-harbour.co.uk.

Cockington

Just a mile behind the seafront is the wonderfully preserved, improbably cute, but usually crowded 'village' of **Cockington**. It has inevitably turned

COCKINGTON VILLAGE,
TQ2 6XA; ☎ 01803 606035;
www.countryside-trust.org.uk
Entry: free; always open.

from a proper picturesque village into a full-time tourist attraction run by a special trust, but it is still worth the walk, drive, cycle or horse-drawn carriage ride to see.

For starters, it's free. The historic manor house, **Cockington Court**, sits among 460 acres of beautiful parkland to explore. The house and its stables are now craft studios, so you can watch glassblowing, pottery, calligraphy and woodcraft (and, of course, buy). The welcoming village pub, the **Drum Inn**, was designed by famous architect Edwin Lutyens who also designed Castle Drogo on Dartmoor. You'll also find tea rooms, gift shops, gardens, restaurants, a historic church, a cricket pitch and a play area for children.

On the seafront between the big old Grand Hotel and the modern Princess Theatre you'll see ancient remains of **Torre Abbey** in extensive gardens. This was once Britain's wealthiest monastery but had become very shabby and has been shut for 2 years for a multi-million-pound refurbishment programme. Bizarrely the town held a special closing ceremony conducted by TV's David Suchet, famous as Agatha Christie's Poirot. Torquay's most historic building is due to open in summer 2008 with a new cloister garden as a major heritage attraction.

> **TORRE ABBEY**, King's Drive, Torquay TQ2 5JE; ☎ 01803 201201; www.torre-abbey.org.uk.

Coastal walks
The **coastal walks** around Torquay are some of Devon's best, particularly heading north and east on the coast path. One great source of routes is www.englishriviera.co.uk where you can download walking guides for printing or as a podcast. Failing that you can get free walking leaflets from tourist information centres.

Babbacombe and St Marychurch
The Torquay suburbs stretch a long way but two former villages now submerged in leafy bungalow-land have managed to retain their sense of identity.

> **BYGONES**, Fore Street, St Marychurch, Torquay TQ1 4PR; ☎ 01803 326108; www.bygones.co.uk
> Entry: adults £5.95, OAP £5, children 4–14 £3.95; open 10am daily; winter: closes 5pm; May to Oct: 6pm, Wed/Thur in July/Aug: 9.30pm.

Babbacombe and **St Marychurch** to the north of the harbour have their own centres, with pretty small independent shops and cafés. They have some good attractions too.

Halfway between the two villages is the entertainingly odd **Bygones**. This is essentially a life-size Victorian street and period rooms, all re-created inside a former cinema. There is also a First World War walk-through trench, 1960s shopping arcade and lots of old model railways.

Paignton
In the wooded countryside just behind Torbay stands the fairytale **Compton Castle**, now a National Trust property. It was once the home of the seafaring

Compton was Sir Humphrey Gilbert's home

Gilbert family. In Tudor times Sir Humphrey Gilbert was an explorer, coloniser of Newfoundland and half-brother to Sir Walter Raleigh. If you storm the dramatic gatehouse and battlements you'll find a flower garden and impressive medieval kitchen inside.

COMPTON CASTLE, Marldon, Paignton TQ3 1TA; 01803 842382; www.nationaltrust.org.uk
Entry: adults £3.90, children £1.95; open Apr to Oct: Mon, Wed, Thur 10am–5pm.

Once the railway reached as far as **Paignton** in the late 19th century the town became renowned as a seaside resort alongside its more established neighbour. Paignton never reaches the glamorous heights of Torquay and unkind Devonians sometimes call it 'Poor quay'. But it still has plenty of family seaside appeal. Think colourful beach huts, kiss-me-quick pier and lots of cheap shops.

Behind the sandy beach is a broad area of grass, **The Green**. This was built by encouraging locals to bring down wheelbarrows full of soil in exchange for sand. The Green is a busy venue for exhibitions and events, informal football (jumpers for goalposts), picnics and donkey rides (if you really need to know they're Rocky, Nosey, Tim, Jack, Blue, Fred, Ashley, Jemma, Charlotte, Daisy, Bambi, Floss and Snowy... and they give children rides every day from Easter to September).

KIRKHAM HOUSE, Kirkham Street, Paignton TQ3 3AX; www.english-heritage.org.uk. Entry: free; open spring/summer bank holidays and every Sun in July/Aug, 2–5pm.

OLDWAY MANSION, Torquay Road, Paignton TQ3 2TD; ☎ 01803 207933; Entry: free; open 9am–5.30pm.

Much of the town has a low-rise, makeshift feel, as if it's all folded up and put away at the end of each summer. But architecturally, Paignton does have some of Torbay's most interesting buildings tucked away and they're free to enter.

Hidden along a small street in the town centre, for example, is the medieval stone building, **Kirkham House**. It has survived unchanged since from the 14th-century and is laid out with replica furniture as if a medieval family still lives there but has popped out for the day.

CELEBRITY CONNECTIONS: THE QUEEN OF CRIME

One of Devon's most famous figures, **Agatha Christie** (1890–1976) was born in modest house on Barton Road, Torquay. The house has been long since demolished but Agatha's legacy has lived on. She became the 'Queen of Crime' with a prolific series of whodunnits and plays, including the Hercule Poirot and Miss Marple mysteries and the long-running West End play *The Mousetrap*.

She honeymooned at the Grand Hotel, Torquay, and worked in a hospital in the town during the war. Many of her books were set in South Devon and she is associated with lots of spots in Torbay, although there is nowhere that quite captures the atmosphere of her writing and era as well as Burgh Island Hotel at Bigbury (see South Hams chapter).

She used to travel on the Paignton to Dartmouth railway, go to dances at Oldway Mansion and the Imperial Hotel, visit Cockington and Kent's Cavern, roller-skate on Torquay Pier and go to concerts at Torquay Pavilion. As a child she was rescued from drowning at Beacon Cove, the tiny beach behind the Living Coasts attraction, although her favourite was Meadfoot Beach further east. Agatha often visited Burgh Island Hotel and wrote at least two books there. It has served as the setting for several film and TV adaptations of her work.

Her family home, Greenway, overlooks the River Dart near Galmpton in South Devon and is now in the care of the National Trust. Torquay Museum has a special Agatha Christie section, and there is also a bronze bust of the writer near the harbourside.

Torbay tourist information centres have a free leaflet describing an Agatha Christie walk around the town. Contact Torquay Tourist Information Centre at 5 Vaughan Parade TQ2 5JG or call 01803 211211.

Just off the main street, **Oldway Mansion**, built in the 1870s, may house the council offices now but it was once the stunning residence of Isaac Singer, boss of the Singer sewing machine empire. Was he rich? Well, his son Paris kept his own private seaplane at the end of Paignton beach, and two of the big seafront hotels were originally houses Isaac had built for two of his other sons. Oldway's interior with its marble staircase is so ornate it earned the nickname of 'Little Versailles'.

The 17 acres of grounds were designed by the French landscape artist Duschesne – they're a good spot for a picnic away from the beach crowds. And

Oldway has appeared in a number of films, including the 2004 *Churchill: The Hollywood Years*, starring Christian Slater.

And Paignton's third great period attraction is a railway. In fact, the 7 mile journey to Kingswear on **Paignton and Dartmouth Steam Railway** is one of Britain's greatest train journeys. The engines and carriages are superbly original and the route is wonderfully scenic, with views of the sea and estuary.

The train was often taken by crime writer Agatha Christie when she lived here and her detective, Hercule Poirot took the same journey in both the *ABC Murders* and *Dead Man's Folly*. The train also stops at **Churston Ferrers**, between Paignton and Brixham, where Agatha often visited the parish church. She paid for the beautiful stained glass east window. She would also lunch at the beautiful Churston Court, an elegant country house hotel (see *The best... places to stay*).

> **PAIGNTON AND DART-MOUTH STEAM RAILWAY**, Queen's Park Station, Torbay Road, Paignton TQ4 5AF; ☎ 01803 555872; www.paignton-steamrailway.co.uk. Price: adult return from £7.40, children 5–15 from £5.10; trains: nine a day in high season; otherwise four a day; Nov to Mar: only occasional 'Santa' trains.

Brixham

The third of Torbay's trio of towns is **Brixham** and it's very different in character. This used to be a hilly fishing village around a working harbour that has grown into a big tourist town. It sometimes feels like a maritime theme park with shops selling paintings of galleons, nautical nick-nacks in every pub and restaurant and brightly coloured 'fishermen's cottages' covered in nets and lobster pots that are really holiday homes for visitors. But make no mistake: Brixham is still a serious fishing port.

The harbour is home to one of UK's biggest fishing fleets; more than 100 boats land and sell their catch at the daily local fish market on the quayside. Every year, more than 10,000 tonnes of fresh fish land on these quays to supply restaurants all over England. Visitors can watch the daily bustle as large beam trawlers and smaller day boats come and go. Day boats can usually been seen working the seas around Tor Bay, especially from Berry Head and Hope's Nose.

But if you think 100 is a lot of boats, this harbour was once home to the country's largest wooden sailing fleet and it was many hundreds strong. They say that the trawler was invented here. Around 300 wooden trawlers were built in Brixham's own shipyard in the 19th century alone. Today there are just six left, known as the **Heritage Sailing Trawlers** (look out for *Pilgrim, Vigilance, Provident, Keywadin, Golden Vanity* and *Regard*).

Many of them offer charter trips, training courses or evening cruises. Some sail round the Bay or moor in the harbour on the Town Pontoon and allow visitors to look round.

They're the oldest boats in the harbour although there is another one that looks a lot older. Drake's **Golden Hind** is actually a modern replica but looks just like a Tudor galleon. It's the ship that Drake took on his round-the-world voyage of 1577. It's moored permanently in Brixham harbour and you can get a hands-on experience of life as Tudor sailor. To most visitors, the Hind seems remarkably small and cramped.

GOLDEN HIND, The Quay, Brixham TQ5 8AW; ☎ 01803 856223; www.goldenhind.co.uk. Price: adults £3, concessions £2; open Mar to Oct: daily10am–4pm.

In 1688, Prince William of Orange landed at the harbour and went on to claim the throne as King William III in what became known as 'The Bloodless Revolution'. William's harbourside statue commemorates the site in both English and Dutch.

Brixham has endless tales of smugglers and pirates. One of the best is how in the 1850s Brixham's enterprising smugglers took advantage of a cholera epidemic to smuggle out booty of tobacco and brandy in coffins. If that appeals to your darker sense of humour, you will enjoy Brixham's **ghost walks**. The 'original ghost walk' runs on various evenings between Easter and Halloween (☎ 01803 857761; myweb.tiscali.co.uk/devondawdlers).

There are ghosts of a different kind if you walk east from the harbour for 30 minutes. You'll reach the long flat headland that marks the end of Torbay. Roman artefacts found at Berry Head suggest it has a long history as a lookout post. During the Napoleonic Wars there were three substantial forts here, which held a total of 40 cannons. Much of the remains can be seen today and the guardhouse is now a café. There is a lighthouse here too, plus fine views across the bay. Wildlife experts pick it as one of Devon's top nature reserves with hundreds of rare plants and thousands of seabirds. Walk on to the next point – Scabbacombe Head – for wilder seascapes and some energetic climbs.

 ## Wet weather

That 'Riviera' tag can seem a bit hollow when the rain is teeming down but there are still plenty of things to do: they start with a pretty good indoor leisure complex, the **Riviera Leisure Centre**, just behind Torre Beach in Torquay. It has an indoor beach with a giant wave machine, 84° Fahrenheit water and a fun slide, café and gym.

RIVIERA LEISURE CENTRE, Chestnut Avenue, Torquay TQ2 5LZ; ☎ 01803 299 992; www.riviera-centre.co.uk. Entry: from £2 to £3.60; open daily; 7.30am Mon to Fri, 9am weekends, closes 4pm Mon/Tues, 8pm Wed, 9pm Thur/Fri, 6pm Sat/Sun.

Another plan B if it's raining is **Kent's Cavern**, a great cave attraction just inland from Torquay's harbour. The guides will show you how Stone Age humans lived incredibly deep

Kents Cavern was home to stone-age families

KENT'S CAVERN, Ilsham Road, Wellswood, Torquay TQ1 2JF; ☎ 01803 215136; www.kents-cavern.co.uk. Entry: adults £7, children 3–15 £5.50, family (2+2) £23.50; open all year 10.30am–4pm daily, guided tours more frequent in summer.

inside the caves. There is a good bit where they turn off the lights for a moment so you realise how dark it really is. There is the usual sound and light show, and in July and August, there are evening ghost shows. It's all very well done – so well done that Kent's is the 'Best Large Visitor Attraction in South West England 2008'.

What to do with children

This part of Devon offers plenty of great activities for children. **Quaywest Waterpark** is enormous, with eight big slides, two toddler pools and a main swimming pool. The slides range from the highest in the country – the scary 65ft plunge in the Devil's Drop to the torrents of the Raging Rapids or the rush of the swirling Sidewinder. The best news is that the water is heated to 80° Fahrenheit and it's all right next to the Goodrington beach and park.

Another great family day out is provided by **Paignton Zoo**. Expecting a few flea-bitten chimps and a dead-looking snake in a box? Wrong! This seaside menagerie is actually one of England's biggest and most beautiful zoos. More than 1,200 animals live among attractive botanical gardens (including lions, tigers, cheetahs, kangaroos, elephants, giraffes, parrots, zebras, baboons and gorillas). The zoo was founded by Herbert Whitley, a shy and eccentric millionaire, and is now owned by a charitable trust dedicated to wildlife conservation.

Goodrington is the ultimate family-friendly beach with tons of activities right

QUAYWAST WATERPARK, Goodrington Sands, Paignton TQ4 6LN; ☎ 01803 555550; www.quaywest.co.uk Entry: adults £8.95, children £7.95, family £31; open May to Sept: daily 10am–6pm.

PAIGNTON ZOO, Totnes Road, Paignton TQ4 7EU; ☎ 01803 697500; www.paigntonzoo.org.uk Entry: adults £9.35, children over 3 £6.25; family (2+2) £28.95; open daily from 10.00 am, closing times vary.

next to the beach. **Goodrington Park** (www.goodringtonpark.co.uk) is really just a general-purpose open space with a mix of activities – crazy golf, quad bikes, swan pedalos, bumper boats, drop slides, boating lake and a large natural picnic area and walking trails with swans, geese and wild birds. For centuries locals believed the lake here was a mysterious 'bottom-less pool' but when the park was built around it, they found it was only 2ft deep. So now it's used as the boating lake. The park area is free to get in but you pay for rides and activities. There is also a Brewer's Fayre pub, go-kart track, a seashore visitor centre, a watersports hire centre (☎ 01803 663243; www.skiwest.co.uk) and a leisure centre with indoor pool, children's play area and sauna (☎ 01803 522240; www.leisure-centre.com).

> **GOODRINGTON SANDS**, Paignton TQ4 6LN; ☎ 01803 555550; www.quaywest.co.uk Entry: adults £8.95, children £7.95, family £31; open May to Sept: daily 10am–6pm.

For something different try **Babbacombe Model Village**. It's quite surreal to wander between thousands of miniature buildings where tiny people and vehicles re-enact scenes from British history. Babbacombe's model village is so big it covers 4 acres and leaves you amazed at the dedication of the people who conceived and created it. The mini-world includes Nessie the fire-breathing dragon, an extensive model railway and a new indoor 3-D cinema.

> **BABBACOMBE MODEL VILLAGE,** Hampton Avenue, Babbacombe TQ1 3LA; ☎ 01803 315315; www.babba-combemodelvillage.co.uk. Entry: adults £7.90, children 3–14 £5.50, family (2+2) £24.90; open daily, hours vary from Jan/Feb,11am–3.30pm to July/Aug 10am–9.30pm.

Quads are a special holiday treat for those brave and rich enough to try and the place to do it is Torquay's **Junior Quad Centre**. Children aged 5–12 use a 50cc Suzuki, older kids use a 90cc Honda. They're all given tuition on an instruction circuit before joining the main circuit – a mix of tarmac and off-road surfaces.

> **JUNIOR QUAD CENTRE**, Moles Lane, Shiphay, Torquay TQ3 1SY; ☎ 01803 615660; www.juniorquadcentre.co.uk Price: six minute ride £3–£5, 30 minute ride £72–£80; open Sat, Sun and school holidays 9.30am–5.30pm.

 ## Entertainment

Theatre and cinema

Thanks to the huge holiday and leisure tradition this is often the liveliest area of Devon – and not just in the summer. This exuberance of entertainment is demonstrated by the number of theatres: **Babbacombe Theatre**, Babbacombe Downs (☎ 01803 322233; www.babbacombe-theatre.com) has traditional variety shows with the longest running summer season in the UK. Babbacombe has launched many careers including Bruce Forsyth who said: 'The atmosphere in this place – you just can't beat it'.

Princess Theatre, Torbay Road, Torquay (☎ 01803 290288; www.princess theatre.org.uk) is a large 1,500-seat venue on the harbourside with a year-long programme of professional large-scale productions from West End musicals to major concerts. **Little Theatre**, St Mark's Road, Torquay (☎ 01803 299330; www.toadstheatre.co.uk) is a pretty converted church that is home of one of the highest-rated amateur dramatic societies in the country and the **Palace Theatre**, Palace Avenue, Paignton (☎ 01803 665800) is a Victorian theatre showing mainly local performances. **Brixham Theatre**, New Road, Brixham (☎ 01803 207930) is friendly local theatre with occasional performances and concerts.

You'll find cinema complexes in Torquay (Abbey Road, TQ2 5NQ; ☎ 01803 292324; www.merlincinemas.co.uk) and there is the Paignton Apollo on the Paignton seafront(☎ 0906 2943456; www.apollocinemas.co.uk).

Clubbing and music

And in the summer particularly, Torbay is the clubbing capital of Devon with dozens of late-night **dance venues**, including:
- **Bohemia**, Torwood St, Torquay ☎ 01803 292079 (serious dance club described by Judge Jools as 'way cool')
- **The Venue**, Torwood Street ☎ 01803 213903 (slick club but young crowd)
- **Valbonne**, Higher Union Street ☎ 01803 290458 (slightly older punters)
- **Club Zig Zag**, Market Street, Torquay, ☎ 01803 200110 (mainstream dance)
- **Bar Med**, Fleet Walk ☎ 01803 209014 (café by day, cocktails and dance by night)
- **Mermaid**, Esplanade Road, Paignton ☎ 01803 558258 (busy, hot and sweaty)
- **Rocky's**, Rock Road, Torquay ☎ 01803 292279 (mainly gay, four different levels)
- **Barcode**, Palk Street, ☎ 01803 200110 (another day-time café where they turn the music up loud at night).

Live music can happen at the theatres, clubs and many of the larger hotels such as the **Recliffe Hotel**, Paignton. And there are plenty of local pubs joining in the action, especially in the holiday season, for example:
- **The Lime Tree**, Dartmouth Road, Paignton
- **The Manor Inn**, Market Street, Torquay
- **Prince of Orange**, Barton Hill Road
- **Torquay and Bolton Hotel**, New Road, Brixham

The best... PLACES TO STAY

With over 500 hotels in Torquay alone you'd think there are plenty to choose from, but even this many can be full on a sunny bank holiday, so it's important to book.

BOUTIQUE

Orestone Manor

Rockhouse Lane, Maidencombe, Torquay TQ1 4SX, ☎ 01803 328098 www.orestonemanor.com

Among steep woods leading to a secluded beach north of Torquay, you'll find this colonial style country house hotel. There is a large garden, terrace and highly-rated restaurant. Orestone was originally the home of artist John Callcott Horsley, designer of the first Christmas card. In 1857 he painted his famous brother-in-law, Brunel, here. That painting now hangs in the National Portrait Gallery.

Price: B&B from £99 to £149 for a single; from £135 to £225 for a double.

Gleneagles Hotel

Asheldon Road, Wellswood, Torquay, TQ1 2QS, ☎ 01803 293637 www.hotel-gleneagles.com

When John Cleese and the Monty Python team stayed here in the 1970s it was so bad and the owner so rude that it inspired John to create the *Fawlty Towers* series. Since then thousands of fans of the show have been to see the shabby guesthouse. But in 2006 it was completely refurbished and turned into a small boutique hotel, reopened by Prunella Scales (who played Cybil in *Fawlty Towers*). It now has contemporary décor, sea views, outdoor pool with Lloyd Loom sun loungers and palm trees. There is still a small display of Fawlty memorabilia, however.

Price: B&B from £75 to £90 for a single; from £150 to £180 for a double.

HOTEL

The Grand Hotel

Sea Front, Torquay TQ2 6NT ☎ 01803 296677 www.grandtorquay.co.uk

This big classic Edwardian hotel is right on the seafront, with the rail station behind. Appropriately it retains an air of grandeur: many rooms have sea-facing balconies, there is a rosette-winning restaurant and formal gardens. The Grand has indoor and outdoor pools, spa and gym. And as a historical note, Agatha Christie spent her honeymoon here.

Price: B&B from £70 to £100 for a single, from £140 to £200 for a double.

Churston Court Hotel

Churston, near Brixham, TQ5 0JE ☎ 01803 842186 www.churstoncourt.co.uk

In this magnificent 12th-century manor tucked away from the seaside bustle you'll find log fires, wood paneling, rich red fabrics, oil paintings and candlelit dinners. Tudor explorer Sir Humphrey Gilbert was a frequent visitor with his half-brother Sir Walter Raleigh; 450 years later Agatha Christie was also a regular and was inspired to write *Death on the Links* here.

Price: B&B from £95 per night in a four-poster double.

INN

Bickley Mill

Stoneycombe, Kingkerswell TQ12 5LN ☎ 01803 873201, www.bickleymill.co.uk

There are neat modern bedrooms with neutral colour schemes above this smart restaurant/pub. The converted mill stands in gardens in a quiet village that's handy for the main roads. There is good food, open fires and history all around you.

Price: B&B from £60 to £65 for a single, from £75 to £80 for a double.

FARM STAY

Chipley Farm

Bickington, Newton Abbot TQ12 6JW ☎ 01626 821486 www.chipleyfarmholidays.co.uk

Louisa, an artist, and Fred, a farmer, own this dairy farm amid rambling gardens. You can sit with the family to eat farmhouse suppers cooked on a green Aga. Choose the four-poster bedroom – it opens onto a wisteria-covered patio. Much of the fruit and vegetables are grown in their garden and much of the meat is home reared, but they don't take credit cards, and children under 3 aren't permitted.

Price: B&B from £60 to £70 for double, dinner £20.

Elberry Farm

Elberry Farm, Broadsands, Paignton
☎ 01803 842939
www.elberryfarm.co.uk

Elberry is a big Victorian family farmhouse, where farmer's wife and horsewoman Mandy runs the B&B. Rooms are simple but the farm is enthralling. Cream teas are served in a sunny walled garden. Beef cattle are reared on the land and there is a farm shop selling free-range eggs, local honey and home-produced vegetables. Babysitting is available by arrangement.

Price: B&B from £18 to £25 per person per night, children £10–£14, dinner from £9, children £4.50–£8.50.

B & B

Sampsons Farm & Restaurant

Preston, Newton Abbot Q12 3PP
☎ 01626 354913
www.sampsonsfarm.com

At this thatched 16th-century farmhouse guests can stay in the main house or the converted stables. The AA dining award menus feature fresh local produce; note that children under 14 are not allowed in restaurant after 6.45pm.

Price: B&B from £59 to £140 for a double.

Thomas Luny House

Teign Street, Teignmouth TQ14 8EG
☎ 01626 772976
www.thomas-luny-house.co.uk

Stop giggling at the name and appreciate

the house, which was built in the late 18th century by an acclaimed marine artist in the old maritime quarter of Teignmouth. The period feel remains, as does a sense of luxury which has earned a Tourist Board gold award.

Price: B&B from £64 to £68 for a single; £80 to £94 for a double.

Potters Mooring

30 The Green, Shaldon TQ14 0DN
☎ 01626 873225
www.pottersmooring.co.uk/

An old seaman's house at the pretty estuary-side village of Shaldon has been refurbished to provide a high standard B&B. In Captain Potter's old home there is now a four-poster room, wifi in a separate cottage, and views of the river and bowling green.

Price: B&B from £55 for a single; from £90 for a double, from £80 to £95 for a family room.

SELF-CATERING

Victorian House

☎ 01647 433593
www.helpfulholidays.com

This Devon-based cottage company has holiday homes in Torquay, Brixham, Teignmouth, Shaldon and Dawlish. The grandest is a Victorian house in Torquay's smart Wellswood area with five bedrooms that sleep up to 12. It's expensive but offers sea views, an acre's garden, quality furniture, chandeliers, range cooker, oil paintings and games room.

Price: from £720 to £2445 per week.

The Old Post Office

☎ 01326 555555, www.classic.co.uk

There *is* something 'classic' about this cosy white-washed holiday cottage in a village near sea, with two bedrooms. It sleeps four and has leather furniture, warm yellow walls and a pretty garden. The house is opposite the church, and a pub and shop are 100 yards away. Short breaks are available but children under 6 or pets aren't permitted.

Price: from £294 to £624 per week.

🛒 Shopping

Torquay has a good reputation among locals for shopping – there are certainly more shops than you'd expect for a town of this size. Around the harbour and leading up **Union Street**, you'll find the grand old Hoopers department store, TK Maxx and most of the big high street names. Next to the harbour, the Pavilion is a converted Victorian theatre, now housing independent shops, as well as a bar and restaurant overlooking the marina.

We've already mentioned St Marychurch and Babbacombe's quieter shopping 'villages'. The **Wellswood** district is also thought of as having rather stylish small shops.

Torquay also boasts a huge out-of-town shopping centre at **The Willows** (Nicholson Road, TQ2 7XA) just north of the town off the A380. As well as a hypermarket, there is an M&S and several other big name clothes shops, furniture stores and electrical retailers.

The best... FOOD AND DRINK

Torbay is clearly more about consumption than production. There is a huge selection of eating places, including French, Italian, Spanish, Indian, Thai, Moroccan and Mexican. There are Michelin-starred restaurants and award-winning fish and chip shops. And Torbay has Devon's most continental café culture, with sunny summer's evenings enjoyed al fresco.

While the region has fewer farms than most of Devon, it does have a fine tradition of seafood. Every day the Brixham fleet land fresh Dover sole, plaice, lemon sole, lobster, crab, scallops and black mussels (usually from Elberry Cove). If farm produce has to travel a few miles from the producers inland, the fish often comes a few hundred yards to your plate.

▶ Staying in

The best place to buy local produce is the new £1m **Occombe Farm** – run by an environmental charity, which ploughs all profits back into local conservation work.

The farm is organic, there is a nature reserve, education centre (built from hay bales), and a farm shop selling locally sourced organic pro-

OCCOMBE FARM, Preston Down Road, Paington TQ3 1RN; ☎ 01803 520022; www.country-side-trust.org.uk/Occombe Open: Mon 9.30am–5pm, Tues to Sat 9am–5pm, Sun 10am–4pm.

duce. You'll also find a traditional butchery, café and organic bakery.

The farm shop won the national Best Farm Retail Newcomer 2008 Award and their excellent website gives photos and details of all their suppliers, including organic lamb from Elbury Farm near Exeter, and fruit and vegetables from an organic farm at Kenn. There is even a farmers' market here on the first and third Wednesday of every month.

At the opposite end of the scale there are some cracking fish and chip shops. At **Hanburys** (Princes Street, Babbacombe, TQ1 3LW; ☎ 01803 329928; www.hanburys.net) you can eat in or out. They've been the south-west fish and chip shop of the year four times and national champion too. Their secret? Groundnut oil, plus the finest Maris Piper potatoes sourced locally in summer and a state of the art Dutch computerised gas range that cost up to £75,000. For something different try the battered brill or smoked haddock. It's open 4.30–9.30pm but closed on Sundays. And to follow, the **Igloo** 57 Torbay Road, Paignton TQ3 3BY; ☎ 01803 521449; www.theigloopaignton.co.uk) is an award-winning ice cream parlour.

🍶 Drinking

TEIGN ROAD, Newton Abbot, TQ4 4AA; ☎ 01626 334734; www.tuckersmaltings.co.uk Entry: adults £5.95, OAPs £4.95, young adults (16–17) £3.95, children 5–15 £3.65, family (2+2) £15.85; tours Easter to Oct: Mon to Sat 10.45am, 12.00 noon, 2pm, 3.15pm.

The best place to start any Torbay drinking tour would be **Tuckers Maltings** – the only traditional malt house open to the public in Britain. It produces enough malt to brew 15 million pints of beer each year and supply more than 30 south-western breweries. Their shop stocks a wide selection of bottled beers brewed using their malt. Teignworthy brewery is based in the Maltings, producing local favourites Reel Ale, Spring Tide and Beachcomber. You can take a tour to see the 100-year-old barley-to-beer process with free tastings.

There is another local brewery on a working farm just outside the village of Bishopsteignton. **Red Rock Brewery** is based in a converted barn and can produce over 400 gallons of beer each week. The beer is made from the water from the farm's spring – there is no mains water or phone line on the farm. Malt is bought from Tuckers Maltings. The two beers made are Red Rock and Back Beach. You can buy the beer at the farm, call 07894 035094 or visit www.redrockbrewery.co.uk for details.

HUNT'S SCRUMPY, Higher Yalberton Farm, Yalberton, Paignton, Devon TQ4 7PE; ☎ 01803 782309 Open daily, Mon to Sat 9am–5pm, Sun 12–1pm.

And cider drinkers can find the source of the local **Hunt's Scrumpy** at a farm near Yalberton, a mile off the A385 Torbay–Totnes road. Look for the cider signs, then ring the bell at the window on the left of the farm entrance. You'll see the cider barrels inside and you can try before you

🍴 EATING OUT

FINE DINING

Orestone Manor
Rockhouse Lane, Maidencombe, Torquay TQ1 4SX , ☎ 01803 328098
www.orestonemanor.com

The restaurant at this relaxed colonial-style country house hotel has an à la carte or brasserie menu. You can eat inside or out, and the chef uses organic herbs, fruit and vegetables from the hotel garden and local seafood from Brixham day boats. Price is £38 for three courses.

The Elephant
3–4 Beacon Terrace, Torquay TQ1 2BH
☎ 01803 200044
www.elephantrestaurant.co.uk

Torquay's highest-rated restaurant has a Michelin star and is Les Routiers South West Restaurant of the Year at the time of writing. It's the sister of Orestone Manor with the same relaxed ambience, this time in a period terrace house alongside the harbour. The first floor is more formal, downstairs is the brasserie. Restaurant: three courses cost £39.50, tasting menu £55; brasserie: a two-course lunch is £15.50, and a three-course dinner costs £21.

The Orchid
Corbyn Head Hotel, Torbay Road, Sea Front, Torquay TQ2 6RH
☎ 01803 213611
www.orchidrestaurant.net

From the outside it looks like a seaside motel but there is exquisite modern food in the restaurant upstairs and fabulous sea views. The Orchid currently holds three AA rosettes and uses all the best local produce, with a daily fish delivery from Brixham. A two-course lunch costs £22.95, a three-course dinner costs £37.95.

RESTAURANT

The Grand Hotel
Sea Front, Torquay TQ2 6NT
☎ 01803 296677
www.grandtorquay.co.uk

A classic grand seaside hotel with an award-winning restaurant. You can expect crisp white linen, formal service and top quality, if traditional, food. A three-course dinner is £25.

Mulberry House
1 Scarborough Road, Torquay TQ2 5UJ
☎ 01803 213639
www.mulberryhousetorquay.co.uk

This Victorian guesthouse stands on a suburban corner but has a cosy top notch licensed restaurant serving modern English dishes. You eat at round tables in front of open fires and fresh flowers. Two courses cost £20.95, three courses are £23.95 and four courses are £26.95.

Number 7
Beacon Terrace, Torquay TQ1 2BH
☎ 01803 295055
www.no7-fish.com

In the same harbourside terrace as The Elephant, this award-wining specialist seafood bistro has plastic tablecloths, bare wood floors and menus on blackboards. The fish is fresh, simple and expertly done. Three courses are about £23.

The Brasserie
The Osborne Hotel
Hesketh Crescent, Meadfoot Torquay TQ1 2LL, ☎ 01803 213311
www.osborne-torquay.co.uk

When the sun shines this is the place to eat – under a parasol and palms on the terrace of a fine period hotel overlooking the sea. Food is relaxed but traditional with barbecues in the summer. And it's good enough to be Michelin recommended. Inside there is the more formal restaurant – Langtry's. A main course is about £13.

GASTROPUB

The Anchor Inn
Cockwood, Starcross EX6 8RA
☎ 01626 890203
www.anchorinncockwood.com

This pretty old pub next to a tiny harbour and winding road on the Exe Estuary is busy and highly rated, especially with locals. Book... and arrive early to get a parking

EATING OUT

space near the pub. There is a big choice of seafood, and the shellfish comes in huge portions. Bar snacks cost from £3.25, and a three-course dinner is £25.

Church House Inn
Village Rd, Marldon TQ3 1SL
☎ **01803 558279**
www.churchhouseinn.free-online.co.uk

This lovely old pub is hard to find, just north of the A380, but it's worth it for its character and atmosphere. The exposed stone walls, beams and flagstones help, as does the good quality, traditional homemade food. Three courses cost around £26.

The Chasers
Stoke Rd, Stokeinteignhead TQ12 4QS
☎ **01626 873670**
www.thechasers.co.uk

An old thatched village pub with surprisingly contemporary cuisine and local ingredients such as South Devon beef, Start Bay crabs and Brixham fish. Eat in or out. Three courses are around £21.

Bickley Mill
Stoneycombe GB – Kingskerswell TQ12 5LN, ☎ 01803 873201
www.bickleymill.co.uk

This family-run freehouse is in a hidden valley where you eat on big wooden tables in front of open fires. The fine homemade food ranges from hot sausage and mushroom sandwich to salmon and spring onion fish cakes. Don't confuse it with the Bickleigh Mill near Tiverton – they are very different restaurants. Snacks cost £3.95 to £8.95, main courses £7.95 to £10.65.

buy. Hunt's is real scrumpy (6% proof) made by traditional methods on this working dairy farm from fruit from the farm's own orchards.

You'll get a discount if you take your own containers.

Kenton Vineyard lies on south-facing slopes on the west side of the Exe Estuary. It was established on an old farm in 2003 by a couple escape hectic careers in law and medicine in London. Now their fine red, rosé and white wine can be tasted, bought and enjoyed at the shop and bar and visitors can take a 'Vine Trail' through the vineyard (£2), when it's open between May and September 12pm–4am daily except Thursdays and Fridays (☎ 01626 891091; www.kentonvineyard.co.uk).

And look out for the products made by the **Real Drink Company** in local shops – this Torbay company makes traditional drinks only from traditional, organic orchards in Devon. Every bottle of the additive-free apple juice, cider, elderflower cordial, and cider brandy identifies the orchard source on the label. You can buy online at www.realdrink.org.

As for good places to go for a drink, there are plenty. We've already mentioned **The Grand Hotel** where the art deco Compass Bar has great sea views and the local 'foodies' pubs:
- **The Anchor** at Cockwood
- **Church House Inn**, Marldon

- **Chasers**, Stoketeignhead
- **Bickley Mill**, Kingkerswell

Add in the **Wild Goose** at Combeteignhead, which seems more remote than it is and serves local ales such as Otter, Red Rock and Teignworthy, and the **Two Mile Oak** at Newton Abbot, a traditional old coaching inn with beer from the cask. **The Maritime** in Brixham is small but big on relaxed atmosphere, including a parrot, open fires and flowery curtains. Nearby the **Blue Anchor** uses an old chapel as a bar and serves Dartmoor Best.

In the hamlet of Maidencombe, the **Thatched Tavern** is a good all-rounder with food, bar and garden just above the beach. In the heart of Torquay the **Crown and Sceptre** is another friendly coaching inn with wide range of real ales.

FURTHER AFIELD

Newton Abbot

Famous to outsiders just for its racecourse, Newton Abbot is well known to locals as one of Devon's best market towns. Most holidaymakers bypass the town on one of the network of trunk roads on the outskirts. But if you do stop, you'll find why all the locals go there: a good **farmers' market** in Courtenay Street in the pedestrianised town centre (Tuesdays 9am–4pm), a **livestock market** in the cattle market on Wednesdays, an indoor food and produce market Mondays to Saturdays at the **Butter Market**, and an outdoor market in **Market Square**, Wednesdays and Saturdays (9am–4pm). And on Sundays there are **carboot sales** in the cattle market car park, or in the multi-storey if it's raining. For more information contact the Tourist Information Centre (6 Bridge House, Courtenay Street, Newton Abbot TQ12 2QS; ☎ 01626 215667).

Just outside town is **Stover Country Park**, a Devon County Council nature reserve with a lake and woods. It's a Site of Special Scientific Interest, mainly because of its varied population of dragonflies (19 different species).

STOVER COUNTY PARK, Newton Abbot TQ12 6QG (signed off the A382); ☎ 01626 835236. Entry: free.

Almost next to Stover Country Park is **Burnham Nurseries** (☎ 01626 352233; www.orchids.uk.com), a family-run plant centre now in its third generation. The exotic undercover collection of orchids is the largest in the UK. And there are also extensive nurseries at **Plant World**, plus a good café and great views of the Teign Valley. Impressive gardens are laid out to represent

PLANT WORLD, St Marychurch Road, Newton Abbott, TQ12 4SE; ☎ 01803 872939; www.plant-world-seeds.com. Entry: £3.00 open Apr to Oct daily 9:30am–5pm.

BRADLEY MANOR, Newton Abbot, TQ12 6BN; ☎ 01626 354513; www.national-trust.org.uk. Entry: adults £3.90, children £1.95; open Apr to Sept: Tues to Thur.

each continent with rare plants to match.

On the riverbank outside Newton Abbot, **Bradley Manor** is one of Devon's most complete medieval houses. The great hall is emblazoned with the royal coat of arms of Elizabeth I. In the wood close to the manor house you will find the 'Puritan Pit' – a natural hollow where non-conformists held secret meetings to avoid religious persecution.

Chudleigh

The small town in the rich valley behind Teignmouth has a couple of great reasons to visit. **Ugbrooke Park**, the home of Lord Clifford, is a stern stone house with lavish interior standing in the Capability Brown parkland with lakes, rivers, orangery, tea shop, statues and magnificent trees.

UGBROOKE PARK, Chudleigh, TQ13 0AD, signed from A380; ☎ 01626 852179; www.ugbrooke.co.uk. Entry: from £4 to £7.50; July to Sept: Tues to Thur and Sun, 1.30pm–5pm; house tours 2pm and 3.45pm.

The GWR

The **Great Western Railway** was built to link London with the West Country. The main line runs across Devon from the east to Exeter and then down the coast to Newton Abbot where it turns inland across the southern end of Dartmoor to reach Plymouth.

Here we want to tell you about the section between Exeter and Newton Abbot, as it's one of the most spectacular rail routes in Britain. This stretch is being considered for World Heritage Site status as the book is being written.

Isambard Kingdom Brunel bravely created a route that hugs the foot of the cliffs and the estuary shore right along the water's edge. Waves crash over the granite rail promenade between Dawlish and Teignmouth, where the track tunnels through red sandstone outcrops and headlands. Along the Exe Estuary the line bridges the entrance to little harbours such as Cockwood and passes along the side of Powderham's deer park. At Dawlish the station is right on the seafront and you have to walk under the track to reach the beach. The rock supporting the track is often damaged by heavy seas and has to be hastily repaired.

The 30-minute trip is a rail wonder of the world and is worth the ticket at any time of year. In fact, if the weather's bad it's even more dramatic (☎ 08457 000 125; www.firstgreatwestern.co.uk; single from £3.90).

Visitor information

Start all queries at the comprehensive Riviera regional website: www.englishriviera.co.uk or call the central Riviera tourism line ☎ 01803 211211.

Tourist information centres:
Torquay Tourist Information Centre, 5 Vaughan Parade TQ2 5JG; *Paignton Tourist Information Centre,* Esplanade Road TQ4 6ED; *Brixham Tourist Information Centre,* Old Market House, The Quay TQ5 8AW.

Hospitals: Torbay Hospital has the 24-hour A&E department for the region, Newton Road, Torquay TQ2 7AA, ☎ 01803 614567.

Supermarkets: Sainsbury's, Willows shopping complex outside Torquay, Nicholson Road TQ2 7HT, ☎ 01803 614689; *Tesco,* Fleet Street TQ1 1DB, ☎ 0845 6779823; *Somerfield,* Union Street TQ1 3UT, ☎ 01803 295384; *Somerfield,* Cherry Brook Square, Paignton TQ4 7LY ☎ 01803 842313; *Morrisons,* Totnes Road, Paignton TQ4 7ET, ☎ 01803 527559; *Sainsbury's,* Brixham Road, Paignton TQ4 7BA, ☎ 01803 666444; *Somerfield,* Fore Street, Brixham TQ5 8JJ, ☎ 01803 853183); *Tesco,* Newton Road, Kingsteignton TQ12 3RN, ☎ 01626 237400; *Sainsbury's,* Keyberry Road, Newton Abbot TQ12 1BN ☎ 01626 333639; *Asda,* Highweek Street, Newton Abbot TQ12 1TG ☎ 01626 882700.

Sport: Torquay United FC (☎ 01803 328666; www.torquayunited.co.uk) currently in the Blue Square Conference, play at Plainmoor Stadium, to the north east of the town (TQ1 3PS). *Torquay Athletic RFC* plays almost on the seafront at the Rec, Rathmore Road TQ2 6NX (☎ 01803 607577, www.torquatrugby.co.uk).

Bike rental: Colin Lewis, *5–7 Manor* Road, Paignton, ☎ 01803 553095, www.colin-lewis.co.uk. An ex-professional cyclist opened this shop after retiring from racing; *Onabike,* 106 Queen Street, Newton Abbot, ☎ 01626 334664; *Simply the Bike,* 100–102 Belgrave Road, Torquay, ☎ 01803 200024; *Bikes N Tools,* Unit 11, The Market, Market Street, Torquay, ☎ 01803 296604; *Bikin' Motion,* 20 Torhill Road, Castle Circus, Torquay, ☎ 01803 214145, www.bikinmotion.co.uk; *Mylor Cycles* 10 Northumberland Place, Teignmouth TQ14 8DD, ☎ 01626 778460.

Taxis: Station Taxis, Newton Abbot, ☎ 01626 33 44 88; *Dawlish Taxis,* ☎ 01626 888111; *Terry's Taxis,* Teignmouth, ☎ 01626 873334; *Torbay Cab Co,* Torquay, ☎ 01803 292 292; Able Taxis, Paignton, ☎ 01803 555200; *Brixham Taxis,* ☎ 01803 853000.

And nestling under the distinctive outcrop of Chudleigh Rocks are the eight acres of **The Rock Gardens**, hidden in a big old stone quarry with tree ferns, carp ponds, inspiring views and an illuminated cave.

Teignmouth

The seaside town at the mouth of one of Devon's major rivers is worth a visit, if only for the panorama of beach, sea and estuary from either bank of the Teign. But the most important thing to know in advance, however, is that all Devonians call it 'tinmuth' and *not* 'taynemouth'.

Teignmouth itself has a quaint old town centre behind the beach with Georgian and Victorian buildings dating from its heyday as a port for Dartmoor granite and early seaside resort. In Regent Street, look for **Ridley's Restaurant**. Local lad Darren Ridley left town to work at as a chef at Buckingham Palace, Gleneagles and the *QEII*, then returned to open this quirky restaurant.

Teignmouth's beach is shingly sand – the old pier once acted as a divider to segregate male and female bathers. There is a green behind, called the Den, with tennis and mini-golf.

On the estuary side of town is **Back Beach**, an interesting world of boats, nautical bits and fishermen's huts. It's too dirty to swim but you can get a passenger ferry to **Shaldon** here. It claims to be the oldest continuously working ferry in England, having been doing its stuff for over 1,000 years. The boat itself is 100 years old. It lands on the beach in front of Shaldon's **Ferry Boat Inn**, which serves food and has a nice riverside terrace.

The other crossing, the long low-lying bridge upstream, was opened in 1931. The views are nice enough to encourage a walk across, although traffic is heavy in summer.

On the west bank, **Shaldon** is a daintier prospect. There is a picturesque village green surrounded by period cottages, some quaint old-fashioned shops and wonderful walks – include the smugglers' tunnel under the great looming red sandstone headland called 'The Ness'. It emerges at a secluded beach on the other side. For more information contact Teignmouth Tourist Information Centre (The Den TQ14 8BE; ☎ 01626 215666).

Dawlish

Dawlish doesn't have Teignmouth's elegance and views. The town that was loved by the Victorians has been spoilt by its high ratio of takeaways and amusements. Nevertheless the red sandstone cliffs and stream-side park with its iconic black swans do retain a period charm and some of the side streets have wonderful old houses tucked away.

Dawlish's beach is small and comprises a sandy shingle mix reached through a tunnel under the seafront railway (see GWR panel). The trains lend excitement but nearby **Dawlish Warren** has a much better sand beach.

The Warren is a 1.5 mile sandy spit sticking out into the mouth of the Exe, with plenty of sea defences to stop it washing away. Around the shore are dunes and holiday camps but the beach is big enough for anyone to escape the crowds. The walk along the GWR granite railway embankment to Dawlish is also popular, but note how often it has to be patched up after sea damage. Further north is the village of **Cockwood** on the Exe Estuary – a tiny pretty harbour hamlet with two good pubs (The Anchor and The Ship). For more information contact Dawlish Tourist Information Centre (The Lawn, Dawlish EX7 9PW; ☎ 01626 215665).

Haldon

Inland from the western bank of the Exe Estuary are the Haldon Hills. Peeping from top of the trees, the Georgian folly of **Belvedere Tower** can be seen from all over south Devon. The woods have been developed as a leisure site, with walking paths, picnic sites, bike trails and an innovative children's adventure trail. And Exeter Racecourse is situated at the highest point on the A38.

BELVEDERE FOLLY,
☎ 01392 833668; www.haldon-belvedere.co.uk
Entry: adults £2.00; open Feb to Oct: Sun and bank holidays 1.30pm–5.30pm; luxurious one-bedroom apartment in the Belvedere Tower with stunning views from £300 for a three-night stay.

The best point of access for the 15 miles of woods and hills is the **Haldon Gateway**, a car park (£2 per day) with access to 30 miles of new trails for bike, foot, or on horseback. And here is the 'Hub', with a play area, toilets, a shower, the Ranger's Office, an art gallery, cycle hire and café (☎ 01392 834251; www.forestry.gov.uk/haldonforestpark/).

The Belvedere folly was built by Sir Robert Palk, one of the richest men in England in the late 1700s. He made a fortune in India then built a grand mansion modelled on Buckingham Palace lower down the hill. But all that remains is the stable block and staff quarters, which have been converted into the rambling old **Lord Haldon Country House Hotel** in Dunchideock.

The Belvedere was used by the Palks to entertain guests, including King George III. Later, Marconi is said to have carried out tests at the site.

Powderham Castle

POWDERHAM CASTLE, Kenton, Exeter EX6 8JQ; ☎ 01626 890243; www.powderham.co.uk Entry: adults £8.50, children 5–14 years £6.50 family (2+2) £24; open Mar to Nov: Sun to Fri 10am–5.30pm; Secret Garden and Courtenay Fort 10.30am–4pm, Woodland Garden and Belvedere open until 1 Aug.

With secret doors, a private deer park and a folly in the woods, Powderham Castle is a good classic English stately home. In some ways it's an iconic Devonshire attraction, as it's the home of the Courtenay family, the Earls of Devon. The Castle stands halfway up the east shore of the Exe Estuary, the grey stone building visible through the trees from the wonderful little-used estuary road north from Starcross.

The castle was featured in the Oscar-winning film *Remains of the Day* and the TV series *Midsummer Murders*. And you can see its opulent interior on a one-hour guided tour. Outside you can wander at your leisure; there is Victorian walled garden now full of pets for children to play with, a big wooden adventure fort, a birds of prey show (2.30 daily in the summer), archery, local produce shop, plant centre and tearooms.

Powderham Castle; still home to the Earls of Devon

DARTMOUTH AND THE SOUTH HAMS

Picture this classic landscape – small sandy coves, wooded estuaries, secluded boating creeks and rolling hills covered in rich green dairy pasture-land. These are the sights that have made the South Hams one of the most sought-after patches of Devon.

While all parts of the county have nice bits, the South Hams seems to have lots, and perhaps most importantly, it hardly has a horrible bit. That's because there are no really big towns, nothing industrial and not even much of a tourist sprawl. It shares Torbay's mild climate yet lacks the Riviera's highly developed tourism. Much of the land is unspoilt – protected either by agriculture, the National Trust or its Area of Outstanding Natural Beauty designation.

Many of the villages are pristine, protected by the wealth of those who can afford to live in some of Devon's most expensive postcodes. So expect to find beautiful scenery, villages of thatched cottages and the relaxed old towns of Salcombe, Totnes, Modbury, Kingsbridge and Ivybridge.

The South Hams is primarily known as a boating haven – thanks to two extensive and beguiling estuaries with lots of navigable inlets and picturesque moorings. But the area includes some of Devon's best and cleanest beaches too. The superlative seasides of Blackpool Sands, Salcombe South and Big-bury-on-Sea are among five Blue Flags in the region.

WHAT TO SEE AND DO

 Fair weather

Salcombe may have posher yachts, Totnes less touristy shops and Kingsbridge the administrative headquarters, but the real heart of the South Hams is **Dartmouth**. It sits at the mouth of one of the great Devon rivers, where steep wooded hills drop to the edge of the Dart's dark water. Coloured fishing boats bob on their moorings as ferries ply to and fro between pastel painted period houses facing the river on either shore. It's one of Devon's finest panoramas.

Dartmouth's sheltered deep water made it one of the busiest English ports. Richard the Lionheart's crusades sailed from here, Sir Walter Raleigh brought back captured Spanish galleons, Henry Hudson called in during his search for the North West Passage and the Pilgrim Fathers dropped by, bound for the New World in the *Mayflower* in 1620. During the Second World War 480 vessels gathered in the harbour before sailing for the D-Day beaches of Normandy in 1944.

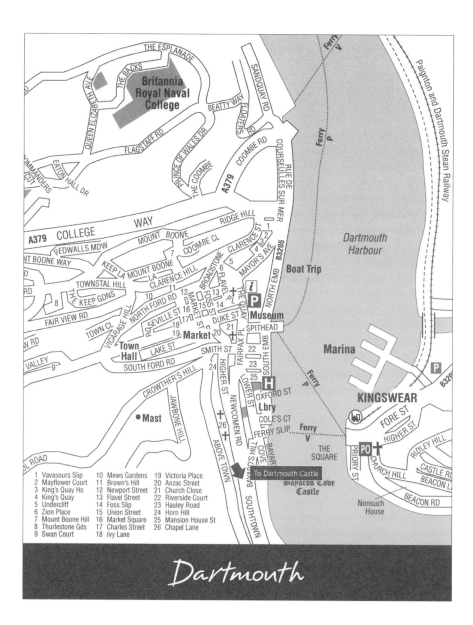

THE ESPLANADE
THE BACKS
Britannia
Royal Naval
College
QUEEN ELIZABETH AVE
FLOATERS RD
BEATTY WAY
SANDQUAY RD
PRINCE OF WALES DR
THE COOMBE
FLAGSTAFF RD
EATON HALL DR
COMMANDERS CT
A379
COOMBE RD
RUE DE COURSEULLES SUR MER
Ferry P
Ferry V
Paignton and Dartmouth Steam Railway
WAY
RIDGE HILL
COLLEGE
A379
MOUNT BOONE
PEDWALLS MDW
COOMBE CL
CLARENCE ST
MAYOR'S AVE
B3205
NT BOONE WAY
KEEP LA
MOUNT BOONE
LA
CLARENCE HILL
BROADSTONE
Dartmouth
Harbour
Boat Trip
TOWNSTAL HILL
THE KEEP GDNS
FAIR VIEW RD
TOWN CL
NORTH FORD RD
SEVILLE ST
VICARAGE HILL
FLAVEL ST
FOSS ST
THE QUAY
NORTH EMB
Museum
i
P
DUKE ST
SPITHEAD
Market
FAIRFAX PL
Town
Hall
LAKE ST
SOUTH FORD RD
SMITH ST
HIGHER ST
SOUTH EMB
Marina
VALLEY
CROWTHER'S HILL
JAWBONE HILL
LOWER ST
NEWCOMEN RD
H
OXFORD ST
Lbry
Ferry P
KINGSWEAR
FORE ST
HIGHER ST
Mast
COLE'S CT
FERRY SLIP
Ferry V
RIDLEY HILL
CASTLE RD
BEACON L
L ROAD
ABOVE TOWN
7TH SC BAYA
COVE
BAYA
THE SQUARE
PRIORY ST
PO
CHURCH HILL
BEACON RD
SOUTHTOWN
To Dartmouth Castle
Dartmouth Cove Castle
Nonsuch House

1 Vavasours Slip	10 Mews Gardens	19 Victoria Place
2 Mayflower Court	11 Brown's Hill	20 Anzac Street
3 King's Quay Ho	12 Newport Street	21 Church Close
4 King's Quay	13 Flavel Street	22 Riverside Court
5 Undercliff	14 Foss Slip	23 Hauley Road
6 Zion Place	15 Union Street	24 Horn Hill
7 Mount Boone Hill	16 Market Square	25 Mansion House St
8 Thurlestone Gds	17 Charles Street	26 Chapel Lane
9 Swan Court	18 Ivy Lane	

Dartmouth

The train that never came

Dartmouth is believed to have the only railway station in the world that a train has never arrived at. The station, now a waterfront restaurant, was built before the railway bridge bringing the line from Torbay. After local opposition, the Dart bridge never got built. The line terminated at Kingswear. Passengers had to take the ferry across to the pontoon at Dartmouth station instead.

You can sense this seafaring heritage everywhere. Hear it in the tinkling rigging of boats, squawking seagulls, and the chugging ferries. On the hill, the Edwardian Naval College dominates the town, and just wandering the bustling narrow streets you'll keep finding names such as Old Rope Walk and the Captain's House.

Some of the old buildings were made from timbers of captured ships and the quayside was built by captured Napoleonic sailors. *The Onedin Line*, a popular BBC TV drama series, which ran from 1971 to 1980, was filmed here (and in Exeter).

In time-honoured tradition, the best way to arrive at Dartmouth is by water. You get a memorable panorama of a town that totally faces the river that is central to its very existence. A trip on the steam train from Paignton to Kingswear, followed by a passenger ferry across the Dart is ideal.

Taking to the water

Whatever, all visitors will want to take to the water at some stage – the good news is you don't need to own a millionaire's yacht to do it. And you don't risk the ultimate locals' verdict on the rich part-time yachting fraternity, which they sometimes call 'The Birmingham Navy'.

The simplest and cheapest method of getting on the water is with those all-year **ferries**. For cars and pedestrians, the *Lower Ferry*, pulled by a tug, crosses to Kingswear, (☎ 01803 752342; car £3.30; 7am–10.55pm Mon to Sat, 8am–10.55pm Sun). The *Higher Ferry*, with its paddle wheels and chains, crosses to Noss. Townsfolk are excited that the *Higher Ferry* is due to be replaced with a bigger new £4m vessel during 2009 (☎ 01803 833351; car £2.50, £4.80 return; 6.30am–10.45pm Mon to Sat, 8am–10.45pm Sun/bank holidays). And the best bargain of all is a passenger ferry that crosses from Kingswear Station to Dartmouth 'station' (adults 60p, children 30p; daily 7am–11pm).

In the summer there are also passenger ferries to Dartmouth Castle or up river. Upstream is probably best if you've only time for one: you'll see ancient woods overhanging the still water and pretty waterside villages suddenly appearing around a bend in the river. Watch for herons, kingfishers and egrets. And many local guides will point out the rock where Sir Walter Raleigh allegedly sat and smoked a tobacco pipe.

There are plenty of **boat trips** to choose from. Look for the old red and yellow fishing boats running the 30-minute Dartmouth to Dittisham route (10am–4.30pm, Mar till the end of Oct). They leave from Double Steps, North Embankment, Dartmouth.

> **DARTMOUTH TO DITTISHAM FERRY**, ☎ 0781 8001108; www.dartmouthdittishamferry.co.uk. Return/single: adults £6/£4, under 16s £4/£3.

Greenway Ferries are more like cruises, with a full commentary. You ring a bell at Dittisham to 'summon the ferry'. The ferry goes to Torquay, Brixham, Totnes, Greenway Estate, Dittisham, Bow Creek and Sharpham Vineyard (☎ 01803 844010; www.greenwayferry.co.uk).

And Riverlink offer a range of cruises, from coastal wildlife expeditions to evening jazz buffet trips. You can even buy a joint return ticket with the steam railway (☎ 01803 834488; www.riverlink.co.uk).

The *Falcon*, operated by owner/skipper Tony Hoyle, specialises in watching seabirds, seals, peregrine falcons, and sometimes basking sharks, dolphins and turtles (☎ 01803 839245/www.dartboat.com). And the *African Queen* offers trips ranging from two-hour evening cruises to weekly charters. You can even sleep on board for a few days. (☎ 07885 246061; www.theafrican-queen.co.uk).

Something really different could be a guided **canoe trip** complete with picnic blankets and hot drinks round a campfire (Canoe Adventures, ☎ 01803 865301) or a selection of **extreme sports** such as coasteering and kayaking with Mountain Water Experience (☎ 01548 550675; www.mountainwaterexperience.com).

Hiring your own boat is easy too. Contact Dartmouth Boat Hire at the Centre Kiosk by the Bandstand, North Embankment, Dartmouth (☎ 01803 834600; www.dartmouth-boat-hire.co.uk) and there are opportunities to charter individual boats including luxury catamarans, fishing boats, speedboats, and sailing yachts.

Back on land

Of course Dartmouth does have an identity away from the water. It's a great place to wander among ancient buildings, browsing boutique shops, art galleries and delicatessens. The cobbled **Old Market** place often features colourful stalls and a farmers' market (every second Sat of the month, 9am–1pm). Look for **Simon Drew's** gallery in Foss Street. Locals love its high-quality but sometimes quirky collections (☎ 01803 832832; www.simondrew.co.uk).

After two French attacks during the Hundred Years War, Mayor John Hawley

Waves crash against the breathtaking Kingswear Castle

started building a castle to defend the town. Eventually there were two, either side of the neck of the river, linked by heavy chains that could be raised every night to prevent access. **Dartmouth Castle** is still largely intact and gives a glimpse of the town's fear of danger from the sea from medieval days to the Second World War. During the Victorian era the castle was equipped with guns that could hit approaching ships 2 miles away. Think of that as you walk/cycle/drive along the estuary to the castle from the town (it's only a mile) or take the castle ferry from the town quayside.

> **DARTMOUTH CASTLE**,
> B3205, TQ6 0JN; ☎ 01803 833588; www.english-heritage.org.uk/dartmouth Entry: adults £3.90, children £2; open Apr to Oct: daily 10am–4pm; Nov to Mar: weekends.

On the other shore, **Kingswear Castle** is now an extraordinary holiday home, restored and let by the Landmark Trust (☎ 01628 825925; www.landmark-trust.co.uk).

As you meander up the Dart estuary, there are plenty of attractions along the way: **Kingswear**, on the east bank of the Dart, is a smaller, quainter reflection of Dartmouth opposite. It's good for a quiet stroll up windy streets with cosy old pubs, (the Ship, Royal Dart and Steam Packet) and great views across to Dartmouth. And you can often buy freshly caught fish on the quayside.

Tucked into the hilly western bank of the Dart, **Dittisham** is a picturesque assembly of cottages around a Norman church with a beautiful carved stone pulpit, and two good pubs (The Red Lion and Ferryboat Inn). It's the start for some excellent walks, including the **Dart Valley Trail**. You must ring the bell near the Ferry Boat Inn to summon a passenger ferry to cross to Greenway. In the middle of the river you'll see the Anchor Stone – village legend has it that unfaithful wives were tied to this as punishment.

Local knowledge

Chef **Kit Noble** owns and runs the award-winning Edwardian guesthouse Nonsuch House with his wife Penny. It stands high above Dartmouth Harbour, on the Kingswear shore. Kit, who moved to the UK from New Zealand, was once judged as cooking Britain's best breakfast by AA inspectors.

Favourite restaurant: The Embankment on the Quayside in Dartmouth, and further afield, The Oyster Shack near Bigbury – the place we go for family celebrations.

Favourite pub: Dartmoor Union at Holbeton, which brews its own beer.

Favourite shop: Luscombes the butchers in Dartmouth, Riverford Organics, Sharpham Vineyard and Mark Lobb's fish stall each Friday at Dartmouth market. My wife Penny would say the Dartmouth galleries, clothes and shoe shops.

Favourite Devon food/drink: Freshly caught fish and shellfish, Sharpham cheese, Blackawton lamb, wine from Sharpham and locally brewed beer.

Favourite Devon activity: Getting into a boat and going up the Dart or out to sea, finding a wonderful beach and having a picnic.

Best view: From our conservatory!

Best thing about living here: The river, the sea, the views, the village...

Best kept Devonshire secret: The River Dart – the most beautiful evocative river with lovely villages, fantastic wildlife, secret places, good pubs and fabulous scenery.

Favourite thing to do on a rainy day: Going for a long walk with my wife and the dogs, coming back to a hot bath, sitting by a roaring log fire listening to good music with a good glass of wine.

Anything else you'd like to recommend to Devon visitors: A trip to Dartmoor, sailing in Dartmouth Regatta, the Dartmouth Food Festival, eating local oysters, the Music Festival, the two local National Trust gardens – Coleton Fishacre and Greenway – and walking on the South West Coast Path.

Wet weather

The **Butterwalk** is an arcade of half-timbered buildings rising above a granite colonnade. Charles II held court in a prosperous merchant's house here once while sheltering from storms, so it's a good place to hide on a drizzly day. Upstairs you can see the wood-panelled rooms he used – they're now the **Dartmouth Museum**. This small but interesting museum includes a superb collection of ships in bottles, and it is said to be haunted.

> **THE BUTTERWALK**, Duke Street, Dartmouth TQ6 9PZ; ☎ 01803 832923; www.devonmuseums.net/dartmouth Entry: free; Easter to Nov: Mon to Fri 10am–4.30pm, Sat 10am–4pm; Nov to Easter: Mon to Sat 12pm–3pm.

Thomas Newcomen, the inventor of the steam pumping engine was born in Dartmouth in 1663, the son of a wealthy shipowner. The site of his house in Lower Street is marked with a plaque. His invention was one of the major advances of the industrial revolution. An 18th-century working **Newcomen engine** is on display in an old electricity sub-station, next to the tourist office.

> **THE ENGINE HOUSE**, Mayors Avenue, Dartmouth TQ6 9YY; ☎ 01803 834224. Entry: free.

Up the hill behind the Engine House, serenely observing the town and the port, is the **Britannia Royal Naval College**. It's where the Queen first met Prince Philip and all Britain's naval officers have attended since 1905. Two-hour guided tours include the chapel, gun-room and quarterdeck, although, for many, the best part is the view. Arrangements are a bit awkward, adults must provide photo ID, a minibus collects you from the town centre and tickets must be booked in advance. The college also runs escorted historic tours of the D-Day preparations in the South Hams and of the woods and gardens surrounding the college.

> **BRITANNIA ROYAL NAVAL COLLEGE**, Dartmouth TQ6 0HJ; ☎ 01803 677787; www.brnc.co.uk. Entry: adults £10.75, children free; Easter to Oct, Wed/Sun; tickets available from Dartmouth Tourist Information Centre(☎ 01803 834224).

What to do with children...

If the children are demanding excitement, **Woodland Leisure Park** is another of Devon's major family theme parks that kids will love and adults will probably grudgingly enjoy. This one has a huge variety at least: twisting water slides, 500m toboggan run, blasting action game, bumper boats, wild west town, small animals zoo, honey

> **WOODLAND LEISURE PARK**, Blackawton, Dartmouth TQ9 7DQ; ☎ 01803 712598; www.woodlandspark.com Entry: per person from £6 low season to £10.75 high season; open daily 9.30am–5pm.

Visit Agatha Christie's family garden at Greenway

farm, tractor yard, soft play, falconry, ferret racing, woodland walks, china painting, a train and a boating lake. There is enough indoor activity to make it worthwhile as a rainy day retreat too. And if you're really sold on the idea – you can stay there on a well-equipped camping and caravan park.

And how to avoid children

The South Hams' mild climate encourages creative horticulture and visitors have some fine gardens to choose from. **Fast Rabbit Farm** is a strangely named woodland garden with a series of ponds linked by waterfalls among camellias, rhododendrons and magnolias.

> **FAST RABBIT FARM,** Ash Cross, Dartmouth TQ6 0LR; ☎ 07813 504490; www.fastrabbit-farm.co.uk. Entry: £3.50; Mar to Oct: Sun/bank holidays, 11am–5pm.

Overlooking the River Dart, **Greenway** is novelist Agatha Christie's family garden. There is woodland with drifts of wild flowers, ancient walled gardens, a peach house and Victorian fernery. It's very pretty but don't expect an Agatha Theme Park – there is nothing about the crime writer to see. It's now in the hands of the National Trust and one of their conditions for opening was limiting the

> **GREENWAY,** Greenway Road, Galmpton TQ5 0ES; ☎ 01803 842382; www.nationaltrust.org.uk Entry: adults £5.20, discount for 'green' transport; open Mar to Oct: Wed to Sat 10.30am–5pm.

traffic. So to arrive by car you have to pre-book a parking space or you won't get in. Far better is to arrive by boat. Ferries run from Dittisham, Dartmouth and Totnes or tickets are available for a circular tour on steam train to Kingswear and ferry from Dartmouth (Riverlink, ☎ 01803 834488; www.riverlink.co.uk).

Finally, **Coleton Fishacre** is an arts and crafts house right on the coast with a luxuriant year-round garden. The gorgeous 1930s house was built for the theatre impresarios, the D'Oyley Carte family, who spent 20 years creating the gardens and they are well worth a visit.

> **COLETON FISHACRE**, Brownstone Road, Kingswear TQ6 0EQ; ☎ 01803 752466; www.nationaltrust.org.uk. Entry: adults £6.40, family (2+2) £16, garden only £5.90/£3, discount for 'green' transport; open Wed–Sun, Mar to Oct 10.30am–5pm.

Entertainment

Compared with Torbay next door, the South Hams are far more relaxed. There is less nightlife and culture but still a few treats if you know where to look. The **Dartmouth Music Festival** in mid-May is surprisingly good – with a mix of musical styles (www.dartmouth-music-festival.org.uk) but the **Regatta** in August is when the town really lets rip. The three days are mostly focused on the water but there is barrel rolling, street fairs, pavement painting, tug of war and the Red Arrows too (www.dartmouthregatta.co.uk).

Theatre, cinemas, dance
The rest of the year the **Flavel Arts Centre** (Flavel Place, Dartmouth TQ6 9ND; ☎ 01803 839530; www.theflavel.org.uk) has a cinema, theatre, live music and workshops.

Further afield there is a surprising quantity and quality of concerts, cinema, theatre and dance at **Dartington Arts** (☎ 01803 847070; www.dartington.org/arts), one of Devon's leading arts and crafts venues despite being almost in the middle of nowhere.

The only other South Hams cinema is **The Reel** in the Town Hall, Fore St, Kingsbridge TQ7 1PG (☎ 01548 856636; www.thereelcinema.co.uk) which has a licence so you can drink while watching.

The terrace at Nonsuch House permits gorgeous views over the River Dart

The best... PLACES TO STAY

BOUTIQUE

Burgh Island Hotel

Bigbury-on-Sea TQ7 4BG
☎ 01548 810514
www.burghisland.com

This unique art deco hotel on its own private island is one of Devon's most famous hotels. Its décor and ambience was set in the 1930s, when Edward VIII wooed Mrs Simpson in the Palm Court bar, Noel Coward played piano in the ballroom, and Agatha Christie wrote bestsellers in the clifftop gardens. The Harry Roy band played the Charleston from a floodlit floating platform in the middle of the seawater rock pool and Burgh was hailed as 'the smartest hotel west of the Ritz'. It's not that state-of-the art now, but you'll go a long way to find a more memorable hotel experience. Alongside modern comforts there are period details such as bakelite telephones and retro radios. Some guests even dress in period costume. At low tide you can walk across a sandy beach to the shore but at high tide that's covered. Unpredictable currents deter boats so Burgh employs a unique 'sea tractor'. This contraption drives across the sea bottom as you perch on a platform 12ft higher. It's a suitably bizarre way to arrive on this surreal island.

Price: Dinner, B&B from £285 for a single, from £355 to £550 for a double.

Buckland-Tout-Saints

Goveton, Kingsbridge TQ7 2DS
☎ 01548 853055. www.tout-saints.co.uk

No-one will be dressing in flappers' costumes to dance the Charleston here... This exquisite William and Mary country house hotel has a 40 acre garden including a croquet lawn, opulent interior and formal dining in the acclaimed two AA rosette restaurant.

Price: B&B from £79 to £135 for a single; from £130 to £295 for a double.

The Dart Marina Hotel

Sandquay Road, Dartmouth TQ6 9PH,
☎ 01803 832580
www.dartmarina.com

Dartmouth's highest rated hotel is this modern boutique hotel on riverside with its own marina. You'll find wonderful views, private balconies and dining alfresco with acclaimed cuisine. There is also a spa, solarium, jacuzzi, gym and indoor pool.

Price: B&B from £110 to £145 for a single, from £190 to £275 for a double.

HOTEL

Thurlestone Hotel

Thurlestone TQ7 3NN
☎ 01548 560382. www.thurlestone.co.uk

Just across the mouth of the River Avon from Burgh Island, this hotel couldn't be more different. Although it has been owned and run by the Grose family since 1896, it concentrates on facilities rather than style. So there is a one-rosette restaurant, indoor and outdoor pools, beauty salon, sauna, solarium, Jacuzzi, gym, snooker, pool table, croquet, putting green, tennis, squash, badminton, games room, children's club and live entertainment. There is even a golf course next door.

Price: B&B from £87 to£175 for a single, from £174 to £350 for a double.

Hazelwood House

Loddiswell, Near Kingsbridge, TQ7 4EB,
☎ 01548 821232
www.hazelwoodhouse.com

This small quirky Victorian country house hotel hosts an impressive programme of concerts and workshops. Not all bedrooms are en suite but there are also self-catering two-bedroomed period cottages in the grounds (£400–£650 per week).

Price: B&B from £45 for a single, from £85 to £112 for a double.

The best... PLACES TO STAY

INN

The Modbury Inn

**Brownston Street, Modbury PL21 0RQ,
☎ 01548 830275
www.modburyinn.co.uk**

In the centre of the attractive small town of Modbury, this old coaching inn has real ale, homemade food (Tues to Sat), Sunday quizzes and four en suite rooms upstairs.

Price: B&B from £40 for a single, from £65 for a double.

Old Chapel Inn

**Bigbury TQ7 4HQ, ☎ 01548 810241
www.oldchapelinn.com**

This whitewashed country pub has an acclaimed restaurant and an ancient chapel with a holy well. It's a strange mix but works nicely here, especially the luxurious bed-rooms with specially commissioned hand-made furniture and art.

Price: B&B from £60 for a single, from £85 for a double.

Red Lion

**Dittisham TQ6 0ES, ☎ 01803 722235
www.redliondittisham.co.uk**

An old village freehouse overlooks the Dart and has bedrooms more like a hotel than a pub. Thankfully it's more like a pub down-stairs, with local real ales, log fire, garden with river views and homely food.

Price: B&B from £60 to £100 for a double.

FARMSTAY

Burton Farmhouse

**Galmpton, Kingsbridge TQ7 3EY
☎ 01548 561210, www.burtonfarm.co.uk**

This family-run working farm has pedigree Holstein dairy cattle and flocks of sheep, but the farmer's wife has created a success-ful tourism business too. The house is big enough to have 14 en suite rooms and two self-catering cottages (£285–£795 per week). The attractive restaurant is open to non-residents and cream teas are made with her homemade clotted cream.

Price: B&B from £45 for a single, from £82.50 to £140 for a double.

B & B

Nonsuch House

**Church Hill, Kingswear TQ6 0BX, ☎
01803 752829
www.nonsuch-house.co.uk**

Relax at an elegant Edwardian guesthouse with splendid outlook across the river to Dartmouth. You can sit admiring the view in wicker chairs in the conservatory and taste why they were winners of the AA's 'Best Breakfast in England' title.

Price: B&B from £75 to £110 for a single, from £100 to £135 for a double.

UNUSUAL

The Retreat Boat

**River Dart, Dartmouth TQ6 9BX
☎ 01803 839339
www.theretreatboat.co.uk**

You board your floating holiday cottage in Dartmouth (choose either a sailing yacht or motorboat). The on-call skipper leaves you in peace when you are safely moored some-where in the estuary, which can be for days. But don't fret – these centrally heated boats have every luxury, sleep six and you can go on day trips wherever you want.

Price: From £240 per night (min 3 nights).

Start Point Lighthouse

**Rural Retreats
☎ 01386 701177
www.ruralretreats.co.uk**

This upmarket holiday cottage company has several attractive properties across the South Hams but the two former keepers' cottages at Start Point Lighthouse are the most distinctive. They're luxurious but remote and exposed, and guests are advised to bring earplugs in case it's misty – the fog-horn will start up. Because of the steep cliffs, no children under 11 are allowed, but babies are fine. The cottages sleep five or six.

Price: from £352 for a two-night break in Jan to £1,110 for a week in Aug.

The best... FOOD AND DRINK

Even in the sumptuous food-lover's county of Devon, the South Hams is a high spot. It has both essential ingredients – good local producers plus top shops and chefs that use them.

Dartmouth's Food Festival (www.dartmouthfoodfestival.co.uk) in October provides five days of food events across the town, including cookery demonstrations, tastings, markets and talks. It's a good way of finding out more about local food.

There are local fishing boats landing in both the estuaries (especially Kingswear and Salcombe) and Brixham is just round the corner, so freshly caught seafood is taken for granted. And there are plenty of acclaimed farms producing high quality meat and dairy produce in the hills around the estuaries.

And what is most noticeable is the innovation and enterprise in the local food and drink industry. From local microbreweries to smokeries, cheese makers to bottled spring water, it seems that every South Hams village has someone producing a top quality thing you can eat or drink.

Look out for local wine, organic fruit juices, liqueurs, ice cream and clotted cream. Tuck into locally smoked chicken and fish, and local grass-fed, free-range lamb, pork and beef.

It's an area with some of the highest quality eateries in Devon – some of that due to the quality of produce, some to the wealth of the average eater in the South Hams.

As the book went to press one Michelin-starred restaurant was closing in Dartmouth, but another celebrity chef was opening one. It shows that whenever you read this, there is guaranteed to be top places to eat in the South Hams. TV chef Mitch Tonks, who runs the successful restaurant and cookery school chain FishWorks, lives with his family in Brixham. He is set to open a restaurant on the quayside in Dartmouth only two doors away from the New Angel. This was run by fellow TV chef John Burton Race but is currently closed after Mr Burton Race's estranged wife, Kim, allegedly locked its doors while he appeared on *I'm a Celebrity Get Me Out of Here*. The latest word is it will now be sold.

▶ Staying in

Again, the South Hams is bursting with great grub... The **Riverford Farm Shop** won *The Observer* newspaper's award as the UK's best food shop in 2007 (presented to the shop's owner by Gordon Ramsay). Riverford now has three outlets (one in the middle of Totnes, one at Staverton and one at Yealmpton dealt with in the Plymouth chapter). Riverford has its own organic dairy herd and bakery but it's success is mainly down to the range of food stocked – including cooked meats, pies, cheeses, local organic fruit and vegetables, plus its own bacon and sausages. Specialities range from goose from a Totnes farm, salmon pâté made by Riverside's own chef, and lamb from local farmer George Welsh in Dartington, whose family has farmed there for 400 years.

> **RIVERFORD FARM SHOP**, Staverton TQ9 6AF; ☎ 01803 762523; and High Street, Totnes ☎ 01803 863959; www.riverford-farmshop.co.uk

Riverford stocks the products of the nearby **Sharpham Estate**. There are two great reasons to visit here: it's a leading English vineyard, producing acclaimed red, white and rosé wines, and it's a creamery, where Debbie Mumford makes soft cheeses from the estate's organic Jersey cows. There is a wine and cheese shop and small alfresco café serving local ingredients including, of course, dishes such as Sharpham Brie tarts with a basil pesto, Dartmouth lobster or local free-range chicken. There are tours available too, you can choose between a self-guided walk and tasting (£5) and a full guided tour, wine tutorial, lunch and free bottle (£49.50; must be booked).

> **SHARPHAM ESTATE**, Totnes TQ9 7UT, follow brown signs from A381; ☎ 01803 732203; www.sharpham.com
> Shop open Mar to Christmas, Mon-Sat, daily June to Oct; café and tours summer only.

Also check out the family-run **Britannia Shellfish** at Beesands. It's an excellent way to find fresh seafood. Britannia's own-caught crab, lobster and scallops are held in large seawater tanks so you can 'pick your own', with the option of having it cooked for you there and then. They also sell local wet fish and dressed Start Bay crab. If you time it right, you could see the crab and fish being landed on the beach at Beesands (The Viviers, Beesands TQ7 2EH; ☎ 01548 581168; www.britannia shellfish.co.uk)

And there is more: considered one of the country's finest smokeries, **Dartmouth Smokehouse** in Nelson Road uses traditional curing and smoking, and the best local raw materials such as marinades of spices, honey and herbs, fruit liqueurs, and Somerset apple brandy and burning pure beechwood, oak, apple and cherrywood. Their products include smoked salmon, trout, eel fillets, bacon, goose, chicken, duck, guinea fowl, kippers, haddock, cherry tomatoes, vegetable medley and shiitake mushrooms. You can buy direct online or by phone and you'll see their produce in shops all over Devon. (☎ 01803 833123/www.dartmouthsmokehouse.co.uk).

You'll find 22 flavours of Dartmouth homemade ice-cream at **The Good Intent** in Lower Street or being sold by traditional street vendors around the town in the summer. They also offer homemade fudge, clotted cream, confectionery, preserves, chocolates and biscuits (Dartmouth Ice Cream Company; ☎ 01803 832157;www.dartmouthicecream.com).

It's also an area well served by **traditional butchers** such as A W Luscombe, Fore Street, Totnes TQ9 5RP (☎ 01803 862119) who have been in business since 1788 and sell naturally fed local poultry and game. Or try **Aune Valley Meat**, Rake Farm, Loddiswell, Near Kingsbridge, TQ7 2DA (☎ 01548 550413) which specialises in well-hung beef reared on the farm. **McCabe's**, also in Fore Street, Totnes, cures its own bacon, makes its own sausages and sells kid, wild boar and venison.

You'll find **Mark Lobb** Fish & Game Merchant from Stoke Fleming at markets in Dartmouth (Fri), Kingsbridge (Tues) and Dartmouth's monthly farmers' market.

Other good local **food shops** in the region include **Dartington Cider Press**, for local cheeses, ciders, wines, ice creams and chocolates (Dartington Cider Press Centre, Shinners Bridge TQ9 6TQ; ☎ 01803 847500; www.dartington-ciderpress.co.uk) and surprisingly, local garages. The local **Holliss Filling Station** chain has convenience stores that have won an award for their stock of local meat, fish, cider and vegetables (☎ 01803 832091; www.holliss.co.uk).

🍷 Drinking

It's worth looking out for the award-winning products of **South Hams Brewery** in Torcross, an independent small traditional beer-maker producing several cask and bottled beers including the popular Devon Pride. And **Quercus Brewery** in Kingsbridge makes its own Prospect and Shingle Bay ales and sells a huge variety of specialist beers and ciders at the headquarters in South Hams Business Park (☎ 01548 854888; www.quercusbrewery.co.uk; Tues to Thur 3pm–6pm, Fri/Sat 10am–6pm).

Other local products to try include **Ashridge Cider** from Staverton. It's the opposite of farm scrumpy, these are refined sparkling drinks using the champagne method. **Heron Valley's** award-winning organic fruit juices and cider come from a farm near Kingsbridge and **Devonia Natural Spring Water** is bottled at source at a farm near Totnes.

And the best **pubs** in the area include: **The Ship Inn** in the winding streets above the Dart at Kingswear, which is renowned for real ales, including Otter. It serves fresh fish straight from the boats too (☎ 01803 752348; www.theshipinnkingswear.co.uk); **The Dodbrooke Inn** in Church Street, Kingsbridge, (☎ 01548 852068) is a friendly local with well-kept real ales and farm cider, log fires and good food.

In Totnes, try the **King William IV** in Fore Street, with St Austell beer, stained glass windows and big screen TV; the **Royal Seven Stars** in Fore Street is an

EATING OUT

FINE DINING

The New Angel
South Embankment, Dartmouth TQ6 9BH
☎ **01803 839425**

The future of South Devon's highest-rated restaurant is in doubt as this guide goes to press. Totnes-based TV chef John Burton-Race has just appeared on *I'm a celebrity get me out of here* but is in dispute with his estranged wife about the relaxed riverside restaurant with rooms. It appears to be closed but may re-open again by the time this book is published. Whatever, if it's open when you're in Devon, it's a chance to try one of the best restaurants in the county. A main course costs from £18 to £25.

Buckland-Tout-Saints
Goveton, Kingsbridge TQ7 2DS
☎ **01548 853055**
www.tout-saints.co.uk

There is a two AA rosette French restaurant in this grand country house hotel. The atmosphere in wood-panelled 'Queen Anne' restaurant is formal but food is top quality. A three-course dinner is around £35.

The Dart Marina Hotel
Sandquay Road, Dartmouth TQ6 9PH
☎ **01803 832580**
www.dartmarina.com

Dartmouth's highest rated hotel has a highly acclaimed restaurant with great views, whether dining inside or out. Food is modern, ambience relaxed. A three-course dinner costs £28.50.

RESTAURANT

The Oyster Shack
Bigbury (Stakes Hill, Aveton Gifford) and Salcombe (Hannaford's Landing, Island Street)
☎ **01548 810876**
www.oystershack.co.uk

This cheery modern seafood bistro uses local produce such as oysters and mussels, and now has two branches in Bigbury and Salcombe. Both restaurants have an alfresco decking area and serve breakfast too (main courses from £10.95 to £19.50).

Burgh Island Hotel
Bigbury-on-Sea TQ7 4BG
☎ **01548 810514**
www.burghisland.com

The food is good, but it's this extraordinary venue that makes the hassle of getting to the island for a meal worthwhile. But the kitchen's championing of local produce is more than lip service: all meat must be born and bred within 20 miles, fish comes from Brixham, shellfish from Bigbury Bay. The hotel even has its own market garden on the mainland for fruit, veg and herbs, while lobsters and scallops are kept fresh in the seawater pool. Lunch costs £38 and dinner is £55.

Thurlestone Hotel
Thurlestone TQ7 3NN
☎ **01548 560382**
www.thurlestone.co.uk

The AA one-rosette restaurant in this hotel has great views across the bay or you can try the alfresco terrace. There is a fairly traditional menu with fish and dairy produce from Plymouth. A four-course dinner costs £35.

Nonsuch House
Church Hill, Kingswear TQ6 0BX
☎ **01803 752829**
www.nonsuch-house.co.uk

Breakfast is the star at this Edwardian guesthouse with views looking down on Dartmouth Harbour but the fresh and imaginative dinner menu for non-residents is good too. A three-course dinner is £32.50.

Restaurant 42
Fore Street, Salcombe TQ8 8JG
☎ **01548 843408**
www.restaurant42.co.uk

This relaxed restaurant/brasserie/bar has lovely waterside views, leather sofas and local ingredients including Salcombe crab, local scallops, locally smoked salmon and Devon apple tart. Three courses cost £27.

EATING OUT

The Embankment
24 South Embankment, Dartmouth TQ6 9BB, ☎ 01803 8333540

The tables are right on the quayside looking across the harbour, close to the lower ferry, and you get twinkling chandeliers, interesting art and excellent, locally sourced food. Three courses are around £25.

GASTROPUB
Old Chapel Inn
**Bigbury TQ7 4HQ, ☎ 01548 810241
www.oldchapelinn.com**

Fish from Plymouth, Brixham and Salcombe and local meat is served on a seasonally sensitive menu in the high-ceilinged Refectory Restaurant. The Old Chapel smokes its own meat and fish, cures ham and even makes its own honey, which is used extensively in the dishes.

Malsters Arms
**Tuckenhay, Near Totnes TQ9 7EH
☎ 01803 732350, www.tuckenhay.com**

The Malsters was made famous as Keith Floyd's creek-side gastropub. The colourful celebrity chef has moved on and it's more like an ordinary pub now, but with good B&B accommodation too. Food is good modern uncomplicated British fare. It costs about £22 for a three-course dinner.

CAFÉ
**Café Alf Resco
Lower Street, Dartmouth
☎ 01803 835880
www.cafealfresco.co.uk**

A Dartmouth institution for 14 years, this is a locals' favourite, serving breakfast and lunch, sometimes to live music, at heated outside tables or a cosy interior. There are colouring books for children and wifi for grown-ups. Note the self-catering and B&B accommodation above too. Everyone in town calls it 'Alfs'.

Venus beach cafés
**Blackpool Sands, East Portlemouth and Bigbury-on-Sea
www.venuscompany.co.uk**

Venus runs award-winning contemporary beach cafés in three great locations in the South Hams. Menus are full of local organic genetically modified (GM)-free ingredients including Occombe Farm burgers, Riverford Farm milk, Sharpham wines and cheeses, Buckfast Bakery pies, flapjacks and brownies, Luscombe juices and cider, Burts chips, Cuckoo Farm free-range eggs and Dartmouth Smokehouse salmon. A full English breakfast costs £5.95 (served until 11am at Blackpool and Bigbury), children's boxed meals cost from £3.95, and coffee costs from £1.50.

atmospheric old coaching hotel that is busy on market days; the **Steam Packet** has a scenic location on St Peters Quay and serves Otter and Princetown Jail Ale plus a good range of food.

From the several good town pubs, we've picked two ancient pubs in Dartmouth. You'll find Dartmoor Best at the **Royal Castle** on the quay and Sharp's Doom Bar at **The Cherub** in Higher Street. Salcombe's **Victoria** has St Austell and Dartmoor ales, and further down Fore Street, the **Ferry Inn** has a choice of local cider.

And it's worth the trek over to Burgh Island to the tiny **Pilchard Inn**. There is good food and Sharps, Teignworthy and St Austell beers... and a unique island atmosphere.

ⓘ Visitor information

Tourist information centres:
Dartmouth Tourist Information Centre, The Engine House, Mayor's Avenue TQ6 9YY, ☎ 01803 834224, www.dartmouthtic.org.uk/www.discoverdartmouth.com; *Salcombe Tourist Information Centre,* Market Street, Salcombe TQ8 8DE, ☎ 01548 843927, www.salcombeinformation.co.uk; *Kingsbridge Tourist Information Centre,* The Quay, Kingsbridge TQ7 1HS, ☎ 01548 853195, www.kingsbridgeinfo.co.uk; *Totnes Tourist Information Centre,* Town Mill, Coronation Road, Totnes TQ9 5DF, [tel]01803 863168, www.totnesinformation.co.uk.

Websites: The South Hams council website www.somewhere-special.co.uk, has some good links and facilities, including full details for nine circular walks in the area. A very handy independent view is available at www.venuscompany.co.uk which has webcams on four beaches showing current weather, temperature, wind speed plus a comprehensive guide to the facilities on all the South Hams beaches.

Hospitals: 24-hour A&E facilities are available at *Torbay Hospital,* Newton Road, Torquay, TQ2 7AA, ☎ 01803 614567; *Derriford Hospital,* Derriford Road, Derriford, Plymouth, PL6 8DH, ☎ 0845 155 8155.

Supermarkets: *Co-op,* Mayor's Avenue, Dartmouth TQ6 9NF, ☎ 01803 835516; *Somerfield,* Fairfax Place, Dartmouth TQ6 9AB, ☎ 01803 832737; *Somerfield,* Cookworthy Road, Kingsbridge TQ7 1QN,☎ 01548 854056; *Somerfield,* Brutus Centre, Fore Street, Totnes TQ9 5RW, ☎ 01803 862078; *Morrisons,* Coronation Road, Totnes TQ9 5DF, ☎ 01803 862943.

Bike rental: *Hot Pursuit Cycles,* 26 The Stables, Totnes Industrial Estate, Totnes TQ9 5LE, ☎ 01803 865301, www.hotpursuit-cycles.co.uk.

Taxis: *Clarks Cars,* Salcombe, ☎ 01548 842914; Devon Taxis, Dartmouth, ☎ 01803 833 778; *Bluebird Taxis,* Dartmouth, ☎ 01803 833 522; Sercombe Cars, Totnes, ☎ 01803 864745; *Robs Taxis,* Kingsbridge ☎ 01548 580580.

FURTHER AFIELD

Slapton Sands

Slapton is a geographical oddity that is so big it never seems to get crowded. There is an extraordinary 3 mile long, dead straight beach that's pebble not sand, and it's backed, not by a row of hotels, but a big freshwater lake and an internationally renowned nature reserve called Slapton Ley. There is a road along the top of this strange bar of pebbles and at either end are the villages of Torcross and Slapton, with shops, cafés and pubs (check out The Tower Inn and Queens Arms at Slapton).

You'll see an odd memorial of a Sherman Tank on the seafront at Torcross. It commemorates a wartime disaster just off the beach. During the Second World War thousands of locals were forcibly evacuated from their homes in this area to allow the American army to practise D-Day landings on Slapton beach. One of these practices went badly wrong when German torpedo boats stumbled on American landing craft one night in 1944. In the one-sided battle nearly 800 GIs died – more than in the Normandy landing they were training for.

Blackpool Sands

Regularly voted one of Britain's top beaches, the Devonian Blackpool is not to be confused with the northern version. They've both got sandy beaches and that's about the only similarity – for Devon's version sits in a pretty unspoilt bay surrounded by pine trees. This private beach has a Blue Flag, Seaside Award and, despite the lack of anything like a town here, fantastic facilities: including showers, beach café and shop, watersports hire, summer lifeguards and daily beach cleaning. There is even a nice garden to visit behind the beach, see *What to see and do* (☎ 01803 770606; www.blackpoolsands.co.uk).

Blackpool Sands is regularly voted one of Britain's best beaches

We fought them on the beaches...

In 1404, during the Hundred Years' War, a well-armed force of 2,000 French knights landed on Slapton Sands carried by a fleet of 300 ships. They planned a daring attack on Dartmouth while most of the fighting men were at sea. They were seeking revenge for the continuous raids on their shipping by the privateers of the region.

The French army marched along the coast until it reached Blackpool Sands. Here the French knights met an unlikely collection of untrained local men, women and children armed with sticks and stones that had been organised by Chaucer's friend John Hawley. This local rag-tag army defended the south side of the Blackpool stream. The knights charged across but they were hampered by their heavy suits of armour. Many ended up floundering in the water. Others were chased in to the sea. The French invaders were roundly defeated and the locals took 25 high-ranking prisoners to be ransomed later. When King Henry IV heard the news he was so impressed he ordered a mass to be sung in Westminster Abbey as a celebration.

Kingsbridge

Kingsbridge is the administrative centre of the South Hams but, superficially at least, the least attractive to visitors. Yet there are some good reasons to stop off here on the way to the more glamorous resorts.

The town centre is laced with interesting lanes and passageways, with specialist shops and plenty of cafés, pubs and restaurants. There is a **farmers' market** on the first Saturday of the month and a Women's Institute (WI) market every Wednesday morning in the Town Hall.

Kingbridge holds **open-air concerts** in the Town Square, every Sunday from June to September, there is a small **Music Festival** in mid-June on the quayside and Fair Week in mid-July, which is a particularly lively time for locals.

If it's raining by the sea, Kingsbridge's **Quayside Leisure Centre** with indoor pool, squash, gym and bowling suddenly becomes more attractive (☎ 01548 857100; www.toneleisure.org.uk). And the **Cookworthy Museum of Rural Life** in the old stone Grammar School on Fore Street is worth a peep for its nine galleries of local social and rural history with everything from costumes to carts.

COOKWORTHY MUSEUM OF RURAL LIFE, ☎ 01548 853235; www.cookworthy@devonmuseums.net. Entry: adults £2, family £5; open Mar to Oct: Mon to Sat, 10.30am–5pm.

The best of... DEVON'S COUNTRYSIDE

YOU'LL FIND THE CLASSIC DEVON RURAL VIEW AROUND EVERY BEND. THE SERIES OF FRIENDLY ROUND HILLS DISAPPEAR INTO THE DISTANCE, COVERED WITH LUSH GREEN PASTURES, PATCHES OF RED SOIL AND TALL THICK HEDGES. IT'S NOT JUST A PRETTY VIEW – THIS WELL-WATERED, FERTILE LANDSCAPE HAS SUPPORTED FARMING FAMILIES FOR THOUSANDS OF YEARS.

Top: Exmoor moss; Middle: Horse drawn barge, Tiverton ; Bottom: Broomhill sculpture

Top: Rosemoor; Middle: Eve Valley; Bottom: Dartmoor ponies

Top: Bretnor church; Middle: Dartmoor; Bottom: Horses in the hills above Woolacombe

Golden Cap Estate, near Lyme Regis, www.nationaltrust.org.uk

Burgh Island

DISCOVERY SURF, Bigbury-on-Sea; ☎ 07813 639 622; www.discoverysurf.com
Single lesson: adults £35, children £30; four lesson beginner course: £120/£105.

Firstly note that locals say 'burr' not 'berg' when describing this 26 acre lump of grassy rock with a couple of cottages, cosy 14th-century pub and great views. Of course, its star attraction is the white and mint-green art deco hotel. The luxury hotel maintains the aura of its 1930s heyday when royalty and celebrities danced the night away.

At low tide the island is joined by a causeway to Bigbury-on-Sea but, when the tide is in, the island is cut off. An ingenious tractor on stilts drives guests out to the hotel through the waves.

Bigbury has good beaches with a summer lifeguard service and great views. It's a popular watersports spot, with an all-year-round surf school.

Dartington

Sitting on one of the main routes in the South Hams, thousands of visitors stop off at Dartington village just north of Totnes. It's an unusual attraction – the whole village has been transformed into a sort of giant arts centre owned by a well-meaning Trust. There is a good cinema and theatre in an old barn, live music, courses, conference centre, restaurant, shops, hotel and some pretty serious arty exhibitions (www.dartington.org).

We've already mentioned Dartington's popular upmarket shopping complex, **The Cider Press**, which has exhibitions and events, a local food shop and restaurant but is especially good for browsing designer goods, crafts and gifts (☎ 01803 864171; www.dartingtonciderpress.co.uk).

You can buy Dartington Glass here, but it is made in Torrington in North Devon (see Torrington chapter). You can also buy **Dartington Pottery** from the workshops here set up by Bernard Leach in the 1930s and still producing high quality avant-garde work (☎ 01803 864163; www.dartingtonpottery.co.uk).

Next door is **High Cross House**, a striking 1930s modernist home with fine art and craft displays inside (☎ 01803 864114; open May to Oct; call ahead for opening days and times; entry £3.50, concessions £2.50). And the centre of the estate is **Dartington Hall**, a fabulous medieval mansion where you can stay and eat at the **White Hart** gastropub (main courses about £10). B&B is £60 for a single, £90 for a double. (☎ 01803 847100; www.dartingtonhall.com). This grand house was once the home of the Champerknownes, a wealthy Tudor family. Katherine Champerknowne was the mother of famous Devonian seafarers Sir Humphrey Gilbert and Sir Walter Raleigh (by her second marriage).

Totnes

This fascinating historic town grew up at the point where the Dart narrows from an estuary to a river. After Exeter, it was Devon's second wealthiest town in the Middle and Tudor ages, thanks to the busy harbour exporting local farmers' wool and tin from Dartmoor's mines.

There is still a harbour and you can take boat trips down the river from the Steamer Quay or steam train trips up the river to Buckfastleigh. (See Dartmouth chapter for details of boats.) The feeling of history is everywhere – there are museums on the High Street, a classic castle, ancient guildhall and church. The prettiest bit is the stretch of old High Street buildings with ancient overhanging arcades, and the tiny alleyways off the top of the High Street known locally as 'The Narrows'. You'll see why the town has been ranked in the country's top 40 towns of architectural interest.

Totnes is also one of the busiest **market** towns in South Devon. On Fridays and Saturdays there is a market in the Civic Square, selling everything from bonsai trees to organic bread. On Tuesdays in summer, the square is home to the small 'Elizabethan market' when some stall holders dress in Elizabethan costumes. And on the last Saturday of every month there is a farmers' market in the Civic Hall.

On top of all this, for some reason, Totnes has grown into one of the country's New Age centres, full of alternative therapies, bohemian shops and unconventional characters. Whatever you think of people chanting 'Om' while sitting cross-legged between scented candles, it's an entertaining place to wander. Browse shops selling crystals and complementary medicines, old books, whole foods, antiques and art or just wander up Fore Street from the river. You'll pass under the distinctive **East Gate Arch**, a Tudor 'bridge' over the main street. **The Elizabethan House** at number 70 serves as the town's lively little museum (☎ 01803 863821; adults £2, concessions 75p; open Mar to Oct weekdays 10.30am–5pm).

Further up the main street in another Tudor house is the **Devonshire Collection of Period Costume**, a fine collection of Victorian clothing (Bogan House, 43 High Street; adults £2, children 80p; open Spring Bank Holiday to end of Sept, Tues to Fri 11am–5pm).

And just along the High Street is the Tudor **Guildhall**, still the headquarters of the town council. Spot the boards in the Lower Hall that list

TOTNES CASTLE, Castle Street, TQ9 5NU; ☎ 01803 864406; www.english-heritage.org.uk. Entry: adults £2.40, children £1.20; open Apr to June and Sept: daily 10am–5pm; July/Aug: 10am–6pm.

BERRY POMEROY CASTLE, Near Totnes, off the A385, TQ9 6LJ; ☎ 01803 866618; www.english-heritage.org.uk. Entry: adults £3.80, children £1.90; open Apr to Oct: daily 10am–5pm.

more than 600 consecutive Totnes mayors in gold leaf. Upstairs is the elegant Council Chamber where Oliver Cromwell sat in 1646 (☎ 01803 862147; adults £1, children 25p; open Apr to Oct, Mon to Fri, 10.30am–4.30pm).

Totnes has a classic Norman motte and bailey **castle**, founded soon after the Conquest to overawe the Saxon town. A later stone shell-keep crowns its steep mound, giving sweeping views across the rooftops to the River Dart.

Another castle in the area worth visiting is **Berry Pomeroy Castle**. Devon's 'most haunted' castle is a dramatic and romantic set of ruins hidden away on a wooded crag. There are sinister legends around what once was the finest Elizabethan home in the county. The audio tour is suitably spooky but there are perfectly unghostly walks in the woods too.

Modbury

At the western edge off the South Hams, Modbury is another historic old market town – a sort of mini-Totnes, without the New Age stuff. Again it has a wonderful main street lined with old buildings and is a gentle place for a wander round antique dealers, art and craft galleries, teashops and pubs. **The Exeter Inn** in Church Street is a classic flagstones-and-beams coaching inn with B&B and homely food.

Modbury's eight-day long fair, held at the start of May, dates back to 1329. In 2007, Modbury gained the unusual but highly commendable accolade of being the first 'no plastic bags' town in Britain. For more details contact Modbury Tourist Information Centre (Modbury Court, Church Street, Modbury PL21 0QR; ☎ 01548 830159; www.modburydevoninfo.co.uk).

Salcombe

Devon's most southerly town is a bit like a smaller version of Dartmouth – a pretty nautical town on the western side of a picturesque wooded estuary. But unlike its bigger neighbour, Salcombe has the feel of a fishing village with steep narrow streets leading down to the water.

Nevertheless, Salcombe is one of Devon's top centres for boating and in the summer the streets are dominated by deck shoes and blue sweaters. It's great to join the boating world, even if it just means browsing boating shops and eating seafood with a view of the river. And you can always visit the **Salcombe Maritime Museum** in Market Street for a glimpse of smuggling, wartime dramas and shipwrecks (adults £1.50, children free; open daily Easter to the end of Oct, 10.30am–12.30pm, 2.30–4.30pm).

Of course, the best way to join the modern seadogs is to take a **boat trip** yourself – and there are almost as many available here as in Dartmouth. The

Gorgeous sea views and exotic plantlife abound at Overbecks

easiest and cheapest water trip is the two-minute passenger **ferry** ride to East Portlemouth on the opposite bank (☎ 01548 842061). The **Venus Café** at the top of the ferry steps is recommended by visitors. Other options are the ferry to Kingsbridge on the Rivermaid (☎ 01548 853607/853525) or Kirby Estuary Cruises (☎ 01548 844475).

Aside from boating, there are great **walks** along the coast path to the iron-age fort on Bolt Head. And walking in the other direction you'll see the Kingsbridge estuary is so sheltered that, in some gardens alongside the estuary, locals are able to grow lemons. From East Portlemouth you can the walk around the headland to see Gorah Rock island and right on to see the views from Start Point.

Salcombe's best attraction is the National Trust house and garden at **Overbecks**, a mix of luscious terraced gardens, tremendous sea views and glimpses of the former owner Otto Overbeck's eccentric inventions. Look out for his homemade 'Rejuvenator' which he thought kept him young. Until his death in 1937 that is...

There are plenty of good beaches and coves around Salcombe. The busiest, **North and South Sands**, both slightly to the south of Salcombe, are at the estuary mouth – a short walk from the town. **The Winking Prawn** waterfront brasserie at North Sands is recommended by locals (☎ 01548 842326; www.winkingprawn.co.uk). They offer a steak and king prawn barbecue in the summer months.

OVERBECKS, Sharpitor, Salcombe TQ8 8LW; ☎ 01548 842893; www.nationaltrust.org.uk Entry: adults £5.80, children £2.90, family (2+2) £14.50; open Mar to Oct: Sun to Fri 11am–5pm, July/Aug Sat too.

Two of the best are at **Hope Cove**, a pretty village with two great sandy coves and a harbour, and **Thurlestone**, where the sandy stretch at South Milton is safest and has a summer lifeguard. **Soar Cove** has a fine sandy beach surrounded by sheltering cliffs but is a mile's walk from the nearest car parking.

The Visitors' Book

From Hope Cove to Slapton

'To start the day we had a freshly ground coffee and pain-au-chocolat at the Sea Breeze Café in the small beachside village of Torcross. It's a gorgeous thatched cottage on the beach, the oldest building in the village. You can sit outside with spectacular views of Start Bay, but we sat inside on the sofas and read the papers.'

'After a lazy start we hired some bikes and cycled to Slapton between a big fresh water lake and the sea along a very narrow stretch of land. It is a haven for birds, otters, adders and door mice. It's a wonderful area to cycle through though we met some ducks along the way that were a bit overfriendly and not shy about standing on your feet.'

'Slapton is a quaint little village. The sun came out and we enjoyed a hearty lunch in the Tower Inn's garden consisting of local cider and smoked haddock and bacon fish cakes with chips. We then returned our bikes in time for a stroll along the beach with the sea lapping over our weary feet and a famous Salcombe dairy ice cream.'

'We drove back through the lanes to Hope Cove for a relaxing barbecue of fresh local fish in the garden of our rented accommodation, Primrose Cottage. We relaxed there with a glass of wine and watched the sun go down over the sea.'

Helen Doran, Surrey

PLYMOUTH AND THE TAMAR VALLEY

If you were arriving in Plymouth in your private jet from France you'd reckon the city's location is world class – with the heights of Dartmoor behind, the lush twisting Tamar valley alongside, the islands and inlets of Plymouth Sound framing the ancient waterfront. It's every bit as good a spot as the landscapes of Vancouver, Auckland or Sydney.

Once you'd landed though, the city could be an initial disappointment. It may be the only big city west of Bristol but it attracts fewer tourists than some Devon villages. It's not that there is nothing to see – it's that you have to look a bit harder to find the good parts.

Driving in through dreary suburbs you finally reach a modern centre hastily built to replace what was flattened in the war. It was one of Britain's most bombed cities... and it still shows. Then there is western Europe's biggest naval dockyard and Devon's most notorious red-light area. So the temptation is to turn around and head for somewhere pretty and inoffensive... but persevere. When you reach the waterfront, suddenly Plymouth seems to be worth the journey.

It's certainly some waterfront. **The Hoe** and **The Barbican** are essential Devon sights... actually, they're essential English sights. The reek of maritime heritage is so clear, you feel like you're walking in very footsteps of Drake and the old Tudor seadogs. Add in the fine aquarium, impressive citadel, lively shopping, eating and culture, and you start to realise that Devon's biggest city really does make it as a tourist destination.

And you won't be able to miss the fact that Plymouth is in the process of ambitious redevelopment, the largest since the city was rebuilt after the Second World War. The council's 'Vision for Plymouth' was recently launched by

Exploring the waterfront is the essential Plymouth experience

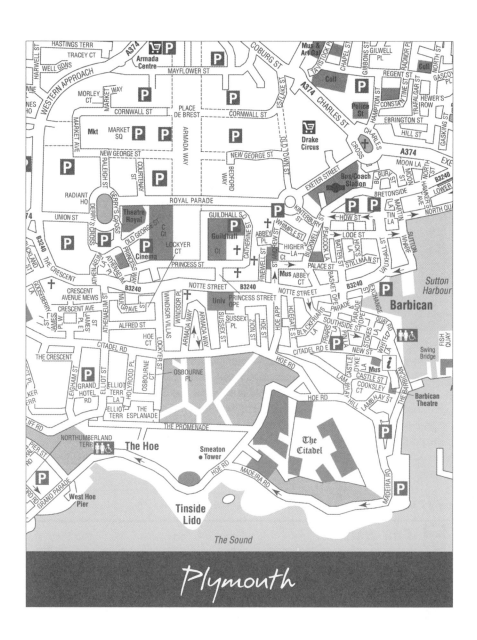

Plymouth

Safe and sound

Plymouth Sound has been the port of arrival and departure for many of the major figures in our history. It was Scott of the Antarctic's departure point on his last fateful voyage, it was where Darwin started a journey that would lead to his theory of evolution and it was where thousands of convicts were shipped off to Australia. Sir Francis Chichester sailed out of Plymouth Sound on his solo round-the-world voyage in his yacht *Gypsy Moth*.

Catherine of Aragon and Pocahontas both arrived in England via the port in 1501 and 1616. The defeated French Emperor Napoleon was brought to Plymouth aboard the *HMS Bellerophon*, which remained in Plymouth Sound for two weeks before sailing him into exile on St Helena in 1815. And the survivors of the *Titanic* disaster disembarked at Millbay docks in 1912.

Plymouth was also one of the principal staging posts for the Normandy landings in June 1944, with Normandy Way (still there, near the Tamar bridges) leading down to one of a series of embarkation points for tens of thousands of US troops. Think what they felt as they sailed out into the Channel and looked back at Plymouth...

internationally renowned architect David MacKay, and is set to have much of the city centre demolished, redesigned and rebuilt by the year 2020.

Apart from that, it's worth noting that many of the best bits of Plymouth are in the countryside around – magnificent stately homes and parks, gorgeous villages, boating havens and pretty estuaries that reward exploration. As the city sits on the border with Cornwall – the Tamar is the boundary – we've ignored the county line in this section and include many sights and spots that aren't technically in Devon at all.

WHAT TO SEE AND DO

 ## Fair weather

Plymouth's nautical heritage is based on the fact that, at the mouth of the Tamar and Plym rivers, is one of Europe's finest deep water anchorages. **Plymouth Sound** is not really advertised as a tourist destination... but we reckon it's one of the major sights of Devon.

There are plenty of vantage points, such as The Hoe, Mount Batten Centre or Mount Edgcumbe, where you can gaze at the huge panorama and watch the constant water traffic. And there are plenty of boat trips too, where you can get close to the water and get a fish-eye view of the city. And while you're doing that, think of the history in front of you. This is where Drake and the Eng-

Smeaton's Tower stood out at sea for 123 years

lish fleet of galleons assembled to sail against the Armada. Or picture the intrepid colonists on the *Mayflower* setting off for America or Captain Cooke embarking on his voyages to discover Australia, New Zealand and the South Pacific. Imagine Raleigh, Hawkins and Grenville sailing their small wooden sailing ships out across the Sound.

All of those voyagers would have glanced back to the grassy clifftop called **The Hoe** just above the waterfront. Today it still makes a perfect spot to picnic or simply look across the Sound, with Cornwall on the far bank, Devon on this side, Drake's Island and the Mount Batten Breakwater in the middle.

THE HOE, PL1 2PA;
☎ 01752 775841; www.english-heritage.org.uk. Entry: adults £3.50, children £3; tours only, May to Sept: Tues/Thur 2.30pm.

Unless you're a slang-loving American rapper, Hoe just means 'hill' and that's all this clifftop plateau is. But it's a hill that acquired legendary status with the story of Francis Drake playing bowls here when the 'invincible' Spanish Armada appeared on the horizon one day in 1588. The story goes that Drake wouldn't be panicked into stopping the game – saying there was plenty of time to finish it... and then tackle the Armada. Historians have speculated that Drake was demonstrating his expert knowledge of tides, winds or distance at sea, but whatever, it's a nice story and helps contribute to Drake's daring reputation.

And ever since then small boys have stood here gazing out to see trying to picture a horizon bristling with hundreds of sails as the fearsome Spanish Armada approached. Today the Hoe is a bright, airy spot, flanked by attractive Victorian and Edwardian buildings... and with a prominent statue of Drake next to a globe.

SMEATON'S TOWER,
Hoe Road PL1 2NZ;
☎ 01752 304775; www.ply-mouth.gov.uk. Entry: adults £2, children over 5 £1; open 10am–12pm, 1–4.30pm, Tues to Fri, closing at 4pm on Sat/bank holidays, closing at 3pm Oct to Mar.

What appears to be a badly-sited lighthouse on The Hoe has become one of the most familiar images of Devon. **Smeaton's Tower**, a classic red-and-white striped lighthouse, was originally built in 1759, on the wave-battered Eddystone Rocks 14 miles out to sea. Smeaton's sturdy tower stood on the reef for over 100 years. As a sort of tribute to the tower and its pioneering builder, it was rebuilt here in 1882. You can climb 93 steps to the top for even higher views. On a clear day

Plymouth Sound is a centre for watersports

you can see the current Eddystone lighthouse on the south west horizon.

On the seaward side of the Hoe is the recently restored **Tinside Lido** (☎ 01752 261915), an open-air seawater swimming pool dating from the art deco era. In the 1930s there were beauty contests here, ladies parading in their swimsuits before smirking male judges. An orchestra would play while families swam and changing coloured lights would illuminate the pool and fountains from below. Sadly, its distinctive semi-circular shape was used as handy landmark by German bombers in the Second World War. Plymouthians meanwhile used it during the war to do their washing. Now, after a multi-million pound refurbishment, it's a stylish place to cool off on hot days. And further down by the water's edge are three more open tidal seawater pools, without the glamour of the Lido but without the entry fee either.

On the headland between the Hoe and the Barbican are enormous fortifications built by Charles II, 100 years after Drake, and in still in use by the military today (as Commando barracks). The **Royal Citadel** is mainly a hardcore gun emplacement but there are interesting guided tours and the views from the ramparts are pretty impressive. The walls are ridiculously thick and with cannons pointing both out to sea and inland, it's meant to look daunting – King Charles' idea was to keep rebellious Plymouthians in their place too.

Stroll round the corner from The Hoe and you'll reach **The Barbican**. This

Eddystone tragedies

Building any lighthouse on the submerged Eddystone rocks was no mean feat – only 3ft of the treacherous reef is above the water at high tide. But it was so dangerous to shipping that sailors would take a 100 mile detour to ensure they missed it. Dozens of ships were wrecked there.

The first lighthouse was an exotic octagonal wooden tower built by architect Henry Winstanley. His structure survived for three years. Winstanley was so confident of its strength he sailed out from Plymouth to be on his creation during a violent storm in 1703. But he, his lighthouse crew and the whole lighthouse were swept off the rocks in the night and never seen again.

The second Eddystone Light was also made of wood. One night it caught fire and

harbourside area is where you'll best sense the maritime flavour of Plymouth's past. It's not just the narrow cobbled streets and Tudor buildings, you can often smell the salty stink from the fishmarket on the quay.

The Barbican is Plymouth's tourist heart, with boat trips, galleries, craft shops, antique traders, the aquarium, a glassblowing workshop, restaurants and bars. Spot the modern metal sculpture on a pole on the harbour wall – locals call it 'The Barbican Prawn'. And look at the old stone warehouses – these were often used to store captured French and Spanish treasure and even prisoners of war. Others stored biscuits for the navy or brewed the ships' essential beer supplies.

THE ELIZABETHAN HOUSE,
New Street, The Barbican, PL1 2NA
Entry: adults £1.50, children £1;
open Tues to Sat and bank holidays
10am–12pm and 1–3pm; Apr to
Sept 10am–5pm.

The best bit is New Street, with its half-timbered homes and public **Tudor Garden** dotted with ancient plant varieties. A peep in **The Elizabethan House** is the best way of capturing the creaky-wood atmosphere of a perfectly intact sea captain's home from Drake's era, with dark panelled walls, ancient oak doors, twisting stairs and low ceilings.

Out on the water

Even if you've seen all that lot you're still missing one vital Plymouth ingredient – a waterbound adventure. The natural bay with its breakwater, tributaries and beach coves make Plymouth one of the best venues in the country for anything from riding on a car ferry to kitesailing.

The easiest and cheapest way across the water is using one of the many ferries. See the *Visitor information* section for details. The passenger trips to Mount Edgcumbe and Cawsand are the most scenic but even the Torpoint

the unfortunate lighthouse keeper Henry Hall ended up as the recipient of the first-ever official autopsy. He heard the fire, looked up to see what was happening and a glob of melted lead from the roof dropped right down his throat. He was rescued and bought back to Plymouth where no-one believed him. So when he died a few days later, they opened him up and found... a big lump of lead.

In 1756 John Smeaton was asked to design the third Eddystone light. He built it like a giant tree – with strong rings of dovetailed stone but able to bend in the wind. It worked so well that it was only when the natural rocks underneath began to be worn away by the sea that his tower was bought back to Plymouth. It's still the model for all lighthouses built on rocks.

car ferry gives a great view from the water that you'll never see otherwise. Watch out too for the big Brittany Ferries vessels crossing the Sound on their way to or from France and Spain.

MOUNT BATTEN CENTRE, 70 Lawrence Road, Mount Batten, Plymstock PL9 9SJ; ☎ 01752 404567; www.mount-batten-centre.com.

For watersports, start at the **Mount Batten Centre** – a former RAF flyingboat camp at the mouth of the River Plym to the east of the city. You can still see giant hangars where Sunderland flyingboats were stored. There is tuition, hire, taster sessions and courses in a range of activities. The Centre has its own fleet of dinghies, catamarans and two racing yachts. You can try windsurfing, kayaking or canoeing or take a course in powerboating. It has expanded into land-based adventure sports too – including trips caving in the limestone caves at Buckfastleigh, gorge walking on the moors and abseiling on their own climbing wall. There is comfortable hotel accommodation and food on site if required.

PLYMOUTH POWERBOAT SCHOOL, Queen Anne's Battery Marina, Plymouth PL4 0LP; ☎ 01752 255700; www.south-west-rib-charter.com.

Also try **Plymouth Powerboat School** for activities using high-powered rigid inflatables (RIBs) including chartered trips and tuition.

If you just fancy a boat trip with someone else doing all the work, then there are lots of operators. Try the blue-and-white vessels of **Plymouth Boat Cruises** (☎ 01752 408590), which sail from Phoenix Wharf at the southern end of the Barbican. You can take a four-hour cruise up the Tamar to Calstock and Morwellham (£11 adults, £8 children); a trip to Saltash Pier including a tour of the naval dockyard (£6 return, £3 children); and a two-hour cruise east to Newton Ferrers and the River Yealm (£7 adults, £4 children).

Other tour operators include the black-and-white boats of **Tamar Cruising**, which also runs the Cremyll Ferry (☎ 01752 822105; www.tamar cruising.co.uk).

And for the most exciting boat trip of all, try a fast and bouncy 30-minute RIB tour of the Sound with **South West RIB Rides** (☎ 01752 777650; www.south-west-rib-rides.co.uk; £10 adults, £6 for under 12) from either the Barbican or Mount Batten Centre.

Finally, it's hardly watersports but it is over the water... the **Tamar Bridge** is the modern toll bridge linking Cornwall and Devon. The views are stunning and you can park at the Plymouth end to have a good look. The older railway bridge alongside was built by Isambard Kingdom Brunel. You pay £1 per car, but only crossing from Cornwall into Devon. It's run by the same body as the Torpoint Ferry, and its website (www.tamarbridge.org.uk) shows webcams of the bridge and Torpoint Ferry so you can see which has the longest queues. A car ride on the Torpoint Ferry also costs £1.

Wet weather

On a rainy day, the quayside offers some interesting diversions. You'll find the **Mayflower Centre**, a contemporary visitor centre with interactive displays about the maritime heritage and telling the story of the Pilgrim Fathers who sailed from the steps outside in 1620 to establish a celebrated colony in New England.

PLYMOUTH MAYFLOWER CENTRE, The Barbican, PL1 2LS; ☎ 01752 306330; www.visitplymouth.co.uk. Entry: adults £2, children £1; open Apr to Oct: daily 10am–4pm; Nov to Apr: closed Sun.

The waterfront may be like living history, but the rest of the city isn't. The centre took the brunt of wartime bombing and was rebuilt as a grid of low-rise shops. These areas are gradually being redeveloped but a few historic treasures survived. **The Merchant's House** is another half-timbered Tudor building, this time a wealthy trader's home. It now features an eclectic museum of local oddments like truncheons, a dolls' house and a re-created apothecary's shop.

THE MERCHANT'S HOUSE, 33 St Andrews Street; www.plymouth.gov.uk. Entry: adults £1.50, children over 5 £1; open Tues to Sat and bank holidays 10am–12pm and 1–3pm; Apr to Sept 10am–5pm.

And nearby **Prysten House** is the city's oldest home, built in 1498 around a courtyard with open timber galleries and smoke-blackened beams. Downstairs is Plymouth's best restaurant, Tanners, and upstairs is the 28ft Plymouth Tapestry.

PRYSTEN HOUSE, Finewell Street, PL1 2AD; ☎ 01752 661414. Entry: £1; open Apr to Oct: daily 10am–5pm.

Nearby on Royal Parade is the Plymouth Parish Church, **St Andrews** which was extensively rebuilt after being firebombed in the Second World War. The highlights of the new church are the stained glass windows by renowned artist John Piper.

THE CITY MUSEUM, Drake Circus PL4 8AJ; ☎ 01752 304775; www.plymouth.gov.uk Entry free, Tues to Fri 10am–5.30pm, Sat and bank holidays 10am–5pm.

City Museum and Art Gallery

Plymouth's museum is probably Devon's finest, but this grand grey stone building is currently shut for a Lottery-funded refurbishment, until at least midway through 2008. If it has re-opened, you should find it's even better than it was when you last visited. Plans include galleries of natural history, 17th-century art, the story of local china and porcelain and a collection of treasures from around the world brought back to Plymouth by sailors. Its collection also includes much acclaimed local art including works by 18th-century portrait artist Sir Joshua Reynolds who was born in Plympton and 20th-century painter Robert Lenkiewicz who lived and worked on the Barbican and produced the giant mural there.

What to do with children...

A guaranteed winner for the children is the **National Marine Aquarium**. This modern attraction near the Barbican is more like a research and education centre that you can look round, and that makes it more interactive and thought-provoking than many ordinary aquariums. You can actually touch fish and talk to experts, as well as gawping at crowd-pleasers such as sharks and seahorses.

NATIONAL MARINE AQUARIUM, Rope Walk, Coxside, Plymouth PL4 0LF; www.national-aquarium.co.uk; ☎ 01752 220 084. Entry: adults £9.50, child (4–15) £5.75, family (2+2) £27; open daily 10am–5/6pm.

And how to avoid children

A great adults-only attraction is **Plymouth Gin Distillery**. Tucked away behind the Quay is the old medieval friary that has become the distillery. There are tours to see the process and learn the drink's interesting history as an official navy ration. Of course there are free samples and a gift shop too. There is also a very stylish new restaurant – see *Eating out*.

PLYMOUTH GIN DISTILLERY, South Side Street, PL1 2LQ. Entry: £6; no admittance for under 18s; open Mon to Fri 9am–5.30pm, Sat 10am–5.30pm, Sun 11am–5pm.

Entertainment

A city as big as Plymouth is sure to have a wide range of entertainment options. With the biggest university in the west and numerous colleges, there are more than 50,000 students – which guarantees there will be plenty going on after dark.

Firstly though, we'd better tackle the **Union Street** strip. This road connects the city centre to the Devonport area and is both legendary and notorious among locals as 'Devon's most dangerous street'. It's has been the favourite of sailors and dockers since Victorian times. There is a scruffy mix of takeaways, casinos, bars and clubs leading to the red-light district and it's not unusual to see Military Police in action here in the early hours at weekends. Lively doesn't quite cover it. If you want a hectic night-out there is nothing to touch it in Devon.

But we suspect that description have put many of you off, but don't worry: in recent years a more chilled entertainment area has developed around the **Barbican**, including a cinema, clubs, restaurants and contemporary bars.

Theatre and Cinema

The Vue is a modern multiscreen cinema complex, with bowling alleys, cafés and night club, at Barbican Approach (☎ 0871 224 0240). There is also an ABC cinema at Derry's Cross, PL1 2SW (☎ 01752 225553) and a screen at **The Arts Centre** in the Barbican at Looe Street, PL4 0EB (☎ 01752 206114; www.plymouthac.org.uk), which has the admirable slogan: 'Art, film, food'.

And Plymouth has an impressive range of theatres: **The Barbican** in Castle Street, PL1 2NJ (www.barbicantheatre.co.uk; ☎ 01752 267131) is small, and artsy, and hosts regular comedy nights. **The Theatre Royal** and its smaller stage, **The Drum**, in Royal Parade in the centre (PL1 2TR; ☎ 01752 668282; www.theatreroyal.com) is one of the south-west's leading drama venues. It claims in fact to be the largest and best attended regional producing theatre in the UK. Plymouth Athenaeum at Derry's Cross (PL1 2SW, ☎ 01752 266079; www.plymouthathenaeum.co.uk) and Devonport Playhouse, Fore Street, Devonport (PL1 4DN, ☎ 01752 606507; www.applausesw.org.uk) are smaller community theatres featuring mainly amateur productions.

Music and other entertainment

Live music happens in pubs, clubs and venues all over the city. **The Plymouth Pavilions** holds 4,000 people and is just off the dreaded Union Street but does have its own safe car park. It's the largest indoor venue in Devon and concerts range from rock to ballet. Recent acts include The Kaiser Chiefs, Jack Johnson and Joss Stone. The Pavilions complex also has a large swimming pool and ice rink (☎ 0845 146 1460; www.plymouthpavilions.com). Nearby, **The Hub** in Bath Street is smaller but another good venue with impressive line-up of acts (☎ 01752 222664; www.plymouthhub.com). Recent stars include Dartmoor folk star Seth Lakeman and US popsters The Thrills.

For classical music, consult the excellent website www.plyclassical.co.uk, which lists all serious music events in the area.

North of the centre, the area of Mutley has a big student population. So there is a good area of entertainment around **Mutley Plain** with some decent contemporary bars. The Fortescue Hotel (☎ 01752 660673) hosts live music (every Thur) and comedy nights (first Sat of each month).

 # Shopping

Plymouth is the 14th largest UK city but a survey in 2006 ranked it only 29th for shopping. And another report found that only 8% of people living to the west and east of the city shopped there, preferring Truro, Torquay or Exeter.

The new £200m shopping mall at the eastern edge of the city centre – **Drake Circus** – has improved the choice of major stores but its looks have been

The best... PLACES TO STAY

HOTEL

The Duke of Cornwall 🏠 🛏 🍴 ♿

Millbay Road, Plymouth PL1 3LG
☎ **01752 275850**
www.thedukeofcornwallhotel.com

Plymouth's grand old Victorian gothic hotel may now be part of a national chain but it retains the style and class of a city landmark with a two AA rosette restaurant and elegant if old-fashioned rooms.

Price: B&B from £99 to £195 for a single, from £115 to £195 for a double.

Langdon Court Hotel 🏠 🛏 🍴 ♿

Wendbury PL9 0DY
☎ **01752 862358**
www.langdoncourt.com

In the countryside south-east of the city, this Tudor mansion is one the area's most attractive hotels and restaurants. It was once the home of Katherine Parr, Henry VIII's sixth wife, and in the late 19th century the Prince of Wales, later to become Edward VII, often came to stay with his mistress, the actress Lillie Langtry.

Price: B&B from £79 to £129 for a single, from £99 to £169 for a double.

B & B

The Dudley Hotel 🏊

Sutherland Road, Plymouth PL4 6BN
☎ **01752 668322**
www.Dudley-hotel.com

For the outside it looks like just another Victorian terrace house, but inside has been renovated to a very high standard. It's almost a boutique B&B with a four-star rating and ambitious décor.

Price: B&B from £32.50 to £37.50 for a single, £54 for a double.

The Four Seasons Guesthouse 🏠

207 Citadel Road East, The Hoe, Plymouth PL1 2JF
☎ **01752 223591**
www.fourseasonsguesthouse.co.uk

There are dozens of guesthouses among the elegant period terraces around The Hoe but many are tired and dated. This is the best of the bunch, decorated in light neutral colours, with four stars from VisitBritain and breakfasts made from fresh local ingredients.

Price: B&B from £31 to £46 for a single, from £47 to £62 for a double.

SELF-CATERING

Mossgara 🏊

Noss Mayo
c/o Rural Retreats
☎ **01386 701177**
www.ruralretreats.co.uk

One of the UK's top quality holiday rental companies has two lovely houses to the east of Plymouth. This one is a new green oak timber-frame structure above the Yealm estuary with superb views and its own private quay. It sleeps up to eight.

Price: from £370 for a two-night break to £1,607 for a week in high season.

UNUSUAL

Danescombe Arsenic Mine 🏊 🏠

Calstock, Cornwall
☎ **01628 825925**
www.landmarktrust.org.uk

The Landmark Trust look after some of the most unusual historic buildings in the country and rent them out for holidays. And this is one of their most unusual holiday homes – the former engine house of a Victorian arsenic mine deep in a steep wooded valley which now sleeps four.

Price: from £325 to £1,287 per week.

controversial with local critics describing it as 'a concrete box'. It even won a national award as the worst building in the UK.

Nevertheless Plymouth does have one of the biggest shopping areas in Devon concentrated in its centre and handily surrounded by car parks. The latest count was 520 shops in this area, many of them in traffic-free spaces. There are three department stores, some big name stores, pavement cafés, and a slightly quirkier 'independent quarter' at the western end of the centre. There is a huge **indoor market**, covering three-quarters of an acre with more than 100 stalls.

But despite the efforts to spruce up the city centre, we suspect most visitors will find the Barbican area is best for souvenirs, gifts, antiques and crafts.

The best... FOOD AND DRINK

Plymouth is well placed to supply its shops and chefs with fresh fish and take advantage of some fine food producers in the countryside around. Fish is landed daily and sold direct on the Barbican quayside and there are also fresh fish stalls in the pannier market in the city centre. This is a good place to find fresh local meat and vegetables too.

It's not a city with a notable culinary heritage but increasingly shops are stocking more natural, local ingredients and restaurants are serving them. And crucially, there are now a few great restaurants in the city. Plymouth still has a lot of fast food and takeaways but at least the fish and chips are often excellent. And if you want to see the water while you eat, The Barbican is the area with most sea view tables.

Staying in

Plymouth's **farmers' market** is held on the second Friday of every month in the pannier market in the city centre with around 25 stalls. Away from those dates, many locals drive a few miles east to Yealmpton for **Riverford Farm Shop**.

RIVERFORD FARM SHOP, Kitley, Yealmpton, Plymouth PL8 2LT; ☎ 01752 880925; www.riverfordfarmshop.co.uk. Open daily.

This food store and café won *The Observer* newspaper's award as the best food shop in 2007. Riverford has its own bakery and stocks cooked meats, pies, cheeses, local organic fruit and vegetables, plus its own bacon and sausages. All the food in the café comes from the shop, there is an outside barbecue in the summer and a seasonal pick-your-own area too.

EATING OUT

FINE DINING

Tanners
Prysten House, Finewell Street, Plymouth PL1 2AE, ☎ 01752 252001
www.tannersrestaurant.com

This modern restaurant housed in Plymouth's oldest building is the spot where the Pilgrim Fathers ate their last meal before setting sail. It's unlikely they were as well fed as today's diners at Tanners. The contemporary British food is as good as you'll find anywhere in Devon and it was the 2007 AA Restaurant of the Year. Chefs Chris and James Tanner have had their own TV series *The Tanner Brothers* and James appears regularly on *Ready, Steady, Cook*. They're so popular locally they've just been awarded honorary degrees from Plymouth University. A two-course dinner is £26.00, three courses cost £32.00, and five courses cost £37.

The Barbican Kitchen
Blackfriars Distillery, Southside Street, The Barbican, PL1 2LQ
☎ 01752 604448
www.barbicankitchen.com

This modern lime and lilac brasserie is a collaboration between two of the city's heroes, the Tanner Brothers and Plymouth Gin. It's housed in the historic distillery at The Barbican but is very contemporary. Food is bright and lively with lots of local traceable ingredients. Main courses cost from £7.95 to £16.95.

The Duke of Cornwall Hotel
Millbay Road, Plymouth PL1 3LG
☎ 01752 275850
www.thedukeofcornwallhotel.com

The city's grandest Victorian hotel has a classic restaurant under a domed ceiling with a huge sparkling chandelier. The food is more contemporary than you'd expect and has two RAC Blue Ribands for quality. Main courses cost from £12 to £15.

RESTAURANT

The Artillery Tower
Firestone Bay, Plymouth PL1 3QR
☎ 01752 257610
www.artillerytower.co.uk

Here's a unique chance to dine in a 500-year-old fort looking out across Plymouth Sound. There is award-winning traditional British cuisine with local ingredients such as Devon duck with cider sauce, Devon beef with red wine and a selection of local cheeses. A three-course dinner costs from £20.50 to £25.50.

GASTROPUB

The Dartmoor Union
Fore Street, Holbeton PL8 1NE
☎ 01752 831288
www.dartmoorunion.co.uk

This acclaimed pub lies in the countryside to the east of the city. It has an AA rosette and has been voted Les Routiers Dining Pub of the Year. Ingredients are very local – vegetables are grown within sight of the inn. A three-course dinner costs around £28.

The Rose and Crown and Seafood Restaurant
Market Street, Yealmpton PL8 2EB
☎ 01752 880502
www.theroseandcrown.co.uk

On one side of the road is the old pub the Rose and Crown, now with a modern Pacific Rim menu, on the other is The Seafood in a minimalist converted barn. Both have AA rosettes for food, the Seafood has two. Main courses cost about £14.

EATING OUT

The Ship Inn
Noss Mayo PL8 1EW
☎ 01752 872387, www.nossmayo.com

This whitewashed pub right on the creek-side is a favourite yachtsmen's port of call. There is a wonderful terrace by the water or eat inside where reclaimed materials have been used beautifully among log fires and bookcases. The light, modern food is recommended by Michelin. Three courses cost about £25.

CAFÉ
Tudor Rose Tearooms
New Street, The Barbican
☎ 01752 255502

Here's another local institution – a classic tea shop in an Elizabethan house. Amid the creaky floorboards and darkened beams,

tuck into old English delicacies such as sticky cakes, Devon cream teas, traditional pasties and cottage pies.

View2
Vauxhall Quay, The Barbican
☎ 01752 252564
www.barbicanleisurebars.com

View2 is a trendy new complex on the far side of Sutton Harbour, with a food terrace overlooking the water. There are pizzas (from £8.95), comedy nights every Wednesday, Salsa nights every Monday, and a late dance club when everything else has finished.

COUNTRYMAN'S CHOICE FARM CENTRE, next to Endsleigh Garden Centre, Cadleigh Park, Ivybridge PL21 9JL; ☎ 01752 895533; www.countrymanschoice.co.uk

Countryman's Choice Farm Centre is also to the east, just off the A38 at Ivybridge. This is owned and run by a local farming family. The stock includes local cheeses, freshly cooked meats, fresh fruit and vegetables, cakes (made on site using local free range eggs), local jams and ice-cream.

Another big local food name is **Burts Chips**, started by Richard Burt in Kingsbridge. Burts Chips' innovative range includes parsnip, lobster and black pepper chips but are all made using as much local and seasonal produce as possible. The chips are now made at Roborough to the north of Plymouth.

FRANCINE'S, North Prospect Road, Milehouse, Plymouth PL2 3HY; ☎ 01752 567577; www.francines.co.uk. Open Fri lunchtime 12–1.30pm, evenings 4.30–8.30pm, closed Sun.

For a takeaway, first choice should be **Francine's** in Milehouse, a multi-award winning chippie that is run by the enthusiastic Francine Baker. It's a Plymouth institution, using natural vegetable oil. It once made headlines by creating the UK's biggest Spam fritter measuring 18 x 12 inches.

Drinking

Plymouth Gin is the best known local tipple – and you can visit the distillery in the Barbican and eat at their new joint restaurant opened with the celebrated local chefs the Tanner brothers. See the *What to do* and *Where to eat* sections above. And we've already mentioned the **Rose and Crown** in Yealmpton and **The Ship** in Noss Mayo in the food section – they're very good drinking pubs too. The Ship's beer comes from Summerskill's just down the road, supported by Princetown beer from Dartmoor.

Summerskills, based in Billacombe, Plymouth (www.summerskills.co.uk), was once owned by Monty Python's Terry Jones. Now it's owned by enthusiastic local brewers and uses Tuckers Malt from Newton Abbot. There is quite a range of beers but watch out for Indiana's Bones, an award-winning dark winter beer that packs a 5.6% punch.

You'll find Summerskills all over Plymouth, from the **Artillery Arms** in Stonehouse to the **Volunteer** in Yealmpton.

And the **Dartmoor Union** in Holbeton has its own microbrewery opposite the restaurant – The Union Brewery – with two real ales, Union Pride and Union Jacks that are only available here. Diners can see the copper and wood clad vats. All the malt is from Tuckers in Newton Abbot too.

In the lanes just outside the village, look for **Borough Farm** (PL8 1JJ; ☎ 01752 830247). Farmer John Walters-Symons' homemade cider is well recommended by locals.

For beer drinkers the best area of Plymouth must be the Barbican. The tiny **Minerva** in Looe Street on the Barbican (PL4 0EA; ☎ 01752 223047) is less touristy than many in this area – the oldest pub in Plymouth retains its low Tudor ceilings, open fire and ancient juke-box, and serves Doom Bar. Locals call it 'The Min'.

And the **Dolphin** on the Barbican itself (PL1 2LS; ☎ 01752 660876) is similarly unspoilt and serves real ale from the barrel. It's one of artist Beryl Cook's favourites. **The Navy Inn**, in Southside Street, round the corner, is an unfussy waterside local, known among Plymouthians for cheap fry-ups.

Across the harbour is the **Thistle Park** (Commercial Road, PL4 0LE; ☎ 01752 204890), a basic but well-recommended pub for beer and food. Look for South Hams beer and live music at weekends.

And in an ancient converted warehouse, **The China House** right on Sutton Harbour (PL4 0DW; ☎ 01752 661592) is a bit more tourist themed but has a reputation for good fish and chips. The **Fareham Inn**, Commercial Road, PL4 0LD; ☎ 01752 201553) is claimed to be the smallest bar in town and is simple friendly place for a quiet drink.

Visitor information

Tourist information centres:

Plymouth Tourist Information Centre, Mayflower Centre, the Barbican, ☎ 01752 306330; *Plymouth Tourist Information Centre, Plymouth Discovery Centre*, Crabtree PL3 6RN, ☎ 01752 266 030, just as you turn from the A38 onto the A374.

Hospitals: 24-hour A&E facilities are available at *Derriford Hospital*, Derriford Road, Derriford, Plymouth PL6 8DH, ☎ 0845 155 8155.

Supermarkets: *Sainsbury's*, Crabtree Road PL3 6RL, ☎ 01752 222748; *Tesco*, Transit Way PL5 3TW; ☎ 0845 6779550; *Somerfield*, Embankment Road PL4 9HY, ☎ 01752 313022; *Morrisons*, Pomphlett Road, Plymstock PL9 7BH, ☎ 01752 480729; Morrisons, Outland Road PL3 5UQ, ☎ 01752 775773; *KW Foods*, Brunswick Road, just off Exeter Street PL4 0NP, ☎ 01752 262688, is worth looking out for. It stocks a range of exotic foods including Chinese, Japanese and Thai ingredients.

Ferries: • *Torpoint Ferry*, car ferry from Ferry Street, Torpoint, Cornwall PL11 2AX to Devonport, ☎ 01752 812233, www.tamarbridge.org.uk. Runs 24 hours, seven days a week, from every 10 minutes at rush hour to every 30 minutes in the night, car £1, motorbike 20p.

• *Cremyll Ferry*, passenger ferry from Admiral's Hard (off Durnford Street, Stonehouse) Plymouth to Cremyll, Mount Edgcumbe, ☎ 01752 822105, www.tamarcruising.com. Up to 21 times a day, adults £1.30, children 70p.

• *Cawsand Ferry*, foot passenger ferry from the Barbican to beach at beautiful village, ☎ 01752 822514, www.cawsandferry.com. In the summer, up to four times a day.

• *Mount Batten Ferry*, yellow water taxis from the Barbican (pontoon next to Mayflower Steps) to Mount Batten, run daily all year, ☎ 01752 408590, www.mountbattenferry.com. Adults £1.50, children £1, bikes free.

• *Saltash Ferry*, the blue-and-white ferries of Plymouth Boat Cruises run from Phoenix Wharf at the Barbican to Saltash Pier, Mount Batten and Calstock but are more like cruises than ferries. See the What to do section for boat trips (☎ 01752 408590).

Park and ride: There are park and ride sites at Coypool, near Marsh Mills roundabout, the George Junction, near Derriford and Milehouse – follow the signs to Plymouth Argyle. Park and ride services do not operate on Sundays and there are no Saturday services from Milehouse when Plymouth Argyle is playing at home. Rail and ride also operates from Ivybridge train station (just off A38) and from Liskeard and Gunnislake train station (on the Cornish side of Plymouth).

Visitor information

Websites: www.plymouth.gov.uk (not the most visitor friendly; www.thisisplymouth.co.uk.
Sport: *Plymouth Argyle*, the city's football team, is currently in the Championship and plays at Home Park, in Central Park PL2 3DQ, ☎ 0845 338 7232, www.pafc.co.uk/tickets. They are sponsored by Gingsters Pasties; *Plymouth Albion RFC* plays at Brick-fields, Madden Road, Devonport PL1 4NE, ☎ 0870 350 0402, www.plymouthalbion.com.
Media: Plymouth is headquarters of *BBC TV South West.* The studios are in Mannamead, north of the city centre. Plymouth's main commercial radio station is *Plymouth Sound FM*

in De La Hay Ave just off Central Park. Tune to 97FM. The main Devon and Cornwall daily newspaper is the Western Morning News, whose headquarters and printworks in Derriford, Plymouth were designed by architect Nicholas Grimshaw. The city's evening paper, printed by the same publisher, is the *Plymouth Herald.*
Bike rental: *The Battery Cycle Works*, Embankment Road, Plymouth PL4 9HY, ☎ 01752 665553, bike hire with delivery/collection service.
Taxis: *Tower Cabs*, ☎ 01752 252525; *Need-a-cab*, ☎ 01752 666222; *Bridge Cabs*, Ivybridge, ☎ 01752 696969; *152 Cars*, Tavistock, ☎ 01822 611152.

FURTHER AFIELD

Around Plymouth Sound

Saltram House
Like a big chunk of wedding cake among the trees, you can spot this whitewashed Georgian mansion to the east of the River Plym. It was built by the famous designer of the time, Robert Adam, and is said to be one of his finest pieces of work. The lavish house and its grand estate with follies and formal gardens were the location for the film *Sense and Sensibility*.

SALTRAM HOUSE, Plympton PL7 1UH; ☎ 01752 333500; www.nationaltrust.org.uk
Entry: adults £8.40, children £4.20, family (2+2) £21; park open daily all year dawn to dusk; house open Easter to Oct: Sat to Thur 12–4.30pm.

MOUNT EDGCUMBE COUNTRY PARK, Cremyll, Cornwall PL10 1HZ; ☎ 01752 822236; www.mountedgcumbe.gov.uk Entry: adults £5, child (5–15) £2.50, family (2+2) £7.50; house/garden open Easter to Oct: Sun to Thur and bank holidays, 11am–4.30pm; guided tours extra cost; joint river-trip/house tickets; park entry free and always open.

Mount Edgcumbe Country Park

The Rame Peninsular on the west of the Sound is dominated by the 865 acres of parkland and 7 miles of coastline belonging to Mount Edgcumbe Country Park. There are follies, forts, churches, formal gardens and a deer park to explore, plus the house itself: the former home of the Earls of Mount Edgcumbe, first built in the 1500s and restored after the Second World War. Inside, there is a collection of antiques, particularly tapestries and paintings. The whole place is jointly owned by Cornwall County and Plymouth City councils. It's one of the most popular spots for locals to take outings, especially using the Cremyll Ferry from Admiral's Hard.

Saltash The bit of Plymouth that sits on the Cornish side of the Tamar Bridge is often neglected by visitors streaming past on the A38. Saltash has recently started arranging itself in an orderly fashion to encourage more people to stop off. A heritage trail has been set up, which includes Brunel's **Royal Albert Bridge** over the Tamar, the wonderfully ancient cottage that was **Mary Newman's House** (the first wife of Francis Drake) and **Elliot's Store**, an oddly preserved slice of 1970s social history.

You can get a guided tour from the tourist office or take a self-guided tour using the signs and information boards. For more information contact the Tourist Information Centre (Town Hall, Lower Fore Street, Saltash, Cornwall PL12 6JX; ☎ 01752 844846; www.saltash.gov.uk).

Kingsand and Cawsand

It's confusing to outsiders, but this beautiful Mediterranean-looking village is really one place. The county border used to run along a stream through the old smuggling village. On one side it was called Kingsand (Devon), the other Cawsand (Cornwall). Now it's one of the West Country's little known gems, hidden on the Rame Peninsular with pastel-painted period houses in narrow streets behind sandy beaches, great views of the Sound and a passenger ferry to Plymouth from the beach (with a little 'bus-shelter' for waiting passengers). **The Halfway House** in Fore Street (☎ 01752 822279; www.halfwayinn.biz) has good rooms to stay, great grub (including local seafood sometimes delivered to the bar by fishermen in oil skins) and atmosphere, including impromptu late-night sing-songs (especially the Cornish anthem 'Shall Trelawney Die').

To the east

Ivybridge

The old mill town of Ivybridge, just off the A38, is a busy regional shopping centre with a handy **leisure centre** for wet days offering an indoor and out-door pool, gym, restaurant and bar (South Dartmoor Leisure Centre, Leonards Road, Ivybridge, PL21 0SL; ☎ 01752 896999; www.toneleisure .org.uk; open daily).

The town is a good centre for walking. It stands at the start of the **Two Moors Way**, the 102-mile trail which crosses Dartmoor to the north of Exmoor and the **Erme Valley Trail** to Plymouth. The tourist information centre is inside the new Watermark Centre, Erme Court, Ivybridge (☎ 01752 893815). Ivybridge **farmers' market** is held on the third Saturday of each month in Glanville's Mill Car Park, off Leonards Road, from 9am to 1pm.

Newton Ferrers and Noss Mayo

The Yealm Estuary 10 miles to the east of Plymouth is like a mini-South Hams, with lots of boating, pretty creekside homes in unspoilt fishing vil-lages and a smattering of great pubs. There aren't great attractions to list, other than saying it's a lovely place for a wander and the views are often marvellous (see www.newtonnoss.co.uk).

To the north

The **River Tamar** has long been the boundary between Devon and Cornwall. To many Cornish, it means the border between Cornwall and the rest of Eng-land. 'Crossing the Tamar' is a phrase used by locals, meaning a lot more than just driving across a river.

The river nearly cuts the south-west peninsula in half – it runs almost 60 miles not quite reaching the north coast near Bude. Along with its tributaries, the Tavy and Lynher, the valley forms a designated area of outstanding natural beauty. It is part of the Cornish World Heritage Site covering spots across the county associated with the origins of the industrial revolution. This means there are industrial remains to spot in the lush landscape and a series of grand his-toric houses built on the proceeds of the tin, copper and arsenic mining (see www.tamarvalleytourism.co.uk).

To see the valley in all its glory take the train from Plymouth to Gunnislake, called the **Tamar Valley Line** (calling at Bere Alston, Bere Ferrers and Calstock too). There are real ale tours on this line, stopping at pubs along the route (see www.railaletrail.co.uk or call 01752 233094 for a free leaflet). Five self-guided walks from the stations are available from Devon and Cornwall Rail Partnership

(☎ 01752 233094; www.carfreedaysout.com). Cheap day returns cost from only £4.

The station at Bere Ferrers has an eccentric **Railway Heritage Centre**, with a visitor centre in an old railway carriage. (Bere Ferrers Station; ☎ 01822 840044). You can even stay overnight here in a converted vintage carriage that was once pulled by the Flying Scotsman (☎ 01822 840044; www.tamar belle.co.uk). B&B costs £25 per person and a five-course evening dinner is available too.

You could even take a trip on the tranquil water itself. We've mentioned plenty of these already – see *What to do* and the section on ferries in *Visitor information*, but here's another option: a guided canoe trip. **Canoe Tamar** offers daily guided canoe expeditions along the Tamar from Morwellham to Cotehele at £20 per person (Canoe Tamar, Old Solomon's Farm, Latchley, Gunnislake, Cornwall PL18 9AX; ☎ 01822 833409; www.canoetamar.co.uk).

Buckland Abbey

This Cistercian abbey was already 300 years old when it was dissolved by Henry VIII. The famous seafarer from Bideford, Sir Richard Grenville, bought it to use as his house. But he fell on hard times just as his friend and rival Sir Francis Drake returned from his round-the-world trip flush with the booty he'd pinched

BUCKLAND ABBEY, Yelverton PL20 6EY; ☎ 01822 853 607; www.nationaltrust.org.uk
Entry: house + ground/grounds only adults £7.40/£3.90, children £3.70/£1.90, family (2+2) £18.50; check website for opening times Feb to Dec; discounts for winter and green transport.

The imposing Buckland Abbey

Sir Francis Drake

Drake was the most famous, successful and swashbuckling of the Tudor seafarers. At various times he was a privateer (or legalised pirate), explorer, vice-admiral, slave trader, politician, all-round English hero and Spanish bogeyman.

His life was full of daring and glory: he was second-in-command of the English fleet against the Spanish Armada and he sailed around the world in the *Golden Hinde* and was knighted on his ship by Queen Elizabeth when he returned. Drake was King Philip of Spain's personal nemesis. Philip offered a huge reward (worth around £6m today) for the Devonian's life – in vain.

Drake was born near Tavistock, a distant relative of Geoffery Chaucer and fellow seadog Richard Grenville. He went to sea early and at 23 made his first trip to the New World with his second cousin John Hawkins. On one trip to Latin America he captured a fortune in Spanish gold and climbed a tree to spot the Pacific in the distance – the first Englishman to see it. He vowed to return to sail it one day. Which he duly did. Drake sailed from Plymouth in 1577 on his four-year epic voyage. Not only did the *Golden Hinde* sail round the world and back to Plymouth, he also sailed his flimsy galleon further south than anyone before (or for 200 years after) and then as far north to Alaska. Considering the equipment available to him, it was an amazing feat.

Every time Drake saw a Spanish vessel on his journey he attacked it, captured its cargo and returned with a massive prize. The Queen took half – and that sum was worth more than the rest of her entire revenue for the year.

Drake himself was so rich he bought Buckland Abbey north of Plymouth and around 40 homes in Devon. He became Mayor and MP for Plymouth.

As a local politician and benefactor he supervised the building of a leat (or watercourse) from Dartmoor to bring fresh water to Plymouth. In true dashing fashion he rode a fine white horse alongside the leat as the water was first channelled into it, accompanying the first wave all the way to Plymouth. Over hundreds

along the way. Drake made Grenville an offer he couldn't refuse. So it is now thought of as Drake's home although he didn't change much of what Grenville had already done. Nevertheless it's an engaging National Trust property with Drake-themed interactive displays, an Elizabethan garden and regular historic re-enactments.

The star exhibit is **Drake's Drum**, which was used on his ships to beat the men to action stations prior to battles. Legend says that Drake ordered the drum to be sent back to Buckland as he died off Panama and vowed that if ever England was in peril and someone beat the drum... he would return. It is said to mysteriously beat itself during times of peril, including once on a British

of years this story has turned into a Plymouth legend that somehow Drake bought water to the town by magic, just by riding his horse from Dartmoor. And the whole story has been amplified into a great civic tradition, which now involves the Lord Mayor of Plymouth holding an annual ceremony at Burrator Reservoir on the moor in mid-June, to give thanks to the delivery of water. A toast is drunk to Drake's memory with the addition: 'May the descendants of him who brought us water never want wine.'

After this did Drake retire to the prosperous life of a county gentleman? Of course not. He was soon off again, attacking Spanish ports in the Caribbean and New World. Then came the famous daring raid on Cadiz, where Drake sailed right into the main harbour of Spain and destroyed the fleet there – a feat he famously referred to as 'singeing the king of Spain's beard'. As a mere commoner Drake was treated in an extraordinary way, becoming a favourite of the Queen and being second-in-command of the English fleet against the Armada. As the huge Spanish invasion force sailed up the Channel, Drake somehow characteristically managed to capture the galleon that carried all the money to pay the Spanish army. Then he organised the decisive attack on the Armada as it moored off Calais. Old wooden hulks were set ablaze and cast adrift among the Spanish fleet. It caused chaos, the Armada scattered in all directions and the threat to England was over.

Drake's seafaring continued into his mid-fifties, with more attacks on Spanish outposts and shipping, until he died of dysentery off Panama. In his lifetime Drake was one of the most famous, or feared, men in the world. His name is associated with many myths and legends – one of which is that his ghost rides across Dartmoor at the head of a pack of 'hell hounds' seeking the souls of the unbaptised. Drake was a determined Protestant throughout his life but the roots of this legend are mysterious.

First World War battleship when the captain ordered the ship to be searched twice for the drum they could all hear, but it was never found.

COTEHELE, St Dominick, Cornwall PL12 6TA; ☎ 01579 351346; www.nationaltrust.org.uk; Entry: adults £8.40, children £4.20, family (2+2) £21; garden only £5, £2.50 and £12.50; house open mid-Mar to early Nov: Sat to Thur 11am–4.30pm; garden open every day 10.30am to dusk.

Cotehele

Yet another stately home in the Tamar Valley – this time an impossibly cute granite Tudor manor in gorgeous riverside gardens. It was the film location for 1996 film *Twelfth Night* and it's easy to picture Helena Bonham Carter and Sir Ben

Kingsley wandering these gardens. Spot suits of armour, ghostly legends and what is believed to be the world's earliest domestic clock. You can take boat trips from Cotehele Quay where there is also a good teashop.

Dingles Fairground Heritage Centre

Follow the Tamar almost as far as Launceston and you'll find this quirky attraction: The National Fairground Collection. Wander round a giant warehouse full of steam organs, traction engines, fairground art and memorabilia. There are a few vintage working rides and stalls and if you're really lucky you'll stumble on one of the occasional wall-of-death riders' reunions.

DINGLES FAIRGROUND HERITAGE CENTRE, Milford, Lifton PL16 0AT; ☎ 01566 783425; www.fairground-heritage.org.uk
Entry: adults £6, concessions £4.50; open 20 Mar to 3 Nov: Thur to Mon 10.30am–5.30pm.

Morwellham Quay

The best way to learn about the industrial past of this area is at Morwellham – a sort of scenic theme park about the early industrial revolution in these parts. There are costumed guides and actors everywhere as you take an underground train ride into a copper mine, board an historic Tamar ketch and stroll around Victorian cottages, farm, school and shop, enjoy horse carriage rides, visit a smithy, waterwheel and quayside.

MORWELLHAM QUAY, PL19 8JL; ☎ 01822 832766; www.mor-wellham-quay.co.uk. Entry: adults £8.90, children £6, OAPs £7.80, family (2+2) £19.50 (without mine train ride £5.95/£3.95/£5); open daily 10am–5.30pm.

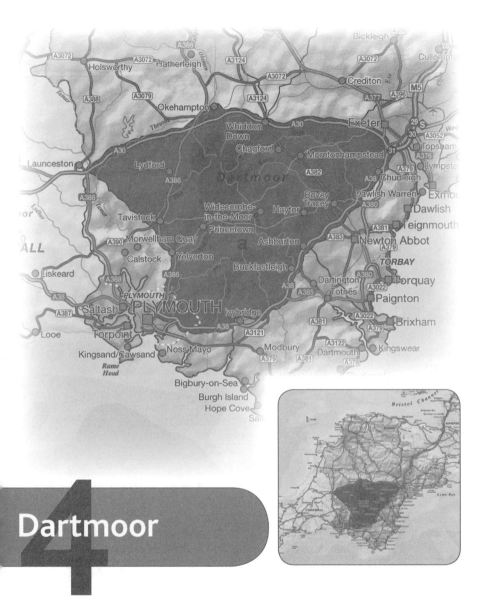

Dartmoor

a. Dartmoor and around

Unmissable highlights

01 Clamber up Haytor for great views right down to Torbay, p.277

02 Discover the ancient stone 'Clapper Bridge' over a beautiful stretch of river at Postbridge, p.277

03 See the forbidding walls of Dartmoor Prison rising out of the misty moorland, p.289

04 Explore Castle Drogo – a unique modern million-aire's medieval fantasy fortress, p.281

05 Enjoy cream tea in the inspiring surroundings of The Garden House near Yelverton, p.283

06 Delve into the mossy depths of Lydford Gorge to find the Whitelady Waterfall, p.284

07 Visit Buckfast Abbey, hear the monks singing in the church and buy some of their homemade honey, p.285

08 Go to Widecombe Fair – with Uncle Tom Cobley and all... p.291

09 Splash out on a Michelin two-star gourmet dinner at Gidleigh Park, p.296

10 Walk away from any car park on the Moor until you can't see the car, the road, any buildings or any other people... p.274

DARTMOOR

If your holiday dreams only involve nightclubs, streetlife and designer beachwear, look away now. Not everyone gets a thrill from a wild empty landscape, an ancient granite boulder crusty with lichen or a mysteriously gnarled, bent tree over-hanging a babbling stream.

Central Dartmoor is certainly a hardcore outdoor attraction – as extreme an environment as you'll find in England. And to many, that's its greatest attraction.

Of course, it's not just for bearded walkers with trousers tucked into woolly socks – even the heart of the Moor contains great pubs, restaurants and memorable sights. But if you're worried about getting your shoes a bit muddy or you tend to get lost going for a walk in the local park, perhaps you'll enjoy the outer rim of Dartmoor more than the 25 mile wide central wilderness. This ring of towns and villages has plenty to see and do, with just a hint of the moor thrown in.

In this chapter we've included everything between the A30 and the A38, whether it's strictly within the National Park boundaries or not. To the west, we've included Tavistock and Yelverton, and to the east, Bovey Tracey and Dunsford.

DARTMOOR AND AROUND

Do you enjoy perching on a lonely lichen-covered granite boulder? What about gazing at a view that hasn't a single building in sight? Would you like to picnic next to a clear stream bubbling between mossy rocks? What about mysterious prehistoric remains or rugged old stone cottages hunched against the wind?

Dartmoor has an appeal that is quite different from the rest of Devon. For some, the moor is the real ancient heart of Devon – the oldest, highest and least spoilt geographic centre of the county. When Devonians refer to 'The Moor', they usually mean Dartmoor, not Exmoor, which is considered mainly the business of Somerset.

The map of Devon shows this huge blob of wonderful nothingness in the middle. That blob is surrounded by a ring of civilisation – the towns and villages around the edge of the Dartmoor. It's roughly a circle, 25 miles across. There are few roads and no towns inside the circle, just scattered villages, Dartmoor ponies and very rugged sheep. It's one of England's wildest areas and the highest land in the country south of the Pennines. Two spots are officially classed as mountains (High Willhays and Yes Tor).

But while it's famous for being forbidding and windswept, Dartmoor does have a softer side too. There are gentle woods, waterfalls, lush valleys and wildlife everywhere. Particularly around the perimeter, visitors will find castles, stately homes, gardens, museums, steam railways, crafts centres and welcoming country pubs.

Throughout the year it is an exceptionally beautiful place to visit, with deep wooded gorges, beautiful lake-like reservoirs and tumbling rocky rivers. Even if you just take an afternoon's drive across the moor it could be one of the highlights of your visit to Devon. After all, there are three essential parts of Devon to see: the famous coastline, the lush rolling farmland ... and Dartmoor.

WHAT TO SEE AND DO

 ### Fair weather

Dartmoor is a big National Park covering almost 400 square miles. Only 30,000 people live on it, making it the largest and least populated patch of wilderness in southern England.

Yet the vast horizons of peat moor and boulders contain thousands of things to see and do. Even in the serious central moor, you'll find nature reserves,

The long trek to Watern Tor is worth it

Sites of Special Scientific Interest, endangered birds, rare plants and more archaeological sites than anywhere else in north-western Europe.

And there are more than 160 **Tors** – Dartmoor's distinctive rocky hill tops. They are chunks of ancient weather-beaten granite that poke out from the peat at the summit like a tooth. You can just stare at them on the horizon but the real temptation is to walk to a tor, clamber up and see what the view is like. Some of the best to see are Haytor (south Dartmoor), Brentor (west Dartmoor), Kestor (west of Chagford), Hound Tor (south of Manaton), Watern Tor (in the centre of the northern moor) and Yes Tor (near Okehampton Common).

Then there are the **prehistoric remains** – standing stones, stone circles and cairns. Across Dartmoor are 5,000 hut circles – the stone foundations of ancient Bronze Age settlements. The best are at **Grimspound**, south of Lettaford. The ruins of this 3,000-year-old farming village cover 4 acres – it's an eerily evocative spot where once at least 24 houses stood.

GRIMSPOUND, on the B3212, 4 miles north east of Postbridge, at Challacombe Cross, take the lane to the right signed to Widecombe; just over a mile down this narrow road there is a tarmac pull-in on the right. Grimspound is a few hundred yards up on the left.

Other prehistoric highlights include **Merrivale**, where the remains of a Bronze Age settlement stand next to sacred sites – three stone rows, a stone circle, standing stones and burial cairns (one mile east of Merrivale). Locals call the long low row of stones 'The Plague Market'. Healthy 17th-century people would bring food here for the poor banished plague victims out on the moor. Take the B3357 to Merrivale – the stones are on the high plateau above the village.

Hound Tor's deserted medieval village, is another spot worth finding. It was probably abandoned 600 years ago (1.5 miles south of Manaton, 0.5 mile from the Ashburton road). And the biggest area of ancient sites is the scattering of

Local legends: the hands of fate

Driving along the B3212 near Two Bridges may seem a harmless way of pottering across Dartmoor. But you could be about to meet one of the moor's strangest and scariest legends... .

The Hairy Hands are two disembodied hands that grab your steering wheel or motorbike handlebars and wrench them to the side, sending you off the road to your terrible doom.

The legend arose from an unusual number of crashes on this stretch after the First World War. Drivers said it felt like invisible hands had grabbed their wheel, but one Army Captain specifically described the hairy hands that did the deed. After that, the legend grew and grew.

Eventually local authorities investigated the road. They found the camber or pitch of the surface was likely to cause skids, where the steering wheel could feel like it was jerked in the wrong direction. The road was improved. More recently a blanket 40mph speed limit was imposed on previously fast moorland roads, mainly to protect livestock that wander freely but without road sense. The legend of the hairy hands however lives on. It is still a great favourite among Devon schoolchildren.

300 Bronze Age and medieval sites, covering 6 square miles in the **Upper Plym Valley** (4 miles east of Yelverton).

The countryside itself can be bleak or spectacular. Lush green **valleys** cut across the moor. The Dart and Teign and their tributaries are like verdant linear oases slicing through the windswept moorland. You'll find pretty woods alongside tumbling rivers in the shelter of these valleys. Dartmoor's rainfall is stupendous; it's often misty or drizzling, so the rivers are always running and the moorland peat never dries out. Walk more than a few yards and you'll discover another Dartmoor speciality – the bogs or, as locals say, 'mires'. Remember the dreaded mires in *The Hound of The Baskervilles*? Thankfully, they're not all dangerous enough to swallow a man like those. Some are rather fun. You can bounce on wobbly tussocks of grass or step from boulder to boulder. Others however are dangerous, so take care, use a map and wear the right boots.

Walking
With all this moorland at your disposal you can **walk** as much or as little as you want. A short stroll may be all you need to catch a flavour of all that wilderness out there. But the sense of space does encourage some serious hiking expeditions. Dartmoor's unique geography means that many of the best bits are simply not accessible unless you own a helicopter... or take a serious walk.

Much of it is a long way from any road and the weather can change very

Local knowledge

Young folk singer, songwriter and musician **Seth Lakeman** lives at Horrabridge near Yelverton. He's the Radio 2 Folk Singer of the Year, with the folk album of the year too and a Mercury Music Prize nomination. Many of his songs are about Dartmoor legends and stories.

Favourite Devonshire restaurant: I've always really enjoyed the Warren House Inn up on the high Moor. The pub is in the middle of nowhere, the food is lovely and Warren House provides a great place to shelter when the weather turns bad...

Favourite pub: I'm spoilt for choice round here but my local for some years has been the Drake Manor Inn in Buckland Monachorum.

Favourite shop: Has to be Yelverton Stores. They sell the best pasty around!

Favourite Devon food/drink: Jail Ale is my favourite around here. The brewery is only just up the road in Princetown.

Favourite Devon activity: When it's hot, it's great going for a long walk and then jumping in one of Dartmoor's fast flowing rivers to cool down.

Best view: Think it has to be the one from Peak Hill near Yelverton. It's where I saw the recent eclipse from. On a clear day you can see all the way past Bodmin and right out to the breakwater in Plymouth.

Quirkiest attraction: All the animals roaming around the moor. You have to have your wits about you when driving, especially at night, as they can jump out of anywhere.

Best thing about living here: The space, the beautiful and varied countryside.

Best-kept Devonshire secret: Double Waters. Can't say more. Wouldn't be a secret otherwise. (It's pretty remote... look it up on a map!)

quickly. So any Dartmoor walking needs to be treated with the same care as a mountain expedition.

Without trying to put off holidaymakers who fancy a stroll, you will get a lot more from Dartmoor if you turn up with a decent map, serious boots and all-weather clothing.

For any exploring on Dartmoor – even by car – we recommend the OS Explorer OL28 Dartmoor map. It's available online from the National Park Authority at: www.dartmoor-npa.gov.uk.

You can wander any of the 450 miles of footpaths and bridleways and if that's not enough there are ancient mining tracks and leats (or artificial water channels) to follow too. Some serious trekkers will just head off with a map and a compass, others will tackle the major moorland trails. These include:

• **Dartmoor Way** – a 90 mile circuit of the moor
• **Two Moors Way** – linking the south of Dartmoor with Exmoor
• **Taw Teign Link**, from Sticklepath to Chagford
• **Templar Way** – from Haytor to the south coast
• **West Devon Way** – from Okehampton to Plymouth

Details of all the walks are available from the tourist offices listed below.

For public transport links to any walking routes visit: www.traveline.org.uk.

Walking is the only way to reach Dartmoor's highest point, **High Willhays** (621m/2,037ft), a rather characterless tor in the midst of the north moor. The neighbouring **Yes Tor** is only slightly lower and much the more memorable sight.

The excellent online walking archive at walkingbritain.co.uk has a good route to Yes Tor, starting at Meldon Reservoir. Visit www.walkingbritain.co.uk /walks/walks/walk_a/1075/ for the details, plus plenty of other Dartmoor routes.

Dartmoor's tors are the focus of an annual event known as the Ten Tors Challenge, when 1,000 young people, aged between 14 and 21 and mostly local, walk for distances of up to 55 miles over 10 Tors.

Long-distance walkers often join in the tradition of '**letterboxing**' on Dart-moor. It started at particularly inaccessible points. Watertight containers, or 'letterboxes', were kept here, each containing a visitor's book and a rubber stamp. The original intention was for walkers to leave a letter or postcard, which would then be collected and posted by the next person to visit the site.

Today there are thousands of letterboxes hidden over the moor, many within easy walking distance of the road. Clues to their locations are placed in other letterboxes or on the internet. It has become a sport in itself, with thousands of walkers gathering for 'box-hunts'. For more details visit: www.dartmoorlet-terboxing.org.

10... great Dartmoor strolls

Not everyone wants to tackle a major expedition on their holiday, but there are plenty of easy Dartmoor strolls for the less adventurous.

1 Walk up to Dartmoor's most popular spot – Haytor Rocks – and clamber around the granite tor admiring the views (from the B3387)

2 Explore the tracks through the gorse to the pretty valley south from the lonely Warren House Inn (on the B3212 between Two Bridges and Moretonhampstead)

3 Climb up to the tiny but spectacular Brentor Church perched on a rocky crag (south of North Brentor)

4 Wander around the intact ancient stone Clapper Bridge over a beautiful stretch of river at Postbridge (by the B3212)

5 Follow Devonport Leat – a 200-year-old water channel descending from the southern moor (off the B3212 north of Yelverton)

6 Enjoy the paths through the wooded Teign valley around Fingle Bridge near Chagford

7 Park at Belstone near Okehampton and follow the old cart tracks onto Belstone Common and the tors at Cullever Steps

8 Walk through the nature trails in Yarner Wood Nature Reserve, just west of Bovey Tracey

9 Discover the remains of a clapper bridge at Dartmeet, where the East and West branches of the river come together (on the B3357)

10 Explore the paths between the mossy, twisted old oaks of Wistman's Wood Nature Reserve in the West Dart Valley, a mile north of the Two Bridges Hotel.

Towns and villages

There are a few settlements on Dartmoor itself. We'll start at the centre with the forbidding village of **Princetown** overshadowed by the grim granite walls of Dartmoor Prison, looming up out of the surrounding hills like some historic fortress. It's a bleak spot with ranks of wardens' houses alongside the prison walls but it's also home to the useful **High Moorland Visitor Centre**, and a few shops, pubs and B&Bs if you need somewhere to recover or relax. **The Old Police Station Café** in Tavistock Road is open daily and is a good place to rest with a pasty and cup of tea. And the Prison Museum is a memorable diversion (see *Attractions* below).

To the north-east, **Chagford** is a small town but has a genteel upmarket air, with nice pubs, quirky shops and a wonderful network of walks. You may spot Jennifer Saunders or Ade Edmondson, who live on a farm just outside.

The trail from Chagford, past its municipal open air swimming pool, and down the Teign Valley is one of Devon's best walks. The riverside trail, known as **The Fisherman's Path**, leads through the steep-sided wooded valley, almost under the ramparts of Castle Drogo to a pretty spot with fairy-tale name of **Fingle Bridge**. Here there is a well-sited inn, 16th-century stone bridge, car park and the start of more fantastic footpaths. You could walk back to Chagford on the crest of the gorge, on the **Hunter's Path**, or set off onto the higher moor further south. A long route incorporating these paths is explained in an archive walk at www.devon.gov.uk/public_rights_of_way/.

To the north-west, **Tavistock** is a bigger, busier centre with a lively pannier market and some interesting old buildings that owe their grandeur to the Duke of Bedford who grew rich on the proceeds of his mining investments on the moor. Bedford Square is the centre of the town, surrounded by granite Victorian buildings, some with ornate crenellated facades. The busy pannier market is just behind and the pretty River Tavy to one side. Tavistock is also known for its individual shops, good selection of restaurants, the lively Wharf arts centre

North Bovey is one of the prettiest moorland villages

Tavistock's Bedford Square

and the Goose Fair in October (see *Entertainment*).

Further north is **Okehampton**, another important regional market town with shops that serve a wide rural area. Off the grand main street is a Victorian shopping arcade, railway station and a museum. The castle lies to the west, alongside the Okement River. To the south, there are pretty villages to explore and many routes up on to the moor.

On the more populated south-western edge, **Yelverton** has a few useful shops, including Yelverton Stores that sell pasties recommended by local folk star Seth Lakeman (see *Local knowledge*). There is the unusual Paperweight Centre, a golf club and a huge distinctive chunk of rock on Roborough Down next to the Plymouth road. **The Burrator Inn** ('The Burrie' to locals) is a good stop for food and drink.

This village is another centre for walkers. The walk up **Peak Hill** to the north of the village is short and steep from the B3212, but the extensive views are a great reward. Nearby is the great Victorian dam that holds back **Burrator Reservoir**, which provides a good circular walk or cycle route. It's about 4 miles. On the south side of the Reservoir, **Sheep's Tor** looms like a small mountain. That's another, more challenging walking opportunity.

On the south-west side, you'll find **Bovey Tracey** on the map, looking rather big and important. When you get there however it's little more than a pleasant big village with a bridge over the River Bovey. First, note that all locals pro-

CELEBRITY CONNECTIONS: NOEL'S HOUSE PARTY

TV presenter **Noel Edmonds** now owns one of the country's greatest landscaped gardens – the Wood Estate at the tiny village of South Tawton, between Sticklepath and Whiddon Down on the north edge of Dartmoor. The man behind *Mr Blobby* and *Deal or No Deal* is spending £1m restoring the 30-acre formal gardens and parkland, and £1m modernising the £3m, 24-bedroom, 'Arts and Crafts' house, which came with 10 resident peacocks.

Noel has told his official fan website: 'Wood is early 1900s and what I fell for were the grounds. In fact, on the first visit I just looked at them and them alone. It wasn't until the second trip that I actually saw the house. I was drawn to the place because the gardens were laid out by Thomas Mawson, a famous landscape gardener.'

Edmonds, who is a deputy Lord Lieutenant of Devon, is a passionate restorer. With his ex-wife Elizabeth, he spent 15 years and millions of pounds improving their former family home, Broomford Manor, a Victorian estate with 950 acres, between Hatherleigh and Okehampton. They sold Broomford for £11m when the marriage ended but Elizabeth and the children still live close by. 'Obviously I was sad to leave Broomford,' says Noel. 'My life has gone through an enormous upheaval over the past couple of years, but I am very happy at the moment and very excited to have a place back in Devon.'

Edmonds, 57, once the highest paid presenter on TV, says he will consider opening his new gardens to the public once they're restored. English Heritage have described his plans as 'terrific news'. 'The gardens at Wood House are of international importance – on a par with places such as Stourhead, Studley Royal and Blenheim,' a spokesperson said.

nounce Bovey (as in Bovey Tracey or North Bovey) as Buvee. There are a few good reasons to stop here, the Craft Centre, Pottery and Marble Museum plus some interesting shops, pubs, teashops and restaurants.

Ashburton, just off the A38, has more nice old shops and places to eat and drink. It originally grew wealthy on the tin industry and somehow it retains that well-to-do feel, with attractive houses with slate facades and antique shops to catch the passing tourists. The River Dart Adventure Park nearby (see *What to do with children*) is a top day out for families, while the more adventurous will find a host of walking, fishing, canoeing and pony trekking opportunities locally, especially in the summer holidays.

Then there are the smaller villages around the edges of the Moor. **North Bovey**, **Lustleigh**, **Widecombe**, **Drewsteignton** and **Belstone** are among the best and worth a potter. There may not be grand specific attractions but it can be just as enthralling to stroll around peeping at lovely old cottages and gardens with a chance for a chat with a local or a stop in a teashop or pub.

Castles

But if you're looking for more 'normal' attractions, this corolla of civilisation around Dartmoor has plenty. From a distance, **Castle Drogo** looks like a magnificent medieval stronghold but was actually built for self-made food retailing millionaire Julius Drewe less than 100 years ago by celebrated architect Edwin Lutyens. That makes it all

CASTLE DROGO, Drewsteignton EX6 6PB; ☎ 01647 433306; www.nationaltrust.org.uk
Entry: adults £6.72, children £3.36, family (2+2) £16.81; open mid-Mar to late Oct, Wed to Mon, from 11am + some winter weekends.

the more interesting to investigate – you'll see the granite grandeur of a medieval castle, like coats of arms and battlements, and the interior of a period

Castle Drogo is less than 100 years old

Okehampton Castle stands just outside the town

country house, like the ingenious early plumbing systems and traditional kitchen. The hilltop gardens are delightful too, perched hundreds of feet above the Teign Gorge. They're the National Trust's highest gardens. And there is usually something happening for children every day during school holidays.

Okehampton Castle was built just after the Norman Conquest as the seat of the new Sheriff of Devon. Originally it was a classic motte and bailey design, with a stone keep on a mound. It became the largest medieval castle in Devon, the home of the Courtenay family until they fell from power in the 16th century. The ruins now stand in a picturesque spot on a wooded spur above the River Okement.

Lydford Castle is another ruin on the moor's fringe. You'll find a 13th-century keep on a mound, which later became a notoriously harsh prison once described as 'the most annoyous, contagious and detestable place within this realm'. To the south is an earlier Norman earthwork castle, and to the north, Saxon town defences.

Gardens

At **Stone Lane Gardens** you'll see a 5-acre woodland garden around streams and ponds with a special collection of birch and alder trees. Buy ones you like the look of in their tree nursery. In

OKEHAMPTON CASTLE, EX20 1JB; ☎ 01837 52844; www.english-heritage.org.uk Entry: adults £3.00, concessions £2.40, children £1.50; open Apr to Sept: daily 10am.

LYDFORD CASTLE, in Lydford off A386, 8.5 miles south of Okehampton; www.english-heritage.org.uk. Entry: free, open all year.

STONE LANE GARDENS, Stone Farm, Chagford TQ13 8JU; ☎ 01647 231311/www.mythicgarden.eclipse.co.uk Entry: adults £2.50, children £1.50; open daily 2–6pm.

summer scores of local artists exhibit sculptures for sale in the woods close to Castle Drogo.

THE GARDEN HOUSE, Buckland Monachorum, Yelverton PL20 7LQ; ☎ 01822 854769; www.the-gardenhouse.org.uk. Entry: adults £5.50, children 5–15 £2; open 1 Mar to 31 Oct: daily 10.30am–5pm daily.

The Garden House is a bit different – its owners are at the forefront of a naturalist movement to keep gardens relaxed and informal. There are more than 6,000 varieties here, intermingled around a quarry garden, acer glade, wild flower meadow, plant centre and tea rooms. Still not sure? The *Sunday Telegraph* called it 'one of the most innovative and exciting gardens in Britain today' and Alan Titchmarsh once said, 'You'd be mad to miss it.'

Stroll through **Lukesland Gardens** and you'll find 24 acres of woodlands with flowering shrubs and wild flowers in a small valley just north of Ivybridge.

LUKELAND HOUSE, Harford, Ivybridge PL21 OJF; Entry: adults £3.50, children free; open 26 Mar to 11 June and 15 Oct to 12 Nov, Wed/Sun and bank holidays.

It's fun for youngsters to explore the streams, islands, bridges, paths and tunnels through bushes. And you can end up with tea in the Old Billiard Room in a grand Victorian Dartmoor hunting lodge.

Hill House Nursery is a classic English garden around a wonderful old vicarage with an adjoining nursery. All pest control is biological – using predator insects to control unwanted visitors like aphids. The garden is right next to the village churchyard that has the grave of a coachman called Baskerville. When visiting his friends near by, Conan Doyle learned of their coachman's name and used it in his famous novel *The Hound of the Baskervilles*.

HILL HOUSE NURSERY, Landscove, Ashburton TQ13 7LY; ☎ 01803 762273; hillhousenursery.co.uk. Entry: free; open daily 11am–5pm, tea room open Mar to Sept.

Waterfalls

Who would have thought that a simple waterfall in south-west Dartmoor could become one of Devon's major attractions but **Becky Falls** has an enduring appeal that has made it popular for generations. It was voted the Top Beauty Spot in Devon for 2007 and has been attracting visitors for over 100 years. It's a privately owned valley that's always a good reliable half-day out without exposing you to the real wilds of Dartmoor. It's

BECKY FALLS WOODLAND PARK, Manaton, Newton Abbot TQ13 9UG, Becky Falls is signed 4 miles west of Bovey Tracy; ☎ 01647 221259; www.becky-falls.com. Entry: adults £6.50, children (4–15) £5.50, family (2+2) £22; open Feb to Nov: daily 10am–5pm.

basically a nice 70ft waterfall but the walks through atmospherically dank wooded valley make it something more. Then there are the add-on bits such as children's entertainment during school holidays, including animal encounter shows (lizards, spiders and snakes) and animal feeding sessions (rabbits,

On the hounds' trail

Any local will tell you that Arthur Conan Doyle stayed in Devon to write his most enduring Sherlock Holmes mystery. The exact inspiration for *The Hound of the Baskervilles*, however, is still the subject of debate among scholars. The story is thought to be based on the legend of squire Richard Cabell, who had an evil reputation among Dartmoor locals. Legend has it that when he died in the 1670s, black howling dogs breathing fire raced across Dartmoor.

Doyle's old friend Bertram Robinson, who lived at Park Hill House in Ipplepen, first told him about the legend and was thanked in the first edition of the book in 1902. And Robinson had a coachman called Henry Baskerville who drove the two of them around the moor sightseeing and researching. The vicar of Ipplepen also helped them with some details of Dartmoor legends. Baskerville Hall itself may be based on either Hayford Hall or Cabell's home at Brook Manor – both of them are near Buckfastleigh.

Some locals claim that Doyle was inspired to write the story by Houndtor's jagged summit, which resembles a pack of hounds, frozen in mid-flight. One thing is agreed, that the *Hound of the Baskervilles* was set in the midst of Dartmoor around Fox Tor Mire, the fictional and deadly 'Grimpen Mire'. The book describes Dartmoor ponies being sucked into the stinking bog, and the story's villain himself disappears, presumed drowned in the 'foul slime of the huge morass'.

For the full story, read *The Hound of the Baskervilles: Hunting the Dartmoor Legend* by Philip Weller (www.amazon.co.uk).

guinea pigs, ponies and goats).

If you're on the other side of the moor there is a more naturalistic alternative to Becky, at **Lydford Gorge**. It's the same sort of thing – with trails through oak woods in a deep ravine alongside the river Lyd to the lovely 'Whitelady' waterfall, but without the animal farm stuff. In fact you have to be careful your children don't fall in the river here, and everyone should wear sturdy shoes to tackle the riverside path.

To complete the trio of waterfalls, try **Canonteign Falls** near Chudleigh. Whether or not it's England's highest waterfall as they claim – and there are several claimants in the north of the country – it's still a nice spot among woodland walks and fern gardens. The artificial stream falls

LYDFORD GORGE, Lydford, near Okehampton EX20 4BH; ☎ 01822 820320; www.national-trust.org.uk. Entry: adults £4.70, children £2.35, family £11.80; open all year from 11am on weekends; mid Feb to Easter: Fri to Sun; Easter to end Oct: daily.

CANONTEIGN FALLS, Near Chudleigh EX6 7NT; ☎ 01647 252434; www.canonteignfalls.com Entry: adults £5.75, children £4.25, concessions £4.75, family (2+2) £18.50; open until end Oct: daily 10am–4pm.

220ft down a leafy cliff to lakes below. There is a picnic area, playground café, shop, and you can even buy a certificate to prove you've walked to the top of the 'highest' waterfall.

Other attractions

Besides the castles, gardens and waterfalls, there are plenty of attractions around the edge of Dartmoor. Perhaps the best known is **Buckfast Abbey**, one of the UK's most visited religious sites.

> **BUCKFAST ABBEY**, Buckfastleigh TQ11 0EE; ☎ 01364 645550; www.buckfast.org.uk Entry: free; open Sun 12–6pm; weekdays 9am (Fri 10am) to 6pm.

Buckfast Abbey monastery was founded alongside the Dart in the 11th century but was abandoned after the Dissolution. Benedictine monks refounded Buckfast in 1882 and rebuilt the present church. It was built by six monks, none of whom had any prior building experience. Little wonder it took them 32 years.

Now the abbey is a well-run business that's financially self-supporting, making and selling its own pottery, stained glass, carvings and tonic wine. You can visit the church, mill, barns, gardens and even join services with the Benedictine monks. The produce shop is open every day selling monks' creations like tonic wine, fudge and beeswax plus crafts from monasteries all over Europe, including beer, icons, soaps, jams, cordials, wine, biscuits, prunes and garden fertiliser.

Buckfastleigh also has a station on the South Devon Steam Railway and an extraordinary pub museum (see *Wet weather*).

> **FINCH FOUNDRY**, Sticklepath, Okehampton EX20 2NW; ☎ 01837 840046; www.nationaltrust.org.uk. Entry: adults £3.90, children £1.95; open mid-Mar to late Oct: daily 11am–5pm except Tues.

Finch Foundry is a glimpse of Dartmoor's forgotten industrial heritage: a 19th-century water-powered forge working amid cottage gardens. In its heyday, the foundry produced farm and mining tools. Regular demonstrations throughout the day show three waterwheels driving the huge tilt hammer and grindstone.

> **KILWORTHY FARM**, Tavistock PL19 0JN; ☎ 01822 614477 Entry: adults: £2.50; opening times and dates not confirmed as we went to press.

There is another waterwheel at **Kilworthy Farm** near Tavistock and it's the biggest waterwheel in Devon. This grey stone Victorian farm was built by the Duke of Bedford in 1851 and still works today. Visitors can examine examples of the most advanced mechanised thinking of the Victorian era. You'll see pioneering examples of a mechanised threshing barn and a blacksmith's shop. There is B&B on the farm too (£30–£35 per person).

Activities

We've covered walking, and there is plenty of horse-riding, cycling, fishing (especially salmon) and canoeing. But most Dartmoor visitors probably don't expect some of the more eccentric activities on offer.

A farm near Widecombe, for example, offers a range of guided treks across lesser known beauty spots on the moor... with a lama to carry your picnic and waterproofs. It includes a picnic of local products or pub lunch.

And a couple of farms offer falconry holidays. **Devon Eagles** were recently used by Channel 4 for a programme with Gordon Ramsay, where they taught the chef to catch a rabbit for his lunch using one of their eagles. Sessions on a one-to-one basis cost from £35 for a one-hour child's experience to £165 intensive day of falconry training including three-course hotel lunch.

And to top it all why not sail away on the wind, with a hawk's-eye view of the moor? If you're in an extravagant mood, **Airtopia Ballooning** offers balloon trips across the moor.

DARTMOOR LLAMA WALKS, Ponsworthy House, Ponsworthy TQ13 7PJ; ☎ 01364 631481; www.dartmoorllamawalks.co.uk. Entry: half-day adults £45, children under 14 £25; open all year.

DEVON EAGLES, Holne Chase Hotel, near Ashburton, TQ13 7NS; ☎ 01364 631471; www.devon-seagles.com

AIRTOPIA BALLOONING, Langford Barton, Ugborough, Ivybridge PL21 0PG; ☎ 01364 73969/www.airtopia.co.uk Price: per person from £130 for 1, £120 for 2–4, £115 for 5–7, £110 for 8 +, £95 children 7–12.

 ## Wet weather

SOUTH DEVON RAILWAY TRUST, The Station, Buckfastleigh TQ11 0DZ; ☎ 0845 345 1427/01364 642238; www.southdevonrailway.org Return ticket: adults £9, children 5–14 £5.40, OAPs £8.10, family (2+2) £26; Easter to end Oct + occasional days including Santa trains, check timetables.

DARTMOOR RAILWAY, Okehampton Station, EX20 1EJ; ☎ 01837 55637; www.dartmoor-railway.co.uk. Return ticket to Meldon: adults £4.75–£5.75, OAPs £3.75–£4.75, children £1.75–£2.75.

Railways

When the rains come, there is no better way to drink in Dartmoor's fabulous scenery, while still staying dry, than to take one of the scenic rail routes. With its pretty route along the Dart Valley and rota of restored steam engines, the **South Devon Railway** (running from Buckfastleigh to Totnes) was voted the best heritage train in the country in 2007. It's certainly a nostalgic way to see the scenery and, for the really enthusiastic, there are opportunities to drive the train as a volunteer – check with the Trust.

Alternatively, there is the **Dartmoor Railway**. Okehampton Station offers short trips on a restored steam train to Meldon Quarry just 2 miles away. It's an interesting little journey past

Local knowledge

Mark Stratton is a professional travel and nature writer and photographer whose work appears in publications like *The Sunday Times, Wanderlust* and *BBC Wildlife*. He been based in Devon since 1998. Despite his worldwide travels he is always 'most content when I return to my home village of Chagford'.

Favourite restaurant: I enjoy the occasional splurges at 22 Mill Street in Chagford. There is fine dining fused with fresh local produce. It's definitely a treat place to go with friends.

Favourite pub: The Drewe Arms, Drewsteignton, has changed a bit since Mabel Mudge, Britain's longest serving landlady retired in the 1990s, aged 99, but the low ceilings, mazy rabbit warren interior, and better – than – most food, make it a great country local.

Favourite shop: Has to be the local institution known as Bowdens. Since the 1860s it has sold everything (and I mean everything) from ironmongery to outdoor wear. I've found souqs in Damascus with fewer items for sale.

Favourite Devon food/drink: Would probably have to be Browne's amazing homemade chocolates from the nearby village of Throwleigh.

Quirkiest attraction: I like taking friends (particularly if they have children) on a steam train ride from Okehampton's lovely old railway station to Meldon Reservoir.

Best kept Devonshire secret: For me, as somebody who has studied and written about butterflies, it's discovering new sites when I go for a walk with these rare delicate creatures. Like the White Admirals flitting between the trees at Yarner Woods or the rare high-brown fritillaries of Aish Tor.

Favourite thing to do on a rainy day: Head up Jurston Way onto the High Moor to be buffeted by winds and enveloped by mist but from within the safe walls of Britain's third highest pub – Warren House Inn.

Anything else you'd like to recommend to Devon visitors: Come down with your car empty of shopping. Eat locally, support the local economy, and buy the local produce – it's superb!

the castle and over a 120ft high Victorian viaduct. Walkers and cyclists can follow the route too. In the other direction is a scenic 15 mile stretch of restored track linked with the Tarka Line just west of Crediton.

Trains run between Okehampton and Meldon every weekend, and certain other days. Connections to and from Crediton and Exeter (operated by First Great Western) only run on summer Sundays.

Eccentric attractions

The **House of Marbles** is one of those places you'd never visit unless you were on holiday: it's a glass-blowing factory with a marble museum. But they do have one bizarre sight you won't easily forget – the UK's longest marble run.

And here's another odd holiday special: **Yelverton Paperweight Centre**, an exhibition of hundreds of glass paperweights, collected by Cornish postmaster Bernard Broughton over many years. They're strangely beautiful but after staring at them for a while you might start worrying about the meaning of life. There is a glass paperweight shop here too.

Museums

A trip to **Dartmoor Prison Museum** is recommended. Don't get too excited, they don't let you into the prison itself. This display of old prison bits and information is across the road in the old dairy buildings. Nevertheless it's certainly more informative than staring at the bleak granite outer walls of the prison. Look for the collection of illicit things made by prisoners over the years. The prison shop here is good – bizarrely, you can buy garden gnomes made by prisoners. At the time of writing they also had real old cell doors for sale (£50 each).

Another slightly offbeat museum is **The Valiant Soldier**. This closed-down pub in the middle of Buckfastleigh is like a time-capsule – nothing has changed since it last called time in 1965, from the coins in the till to the labels on the bottles, the dominoes on the table to the old cider jars. The landlord and lady simply went upstairs to live and left the downstairs untouched. It was the

HOUSE OF MARBLES, Pottery Road, Bovey Tracey, TQ139DS; ☎ 01626 835358; www.houseof-marbles.com; free Easter to Sept: shop open daily, glassworks Mon to Fri 9am–5pm, Sun 10am–3pm.

YELVERTON PAPERWEIGHT CENTRE, Buckland Terrace, Leg O'Mutton Corner, Yelverton PL20 6AD; ☎ 01822 854250; www.paperweightcentre.co.uk; free; open Apr to Oct: daily 10.30am–5pm; other months check before visiting.

HMP DARTMOOR, Princetown PL20 6RR; ☎ 01822 892130; www.dartmoor-prison.co.uk; adults £2, OAPs £1, children under 5 £1; open daily except Christmas week, 9.30am–12.30pm, 1.30–4.30pm (4.00pm Fri/Sun).

THE VALIANT SOLDIER, 79 Fore Street, Buckfastleigh, Devon TQ11 0BS; ☎ 01364 644522; www.buckfastleigh.org/valiant.htm; entry: not confirmed as we went to press; open Good Friday, Easter Saturday and Easter Monday 12.30–4.30pm, then Tues to Fri 12.30–4.30pm until end Oct.

Dartmoor prison

In 1805, during the Napoleonic War, thousands of French prisoners were held in floating hulks on the Tamar at Plymouth. Conditions were appalling and many died, so the prisoners were marched up to the middle of Dartmoor to build a new jail.

They were joined by American prisoners of war taken in the war of 1812 and at one time the prison population numbered almost 6,000. In the cold harsh conditions, many died and were buried on the moor. On one occasion a drunken officer ordered guards to open fire and seven prisoners were killed and 31 wounded.

Later the prison became a general prison, considered the harshest in Victorian England. In 1917 all convicts were withdrawn from Dartmoor, which was then used to confine 1,100 conscientious objectors who refused military service and were forced into hard labour. In 1932 the quality of the food was so bad it led to an explosive uprising in which much of the prison was seriously damaged.

Until recently, Dartmoor Prison's inmates have been some of the most dangerous and notorious in Britain. But now it has a woman governor and 600 inmates of a less stringent category.

Over the years hundreds tried to escape, especially from work parties on the prison's moorland farms. Most are caught, wandering lost, hungry and cold on the moor.

village inn for 200 years and although it's fascinating to see the snapshot of social history, it's also a bit sad that it's no longer a real pub...

 ## What to do with children

The family-run **Dartmoor Zoo** was featured in its own series on BBC2 in 2007. You'll find more than 200 animals, from tiny stick insects and spiders to lions, tigers and bears. Compared with a big city zoo it's slightly shambolic but still entertaining.

DARTMOOR ZOOLOGICAL PARK, Sparkwell, PL7 5DG (signed from A38); ☎ 01752 837645; www.dartmoorzoologicalpark.co.uk; adults £7.95, OAPs £6.95, children 4–15 £5.95, family (2+2) £24; open Nov to Mar: daily 10am–4pm; Mar to Oct: 10am–6pm.

The River Dart Country Park is an adventure centre offers everything from jungle ropes to fishing. Among the adventure parks, children have a wooden pirate ship to capture and there is a toddlers' beach too. In summer there are instructors showing how to tackle zip wires, canoes and climbing on Dartmoor. It's green enough to have its own hydro-electric generator, use biodegradeable materials and source

RIVER DART COUNTRY PARK, Ashburton TQ13 7NP; ☎ 01364 652511; www.riverdart.co.uk; adventure park £6.50, day adventures £30; open Mar to Oct.

PENNYWELL FARM, Buck-fastleigh TQ11 0LT; ☎ 01364 642023; www.pennywellfarm.co.uk; adults £9.50, OAPs £8.50, children 3–16 years £6.90; open Feb half-term to the end Oct: daily 10am–5pm.

MINIATURE PONY CENTRE, Wormhill Farm, North Bovey TQ13 8RG, on the B3212, two miles west of Moretonhampstead; ☎ 01647 432400; www.miniatureponycen-tre.com; adults £6.50, concessions £5.00, children over 3 £5.50, family (2+2) £22.00; open 19 Mar to 28 Oct: daily 10.30am–4.30pm.

food locally. There is B&B available in the manor (summer and spring/autumn weekends), self-catering lodges and a campsite.

You can see why **Pennywell Farm** near Buck-fastleigh won the 'National Farm Attraction of the Year' award: it is packed with activities such as quad bikes, rides, go karts, maze and miniature railway. Children can hand-feed lambs, deer and hedgehogs and there are sheep dog trials, fal-conry displays, play areas inside and out, and a licensed café.

The Miniature Pony Centre in North Bovey offers a chance to sidle up to more than 150 child-sized animals, including miniature Shetland ponies, tiny donkeys and foals. Children will love the pygmy goats, pigs and lambs, pony-riding arena (extra charges apply), plus indoor and out-door play areas.

Entertainment

Sorry, people come to the Dartmoor to get away from what generally passes for entertainment in the rest of the world. Expect precious little nightlife apart from isolated pubs.

THE WHARF, Canal Road, Tavistock PL19 8AT; ☎ 01822 611166; www.tavistockwharf.com

At least the ring of towns around the edge of the moor have some leisure facilities. The best is **The Wharf** at Tavistock, an old industrial building between the River Tavy and Tavistock canal that's now an arts centre. There is a handy programme of theatre, concerts, cinema and art, plus a decent waterside coffee shop and bar.

The only other cinema near the Moor is the **New Carlton** in Market Street, Okehampton (☎ 01837 658586; www.merlincinemas.co.uk). It's licensed and has armchairs and sofas.

Tavistock is famous for its annual **Goose Fair** on the second Wednesday of October, dating back to the 12th century. There is a fun fair and hundreds of stalls are spread along the Plymouth Road. You may even see some geese for sale or eat goose at some of the town's restaurants. Locals usually call it the Goosey Fair.

For locals the big events of the summer are the **agricultural shows**. Expect livestock competitions, shows of local flowers and vegetables, perhaps crafts and trade stands, which usually mean young boys gawping at shiny tractors

Uncle Tom Cobley and all

There isn't an accepted Devonshire anthem. Local football supporters sing 'Drink up the cider', the county's radio listeners love local duo Show of Hands' stirring hit single 'Roots'. But perhaps the strongest contender is a strange little song from the heart of Dartmoor. The song **Widecombe Fair** has a famous chorus:

"Tom Pearce, Tom Pearce, lend me your grey mare,
All along, down along, out along lee.
For I want to go to Widecombe Fair.
With Bill Brewer, Jan Stewer, Peter Gurney,
Peter Davy, Dan Whiddon. Harry Hawk,
Old Uncle Tom Cobley and all...
And Old Uncle Tom Cobley and all."

No-one really knows who all these Devonian characters were but there is a grave marked Tom Cobley in the village Spreyton just north of Whiddon Down. Cobley lived at Butsford Farm and his descendants still live in the village today. And historians have found a Bill Brewer and Tom Pearce who lived in nearby Sticklepath at the same time. Predictably Spreyton's pub is now called the Tom Cobley. It's a real ale mecca, and was voted CAMRA's UK pub of the year in 2006.

Widecombe Fair is still held on the second Tuesday in September and, because of the song, attracts thousands of visitors. Even in the rest of the year the tiny village of granite cottages is a popular spot for tourist coaches.

At the fair expect the usual programme of livestock classes, dog show, vintage vehicles, gymkhana, maypole dancing, bale tossing, tug of war, local produce stands and a beer tent. Drinking and dancing can continue late into the night. Entry costs £6 but parking and vehicle access in the tiny lanes around Widecombe can be very difficult. The village website (www.widecombe-in-the-moor.com) publishes a traffic plan in advance to try to ease congestion.

and combine harvesters. Traditionally there is entertainment from local groups like marching bands, Morris dancers and dog handlers. Okehampton Show (www.okehamptonshow.com), Cornwood Agricultural Show (www.cornwood-show.co.uk), and Chagford Show (www.chagfordshow.com) all take place in August. And Widecombe Fair on the second Tuesday in September is a major attraction (see panel).

The best... PLACES TO STAY

BOUTIQUE

Bovey Castle

North Bovey, TQ13 8RE, ☎ 01647 445000
www.boveycastle.com

Formerly owned by the W H Smith family, this grand house is now hotelier Peter de Savary's latest exclusive property. It's one of Devon's top places to stay, a 'luxury hotel and sporting estate' with every country house convenience, including spa, pool, free bikes, children's play room, snooker room and piano bar all set amid vast parkland. The golf course is so sought after the membership includes Freddie Flintoff, Greg Norman, Colin Montgomerie, Sam Torrance, Darren Clarke and Jimmy Tarbuk.

Price: from £295 to £1750 for a double.

Hotel Endsleigh

Milton Abbot, Tavistock PL19 0PR
☎ 01822 870000
www.hotelendsleigh.com

You'll find this former hunting lodge on the western edge of the moor, down a mile-long private drive. It was built for the Dukes of Bedford 200 years ago and the building has been refreshed with a striking interior redesign by Olga Polizzi. Inside you'll find crisp linen, contemporary art and period Regency panelling. Outside there are over 100 acres to explore.

Price: B&B from £200 for a double.

Gidleigh Park

Chagford TQ13 8HH
☎ 01647 432367
www.gidleigh.com

One of Devon's highest rated hotels – a mock-Tudor mansion built for an Australian shipping magnate now owned by greeting card magnate Andrew Brownsword. Food is by celebrity chef Michael Caines (and currently rates two Michelin stars), bedrooms are full of exquisite luxury features and the 45-acre gardens include tennis, golf and heated dog kennels.

Price: B&B from £340 to £480 for a single, from £440 to £1,200 for a double (including dinner).

HOTEL

The White Hart

The Square, Moretonhampstead TQ13 8NF, ☎ 01647 441340
www.whitehartdartmoor.co.uk

A 300-year-old coaching inn in the centre of this moorland town was where mail coaches changed their horses on the way to London. It now offers neat rooms, fine food and, as part of the de Savary empire, free use of Bovey Castle's leisure facilities.

Price: B&B from £70 to £85 for a single, from £118 to £140 for a double.

INN

Abbey Inn

Buckfast TQ11 0EA, ☎ 01364 642343
www.Abbeyinn.net

Some bedrooms overlook the River Dart – they're the ones to go for. You'll see trout leaping for flies from your window. The pub has fine food, cosy ambience and local beer and cider.

Price: B&B £50 for a single, £80 for a double.

The Rock Inn

Haytor TQ13 9XP
☎ 01364 661305, www.rock-inn.co.uk

The Rock is now halfway between a pub and a restaurant with rooms. Food is highly rated but the beamed bedrooms are full of historical details too.

Price: B&B £66.95 for a single, from £86.95 to £116.95 for a double.

Gidleigh Park houses Michael Caines' highest-rated restaurant

The best... PLACES TO STAY

Church House Inn

Holne, near Ashburton, TQ13 7SJ,
☎ 01364 631208
www.church-house-inn.co.uk

This half-timbered medieval pub is close to the open moor and retains its ancient atmosphere with dark wood panelling, antiques and open fires. Favourite Devon author Charles Kinglsey (*The Water Babies* and *Westward Ho!*) was born in the village. Most rooms have great views and the homemade food is popular with locals.

Price: B&B from £28.50 to £34 per person per night.

FARMSTAY

Bush Park

Lydford, near Tavistock PL19 0NE
☎ 01822 820345
www.totaltravel.co.uk

Stay next to the National Trust's Lydford Gorge, with the Hepworth family, their flock of sheep, some chickens, goats and a cat. The décor is quirky and the owners offer to drive guests to and from the pub for dinner. On-site dinner is by prior arrangement and accommodation for children is 'negotiable'.

Price: B&B £30 for a single, £50 for a double.

B & B

Gate House

North Bovey TQ13 8RB, ☎ 01647 440479
www.gatehouseondartmoor.co.uk

This ancient thatched long house with oak beams and huge granite fireplaces has its own outdoor swimming pool. Eat breakfasts together on a big table next to the Aga. Bedrooms are pretty and old-fashioned.

Price: B&B £33–£37 per person (including afternoon tea).

SELF-CATERING

Beckwood Cottage

Becky Falls Woodland Park, Manaton,
Newton Abbot TQ13 9UG
☎ 01647 221259
www.beckyfalls.com

You can wake to the sound of the waterfall at this stone cottage furnished with antiques that sleeps six in three bedrooms. The poet Rupert Brooke and author Virginia Woolf both stayed here while visiting the Falls.

Price: from £386 to £850 for a three/four-night break, from £498 to £1,142 for a week.

Manaton cottage

Helpful Holidays, ☎ 01647 433593
www.helpfulholidays.com

This family-run holiday cottage agency have the best selection of Dartmoor properties, probably because they're based in Chagford. One of the best is a thatched stone cottage on the village green in Manaton. The three-bedroomed cottage sleeps six, has a range cooker, 'Country Living' style décor and sunny cobbled courtyard.

Price: from £355 to £1,110 for a week.

UNUSUAL

Rock Valley Farm

Rock Valley Farm, Doccombe, Moreton-
hampstead TQ13 8ST, ☎ 01647 441175
www.horsecaravans.co.uk

Sleep in beautifully decorated gypsy caravans in a field, with an open fire and cooking utensils, but no electricity. The farm has a New Age aura, with alpacas and a bluebell wood. Tents are available too.

Price: £55 a night for the caravan that sleeps two adults and two kids.

Shopping

At the south edge of Dartmoor is a long-standing local shopping institution. Locals simply wouldn't believe you if you said you'd never heard of **Trago Mills**. It's a vast family-run discount shopping complex on the A38 between Bovey and Newton Abbot. For years Trago bosses haven't taken full-

TRAGO MILLS, Liverton, Newton Abbot, TQ12 6JD; ☎ 01626 821111; www.trago.co.uk; open seven days a week.

page adverts in every local paper promoting their bargains and ranting about local politics. Sometimes they have decorated their car park with comical statues of local councillors they disapprove of.

The shopping bit has discontinued lines of everything from furniture to clothes – Trago boasts 80,000 products for sale – and it's surrounded by a leisure park with attractions like go-karts, skating, bumper boats and animal park (10 rides for £4.99).

In complete contrast, the biggest craft gallery in Devon is the **Riverside Mill** in the centre of Bovey Tracey. The 19th-century mill is now a showroom for jewellery, furniture, textiles, ceramics and prints made by the 230 members of the Devon Guild of Craftsmen.

THE RIVERSIDE MILL, Bovey Tracey TQ13 9AF; ☎ 01626 832223; open seven days a week.

In the heart of the Moor, **Powdermills Pottery** was once a Victorian gunpowder factory. Now it is a small family business making and selling pottery made from materials found on Dartmoor, plus local baskets, handspun woollen clothes and furniture. And there are clotted cream teas at the weekend from June to September.

POWDERMILLS POTTERY, Postbridge PL20 6SP, on B3212 which crosses the moor east-west; between Two Bridges and Postbridge; ☎ 01822 880263; www.powdermillspottery.com

Okehampton, Bovey Tracey and Tavistock are the bigger regional shopping towns but little Chagford is proud of its 34 quirky shops, which include a thatched bank and two extraordinary traditional family-run hardware shops side-by-side in The Square. **James Bowden & Son** and **Webber & Sons** have been in existence for over 100 years, and both stock a huge range of household goods. Bowden's also houses a small museum illustrating the history of the shop.

The best... FOOD AND DRINK

It's a tradition of Dartmoor to buy and eat good local produce, and it's easy for visitors to do that too. Some of Devon's finest restaurants are around the moor and there are scores of great places to eat. There is less fast food here than in any other part of Devon.

The ring of towns round the moor host plenty of farmers' markets and there are dozens of suppliers of good local fresh meat and vegetables. Pubs, hotels and restaurants across the area always try to use local ingredients. Some even grow their own vegetables. The farms generally keep sheep or cattle because the wet climate and thin peaty soil makes arable production difficult.

Look out for specialities such as the tastier local wild Dartmoor rabbit, and beef and lamb grazed on heather moorland. And if you're lucky you'll be served salmon and trout caught from the Dartmoor rivers.

▶ Staying in

RIVERFORD ORGANIC VEGETABLES, Wash Barn, Buckfastleigh TQ11 0LD; ☎ 01803 762074; www.riverford.co.uk; tours: guided adults £4, children 3–12 £3, self-guided free; open Apr to Oct: school holidays, weekends, selected weekdays; tours 11am (some days 4.30pm).

It's surprisingly interesting to visit the farm at the heart of one of the UK's biggest organic vegetable box delivery schemes. **Riverford Farm** grow more than 85 types of vegetable so there is something to see all year round: watch spring crops being planted, visit strawberry fields in June, enjoy salads in July, crops in August, sweetcorn in September, and the pumpkin harvest in October. Try an informal guided tour on a tractor trailer. You can also see cookery demonstrations and eat in the licensed restaurant that uses produce right from the fields – this means five or six fresh vegetables with every dish. A two-course lunch is £14 (children £7), dinner is £15 (children £7.50). You must book to eat in the restaurant. A cookery half day with the chef is £50.

There are four regular farmers' markets around the edge of Dartmoor. Watch out for:
• **Buckfastleigh**, town centre, Thursdays weekly, 10am–1pm
• **Bovey Tracey**, town centre, Saturdays fortnightly, 8.30am–2pm
• **Okehampton**, St James Chapel Square, third Saturday in the month, 9am–1pm; www.okehamptonfarmersmarket.co.uk
• **Tavistock**, Bedford Square, second and fourth Saturday in the month, 8am–1pm; Bedford Square, WI market, pannier market, Fridays 8am–1pm; www.tavistockfarmersmarket.com

Dean Court Farm Shop in Buckfastleigh, run by a partnership of butchers and farmers, is a good source of homemade sausages, burgers, faggots, pasties and organic vegetables (Lower Dean, Buckfastleigh TQ11 0LT; ☎ 01364 642199).

And other Dartmoor shops that sell local produce include:
• **Val's Stores**, Court Street, Moretonhampstead
• **D and T Wannell Fruit and Veg Stores**, The Square, Chagford

EATING OUT

FINE DINING
Bovey Castle
North Bovey, TQ13 8RE
☎ **01647 445000**
www.boveycastle.com

The fabulous Palm Court restaurant in Peter de Savary's five-star art deco hotel has a 1920s theme, with a pianist most evenings. It's suitably expensive, but expect lots of quality local produce, impeccable service and a smart casual ambience. A three-course dinner costs £42.50.

Gidleigh Park
Chagford TQ13 8HH
☎ **01647 432367 www.gidleigh.com**

Four AA rosettes and two Michelin stars for celebrity chef's Michael Caines' restaurant tell their own story. *And* he's got an MBE and was voted the best chef in Britain for 2007–8. This mock Tudor hotel clearly offers some of the best dining in the UK. You'll find three dining rooms each with different atmospheres: contemporary, traditional and the garden terrace. It's pricey but you'll get beautiful views, luxury garden strolls, and the best possible use of the finest local ingredients. Lunch costs from £27 to £41, dinner costs £75.

Mill End Hotel
Chagford, TQ13 8JN
☎ **01647 432282 www.millendhotel.com**

The former home of the inventor of the jet engine, Sir Frank Whittle, is now a modern French-style restaurant with two AA rosettes. They use lots of Dartmoor produce, including free-range eggs, vegetables, local beef and the finest, freshest fish caught off the Devon and Cornish coasts. All meat comes from traditional butchers in Moretonhampstead and the cheese from Country Cheeses in Tavistock. A two-course dinner is £28 and three courses cost £38.

Prince Hall Hotel
Two Bridges PL20 6SA
☎ **01822 890403, www.princehall.co.uk**

Stunning views, exposed granite walls and modern art give this country house hotel dining room a mix of rural, contemporary and historic. The food is highly rated locally, with a lot of local ingredients such as Crediton pigeon, Dartmouth smoked duck, River Yealm mussels and Tavistock pork. Dinner costs £35.

Lewtrenchard Manor
Lewdown, near Okehampton EX20 4PN
☎ **01566 783222**
www.lewtrenchard.co.uk

This Jacobean hotel was once the home of the eccentric clergyman who wrote 'Onward Christian Soldiers'. Eat in a candlelit, panelled room facing a pretty courtyard. The highly rated modern British menu has plenty of Devonshire game, local fish and vegetables and herbs from the hotel's walled garden. A three-course dinner costs £40.

The Horn of Plenty
Gulworthy, near Tavistock PL19 8JD
☎ **01822 832528**
www.thehornofplenty.co.uk

A small creeper-covered country house hotel in the Tamar Valley has the highest rated restaurant around east Dartmoor. The Horn has a Michelin star and the 2007 Good Food Guide actually picked it as Devon's best restaurant. Expect unfussy presentation of superb ingredients, a relaxed atmosphere and more great views. Lunch is a bargain. The kitchen uses mostly local produce, including the fruits of the hotel's organic garden. Lunch costs £26.50, and dinner costs £45 (£28 on Mondays).

RESTAURANT
Agaric Restaurant with rooms
North Street, Ashburton TQ13 7QD
☎ **01364 654478**
www.agaricrestaurant.co.uk

A relaxed, quirky old place with a cookery school, nice rooms to stay upstairs and an acclaimed restaurant using a wide assortment of local produce, such as mushrooms from the woods, shellfish from the beach and plants from their own and next-door's gardens. Lunch costs £12.95, and a three-course dinner is about £31.

EATING OUT

Browns Hotel
West Street, Tavistock PL19 8AQ
☎ **01822 618686**
www.brownsdevon.co.uk

This cosy old coaching inn has a brasserie that has won local awards for its excellent food. Note that both still and sparkling water is bottled on the premises and drawn from an ancient well under a glass panel in the Orangery. And the same team also owns 22 Mill Street Restaurant in Chagford, a relaxed restaurant with rooms, which is recommended by locals (☎ 01647 432244). Lunch costs £18.50, and dinner costs £37.

GASTROPUB
The White Hart
The Square, Moretonhampstead TQ13 8NF, ☎ 01647 441340
www.whitehartdartmoor.co.uk

This affordable outpost of Bovey Castle has fine, nicely presented pub food and a popular Sunday lunch with live jazz right in the centre of this moorland town. Main courses cost from £11.95 to £17.95.

The Sandy Park Inn
Chagford TQ13 8JW, ☎ 01647 433267
www.sandyparkinn.co.uk

The latest part of Peter De Savary's hospitality empire is this 17th-century thatched inn with beamed ceilings, log fires and blackboard menus. Expect a hearty, pubby atmosphere and good value top notch nosh. There are lots of local ingredients – such as the meat, much of which is reared and grazed just a mile away. Main courses cost from £8 to £12.25.

Abbey Inn
Buckfast TQ11 0EA, www.Abbeyinn.net

It's not unusual to find a pretty village with a great old pub on Dartmoor. This one has a particularly cosy restaurant with tall windows, open fires and wood panelling. Food is inventive modern British but the more traditional Sunday lunch carvery is so popular with locals you have to book. Main courses cost from £7.50 to £12.95.

The Rock Inn
Haytor TQ13 9XP
☎ **01364 661305, www.rock-inn.co.uk**

Another old country pub just below Dartmoor's most popular tor flies the Devonshire flag outside and serves top quality hearty pub food inside. There are old beams, flagstone floors, candles and blackboards, and look out for the whisky and sultana bread and butter pudding. Three courses cost £29.

Dartmoor Inn
Lydford EX20 4AY, ☎ 01822 820221
www.dartmoorinn.com

On the western fringe of the moor, next to the National Trust's Lydford Gorge, this old place has a surprisingly modern interior with small rooms like a Swedish home. It's like something from a magazine, with open fires, white walls and unfussy décor. The menu is a mix of the finest pub grub and gourmet restaurant-type dishes. Local celebrity chef Michael Caines is a regular and it's a former *Good Food Guide* Country Restaurant of the Year and Devon Life dining pub of the year. Main courses cost from £12.75 to £22.50.

CAFÉ
Dartmoor Tearooms
Cross Street, Moretonhampstead TQ13 8NL, ☎ 01647 441116

In the heart of this moorland town there is a traditional old tearoom by day that becomes a candlelit bistro by night. It serves cream teas with homemade scones and cakes, then later meals using meat, fish and cheeses from across Devon.

Café Green Ginger
East Street, Ashburton TQ13 7AZ
☎ **01364 653939**
www.ashburton.org/directory/greenginger/index.htm

In Ashburton's attractive town centre is this Victorian townhouse with a quirky menu including cream teas, apple strudels and inventive salads. There is a log fire in winter and garden tables and conservatory in summer.

• **Moorland Stores**, Whiddon Down

Country Cheeses in Market Road, Tavistock (PL19 0BW), stocks more than 100 different cheeses, all from Britain and most from the West Country. It's become something of a local cult, selling its own 'Real Cheese' t-shirts and attracting customers such as two Michelin starred chef Michael Caines (☎ 01822 615035; www.countrycheeses.co.uk).

And look out for these prime Dartmoor meat producers: **Brimpts Farm** (☎ 01364 631450; www.beefbox.co.uk) sells beef direct from its herd reared on heather-clad moorland near Dartmeet. So does farmer Phil Coaker at **Runnage Farm**, Postbridge (PL20 6TN; ☎ 01822 880222). He sells lamb too but ring before turning up at the gate. The Powell family at **Holne Court Farm**, Holne (TQ13 7SL; ☎ 01364 631271) sell home-reared beef, lamb and eggs from the farm gate but ring first. There is lamb, beef, pork and poultry from **Lower West Combe Farm** at North Bovey too. Call 01647 221453 before coming to the gate or see the Perrymans at Bovey farmers' market. **Sherberton Farm** near Princetown has been in the Coaker family since 1843 and now sells its beef and lamb direct from the gate, as well as the animals' hides and sheepskins (☎ 01364 631276; www.anton-coaker.co.uk). Beef and lamb from **Lizwell Farm** at Widecombe (☎ 01364 631238) can be bought from the farm or from the village post office.

As a treat, locals recommend the exclusive Browne's handmade chocolates from a small shop in the village of Throwleigh near Chagford (☎ 0845 4560568; www.brownes-chocolates.co.uk).

Drinking

Here's another Devonshire area where it's hard to choose between the local cider and beer. There are great examples of both.

You'll find the home of **Brimblecombe's Cider** on the east of Dartmoor. It's made the old way, by pressing milled apples through straw. Visitors can buy some and can see the old cider press and other original cider-making equipment.

BRIMBLECOMBE'S CIDER, Farrants Farm, Dunsford EX6 7BA; ☎ 01647 252783; www.brimble-combescider.co.uk; open Easter to end Oct daily; Nov/Dec during cider making.

Princetown Brewery makes the popular Dartmoor IPA and 'Jail Ale', which is now available at Asda stores. At 1400ft it's the highest brewery in the country but sadly not open to the public at the moment. The brewery's website (www.princetownbreweries.co.uk) has a good pictorial explanation of the process though and polypins of their beer are available at local shops such as Fox Tor Café, Princetown, Darts Farmshop, near Topsham, Occombe

The Visitors' Book

Visiting Dartmoor

'With its own wild beauty and plenty of places to stop the car, I found Dartmoor a welcome escape from the seaside. We stopped at Dartmeet for a walk and to get up close to the Dartmoor ponies. We had to slow down while driving around the moor because of the sheep and the ponies. After all, you are on their territory!'

'We kept pulling into the many layby areas to catch the spectacular views. Taking a camera really is a must as it is a very beautiful place to visit. We have fond memories of the moor as many years ago we visited and while trying to cross the river my then boyfriend, now my husband, fell in trying to retrieve a shoe that I'd thrown but which missed its landing on the other side. Needless to say, we didn't repeat that this time around.'

'Dartmeet is popular with dog owners and families, has plenty of parking spaces and a café with plenty of outdoor seating alongside the babbling river. We thought Princetown was a charming, picturesque little town to wander around. Dartmoor prison looms large and grey in the distance and the car park operates on an 'honesty box' policy — very quaint.'

'Head for The Old Police Station café, which serves excellent home cooked meals and cream teas. Many of the items displayed around the walls and shelves are for sale.'

Jayne Rowe, Beijing, China

Walkers can admire the scenery surrounding Widecombe-in-the-Moor

Farmshop, Paignton, and Tuckers Maltings at Newton Abbot. Good places to try their beers are: the **Prince of Wales Inn**, Princetown; **Tradesmans Arms**, Scorriton, near Buckfastleigh; **Peter Tavy Inn**, Peter Tavy; and **Trout and Tipple**, Tavistock.

The Royal Oak, Meavy, serves Princeton's beer and is worth a visit for other reasons too. First, it's a cute whitewashed pub on a village green and, second, it's owned by Burrator Parish Council. There is Jail and Dartmoor ale, plus Royal Oak beer brewed by O'Hanlon's in East Devon. This must be the best parish council in Britain because it even provides local scrumpy on tap and there is good homemade food too (The Royal Oak Inn, Meavy, PL20 6PJ; ☎ 01822 852944; www.royaloak inn.org.uk).

We've mentioned some excellent pubs already. Even if you don't want to stay or eat, these are lovely places to have a drink:

• **The White Hart**, The Square, Moretonhampstead TQ13 8NF

CELEBRITY CONNECTIONS

Award-winning young singer-songwriter **Seth Lakeman** comes from Yelverton and often pays tribute to Dartmoor as the inspiration for much of his music. Seth was shortlisted for the prestigious Mercury Prize in 2005 alongside KT Tunstall, Kaiser Chiefs and Coldplay (led by Exeter-born Chris Martin). He also won Radio 2's Folk Singer of the Year award and Best Folk Album.

Seth launched one CD with a live concert inside Dartmoor Prison and another by playing at Princetown Brewery. In 2007 he was awarded an honorary degree from Dartington College of Arts.

Much of Seth's music and lyrics are inspired by the old tales, legends and mysteries of Dartmoor. For example, the title track of his hit album Kitty Jay, tells of the local legend of a servant girl who got pregnant and hanged herself in a barn. Because suicides were never buried in consecrated ground, she was laid to rest at a crossroad near Hound's Tor. Even today, there are always fresh flowers on the grave but no one is ever seen putting them there.

Seth still lives on the moor at a cottage in Horrabridge near Yelverton. He recorded his second CD in his kitchen there. He told BBC Devon: 'I've always been interested in the legends and mysteries of Devon and Dartmoor. All the old boys in the pubs would mention these stories and it's a great theme to write about.'

For more about Seth visit: www.sethlakeman.co.uk

- **The Abbey Inn**, Buckfast TQ11 0EA
- **The Rock Inn**, Haytor TQ13 9XP
- **Church House Inn**, Holne, near Ashburton TQ13 7SJ
- **The Sandy Park Inn**, Chagford TQ13 8JW
- **Dartmoor Inn**, Lydford EX20 4AY

Dartmoor has more good pubs than you'd expect, considering the sparse population. In fact there are more good pubs and fewer bad pubs here than anywhere else in Devon. Other good pubs to try on and around the moor are:

- **The Rugglestone**, Widecombe TQ13 7TF – a tiny country pub with Dartmoor IPA, farm cider and wild ponies in the garden.
- **The Drewe Arms**, Drewsteignton EX6 6QZ – it's not like a modern pub at all, more like sitting in an old person's house. A recommended Dartmoor experience, especially Sunday lunchtime.
- **Warren House Inn**, Postbridge PL20 6TA – an extremely remote pub without mains water or electricity, has an open fire reputed to have been burning since 1845 although many locals are sceptical. It's a great spot for

local beer and cider, traditional pub grub and excellent walks.

- **Tavistock Inn**, Poundsgate TQ13 7NY – this picturesque old beamed pub deep in the moor serves Otter and St Austell ales, baked potatoes and pies. And Arthur Conan Doyle wrote some of *The Hound of the Baskervilles* while staying here.
- **The Cleave Inn**, Lustleigh, near Moretonhampstead TQ13 9TJ – a thatched pub with Otter ale, local organic soft drinks and pretty garden.
- **Castle Inn**, Lydford EX20 4BH – a Tudor inn near National Trust gorge with reviving open fires, real ale and good value bar food.
- **The Drake Manor Inn** at Buckland Monachorum has good food, beer and a very stylish two-bedroomed self-catering holiday flat to rent, from £250 for two nights (☎ 01822 853892; www.goldenhindapartment.co.uk/). It's folk star Seth Lakeman's favourite pub.
- **The Elephant's Nest** at Horndon near Mary Tavy, PL19 9NQ – flagstones and stoves set the atmosphere, sit back and enjoy local beers on hand-pump, farm cider and homemade bar food.

Watch out too for the local sloe gin. Sloes are the fruit of blackthorn, which grows in many Dartmoor hedges. At **Bramley and Gage** in South Brent, you'll find handmade sloe and damson gin and you can buy it in local National Trust shops, Powerdham Castle and Dartington Cider Press.

Moorland Mist Ltd at Mitchelcombe Farm, Holne near Buckfastleigh bottle the widely available Clearly Devon and Pure Dartmoor mineral water.

Visitor information

Tourist information centres: Dartmoor National Park Authority manages a network of information centres including the *High Moorland Visitor Centre* in Princetown, which is open throughout the year. You can get a free *Dartmoor Visitor Guide* from this Centre. Call 01822 890414 or write to: The High Moorland Visitor Centre, Tavistock Road, Princetown, Yelverton, Devon, PL20 6QF. Other tourist information centres: *Okehampton*, Museum Courtyard, West Street EX20 1HQ, ☎ 01837 53020, www.okehampton devon.co.uk; *Tavistock*, Town Hall, Bedford Square PL19 0EA, ☎ 01822 612938; *Moretonhampstead*, New Street TQ13 8PE, ☎ 01647 440043, www.moretonhampstead.com; *Ashburton*, Town Hall, TQ13 7QQ, ☎ 01364 653426, www.ashburton.org; Bovey Tracey, The Lower Car Park, Station Road, ☎ 01626 832047; *Buckfastleigh* (open Easter to Oct) The Valiant Soldier, Fore Street TQ11 0BT, ☎ 01364 644522.

Hospitals: Royal Devon and Exeter Hospital (Wonford), Barrack Road, Exeter, EX2 5DW, ☎ 01392 411 611; *Torbay Hospital*, Newton Road, Torquay, TQ2 7AA, ☎ 01803 614567; *North Devon District Hospital*, Raleigh Park, Barnstaple, EX31 4JB, ☎ 01271 322577; *Derriford Hospital*, Derriford Road, Derriford Plymouth, Devon, PL6 8DH, ☎ 0845 155 8155.

Websites: www.dartmoor-npa.gov.uk (not very useful); www.discoverdartmoor.co.uk (much better); www.virtuallydartmoor. org.uk (excellent: full of virtual tours and local insights).

Supermarkets: Predictably they're all sited in a circle around the edge of the Moor:
Co-op, Moorland Villas, Yelverton PL20 6DT, ☎ 01822 853372; *Waitrose*, School Way, Okempaton EX20 1WL, ☎ 01837 659008; *Somerfield*, Market Street, Okehampton EX20 1HN, ☎ 01837 53996; Co-op, Trago Mills, Liverton TQ12 6JD. ☎ 01626 821888; *Somerfield*, North Street, Ashburton TQ13 7QD, ☎ 01364 652269; *Somerfield*, Brook Street, Tavistock PL19 0BJ, ☎ 01822 616378; *Morrisons*, Plymouth Road, Tavistock PL19 9DS, ☎ 01822 610743.

National Park infromation centres: *Newbridge*, in the car park, west of Ashburton on the B3357, ☎ 01364 631303; *Postbridge*, in car park on the B3212, ☎ 01822 880272; *Haytor*, at the lower car park on the main road, the B3387 3 miles west of Bovey Tracey, ☎ 01364 661520.

Military firing ranges: A big chunk of north Dartmoor is used by the Ministry of Defence for training (the areas are called the Okehampton, Merrivale and Willsworthy ranges). The public has access to these moorland areas except, obviously,

Visitor information

when they're being used for live firing. There is no firing on public holidays and the whole of August. The three danger areas are marked by red and white posts with warning notices. If you're on a path you'll see them. If you're not, you may miss them. If you want to walk into the 'danger' areas, check firing times. The firing programme is published in local newspapers, at information centres, and is available on freephone 0800 4584868 and www.dartmoor-ranges.co.uk. BBC Radio Devon broadcasts daily updates. And as a final safeguard there are warning signals on the moor too (red flags by day and red lamps at night). And for any emergency queries, call 01837 650010 for the 24-hour MOD Duty Officer. Incidentally, the main users of the firing ranges are locally based units: the Royal Naval Base at Devonport, *HMS Raleigh* (the Navy's main shore training establishment) at Torpoint, Britannia Naval College at Dart-

mouth; Royal Naval Air Stations at Culdrose and Yeovilton; Royal Marine Commandos from Plymouth, Taunton and Barnstaple; Commando Training Centre at Lympstone; 43 Wessex Brigade; and the Royal Air Force Regiment and Joint Survival School at St Mawgan.

Bike rental: The best is right on Devon's traffic-free Granite Way Cycle Trail. **Devon Cycle Hire** was even named as the Best Activity to do on Dartmoor by *The Guardian*. Bike locks and route guides are provided free. (Devon Cycle Hire, Sourton Down, Okehampton EX20 4HR, ☎ 01837 861141, www.devoncycle-hire.co.uk.)

Taxis: Finch's, Princetown, ☎ 01822 890224; *Chard Taxis*, Chagford, ☎ 01647 433219; *Okehampton Taxis*, ☎ 01837 53555; *152 Cars*, Tavistock, ☎ 01822 611152; *VIP Cars*, Yelverton, ☎ 01822 852975; *Ashburton Taxis*, ☎ 01364 652423; *Bovey Cars*, Bovey Tracey, ☎ 01626 834163.

H

I

This first edition published in Great Britain, 2008 by
Crimson Publishing a division of Crimson Business Ltd
Westminster House
Kew Road
Richmond
Surrey
TW9 2ND

A catalogue record for this book is available from the British Library

ISBN: 978 1 85458 426 7

The author and publishers have made every effort to ensure that the information in *The Best of Britain: Devon* is up-to-date and accurate at the time of writing. However, the publishers shall not be liable for any loss, injury or inconvenience sustained by any traveller as a result of information or advice in this guide.

Printed and bound by Mega Printing, Turkey

Series editor: Guy Hobbs
Layout design: Nicki Averill, Amanda Grapes, Andy Prior
Typesetting: Amanda Grapes
Cover design: mccdesign ltd and Andy Prior
Picture editor: Lianne Slavin
Production: Sally Rawlings
Proofreader: Kate Kirkpatrick
Town map design: © Chartwell Illustrators
Inside cover design: Tom Hulatt
Regional map design: Tom Hulatt
Regional map source material: © Maps in Minutes™/Collins Bartholomew, 2008

Acknowledgements
The author would like to thank everybody who helped with, and contributed to, this book, particularly Michael Caines, Local Knowledges: Stuart Nuttall, Steve Perryman, Steph Bridge, Lawrence Raybone, Frank Adey, Kit Noble, Seth Lakeman and Mark Stratton, Visitors' Books: Annette Roffey, Graham Brown, Isabelle Utley, Helen Doran and Jayne Rowe.

Help us update
While every effort has been made to ensure that the information contained in this book was accurate at the time of going to press, some details are bound to change within the lifetime of this edition: phone numbers and websites change, restaurants and hotels go out of business, shops move, and standards rise and fall. If you think we've got it wrong, please let us know. We will credit all contributions and send a copy of any Best of Britain title for the best letters. Send to: Best of Britain Updates, Crimson Publishing, Westminster House, Kew Road, Richmond, Surrey TW9 2ND.

Devon picture credits

Front cover: Blackpool Sands, near Dartmouth, South Devon. © 2008, all rights reserved. Alamy Stock Photography; **Inside flap**: A terrace of colourful houses perched on top of the seawall in Dawlish, Devon, iStockPhoto; **Back cover**: Salcombe Bay, mccdesign Ltd; Brentor Church, www.discoverdevon.com, Devon County Council; **Inside cover**: Braunton Burrows, AONB: credit Neville Stanikk; **Contents**: Westard Ho! at low tide: AONB: Neville Stanikk; **Foreword**: Michael Caines Restaurants; **Introduction**: North Devon AONB: Neville Stanikk; **Introduction**: Rosemoor: Simon Heptinstall; **Unmissable Highlights**: **1**: www.discoverdevon. com; Devon County Council; **2**: www.discoverdevon.com, Devon County Council, **3**: Plymouth City Council; **4**: Landmark Trust; **5**: www.discoverdevon.com, Devon County Council; **6**: www.discoverdevon.com, Devon County Council; **7**: Burgh Island Hotel; **8**: iStockPhoto; **9**: Torridge District Council; **10**: English Riviera Tourist Board; **Local Recommendations**: Title picture: Britain on View **2**: John Tweddell; **3**: The National Marine Aquarium; **5**: Britain on View; **Factfile**: www.discoverdevon.com, Devon County Council, **p.62**: Exeter City Council; **p.63**: Stuart Nuttall; **p.64**: Exeter City Council; **p.65**: Exeter City Council; **p.66**: Exeter City Council; **p.72**: Michael Caines; **p.77**: Exeter City Council; **p.79**: Tiverton Canal Company; **p.80**: National Trust/ Rupert Truman; **p.82**: National Trust/ Andrew Butler; **p.93**: Pinnacle Photo Agency; **p.94**: Landmark Trust; **p.94**: Phyllis Baxter at Ottery Information Centre; **p.103**: Simon Heptinstall; **p.104**: National Trust/ Rupert Truman; **p.105**: Steph Bridge; **p.108**: Shutterstock; **p.117**: John Tweddell; **p.126**: www.discoverdevon.com, Devon County Council; **p.127**: Britain on View/ McCormick-McAdam; **p.129**: Lynton & Lynmouth Tourist Information; **p.134**: www.discoverdevon.com, Devon County Council; **p.136**: Simon Heptinstall; **p.138**: Simon Heptinstall; **p.139**: Lawrence Raybone; **p.146**: www.discoverdevon. com, Devon County Council; **p.153**: Shutterstock; **p.154**: National Trust/ Matthew Antrobus; **p.156**: North Devon Marketing Bureau, www.northdevon.com; **p.160**: North Devon Marketing Bureau, www.northdevon.com; **p.165**: North Devon Marketing Bureau, www.northdevon. com; **p.167**: North Devon Marketing Bureau, www.northdevon. com; **p.172**: Simon Heptinstall; **p.172**: www.discoverdevon.com, Devon County Council; **p.174**: Dragon Archery Centre; **p.176**: North Devon Marketing Bureau, www.northdevon. com; **p.181**: South Molton Tourist Information Centre; **p.182**: South Molton Tourist Information Centre; **p.183**: Frank Adey; **p.184**: Cobbaton Combat Collection; **p.192**: Simon Heptinstall; **p.200**: Simon Heptinstall; **p.203**: National Trust/ Andrew Butler; **p.207**: Kents Cavern Ltd; **p.221**: Powderham Castle; **p.226**: Landmark Trust; **p.227**: Kit Noble; **p.229**: National Trust/ Nadia Mackenzie; **p.230**: Nonsuch House; **p.239**: www.discoverdevon.com, Devon County Council; **p.244**: National Trust/ Andrew Butler; **p.246**: Plymouth City Council; **p.249**: Plymouth City Council; **p.250**: Plymouth City Council; **p.265**: Britain on View; **p.273**: Simon Heptinstall; **p.275**: Glass Ceiling PR; **p.278**: Simon Heptinstall; **p.279**: www.discoverdevon.com, Devon County Council; **p.281**: National Trust/ Chris Gascoigne; **p.282**: English Heritage; **p.287**: Mark Stratton; **p.292**: Gidleigh Park; **p.300**: www.discoverdevon.com, Devon County Council; **Colour section: Coastline** Jurassic coast: Exeter City Council; Brixham Heritage Fleet: English Riviera Tourist Board; Sidmouth: Simon Heptinstall; Bucks Mills at low tide, Neville Stanikk; Woolacombe coast: www.discoverdevon.com, Devon County Council; Plymouth Hoe lighthouse: www.discoverdevon.com, Devon County Council; Hoe: Plymouth City Council; Clovelly Christmas: www.discoverdevon.com, Devon County Council; Budleigh: Exeter City Council; **Colour section: Countryside** Exmoor moss: Simon Heptinstall; Horse drawn barges, Tiverton: Tiverton Canal Company; Broomhill Sculpture: Simon Heptinstall; Rosemoor: Simon Heptinstall; Exe Valley: www.discoverdevon. com, Devon County Council; Dartmoor Ponies: www.discoverdevon.com, Devon County Council; Bretnor church: www.discoverdevon.com, Devon County Council; Dartmoor: www.discoverdevon.com, Devon County Council; Horses in the hills above Woolacombe: Neville Stanikk; Golden Cap estate: National Trust/ David Noton; **Inside back cover:** beach at Dawlish Warren, iStockPhoto.

The best of Britain Icons & Symbols

GENERAL ICONS

Fair Weather

Wet weather

What to do with children

How to avoid children

Entertainment

Shopping

Celebrity connections

The best places to stay

Food and drink – staying in

Food and drink – eating out

Food and drink – drinking

Visitor Information

ACCOMMODATION SYMBOLS

Children friendly

Pet friendly

Licensed premises

Evening meal available

Working farm

Swimming pool

Tennis courts

Bikes for hire

Full/approved wheelchair access